WHITE LIES

Canon Collins
and the secret war against apartheid

GW00750172

DENIS HERBSTEIN

James Currey
Publishers

HSRC
PRESS

First published in South Africa in 2004 by HSRC Press
Private Bag X9182, Cape Town, 8000, South Africa
www.hsrcpress.ac.za

Published in the United Kingdom by James Currey Publishers
73 Botley Road, Oxford, OX2 0BS, United Kingdom
www.jamescurrey.co.uk
© Denis Herbstein

Cover design and setting by Jon Berndt
Production by comPress

Distributed in Africa by Blue Weaver Marketing and Distribution,
P.O. Box 30370, Tokai, Cape Town, South Africa, 7966,
South Africa.
Tel +27 +21 701-4477
Fax: +27 +21 701-7302
email: orders@blueweaver.ac.za

Distributed in the United Kingdom and Europe by James Currey
Publishers
73 Botley Road, Oxford, OX2 0BS, United Kingdom
Tel +44 +1865-244111
fax: +44 +1865-246454
email: mary.tinker@jamescurrey.co.za

Distributed worldwide, except Africa, the UK and Europe, by
Independent Publishers Group
814 North Franklin Street, Chicago, IL 60610, USA
www.ipgbook.com
To order, call toll-free: 1-800-888-4741
All other inquiries, Tel: +1 +312-337-0747
Fax: +1 +312-337-5985
email: Frontdesk@ipgbook.com

Worldwide, except UK
ISBN 0 7969 2088 5
United Kingdom
ISBN 0 85255 885 6

This book is dedicated to four remarkable women –
Diana Collins, Phyllis Altman,
Rica Hodgson and Ethel de Keyser.

About the author

Denis Herbstein was born in Cape Town, where he studied law and began his career as a journalist on the Cape Times. He has since worked for several British newspapers. In 1976, while in South Africa reporting for the London Sunday Times and Guardian newspapers, he was deprived of his South African citizenship and expelled by the apartheid government. He now works for the *Financial Times*. He is married and has two children.

Also by Denis Herbstein

White Man, We Want to Talk to You, 1979
The North Downs Way, 1982
The Devils are Among Us: The War for Namibia, with John Evenson,1989
The Porthole Murder Case, 1991

Children's book
My Friend, Mandela: A Grandfather's Tale, 2003

Contents

Foreword by Per Wästberg

Denis Herbstein's book recounts an epic of human courage and inventiveness, of creative bureaucracy, of a commitment to human rights that never wavered. He has narrated Canon John Collins's story as a parallel to more luminous lives in the liberation struggle. Through Herbstein's in-depth research and his talent for laying bare the threads in an intricate, sometimes hardly visible web, an important piece of contemporary history has been preserved. While generally nothing is more boring than monographs about organisations, the story of IDAF is a low-key heroic tale which confirms that good and decisive deeds are possible provided you have the ability to identify with injustice and suffering and to react against senseless and cruel evil.

IDAF could not be seen on posters, or sign appeals like Oxfam or Amnesty. It had to work in the shadows to get things done. So it was underestimated, mistrusted, sometimes overlooked. Yet its significance was immense. While acronyms are abstract and soon forgotten, the actions of John Collins, in the framework of his fund remind us that change is always possible, that dictatorial silence can be broken and propaganda and hypocrisy revealed as lies.

John Collins had a restless energy and a sense of urgency: his own life was running out, but worse, he felt, were the wasted years of the South African political prisoners, of the banned and detained, of the children denied education simply because of their skin colour. Peace not based on freedom, justice and human rights for all is merely a buying of time, said John.

•

My involvement with IDAF began in 1959 when I was expelled from Rhodesia, Angola, Mozambique and South Africa because of my writings on racism and my contacts with the budding liberation movements. In Johannesburg, I met and interviewed Joe Slovo, Ruth First, Walter Sisulu and Oliver Tambo. Back in Sweden I took the initiative and started The Fund against Racial Oppression in South Africa, which soon became Swedish Defence and Aid. I also co-founded the Swedish South Africa Committee and saw it grow into the Swedish Anti-Apartheid Movement.

John and I became close friends; indeed, I had not known such friendship before. We found a common wavelength: humour and slapstick, daring and playfulness, commitment and a penchant for good living. We talked of anything and everything; no inhibitions between us, no taboos. A week younger than my father who died young, John was a father figure but also one of the lawless boys in Richmal Crompton's William books that we both loved.

I acted as an unofficial assistant to John and as a confidential link between IDAF, the Swedish-affiliated fund and the Swedish government. It was a measure of the trust that many governments placed in the person of Canon Collins that they did not ask how their money was handled. Before auditors were called in, the Swedish government held John and me responsible for how millions of Swedish taxpayers' money was channelled into South Africa.

As Denis Herbstein has mentioned, John and I went every year to banks in Zürich to set up pseudonymous funds – Freedom from Fear, Freedom from Hardship, Freedom from Hunger. Under solemn portraits on mahogany walls, we signed papers and changed account numbers with the help of an inscrutable bank manager to whom nothing seemed strange. When we asked our man to join us for lunch, he always declined. He referred to the Swiss mastery of silence and assured us that no client knew any other client. In 1970 John gave me the codes and keys to the safe in Zurich in case anything happened to him. It was a solemn moment of trust.

He liked his gin and tonic and his Sancerre, and his fine

baritone voice filled the vaults of St Paul's. He relished being called the turbulent priest. The fact that he was immensely liked in Sweden outweighed the wrath other governments bestowed on him. His four sons, none of them theologians, kept him busy with their life schemes. In their working marriage of nearly half a century John was the emotional one, Diana the more intellectual – traditional gender roles reversed. Diana's memoirs were aptly named *Partners in Protest* for, except for his external fame, she was his equal in all things.

John's scope was both narrow and immense. We walked in the Chiltern Hills, heading for a ploughman's lunch at a local pub. He did not pay much attention to nature, and when in the midst of a discussion we came up against a white bull he exclaimed: 'Good Lord, where are we, how did this ferocious beast manage to get here?' The bull retreated cautiously. John could be equally absentminded in the theatre, noting down figures for the next dispatch of money to lawyers; consequently, at supper afterwards, he would query whether we had seen a Shakespeare or a Noel Coward. At breakfast, he boiled his eggs green while reviewing strategies and condemning or praising people according to their loyalty to his cause.

He had an appetite for action and swift decisions, a loathing of indifference and compromise. Like Bertrand Russell, he refused to keep silent. John with IDAF was like a dog with a bone; the more somebody (like the International University Exchange Fund in Geneva) tried to take away the sacred bone the more eager he was to resist.

He was the most hated man in white South Africa. He preached against apartheid in St Paul's, and through IDAF his spirit was in every trial and every prison cell in South Africa. The IDAF-funded trials put South Africa in the dock and into the limelight. Without John – as Denis Herbstein vividly shows – apartheid would have stayed longer.

Thabo Mbeki, Albie Sachs and Dennis Brutus were among those I met for the first time in Amen Court. John had friends all over Africa: Kwame Nkrumah, Julius Nyerere,

Kenneth Kaunda, Seretse and Ruth Khama. But he was unknown to the many thousands he helped to survive. When he was nominated for the Nobel Peace Prize, few knew what he was doing to deserve it. As late as 1987, IDAF funded a conference in Harare on South Africa's imprisoned and tortured children, but officially it was paid for by the Bishop Ambrose Reeves Trust. It was the first time that ordinary people from South Africa, most of them black mothers, met the ANC leadership in exile. I remember Joe Slovo getting most of the songs and applause.

To Herbstein's account of Craig Williamson, the spy, I can add that he was suspected by some Swedish members of the IUEF board, but Eriksson frantically defended his friend. Williamson even wrote drafts for a Swedish cabinet minister answering questions from the opposition in Parliament about the purpose of anti-apartheid assistance. I was present in the Russell Hotel when Eriksson turned up with a message informing John that, in view of his age, IDAF and IUEF should merge – it was the wish of the Swedish government, the main donor of both. Collins was upset but inclined to believe it. I phoned Olof Palme, the Swedish Prime Minister, and had him talk to John. The act was of course a preposterous lie.

•

John came for Midsummer festivities in the Swedish country-side. We picked mushrooms in the forest where Sally Mugabe (exiled in Sweden) claimed that only white mushrooms were edible, all others poisonous. Writing this, I remember the memorial service in St Paul's after his death when Mazizi Kunene read his poem for John about the children of the sun who carry the sufferings of others and about the mushrooms:

> You planted green mushrooms in the bowels of a cave
> To be reaped in the quiet season;
> Like the moon-flower that is born a thousand years in secret,
> To feed and nourish each new generation with the ancestral dream.

In the kitchen with Diana's leek pudding, in a private room in the Whig & Pen, in front of the fire in the Amen Court library, or on a rainy walk across Hampstead Heath, we planned inventive aid programs for the victims of apartheid. The strong tea and the oatmeal biscuits crushed between heaps of cryptic letters and blackened stencils in the basement where Phyllis Altman and Rica Hodgson resided are to me what the Madeleine cake was to Marcel Proust – a flavour utopian, fiery and rebellious, evocative of extraordinary moments that are resurrected from oblivion and from what then seemed merely a dutiful routine, a farewell music from an epoch gone.

Per Wästberg was president of International PEN 1979–86. He has been a member of the Swedish Academy and its Nobel Committee on Literature since 1997.

Acknowledgements

My single contact with John Collins – other than hearing him speak at nuclear disarmament and anti-apartheid meetings in Trafalgar Square – occurred on a wintry morning in St Paul's Cathedral some time in the early 1970s. A cultivated male voice came through on the phone and said Canon Collins would like to see me. I was on the *Sunday Times*, trying hard to write more about South Africa, and though it did not seem to have the makings of a scoop, this was, after all, the celebrated Canon of St Paul's. He was waiting inside the West Door. He walked ahead, briskly, along the darkened nave, weaving in and out of pillars, keeping his distance from the few tourists as if they might be carrying an infectious disease. He slowed down, related some incident *sotto voce*, and marched on again, repeating the pattern several times. It was a scene out of the film *Our Man in Havana*. I cannot recall what we talked about. It was icily cold and my thought processes would not have been at their best. He might have been sounding me out on a political trial I had written about. I never heard from him again. I thought I knew a fair amount of what was going on between Britain and South Africa but, other than his well-publicised fundraising events, I had no inkling of his creative role in the struggle against apartheid. This book is an attempt to fill the gap

I want to thank in particular the United Nations Special Committee against Apartheid and the Sigrid Rausing Trust for the generous financial contributions that helped me research the book and have it published.

Lewis Chester, who edited an earlier version of the book.

The staff of the Public Record Office in Kew; the British Library newspaper library, Colindale; the Lambeth Palace library; the United Nations Information Centre in London;

the Mayibuye Centre at the University of the Western Cape; the University of Cape Town Jagger Library; and the statistical department at the *Financial Times*.

Louise Asmal, John Battersby, Geoffrey Bindman, Yetta Bonavie, Al Cook, Ginny Cumming, Saul Dubow, Boris Ersson, Barry Feinberg, Susan Frances, Bill Frankel, Cyril Glasser, Eve Gray, the late Elaine Greene, Christabel Gurney, Nick Guthrie, Verne Harris, Lily Herzberg, Michael Holman, George Houser, Paul Joseph, Gary Kilgallon, Mike Kirkwood, Horst Kleinschmidt, Bjorn Kumm, Margo Levy, Hugh Lewin, Bob Low, Tony McGrath, Jenny Maimane, Shula Marks, Berend Meijer, Anne Mitchell, Bert Musschenga, André Odendaal, Peter Plouviez, Elaine Potter, John Prevett, Terence Ranger, Enuga Reddy, Ronald Segal, Fr John Sherrington, Peggy Stevenson, Raymond Tucker, Randolph Vigne, the late Donald Woods and Paul Yule, for their ideas and/or comments on the progress of the manuscript.

The scores of those interviewed, listed at the end of the book, whose special knowledge I have valued.

And finally the editorial team for meeting the challenge of editing a book 6,000 miles away – helped by the wonder of e-mail: Mary Ralphs and John Daniel of the HSRC Press, and Louise Torr and Jon Rash, working with John Daniel in the Durban sub-tropics.

Acronyms

AAM	Anti-Apartheid Movement
ACOA	American Committee on Africa
ANC	African National Congress
ARM	African Resistance Movement
BBC	British Broadcasting Corporation
BDAF	British Defence and Aid Fund for Southern Africa
BMA	British Medical Association
BOSS	Bureau of State Security
CCJP	Catholic Commission for Justice and Peace
CCSA	Christian Concern for Southern Africa
CIA	Central Intelligence Agency
CIDA	Canadian International Development Agency
CND	Campaign for Nuclear Disarmament
COSAS	Congress of South African Students
COSATU	Congress of South African Trade Unions
COSAWAR	Committee of South African War Resisters
CP	Communist Party
CUSO	Canadian University Students' Organisation
D&A NZ	Defence and Aid New Zealand
DAF	Defence and Aid Fund
DAFN	Defence and Aid Fund Nederland
DANIDA	Danish International Development Agency
DRC	Dutch Reformed Church
ECC	End Conscription Campaign
EDA	Environmental Development Agency
EIRIS	Ethical Investment Research Service
ELTSA	End Loans To South Africa
FO	Foreign Office
FREE	Foundation for the Relief and Education of Exiles
FRELIMO	Front for the Liberation of Mozambique
IDAFSA	International Defence and Aid Fund for Southern Africa (commonly called IDAF)
IMO	International Money Order

IUEF	International University Exchange Fund
MK	*Umkhonto-we-Sizwe* ('Spear of the Nation')
NUPE	National Union of Public Employees
NUSAS	National Union of South African Students
OAU	Organisation of African Unity
PAC	Pan Africanist Congress
PAIGC	*Partido Africano da Independência da Guiné e Cabo-Verde*
PEBCO	Port Elizabeth Black Civic Organisation
RAF	Royal Air Force
SACC	South African Council of Churches
SACP	South African Communist Party
SACTU	South African Congress of Trade Unions
SAIC	South African Indian Congress
SALDEF	South African Legal Defence Fund
SANROC	South African Non-Racial Olympic Committee
SASO	South African Students' Organisation
SATIS	South Africa The Imprisoned Society
SERF	State of Emergency Relief Fund
SIDA	Swedish International Development Agency
SOMAFCO	Solomon Mahlangu Freedom College
SWAPO	South West African People's Organisation
TASS	Technical, Administrative and Supervisory Section
TRC	Truth and Reconciliation Commission
TUC	Trades Union Congress
UCT	University of Cape Town
UDF	United Democratic Front
UDI	Unilateral Declaration of Independence
UN	United Nations
UNESCO	United Nations Educational, Scientific and Cultural Organisation
WCC	World Council of Churches
ZANLA	Zimbabwe African National Liberation Army
ZANU	Zimbabwe African National Union
ZAPU	Zimbabwe African People's Union
ZIPRA	Zimbabwe People's Revolutionary Army
ZNP	Zimbabwe National Party

TWO MEN CAME TO LUNCH

Two men in lounge suits mingled with the summer tourists on the steps of St Paul's Cathedral. The taller of the two, Nelson Mandela, 'the Black Pimpernel', was being sought here, there and everywhere by South Africa's ubiquitous security police. His companion, and host in London, was Oliver Tambo, leader in exile of the African National Congress (ANC). The 'tourists' admired the cathedral's great dome, before setting off briskly down Ludgate Hill, veered right into Ave Maria Lane, took a sharp left at Amen Corner and emerged in the late 17th century tranquillity of Amen Court.

Waiting for them at number 2 Amen Court was John Collins, Canon of St Paul's Cathedral, tall, patrician, with a shock of whitening hair. Collins, at 57, enjoyed a reputation as Britain's most unconventional priest, but he still liked to observe the niceties. Some years earlier when visiting South Africa, Mandela had welcomed him into his township house in Soweto. The Amen Court lunch was a return social engagement. Diana Collins, the Canon's wife and partner in political activism, laid on the spread.

There was no shortage of matters about which polite table talk could be made. It was July 1962, and until six months earlier, Mandela had never set foot outside South Africa. He could relate tales of cloak-and-dagger visits to ten African countries where he had extolled the importance of the ANC in its war against apartheid. And though the reach of Pretoria's police extended to London, he had managed unobtrusive meetings with Hugh Gaitskell and Joe Grimond, leaders of the British Labour and Liberal parties. There had even been a spot of undercover sightseeing – the statue in Parliament Square of Jan Smuts, renowned South African premier and staunch wartime ally of Britain, had produced an exchange with Tambo about how one day it might be replaced by a more appropriate figure.

Collins found the shoptalk beguiling, but the real business of the occasion was transacted in his study over coffee. Although best known as the controversial chairman of the Campaign for Nuclear Disarmament (CND), much of the Canon's time and energy over the previous six years had been devoted to raising funds for activists on trial for political offences in South Africa, and providing welfare payments for the families of those in prison. Mandela and Tambo, along with scores of opponents of apartheid, had benefited directly from the fund-raising efforts of the Defence and Aid Fund (DAF), which was part of Collins's Christian Action movement.

Collins deemed the money well spent, but it had to be appreciated that most of it was drawn from a constituency of concerned Christians, Quakers and pacifists. The Canon had served in the war as a chaplain in the Royal Air Force (RAF), but the atomic bombs dropped on Hiroshima and Nagasaki had turned him into a 'reluctant pacifist'. Non-violence came to be at the core of his personal and political philosophy, although assertive forms of passive resistance (such as the Gandhian *Satyagraha* and CND's annual four-day Easter marches to the nuclear weapons research centre at Aldermaston, 50 miles west of London) met with his approval. The ANC's rigorously enunciated commitment to non-violent political action had equal appeal to Collins.

A few months earlier, however, the ANC had given up on turning the other cheek and had launched a sabotage campaign against the apartheid regime. In December 1961, a recently formed clandestine organisation, *Umkhonto-we-Sizwe* ('Spear of the Nation', or MK), had blown up a number of government installations. A leaflet campaign accompanying the first acts of sabotage proclaimed MK as 'a new independent body' resolved 'to carry on the struggle for freedom and democracy by new methods, which are necessary to complement the actions of the established national liberation movement' (Mandela 1994: 274). The implications of this new militancy naturally disturbed some in London. Collins had been obliged to pacify a Quaker member of Christian Action's ruling council who expressed unhappiness at being associated with a fund that 'underwrote violence'. Although the ANC had not yet publicly acknowledged a connection between itself and the MK saboteurs, the link could hardly have been closer. MK's commander-in-chief was Collins's lunch guest, Nelson Mandela.

Recalling the events of that day 30 years later, Mandela spoke of having to weigh his words carefully, but communication was made easier by a measure of common feeling between Collins and the ANC's two leading figures. Both Mandela and Tambo, who had become a close friend of the Collinses, had been educated at schools founded by Christian missionary societies, so that there was an intrinsic sense of operating within a Christian tradition. Tambo, in fact, had been on the verge of taking orders in the Anglican Church before deciding on a career in law, which led to the founding of South Africa's first all-black legal practice, Mandela & Tambo. However, there was no disguising the fact that while Collins's Christian commitment had led him, in middle life, to a very public pacifist position, the ANC was now proceeding in the contrary direction.

It was critical for Mandela to ensure that Collins kept up 'the absolutely formidable work' of Defence and Aid. Many of the Canon's followers who had been giving funds for non-violent resistance might be wary now of underwriting sabotage. And, although MK's campaign had not yet resulted in loss of life (save for one of its own bombers), it had embarked on a course that could lead to bloodletting. Mandela did not ask Collins to condone what was being done, but he thought he was entitled to an explanation 'as a non-violent man committed to peace, but also as our close friend' (Yule interview 1993).

Mandela sketched his personal odyssey from a position of non-violent protest to the point where he had become the ANC's instigator of armed struggle. As he saw it, the space for peaceful protest no longer existed in South Africa. The government had intensified its repression to a degree that closed off all peaceful channels of black political expression. Non-violent protest, as defined by Gandhi and others, was intended to inspire a change in the hearts and minds of the oppressor. In South Africa, no such change could be detected. On the contrary, the mildest form of political activity was visited with official brutality. The banning of the ANC sought to deprive the people of their voice as well as their power to act. In this situation Mandela felt the African leadership had not only the right, but also the duty, to explore armed struggle as an alternative way forward. This, he explained, was the reason why the ANC had taken the decision to end its near 50-year-long commitment to non-violence.

In his response, Mandela recalled that Collins made it clear that 'he was against violence, but understood our form of violence, that we were forced to resort to what were purely defensive actions' (Mandela interview 1992). While not endorsing violence itself, Collins was prepared to give his support to help the victims of what might happen in that conflict. 'He left (to us) the actual form of the struggle that should be adopted by the leadership inside the country. He said that he did not think it was his duty to interfere' (Yule interview 1993).

Collins went on to argue that none of the money he raised should be used to promote violent political activity, but the formula he endorsed amounted to a pledge of support – through trial defence, or family welfare payments, or both – for any activist, violent or otherwise, who was in trouble with the authorities. If the logic of the distinction between violence and defensive violence was a shade ambiguous, Collins and Mandela both felt that a valuable measure of mutual understanding had been achieved. They could go on working together.

It had been an excellent lunch, but the visitors had to move on to other business. The 'Pimpernel' would surface a few days later in Addis Ababa where, as a guest of the Ethiopian government, he was given the opportunity to hone his skills as a guerrilla leader with a crash course in the arts of demolition, weaponry and mortar firing. Within a few months however, he was in prison, a confinement that he would endure for 27 years, most of it on Robben Island, the former leper colony off Cape Town that was South Africa's version of Alcatraz.

Collins and Mandela never met again, but the understanding stitched together at Amen Court was to have a profound effect on how southern Africa waged its freedom struggle. The epic saga of Mandela's ultimate triumph after the long years in prison has been told many times since, most graphically by Mandela himself. This is the lesser known, but no less dramatic, parallel story of John Collins and his decades-long clandestine funding war on the perpetrators and practices of apartheid.

Chapter 1

JOHN COLLINS: CHURCHILL'S 'DUPE'

The British public's perception of Canon John Collins was reflected in a sketch in the BBC's satirical programme *That Was the Week That Was*, which flourished in the early 1960s. Three unwashed 'beatniks', the term used at the time to describe today's hippies, are in earnest conference about who might best represent their interests in a new national protest organisation. They settle for Collins who, they feel, can be relied upon to make a hash of the enterprise. As one of them puts it, 'He's always in a muddle, you see, muddle, muddle, muddle'.

The joke, though not entirely misplaced, overlooked two key aspects of the man – his practical effectiveness and his single-mindedness once his sympathies were engaged in a cause. From his home in Amen Court and later, out of a shabby four-storey office block in the Borough of Islington, Collins's Defence and Aid Fund injected tens of millions of pounds into the struggle against apartheid. It was money raised by the fund that underpinned almost every political trial of importance to come before the South African courts, from the defence of Nelson Mandela and his co-accused in the five-year-long Treason Trial of the late 1950s and early 1960s; the historic 1964 Rivonia trial; representing Steve Biko's family at the dramatic inquest into his prison death in 1977; through to the gigantic effort required to combat the prosecuting frenzy of the 1980s that heralded the end of white rule. At the same time, funds were directed to the dependants of political prisoners, in South Africa, South West Africa (Namibia) and Rhodesia (Zimbabwe). In each case,

Collins's initiative was crucial to the morale, and often the actual physical survival, of an African resistance leadership in and out of jail.

Lewis John Collins's background offered no waymark to an unorthodox political career. He was born at Hawkhurst in Kent on 23 March 1905, the youngest of four children of a moderately successful builder. The Collinses were at the respectable lower end of the middle class and afraid of sinking lower, but John was brainy and his future promising. It was a church-going home, and at the age of six the boy is said to have expressed the wish to become a priest; not long afterwards this ambition was elevated to Archbishop of Canterbury. He moved smoothly through a minor public school, Cranbrook, and proceeded to Cambridge, where he took his first degree at Sidney Sussex College, Oliver Cromwell's *alma mater*. Sure of his vocation, he stayed on at Cambridge to train for the priesthood at Westcott House theological college. There was no doubting his equipment for the job. He had a large, reassuring presence, a fine baritone voice for singing responses, and he was no troublemaker. His single remembered political flourish during this time was wholly in tune with his conformist, Tory upbringing – in the 1926 general strike, he took the part of the strike-breakers by enlisting as a special constable. It was his patriotic duty.

His first parish in a conservative enclave of Kent was not a success. Collins was not cut out for the quotidian niceties of a country curacy. The stage was too small, and the tea parties and tennis afternoons were too draining. His old college, Sidney Sussex, rescued him, head-hunting him as its chaplain. This was followed smartly by a move to London to a minor post at St Paul's Cathedral, doubling it with a job as Priest-in-Ordinary to the British monarch George V. He was advised before he went off to Buckingham Palace to 'keep the sermons down to seven minutes and you'll be popular with the King' (Collins 1992: 83). He found that ten minutes was just permissible. In ecclesiastical terms, he was an upwardly mobile young man, but then his latent impetuosity got him in a spot of bother.

While his own house was being done up, Collins lodged with a theology professor, the Rev. Maurice Relton. One night, returning from the theatre with Relton's stepdaughter, John kissed her goodnight. Next morning at breakfast Mrs Relton warmly congratulated the young priest on his engagement, which her husband precipitately announced in *The Times*. Collins dithered, and when he gave up the tryst, Relton vowed publicly to 'break you for this'. Collins first came to the notice of Fleet Street under the headline 'Priest-in-ordinary to the King breaks engagement'. Happily, the church had academic ambitions for him. He was eased out of the firing line back to Cambridge, as Vice-Principal of Westcott House. Three years later, moving ever upward, he was Dean of Oriel College, Oxford. But by now the obedient, strike-breaking churchman was developing a Christian conscience.

These were the tumultuous thirties. Unemployment and squalor at home and the rise of the dictators in Europe made Collins revise many of the conventional beliefs he had once accepted about order and society. After a visit to the family of a student in south Wales he described the 'hopelessness and despair revealed in the faces of the unemployed, sitting outside their wretched cottages with nothing to do, and the anger and rebellion burning in the eyes of their womenfolk, and when I saw those slagheap playgrounds... upon which no middle-class parents would ever allow their children to play... a great sense of indignation arose within me'. He realised furthermore 'what a humbug the Establishment is, and how feeble and how at fault is the Church in its social and political witness' (Collins 1966: 62).

He now came under the spell of Albert Loisy, a French Roman Catholic priest excommunicated for his modernising ideas. Collins visited Loisy on several occasions, causing him to question further his conservative approach to politics and social organisation. His disdain for the Church of Rome was reinforced when Cardinal Pacelli, the future Pope Pius XII, blessed, in the name of Christ, Italian troops equipped with mustard gas embarking on their 'civilising' mission to Abyssinia, one of the most ancient of Christian countries (Collins 1966: 63).

As the decade progressed, colleagues in the Oriel common room came to refer to Collins as 'fire-eating John'. There was further evidence that the strike-breaker of the 1920s was changing his spots when he advised the college servants, then on pitifully low wages, that they might improve their lot by joining a trade union. Collins was also discovering a gift for publicity. The King and Queen were due to visit Oxford, but would only formally enter colleges of royal foundation. Oriel was not one of these, though a walk through its grounds was on the itinerary. In league with a *Daily Mirror* photographer, Collins had an undergraduate paint a tortoise in the college colours and place it in the path of the royals. They stopped, and they were amused. As far as the newspapers were concerned the following morning, it might have seemed that George and Mary were in town solely to visit Oriel. The episode, Collins wrote, gave him 'an early insight into the Public Relations racket which, though sometimes perhaps tempting me into indiscretion, has often proved useful in my work' (Collins 1966: 260).

By the time of the outbreak of hostilities with Germany in 1939, Collins had joined the Labour Party and was proclaiming himself a Christian socialist. He had by now married into a die-hard conservative family. Diana Elliot, 12 years his junior, had given up her English studies at Oxford to marry Collins and, incidentally, bring him into contact with a constellation of empire-building relatives. They were Suffolk high-Tory stock that traditionally looked to the colonies for careers as soldiers, lawyers, doctors, civil servants and businessmen. Diana's paternal grandfather had been an army doctor in the Boer War and was besieged at Ladysmith. Her maternal grandfather, James Oliver Fison, founded the firm whose fertilisers enriched the soil of many lands, not excluding the veld usurped by the Boers in South Africa. But Diana's stepmother had her doubts about the marriage to a priest and said to her, 'You'll have such a dull life' (Collins 1992: 104).

Collins joined the RAF and was posted to Yatesbury in Wiltshire where Bomber Command radar and radio operators were trained. He was a non-flying chaplain charged with responsibility for organised worship in a camp with a sharper than average awareness of impending mortality. Although military chaplains have a high status in time of war, they are not expected to be obtrusive. Collins was the exception. He founded an apostolic cell, the Fellowship of the Transfiguration, which was designed to raise the spiritual awareness of officers and men. No one was excluded from its reach, which tended to be egalitarian as well as evangelical. One Christmas Eve, the camp commanding officer called to reserve front-row seats for himself and senior officers at the midnight carol service. Collins explained that this would not be possible, as the fellowship did not recognise rank at church functions. The officers would be welcome to find their own seats – provided they were sober.

Collins's most telling contribution to camp life was to draw eminent speakers from the outside world. Among those who came to talk on the social implications of the Gospel and their hopes for post-war Britain were the Labour Party titans, Clement Attlee and Stafford Cripps; the radical Archbishop of Canterbury, William Temple; and Lord Beveridge, father of the National Insurance scheme. The glittering list even attracted the attention of the prime minister. Shown a memorandum indicating that the Russian ambassador Maisky was scheduled to speak at Yatesbury, Winston Churchill paused long enough in his conduct of the war to minute in the margin that Collins was 'either a communist or a dupe' (John Collins's interview in *The Irish Times* 10.05.75).

In July 1944, Collins was transferred to Bomber Command's headquarters at High Wycombe, where there was a family connection. Diana was a second cousin of Arthur 'Bomber' Harris, the hard-driving boss of the operation. For a while, she and the Collinses first child, Andrew, were lodged in Harris's official residence. Proximity, however, failed to temper the Canon's radicalism. The relationship with Harris was placed under strain when Collins, following a request he could not refuse, featured Harry Weldon an Oxford philosophy don and one-time personal assistant to Harris, as guest speaker on the topic of 'The Ethics of Bombing'. Collins made it known about the camp that a more appropriate title would have been 'The Bombing of Ethics'.

With the war over, Collins brought a crusader's touch to the widespread national desire for spiritual as well as political rejuvenation by launching Christian Action. Those assembled at a packed founding meeting in Oxford town hall on the evening of 5 December 1946 included Protestants, Catholics, Quakers and a sturdy minority of atheists and Jews. Further meetings at Central Hall, Westminster, the left's debating chamber near the Houses of Parliament, and at venues across the country, broadened the appeal and the number of disciples. By no means all were of the left. Tory supporters included Rab Butler, the 'almost' future Prime Minister, and Quintin Hogg, a future Lord Chancellor.[1] Another leading Tory, Lord Halifax, was a patron of Christian Action, as was Britain's foremost filmmaker at that time, J Arthur Rank.

Collins's objective was to make the church more responsive to social issues. 'And it did just that, for a time', recalled Raymond Andrews, a Quaker who served on Christian Action's first ruling council. 'I met people starry-eyed with the enormous hope that the Church would mend its ways overnight and all would follow John' (Andrews interview 2004).

The heady enthusiasm would recede in time, but Christian Action lived on to become an idiosyncratic and often effective pressure group, which was in large measure due to its founder. Collins received crucial support from Stafford Cripps, later Chancellor of the Exchequer in Attlee's post-war Labour government. Cripps encouraged Christian Action's national crusade and used his influence, in the teeth of church opposition, to have Collins appointed to one of the four canonries at St Paul's Cathedral. Sternly against the appointment were the new Archbishop of Canterbury, Geoffrey Fisher, who was no radical; and the Bishop of London, Dr JWC Wand, who had known and disapproved of Collins at Oriel. They feared Collins would be too busy with his interests outside the cathedral. But the office was in the gift of the Prime Minister and Attlee was having difficulty finding socialists to fill his allocation of ecclesiastical vacancies.[2] Collins got the post and with it an undreamed of degree of independence. 'You can't be removed', he used to say cheerfully, 'so they have no blackmail power against you' (*Irish Times* 10.05.75). In January 1949, John, Diana and their by now three young sons moved into residence at 2 Amen Court – in a discreet terrace of fine houses built by Sir Christopher Wren after he had completed St Paul's. Collins was now well positioned strategically, a minute's walk from the Cathedral and three minutes from Fleet Street.

St Paul's had known radicals before. The Very Reverend WR Inge[3], dubbed 'the gloomy dean', had once brought a degree of attention to the Cathedral, not all of it welcome. Inge befriended Collins before the war and had given the young man an inkling of the kind of passions that may be stirred by left-wingers in high Anglican office. Inge's favourites from a wide selection of 'hate mail' were words from a pious lady correspondent who wrote, 'I am praying for your death; I have been very successful on two former occasions' (Diana Collins 1992: 72).

At St Paul's, Collins fine-tuned those attributes that would make him an effective campaigner. He did not moderate the combative sermons, but learnt how to conciliate people, if not principle. The commodious basement at 2 Amen Court provided an operations centre for Christian Action and its numerous causes. Collins also came to realise that his supportive wife was also his most efficient critic. Diana had grown to share her husband's world view, perhaps not with so much force but certainly with greater circumspection. She was her husband's intellectual match, drafting his speeches, settling him down when his flights of fancy threatened to spiral out of control and even, at times, advocating a more radical path than the one he favoured. Collins's notoriety at that time stemmed partly from his controversial views on the issues of the day, but also from his readiness to take on challenges that were not deemed generally exciting, such as road safety and the plight of foreign donkeys.

One early challenge was to haul the Cathedral into the twentieth century. Collins saw the need to liven it up with contemporary artists, craftsmen and dramatists, and by experimenting with modern choir music. An outraged Cathedral organist who threatened to resign found instant support. There followed a chapter meeting where Collins was confronted with a petition signed by all his colleagues suggesting that he should resign. This was the first, though not the last, occasion on which Collins had reason to be grateful for his security of tenure. His geniality was such, however, that few people were angry with him for long. He and the organist became firm friends – and under the Canon's guidance a few of St Paul's cobwebs were in time dusted off.

Racial prejudice in British society was an early front-line issue for Collins, along with denunciations of capital punishment and the arms race, but it was some while before he came to focus on racial segregation in South Africa. In 1947 he caused a stir by speaking out against King George VI's visit to South Africa, but this seemed more a product of scattergun radicalism than a considered campaign. Indeed, Collins later acknowledged, South Africa did not engage much of his attention until later in the decade.

It is difficult to remember now how indifferent Britain was to racial injustice in South Africa in the immediate post-war years. The Church held its tongue, the traders traded, the Labour government steadfastly looked the other way. And most people thought, why not? South Africa's wily Prime Minister, General Jan Smuts, had become an admired figure after joining the Imperial War Cabinet at Churchill's invitation. His country had aligned itself with Britain in its hour of need and it seemed positively ungrateful to find fault. As for South Africa's treatment of its large subject black population, it did not seem much different to Britain's behaviour in its own African colonies. Newspaper coverage of politics in the Union of South Africa tended to focus on the rivalry between the two white tribes, the English and the Afrikaners, still trying to resolve the legacy of the 'Boer War'. Blacks were a side-show lost in a white mist.

The mist began to clear for Collins with the late 1940s publication of Alan Paton's novel, *Cry, the Beloved Country*. The story itself is slight, almost delicate in construction. A black country priest goes to Johannesburg, the city of gold, to look for his delinquent son. Along the way he meets all the deformations of a society sundered by racial hatred and unthinking greed. Paton, a teacher by training and principal of a reformatory in the then Transvaal for thirteen years, had written the book in a spirit of reconciliation. But to many, Collins among them, it read like a call to arms. In 1950, Paton came to Britain on a speaking tour organised by the Quakers. Collins invited him to preach at St Paul's and the two men became firm friends.

In that same year, Collins met the Anglican monk Michael Scott for the first time. Scott, described by Diana Collins as 'a kind of holy vagabond', was a travel-stained veteran of the anti-racist cause in Africa. (Collins 1992: 184). Before Pretoria declared him a prohibited immigrant, his radicalism had earned him time in a South African jail and friendship with Nelson Mandela and other young black nationalists. Most recently, Scott had been to New York to plead the cause of the Herero people of South West Africa (Namibia) at the United Nations (UN). In the First World War, the South African army had seized control of German South West Africa as part of South Africa's contribution to the British war effort. As a result, at the 1919 Versailles peace conference, the colony was entrusted to South Africa's stewardship, with British approval and within the framework of the League of Nations. But after the Second World War, Pretoria rejected the notion that the UN had inherited the responsibilities of the League. Its objective was to incorporate the territory and its one million inhabitants into the Union as a fifth province. Labour Prime Minister Attlee thought it a sound idea. Indeed, few people in Britain would have cared much about what went on in that far-off country but for Michael Scott's resolute pricking of the international conscience.

On his return from New York, Collins invited Scott to speak at Central Hall on 'Christ and the Colour Problem'. It was a Christian Action full house, and Scott did not disappoint. Apartheid, he said, was 'obstructing the natural, social and economic development of all races, the white races included'. But in opposing it, Christians should realise that it might be necessary to 'resist the lawlessness of the law' (Collins 1992: 185).

The manipulation of the legal system in South Africa had by now become an important issue. Since 1948, the National

Party led by Dr Daniel Malan had dominated the political landscape. The former Dutch Reformed Church (DRC) pastor was bent on the defence of the purity of the Afrikaner culture. Elected on a mandate to combat the '*swart gevaar*' (black threat), Malan, without further ado, embarked on a range of legislative initiatives designed to ensure the systematic separation of the races, baptising the policy with no-nonsense directness, *apartheid* (apartness). Three years after the defeat of fascism in Europe, legally entrenched racism had become the prevailing ethic of Africa's deep south.

By now Collins was beginning to think that his own resistance should take a more constructive form. But when he tried to set up a Christian Action group specifically to advance the anti-apartheid cause he was rebuffed. Its distinguished backers viewed the proposal as an unwarranted intrusion into the internal affairs of a fellow Commonwealth country. Diana Collins remembers a meeting of the Christian Action board where 'people got up one after another and said, "Oh no, we shouldn't touch it, it's the most explosive thing, it will be the death of Christian Action". That made John feel it was the one thing we should go for' (Diana Collins interview 1992).

Chapter 2

ACTS OF DEFIANCE

In the wintry dawn of 26 June 1952, thirty-three men and women wearing ANC armbands walked through the 'Europeans Only' entrance of a Port Elizabeth railway station – to be arrested by the waiting police and driven away in *black marias* (police vans), chanting '*Mayibuye Afrika*' (Come back, Africa). They were the first group of peaceful volunteers detained in the ANC's Campaign for the Defiance of Unjust Laws. They filed into the prison cells to the refrain 'Hey Malan! Open the jail doors. We want to enter.'

Within weeks, as acts of defiance spread to other South African cities and towns, the numbers arrested escalated into the thousands, creating the opportunity that John Collins had been waiting for – to be directly involved in the struggle. Some weeks after of the launch of the campaign he received a letter from Father Trevor Huddleston, an Anglican priest in a mission parish in the predominantly black suburb of Sophiatown in Johannesburg. The two priests had not met, but Huddleston had heard about Collins's uncompromising sermons against apartheid in St Paul's Cathedral. Collins, in turn, knew from Alan Paton that Huddleston was the model for Father Vincent, the sympathetic white priest in *Cry, The Beloved Country*.

Huddleston explained that he ran a committee, together with Paton and Ambrose Reeves, the Bishop of Johannesburg, that raised funds for the dependants of jailed campaigners. Volunteers were under instructions not to accept bail or pay their fines. But prison was far from their only worry. Many defiers had held down good jobs as teachers, priests, lawyers, doctors, and factory and office workers. On release, they found their names on employment blacklists. The relief committee did not have the financial resources to help them. Huddleston enquired whether Christian Action could assist. Collins, though by no means certain of Christian Action's attitude, wrote back immediately promising to do what he could.

The 'no-bail, no-fine' Defiance Campaign was an orderly, almost decorous phenomenon, by the standards of what was to come. Led by the ANC and its ally, the South African Indian Congress (SAIC), it represented the culmination of 40 years of earnest, non-violent political endeavour. Since its foundation in 1912, the ANC had put its faith in peaceful persuasion, and it was not disposed in 1952 to give up on non-violence. This campaign, however, represented a shift towards greater militancy in one significant respect. For the first time in its history, the ANC leadership was espousing the deliberate breaking of the law. This was a classic non-violent campaign of civil disobedience in the Gandhian tradition and it reflected the growing influence of a new, younger, more radical element in the ANC. Most conspicuous in this group were Nelson Mandela, Oliver Tambo and Walter Sisulu, products of the ANC's Youth League, formed in the latter stages of the Second World War.

In outlook, Mandela and Tambo were closest. Both Transkeian-born and mission-educated (Methodist in Mandela's case, Anglican in Tambo's), they were also university-trained lawyers. Physically they were unalike. Tambo was short with a face that bore the distinctive scars of his tribe. Mandela was smooth-skinned and tall with a regal bearing that offered a clue to his aristocratic Thembu descent. Sisulu, also from the Transkei, was the son of a white magistrate who had abandoned his black mother. With limited formal schooling, Sisulu was educated in the 'university of life', starting out as a cowherd before moving to Johannesburg where he worked as an estate agent. Within the ANC, his street wisdom and organising skills propelled him to the rank of general secretary. By the early 1950s, the three men were entertaining doubts about the efficacy of the ANC's non-violent credo, but for the time being there was to be no dramatic shift to armed struggle.

As a prelude to the campaign, the ANC wrote a formal letter to Prime Minister Malan asking him to repeal six 'unjust laws'. There was a plethora of choice but the ANC selected:

• The Group Areas Act, described by Malan as 'the very essence of apartheid', which empowered the government to uproot entire communities in order to create separate urban areas for each racial group;

• The Separate Representation of Voters Act, which deprived the coloured community of their right to vote on the common roll;

• The Bantu Authorities Act, which imposed on rural Africans a hierarchical system of tribal governance;

• The Suppression of Communism Act, a measure so broad as to allow the government to outlaw any political organisation or restrict any individual, communist or not;

• Stock limitation laws, ostensibly designed to reduce over-grazing but which had the effect of further reducing the amount of land available for Africans;

• The most detested of all the control measures, the Pass Laws, by which every African male over the age of 15 faced summary arrest if unable to produce his 'pass' on demand by a policeman. The passbook had to contain a monthly signature by the employer, poll tax receipts, official endorsements for work and residential permits in specified areas, and a photograph of its owner. Here was a totalitarian mechanism of control of African movement and employment that the National Party argued was necessary 'for the Bantu's own protection'.

The Defiance Campaign represented the most broad-based assault on official race segregation in South African political history. Yet, it could be argued, it was striking only at the surface manifestations of apartheid, rather than at a structure which long pre-dated Malan's orgy of separatist legislation. The Afrikaners traced their ancestry and their passion for the land back to 1652 when the Dutch East India Company dropped anchor at the Cape and established a settlement behind a stockade to protect them from the local inhabitants, the Khoikhoi. The English were nineteenth century 'Johnny-come-latelies', aiming to secure the sea route to India, then settling and finally exploiting the land. At the root of the 'Boer War' (1898–1901) was Britain's imperialist determination to secure political control of the gold- and diamond-bearing territories of the South African interior then in the hands of the Boers. In the course of the war, thousands of Afrikaner women and children, and their black farm labourers, died from disease and starvation in British concentration camps. The Boers lost the war and deep-rooted seeds of bitterness and hatred ensued from the conflict.

Compensations for the Afrikaners in the peace, which led to the establishment in 1910 of the Union of South Africa, contrived to balance the economic interests of the English mine owners with the political ambitions of the Afrikaners. The understanding was that black rights would be kept, not on the backburner, but in cold storage. When independence was granted, Herbert Asquith, the British Liberal Prime Minister, was able to assure a multi-racial delegation that had come from Cape Town to plead the black cause that in time the Union Parliament could 'by its own gracious and spontaneous act' see its way to improving the lot of the country's black citizens (British *Hansard*, House of Commons second reading debate, 16.08.09).

Instead, the Union Parliament became the statutory vehicle for black repression. The 1913 Land Act excluded blacks from owning land in more than 90 per cent of South Africa's territory. In 1926, an industrial colour-bar excluded Africans from exercising skilled trades. In 1936, the Representation of Natives Act removed the small number of qualified Cape-based African voters from the common roll. Malan's post-war contribution, as leader of the first Afrikaner government able to rule without English-speaking support, was to clothe an old exploitation with a new philosophy and a more ruthless management system.

The Malan regime managed the Defiance Campaign by imprisoning its foot soldiers – who numbered well over 8,000 by the end of 1952 – and charging its leaders under the Suppression of Communism Act. Although very few were, in fact, communists, Judge Rumpff was satisfied in his court judgement that Mandela and his twenty co-accused were guilty of 'statutory communism', though acknowledging that that had 'nothing to do with Communism as it is commonly known'. He was satisfied that they had consistently advised their members 'to follow a peaceful course of action and to avoid violence in any shape or form'. The sentence was nine months hard labour, suspended for two years. Compared to what was to come, it was a light rap across the knuckles.

Discipline remained intact during the six months of the campaign. No single act of violence was proven against the volunteers, though the final weeks were marked by unrelated outbreaks of rioting in Port Elizabeth, East London and Kimberley, which were adroitly used as propaganda against the ANC. The government extended its roster of unjust laws with the Public Safety Act, equipping itself with powers of arrest without trial. Another law aimed at 'any person who encourages, or uses language calculated to cause others to commit an offence by way of protest', faced five years' imprisonment, a £500 fine or ten strokes of the cane (Dugard 1978: 175). The campaign achieved none of its stated objectives, but the ANC's popularity soared, achieving for the first time a membership of more than 100,000. Mandela observed that going to prison had become the new badge of courage for its members.

The 'meddlesome English priest' has an honourable place in colonial demonology. Few have been depicted with such venom in South African school history books as Dr John Philip, superintendent of the London Missionary Society at the Cape, albeit a Scot. On a visit to England in 1827 he rallied support for the San of the Cape Colony. A persuasive speaker, Philip knew which political strings to pull. Soon afterwards, the Hottentot Charter had established the 'no colour bar' principle in the new British South Africa. Now, a century and a quarter later, white South Africa was about to be annoyed by another meddlesome priest.

Collins launched his appeal for funds for the defiers of unjust racist legislation in a Sunday evening sermon on apartheid. It was bludgeon, rather than rapier. 'Let me sympathise with Dr Malan and his difficulties,' he intoned. 'Let us be charitable to him, poor, wretched man, hag-ridden with fear.' He called on his congregation to 'support the cause of the ANC with love

in order to cast out the fear of the Nationalists, and ultimately
to usurp the illusion of white superiority' (Collins 1966: 187).
A friend, the archaeologist, Jacquetta Hawkes, recalled that
when John 'preached brotherhood and love, the congregation
would be happy, but when he particularised it to denouncing
apartheid some would rise and stomp out' (Henderson 1976:
104). Collins's contribution to the rhetoric of the Defiance
Campaign soon made him the Englishman white South Africa
most loved to hate.

Now Collins delivered on his pledge to Huddleston to
raise funds for the cause, an initiative that involved him in
a defiance campaign of his own. St Paul's is a comparatively
short step from Lambeth Palace, official residence of the
Archbishop of Canterbury. Collins's initial plan had been
to draw Geoffrey Fisher into an appeal, thus giving it the
full weight of the authority of the Anglican hierarchy. But
Fisher was cool to the point of hostility. It seemed to Collins
that he 'did not hold with law breaking, however just the
cause' (Collins 1992: 189). So, without his Archbishop's
blessing, he put Christian Action to work, rustling up
£1,450 in quick time.

Huddleston was overjoyed with the cash, as he was with
Collins's public crusading. He later spoke of Collins's impact
in the Defiance Campaign as an awakening to be compared
with the beginning of the crusade against the slave trade:

> So many upright and honourable men in church and state
> opposed Wilberforce and his colleagues, and found moral ar-
> guments for doing so, because they had long since persuaded
> themselves that slavery was part of a divine and providential
> purpose that had continued through the ages. Similarly in
> Britain, honest men and women in positions of authority in eve-
> ry sector of society believed it to be wrong to attack the South
> African Government because it represented authority, law and
> order, and was so closely involved in the Commonwealth that it
> must surely be left to manage its own affairs. There was a strong
> feeling that the values of the union of Boer and Britain were,
> in all essentials, the same: and they were *ipso facto* Christian
> values. (Henderson 1976: 49–50)

Collins, said Huddleston, exercised 'a prophetic role' in demolishing these comfortable myths.

In the short term however, Collins's prophetic gifts alienated a number of erstwhile supporters. He had been able to carry the core of his Christian Action council in support of the Defiance Campaign appeal, but there were significant defections. Archbishop Fisher made his displeasure explicit by withdrawing his representative, while the most august patron, Lord Halifax, once Conservative Foreign Secretary and Viceroy of India, also took his leave. Halifax explained that as someone who had experienced Gandhi's passive resistance movement in India, he did not feel he could countenance similar law breaking in South Africa (Collins 1992: 190). He may also have had access to the cable from Sir John Le Rougetel, Britain's High Commissioner in Pretoria, which complained that funds from the United Kingdom and India providing relief for the dependants 'are directly helping to keep the campaign alive'.[1]

There were other resignations, although not all were related to South Africa. The Roman Catholic Archbishop's delegate to Christian Action took exception to a Collins sermon on birth control. The Tory Quintin Hogg, the civil servant Burke Trend, the writers Bernard Newman and Leslie Paul, and the miller-turned-film producer, J Arthur Rank, were others who disappeared from the scene. Collins himself came under increasingly vitriolic attack from the radical right, though he did extract an apology from William Brittain, editor of the ultra-nationalist *Recorder*, for writing that the Canon's 'preachings from the pulpit are along Party lines' (*The Times*, 17.10.53). The £500 damages went to charity – Christian Action, to be sure. Some years later Collins was forced into an apology of his own to the League of Empire Loyalists for slanderous remarks made from the St Paul's pulpit (*The Times*, 17.04.59).

The effect on Christian Action was not wholly bad. Collins had never been entirely comfortable with the across-the-spectrum range of its political patronage. With the loss of at least some of the great and the good on the right, the enterprise was being fine-tuned. The Council and an increasingly active Race Relations Committee consisted of the kind of people Collins was most happy to do business with – Christian activists, Quakers and the lay left-of-centre. At the same time, as a churchman with ambitions, he ran the risk of making a permanent enemy of his boss, the Archbishop of Canterbury. A showdown could not be long delayed.

In the religious debate about apartheid, a Christian God appeared to be on everybody's side and no-one's. The Dutch Reformed Church (DRC), which served most of the Afrikaner community, provided confident theological justification for apartheid, based on textual scrutiny of the Old Testament. If you believed, as the *dominees* (DRC ministers) did, that blacks were the descendants of Ham (Joshua 9:21), then there was Biblical authority for their having been put on this Earth to hew wood and draw water for the benefit of the white madam and master. Across the spectrum, worshipping the same deity, were those – Collins and Michael Scott in England, Huddleston and Ambrose Reeves in South Africa – who believed with equal fervour in the social message of the New Testament, however destabilising the threat to the existing social order.

Between these polarities stood Geoffrey Fisher and most of South Africa's white Anglican hierarchy. While the Anglicans had little time for the biblical sophistries of their Dutch Reformed brethren, they were themselves divided on racial lines. The many black priests, a consequence of the powerful missionary tradition, were restricted to black congregations. The considerably higher salaried white clergy had white congregations. There were as yet no black bishops. In sociological and racial terms, if not in their ethos, much separated the Anglican and Dutch Reformed churches. If the Anglican Church, representing as it did the 'English' tradition, was instinctively critical of the National Party, its years of inaction in the face of racial injustice had made it timorous in the face of state authority. During the Defiance Campaign, the Archbishop of Cape Town and the Bishop of Pretoria did agree that there could be circumstances in which Christians might properly oppose unjust laws, but both shrank from the suggestion that their own flocks should participate in any way.

Geoffrey Clayton, the formidable Archbishop of Cape Town, British-born like every one of his predecessors, was certainly no apologist for apartheid, but his considered view was that the church would be better employed addressing the deep problems of segregation in its own ranks, rather than inviting retribution by seeking to put the state to rights. The likes of Huddleston and Collins, he complained, were inflaming a situation that needed the healing powers of time and patience. Clayton was convinced that Christians inside South Africa should fight the evil of apartheid. It was, he felt, counter-productive for outsiders to protest. Fisher went along with this view.

So every word and deed of the likes of Collins, Huddleston and Scott were thorns in the official Church's flesh. Huddleston believed all his life that it was Clayton who persuaded the Community of the Resurrection, the order of absolute obedience to which he belonged, to recall him from South Africa in 1955, forcing him to leave his beloved Sophiatown at a time when the community was being systematically destroyed by the forced clearance of blacks from the area in terms of the Group Areas Act.

These issues were given a full airing at Lambeth Palace when Fisher summoned Canon Collins to his presence for an ecclesiastical hauling over the carpet. Citing Archbishop Clayton as his authority, Fisher came as close as he could to ordering Collins to desist from his assault on the South African government. He was not, he said, helping the church in South Africa. Collins countered with Huddleston's view that pressure from outside South Africa was not merely desirable but essential to the achievement of racial justice. When it became clear that Collins would not back down, the atmosphere deteriorated. Harsh words were exchanged and an enraged Fisher seized the lapels of Collins's jacket hoping to shake some sense into him, which, given the Canon's considerable height advantage, amounted to an act of archepiscopal desperation.

On his release, a flushed Collins observed that Fisher was behaving like a headmaster towards a recalcitrant schoolboy. Once again Collins had cause to give thanks for the security of tenure that protected him from dismissal. Neither man won the argument, but the next day they exchanged graceful letters of contrition in which, essentially, they agreed to differ.

Chapter 3

COLLINS IN SOUTH AFRICA: 'THE MOST PLEASANT MADHOUSE IN THE WORLD'

Archbishop Fisher's unsuccessful attempt to show Collins the error of his ways was followed in early 1954 by an initiative from the enemy's heartland. A Durban paint manufacturer, Jack Shave, invited Collins to South Africa to witness at first hand the many good things whites were doing 'for the natives', as polite society referred to Africans in those days. All he asked was that the Canon, on his return to England, speak out truthfully and publicly about what he had learned.

Collins accepted with little hesitation, but Huddleston, who was yet to meet Collins, was alarmed. He wrote later:

> I was afraid that John might all too easily succumb to the deceptive warmth of hospitality which I knew would be offered him in Natal, that he would only see the surface things in a society well provided with a veneer of western Christian civilisation. I was doubtful whether any English ecclesiastic, however well-disposed, could at all assess the reality of such a complex situation in one short visit, more especially when it would make life so much easier to return to St Paul's Cathedral with some bromide assertions about the need for patience, understanding and the desirability of avoiding rash judgments... but in those days I did not know John. (Henderson, 1976: 48)

Huddleston's pessimism was deepened by the fact that he was engaged in two demoralising battles. The previous year, 1953, Parliament had passed the Bantu Education Act, a measure designed to institutionalise the inferior status of the African people. The Minister of Native Affairs, Dr Hendrik Verwoerd, had explained to Parliament, when introducing the Bantu Education Bill, that 'there is no place for the Bantu in the European country above the level of certain forms of labour... There are green pastures in which he has no right to graze'. In terms of the Act, African primary and secondary schools run by the churches and missionary societies were to be turned over to the detested Native Affairs Department, failing which they would lose their annual state subsidy. The Act was due to be implemented in 1955, and Huddleston was in the vanguard of the opposition to it.

The other battle was closer to home. Sophiatown, where Huddleston's mission was located, was one of the few urban areas where Africans could legally own property. In 1953, along with the neighbouring suburbs of Martindale and Newclare, it became the prime Group Areas Act target. Slum clearance was given as the rationalisation for the uprooting of a long-established community of 100,000 people and their relocation to Meadowlands, a new but barren location several miles away. The real purpose, of course, was to whiten Johannesburg by eradicating this 'black spot' in its midst. Huddleston wrote the story of the Sophiatown removals indelibly into history in *Naught for Your Comfort* (1956), which became an international best-seller. The title – from Chesterton's *Ballad of the White Horse* – underlined his profound pessimism: 'I tell you naught for your comfort, yea, naught for your desire, save that the sky grows darker yet, and the sea rises higher'.

Collins's arrival in South Africa caused a stir among friend and foe. He had placed only one rider to his deal with Shave – he would stay a month enjoying his hospitality, then spend a second month touring the country, following his own inclinations and at his own expense. The rules of engagement agreed, Collins settled into the comfortable home of the Shaves, both devout Methodists, and their seven children. The servants, all black, appeared politely grateful to be working in such a happy household – although the Shaves would not, for social reasons, allow Collins to receive black guests in the house. Jack Shave knew everyone who mattered. Collins was a guest of honour at a dinner with the Administrator of the Province of Natal, who told the Canon that Pretoria had instructed him to lay on any facilities he might require. There followed a round of model hospitals, schools, game parks, and African townships where tribal chiefs expressed gratitude for the regime's fine work. For the most part Collins kept his counsel, though, when irritated by one chief who insisted on speaking through an interpreter, he asked, 'So you wish me to return to England and report to our Queen and government that you are perfectly happy with things as they are and wish for no changes?' Caught by surprise, the chief replied in impeccable English, 'No, no, you mustn't do that, things could be improved'. The month up, he thanked the Shaves for their hospitality and went in search of the other South Africa (Collins 1966: 191, 194).

It certainly was a voyage of enlightenment. It was his first (and as it turned out last) visit to the country that was to dominate his life, and he made the most of it. There is the feeling of an adventurous spirit stepping through no-man's-land into a hidden world. The cosseted whites, keenly aware of the boundaries they had imposed, could not conceive of a respectable priest wanting to break the rules to spend time with 'them'.

He came away from his meeting with Chief Albert Luthuli, president of the ANC and recently deposed from his chieftainship by the government, with the impression of a wise and courageous man. 'It is quite fantastic', he said, 'that he should be treated as an inferior person' (Collins 1992: 204). In Soweto, he lunched with Nelson and Winnie Mandela in their Orlando home, and met Oliver Tambo and Walter Sisulu.[1] These men made an enduring impact. He met liberals and communists, Indians and coloureds, and the Mahatma's son, Manilal Gandhi. In Cape Town, Archbishop Clayton was out of town, on a mission in Mozambique.

Collins was especially drawn to Bram Fischer, a man of impeccable Afrikaner lineage – both his father and grandfather had occupied high office in the Orange Free State – who as a Rhodes scholar, had acquired a degree in economics at Oxford University before qualifying for the

Bar. He enjoyed a notable reputation as a defence advocate in political trials. Privately, he was a clandestine leader of the banned and underground South African Communist Party (SACP). In Afrikaner terms Fischer was a traitor to class and race, but Collins said that 'he understood the meaning of the Christian Gospel far better than do those hard Calvinists who, by their fierce and cruel insistence upon the preservation of white supremacy, drive good men to seek in communism rather than in Christianity a way to a better and happier world' (Collins 1966: 210). Fischer and Collins became friends, and Collins would say of Fischer's primarily communist entourage that, 'I felt more in common with this group than with, say, the clergy group in Durban'. (Collins 1992: 208) Collins formed the impression, crucially important in relation to his subsequent work, that South African communists were more interested in overthrowing apartheid than in advancing the cause of international Marxist-Leninism. And he was impressed by the fact that the communists were the only grouping he encountered in South Africa in which blacks and whites mixed and operated on equal terms.

In Johannesburg, Collins lodged at Bishop's House, residence of Bishop Ambrose Reeves, the most trenchant of the senior church critics of Bantu Education. Reeves felt the need to measure his words carefully in public but in the privacy of his home he gave Collins the benefit of his unvarnished opinion. 'The cruelty and beastliness of this place is beyond belief', he told his guest (Collins 1992: 206).

While in Johannesburg, Collins was invited to address a group of black clergymen. A white priest advised him that his black brethren were by and large non-political and it would not be advisable to mention the ANC. Midway through his address Collins asked if anyone supported the ANC. There followed an embarrassed silence, then a priest at the back of the hall hesitantly produced his ANC membership card. Others were emboldened to do likewise. The final census established that all but one of the 40 priests were members. Their white diocesan superiors were astonished.

At the first meeting with the Sophiatown priest in Bishop's House, Huddleston was relieved to observe that Collins had emerged unscathed from his ordeal of indoctrination by official hospitality. If Collins did see himself as a changed, or changing, man it was not in the direction desired by his Durban hosts. He wrote later: 'My visit turned what had previously been a somewhat impersonal approach to race relations into a deep personal involvement' (Collins 1966: 209). The two men were on the same wavelength, as they ranged over Bantu Education, the depredations of the Group Areas Act, and the importance of keeping up the anti-apartheid barrage from overseas. They discussed the prospects for exerting pressure in novel ways through sports and cultural boycotts. Huddleston said that white South Africa gave the impression of being impervious to criticism – and this could well be true within its frontiers – but it was acutely sensitive to censure from abroad. The generous hospitality accorded Collins was proof of this.

Midway through his tour – and with characteristic lack of caution – Collins delivered 'an interim report'. It was nonsense, he told the assembled journalists, to think that anywhere in the world only Marxists and a few cranky Christians were in favour of racial equality. In the long run, 'an integrated state is the only possibility'. But, enquired a reporter, was not this final solution to the racial issue a coffee-coloured race? Collins suggested that the fear expressed by so many of a coffee-coloured nation 'seems to be contradicted by the same people's own insistence that the whole idea of inter-mixture is abhorrent'. It was a neat put down, though better suited to an Oxford common room than his target audience. The *Cape Argus* (24.07.54) called the Canon a 'relentless ecclesiastical Torquemada' and wanted him to know that 'through three centuries there have always been many devoted White people eager to raise the primitive Native above the consequences of his barbarism'.

On the eve of his return, Walter Sisulu invited Collins to address an ANC meeting in the Johannesburg Trades Hall. In the course of detailing his experiences around the country, Collins described South Africa as 'a pleasant madhouse'.

The next day, a photograph of him giving the ANC's clenched fist salute appeared in the press above a caption 'The Communist Canon Collins'. Collins claimed that the presumed affront was in no way intended – he was simply giving the thumbs up sign, but his thumb had escaped the angle of the camera's lens.

Back in England, he delivered on his promise to Jack Shave to speak honestly of his impressions. Black ANC leaders he had met would make an excellent British cabinet, he said. The other pledge, to Huddleston, to mobilise overseas opposition to the Bantu Education Act, proved less easy to discharge. He did make a few speeches on the subject, but with little headway, as opposition was crumbling inside South Africa. Bishop Reeves, with Huddleston's support, took the brave step of closing schools under his control, with a catchment of 10,000 children, rather than surrender control to the state. It proved an isolated act of Anglican Church resistance. Reluctantly, but obediently, Archbishop Clayton handed over the bulk of Anglican schools, as did the Methodist and Lutheran missions. The only churches to soldier on independently without state aid were the Seventh Day Adventists and the Roman Catholics, a small minority of the school population. It was a blow to Collins, who saw Bantu Education as a campaigning issue with the potential to unite the churches and the African leadership in opposition to apartheid. There was no mistaking the finality of the defeat – 'The state marched over us', was Mandela's epilogue on Bantu Education (Mandela 1994: 156).

In March 1956, Collins lost his most cherished contact in South Africa when Huddleston was obliged to accept the recall to England by his order, the Community of the Resurrection. Both were heartbroken. Unlike Collins, Huddleston had taken monastic vows of obedience. There was no choice but to obey and to relish, as best he could, the role assigned to him as Guardian of Novices at the community's home base in Mirfield, West Yorkshire. He would ascribe his recall not so much to the needs of the order but to the machinations of two archbishops, Clayton in Cape Town and Fisher in Lambeth Palace, who wanted him out of the frontline.

Chapter 4

HIGH TREASON

In April 1956, within weeks of Trevor Huddleston's reluctant leave-taking, Minister of Justice CR Swart told the South African Parliament that the police were investigating a serious case of treason and that as many as 200 people could be arrested. But as the months ticked by, the tension eased. The success of the Bantu Education Act had made the regime more confident of its ability to see off its enemies once and for all. The Minister's threat, it seemed, was a spot of early National Party electioneering designed to maintain white apprehension of the 'swart gevaar' ('black threat').

Then, one day early in December 1956, travelling by train in the north of England, Collins read in a newspaper that 156 South Africans had been arrested in dawn raids and charged with High Treason. He knew they faced the death penalty. As soon as he was able, he cabled Ambrose Reeves in Johannesburg: 'I will send you tomorrow a gift, as an earnest of my intention to see that we help you to defend this trial to its end. So please feel free to get the best barristers that you possibly can' (*Isitwalandwe: the story of the Freedom Charter,* (Dir Barry Feinberg, IDAF, 1980). As an earnest of his pledge, he wired all the available Christian Action funds, amounting to £100, so that a defence fund could be started.

Who in the government would have registered the irony of the 105 African, 23 white, 21 Indian and 7 coloured 'traitors' constituting almost exactly the racial breakdown of South African society? The Africans included men Collins had met on his visit – Luthuli, Mandela, Tambo and Sisulu – and others on the ANC executive, including Lilian Ngoyi, president of its Women's League. The academic world was represented by ZK Mathews, one of the country's most distinguished black professors, and the Zulu philologist, MB Yengwa, provincial secretary of the Natal ANC, while from the literary world there were the writers Alex La Guma and Alfred Hutchinson. Fifteen of the accused had professional qualifications, as medical doctors or lawyers. The white 'politicals' included the former 'Desert Rat' Jack Hodgson and the lawyer Joe Slovo and his journalist wife Ruth First, who both knew Mandela from his days as a law student at the University of the Witwatersrand. Most of the whites were communists, but their ranks also featured the social worker Helen Joseph, secretary of the South Africa Women's Federation; and a Londoner, Len Lee-Warden, a trade unionist elected in 1954 to represent Africans in Parliament.[1] There were clergymen too – an African, the Anglican James Calata, and the white Methodist, Douglas Thompson. Huddleston's response to the arrests was to regret that he was not in South Africa to stand trial with his friends. The bail conditions reflected apartheid's values. Whites had to pay £250 and Indians £100, while coloureds and Africans, including public enemy number one, Mandela, paid £50.

The core of the treason charge related to a momentous – and for the government, disconcerting – event at Kliptown, on the outskirts of Johannesburg, on 25–26 June 1955. Huddleston likened the two days of the Congress of the People to a bank holiday on Hampstead Heath. Men with wide-brimmed hats, flapping grey trousers, jackets and ties, women with handbags, sensible skirts, their heads wrapped in colourful *doeks* (scarves), refreshed themselves at booths advertising 'Soup with meat', 'Soup without meat' and 'Comrades Tea 3p – Tea and Sandwich 6p'. All this masked an event of high political purpose. The delegates were drawn from the ranks of the Congress Alliance, a coalition of race-based anti-apartheid groups – the ANC (still Africans only), the Indian Congresses, the Coloured People's Congress and the white mix of communists and non-communists. They had come together to draw up the country's first democratic constitution.

Almost all those charged with treason had been at Kliptown or could be shown to be in sympathy with its aims. Though technically they had not been there, Mandela and Sisulu had hovered on the fringes of the great gathering because they were banned under the Suppression of Communism Act – a banning order that made participation in politics a serious offence. Out of the deliberations came the endorsement of a Freedom Charter, which to western eyes was an unexceptionable statement of democratic principles and equal rights, owing something to the UN Charter but virtually nothing to the Communist Manifesto. Its preamble declared 'that South Africa belongs to all who live in it, black and white', that 'our country will never be prosperous or free until all our people live in brotherhood, enjoying equal rights and opportunities', followed by the assertion that 'only a democratic state, based on the will of the people, can secure to all their birthright without distinction of colour, race, sex or belief'.

In the context of apartheid, of course, the across-the-board pursuit of equal rights by subordinate racial groups smacked of subversion. More, and worse, was to follow. In a society possibly as male chauvinistic as its Afrikaner counterpart, urban black women now asserted themselves. In August that year, mothers and daughters from throughout South Africa converged on the Union Buildings, the seat of government in Pretoria, to protest against the impending extension of passes to women. 'Strijdom,' they sang, 'you have tampered with the women, you have struck a rock'. Five of them were allowed into the Prime Minister's office to present a petition. Johannes Strijdom was away and so the petition was left on his desk. Then, watched by an astonished audience of white civil servants and typists, the 20,000 demonstrators stood in complete silence for half an hour, before marching off in disciplined formation.

Rarely in the history of treason trials can a more comprehensively successful defence have been mounted. John Collins was the financial enabler, although accounts of the period accord him less credit than he deserves, and in some cases none at all. The link between the lawyers and their paymasters was the Treason Trial Defence Fund, run by Bishop Reeves, with Alex Hepple, a former South African Labour MP, its full-time administrator, and Alan Paton active in Durban. Its impressive patrons included Joost de Blank,

Geoffrey Clayton's successor as Archbishop of Cape Town, and Richard Feetham, a retired Appeal Court judge. Mary Benson was one of a group of volunteers who established a close rapport with the defendants on behalf of the fund – an experience she would draw on for her early history of the ANC, *The African Patriots* (1963). With a rallying cry of 'Stand by your leaders', substantial funds were raised within South Africa despite the antipathetic political climate.

In Cape Town, Ronald Segal, publisher of the radical pan-Africanist journal *Africa South*, raised £13,000 at an auction of paintings arm-twisted out of business friends of his family.[2] Rica Hodgson, banned wife of one of the trialists, traversed the country raising funds from Jewish and Indian businessmen. She tapped shopkeepers in Port Elizabeth's New Brighton African location. Indeed, much of the internal £100,000 came from those who could least afford it, the ANC rank and file.

But it was nothing like enough. Over the years the Reeves's fund processed some £260,000 (more than three million pounds in today's values), most of it for defence costs. About two-thirds of this arrived from Collins in London. His contribution was not simply a matter of cash. Having given the fund the initial thrust that enabled it to engage the best lawyers, his unstinting and very public support left the prosecution in no doubt that it was not about to have a walk-over. Indeed, Collins saw the trial as an opportunity to expose apartheid through the state's own tribunal.

The defence leader was Israel (Issy) Maisels, the highest earning QC at the commercial bar. He was assisted by Bram Fischer and Vernon Berrangé, a fearsome cross-examiner, former racing driver and disillusioned communist who had left the party after the Soviet invasion of Hungary in 1956. Berrangé donated smoked trout from his farm in Swaziland to be auctioned for the Defence Fund. The backroom brains of the defence was Michael Parkington, a quirky and acidly anti-communist British attorney who had impressed Fischer with his work in insurance cases. A junior in the defence team, Sydney Kentridge, would in time become a star human rights defender. The lawyers, who were paid monthly by Dr Ellen

Hellman at the Fund's Johannesburg office, marked their briefs at considerably reduced rates.

There were impediments to Collins's injunction to Reeves to get the best barristers. Some, like Joe Slovo, were otherwise engaged as defendants – although he did appear for himself in the trial. The country's sole African advocate, Duma Nokwe, was also in the dock, listed as accused 117. Certainly, with Mandela and Tambo, both practising attorneys,[3] the defendants were not short of legal expertise.

Mandela and his lawyers took the view that the trial was a frame-up, a plot to put the Congress leadership out of action for years, perhaps permanently, while the apartheid programme was set in place unhindered. In this the government might have been partially successful, but the trial became a radicalising event in the unfurling of the struggle. The prosecution intended working through the recorded statements of each accused to establish that they intended to pursue the aims of the Freedom Charter by violent means. Some 12,000 exhibits – pamphlets, police notes, press clippings, pieces of paper seized over the years at political meetings, in police raids or fiddled from trouser pockets and handbags – were fed undigested into the court record. Few could have predicted how interminable this process would be. The last of the accused were acquitted four years and five months from the day of their arrest.

The defence lost no time in attempting an exercise in role reversal by putting Pretoria's policies on trial. In his opening address, Berrangé declared that the defence would contend that the ideas and beliefs expressed in the Freedom Charter, 'although repugnant to the policy of the present government, are such as are shared by the overwhelming majority of mankind of all races and colours, and also by the overwhelming majority of the citizens of this country'.

Much turned on whether sentiments expressed by the defendants over the years could be described as communist in tone. The State's expert witness, Andrew Murray, Professor of Philosophy at the University of Cape Town, considered that many statements attributed to the accused were communistic in nature, including the Freedom Charter itself.

Cross-examining, Maisels led Murray through a number of anonymous quotations, three of which he identified as 'communistic'. To the considerable mirth of the accused and some sections of the court, Maisels revealed that two of the quotations were from American presidents, Abraham Lincoln and Woodrow Wilson, while Dr Malan, the begetter of apartheid, had spoken the third. Maisels then read out a passage that the professor affirmed was 'communism straight from the shoulder', to which Maisels responded, 'No sir! – those were your very own words, from the 1930s'.

With the Treason Trial, Collins the fundraiser moved into top gear. During the Defiance Campaign he had done no more than touch his wealthy friends and solicit contributions through the church press. Now he placed large advertisements in the secular press, especially *The Observer*; he held public appeals at Central Hall and venues outside London, and mail shots were directed at a wider stratum of donors. The 40 sponsors whose names headed Christian Action's appeal letters reassuringly featured luminous figures in British public life – the up-and-coming Labour politicians Harold Wilson and Jim Callaghan; the philosopher Bertrand Russell; the novelists Compton McKenzie and Laurens van der Post; the sculptor Henry Moore; England's cricket captain (later Bishop of Liverpool) the Rev. David Sheppard; and the elderly left-wing Earl of Lucan, whose son infamously disappeared years later after involvement in a lurid murder.

Collins's aptitude for attracting crowd-pleasers was now directed at the recruitment of stars of stage, screen and popular music to enliven his public meetings. The artistic world lent a hand as well. John Piper's Christmas card design raised £600. When Paul Robeson sang spirituals in the Cathedral at Evensong, the bulging collection boxes were for Christian Action. The jazz musicians Johnny Dankworth and Humphry Lyttleton donated their brass skills. Forty years on, Lyttleton recalled his first meeting with a man who knew little about jazz and had misgivings about the concert, though the artists and musicians were performing gratis. They had booked the American vibraphonist Lionel Hampton, but Collins was worried about his reputation for working audiences into a frenzy. The evening was a great success and the audience clamoured for more. As the Royal Festival Hall exacted a £50 surcharge for every half-hour of overrun, Collins, apart from his fears of an unseemly riot, now saw the profits for the evening going up in smoke. He addressed the audience in a 'forthright and testy manner, telling them that if they wanted more, they'd jolly well have to pay for it themselves'. They did, and the melodies lingered on for another half an hour (Lyttleton letter to author, 24.09.96).

Abdul Minty, who arrived in London from Johannesburg in the late 1950s, was impressed by the potency of a Collins event that mixed showbiz with evangelical fervour and an unbridled appetite for the contents of people's wallets. Minty, later a mainstay of the Anti-Apartheid Movement, recalls: 'Trevor and John were complementary in building up a massive campaign in Britain. It was not easy, not yet the period of full-blooded African decolonisation. There was still a debate in Britain as to whether blacks were fit for self-government. Yet Collins did not ask for money, he exhorted it' (Minty interview 1992). The final act of a rousing evening would have the Canon reminding his audience of their moral obligation to support this noble cause. 'We need funds to keep up our work. Who will give me £1,000?' He would stare unembarrassed at the audience, which sat all the more stiffly, fearing that the slightest twitch might be interpreted as a willingness to volunteer so huge a sum. A minute, or more, passed. Sometimes it worked, and Diana Collins or a cohort would bucket the donation. Or he dropped to £500, at which point a well-heeled sympathiser might be relied on to set the ball rolling. Thereafter no donation was too small.

Collins was not operating alone. There was help too from other sources. The New York-based American Committee on Africa, representing liberal churchgoers, academics and a rare socialist or two, raised $75,000 for the trial. Eleanor Roosevelt, the former first lady, sent an autographed copy of her latest book for auction. Despite reservations about communists in the Defiance Campaign leadership, a US Methodist group raised $5,000 in response to a letter from Sisulu. One donor calculated the proportion of his tax bill that went towards military spending and paid $100 instead to the Committee.

Collins sent Gerald Gardiner, the most eminent Labour barrister of the day and a future Lord Chancellor, to observe the early stages of the Treason Trial. Fearing that Pretoria would see a connection with Collins as a provocation, Gardiner arrived as the representative of the Bar Council. Reporting back to a Central Hall meeting, Gardiner remarked on the irony of the Church of England, for the first time in its history, openly assisting in the organisation of a fund to defend men and women charged with High Treason in a foreign land.

The stirring image was not strictly accurate. Christian Action, with a paid-up membership of some 2,000, remained on the fringes of the Church of England. And Collins appears to have been a shade unsure of winning the support of his committee. The minutes of the first meeting after the arrests record him as saying that the £3,000 so far collected was for 'the welfare of those arrested and their dependants', suggesting that, initially at least, he needed to downplay the bankrolling of lawyers, though it was the *raison d'être* of his appeal. Freda Nuell, keeper of the minutes for 30 years, said Collins didn't like to put in too much – 'decisions rather than discussions' (Nuell interview 1992).

While the funding effort for the Defiance Campaign had produced some defections, no one deserted this time, mainly because Collins now had a council in his own image. But not a bunch of yes-men, insisted Raymond Andrews. 'We were intelligent and strong-minded and John was open to persuasion. If he didn't get full support from his inner circle of friends, he didn't go ahead' (Andrews interview 2004). His council later drew the line at taking the Campaign for Nuclear Disarmament on board, which Collins then ran separately, outside the Christian Action fold. Collins used to sound out controversial matters with trusted friends who were not often seen at meetings. They included Lord Longford, a former Labour colonial secretary; the publisher Victor Gollancz; the theologian Edward Carpenter; and John Drewett, Vicar of St Margaret's Lothbury in the City.

For most of the time, however, he could rely on a strong strand of support on the council. John Prevett, a young

London actuary; Michael Graham-Jones, a friend since
Oxford days; and the Quakers, Raymond Andrews and John
Fletcher, who were powerful guides in matters of race; were at
times concerned about the Canon's impetuosity but they had
no qualms about the appeal's overall objectives.

The campaign benefited from a generation freshly exposed
to the drama of South Africa. They had read Paton's novel
and now, in its first year of publication, they bought 100,000
hardback copies of Huddleston's momentous account of
the Sophiatown removals. The priest's Treason Trial appeal
letter in *The Observer* must have seemed like a request from a
semi-deity. During the Defiance Campaign, donors had been
willing to take on board a mildly complicated justification
for supporting the families of convicted law-breakers, but
now the Treason Trial could be more simply presented as
state persecution of men and women denied rights that were
automatically enjoyed in Britain. While many in the Church of
England hierarchy frowned on Collins and his methods, they
could not reasonably be seen to oppose him on this issue.

Collins was able to take the campaign into areas that the
Anglican Church could not reach. Diana Collins recalls
the scene as the post was opened around the Amen Court
breakfast table: 'The family had bets on the amounts... and
the daily score rose steadily enough to meet the requests
that arrived regularly from Ambrose Reeves' (Diana
Collins interview 1992). The donations were from people
of every colour, creed and class. Abdul Minty inquired if a
Muslim might 'join' Christian Action (though there was no
membership card or book of rules). 'Do you respect the life
and teaching of Jesus of Nazareth?' Collins asked. 'Sure,' said
Minty, 'we regard Jesus as a great prophet'. 'Then you're more
than welcome', came the reply (Minty interview 1992).

Collins once advanced the proposition that there were
more Christians outside the church than within it, which
may not have helped his career prospects and might not even
have been true. But his skill in tapping into that nebulous
area characterised as 'Christian conscience', wherever and in
whomever it might be found, was what gave impetus to the
Treason Trial appeals.

As the trial ground on into its second year, Bishop Reeves warned Collins that, whatever the outcome, there would be more trials to come. Was it possible for Christian Action to extend its remit to cover these and other unforeseen crises? Rather than negotiate a new set of complicated contingency arrangements with his council, Collins responded by setting up a legally distinct British Defence and Aid Fund for Southern Africa (BDAF). The fund remained under the umbrella of Christian Action for a while, but in practice it was easier to operate on its own without being buffeted by the eddies of public opinion to which Christian Action would always be subject. So the spin-off supplanted Christian Action as the source for funds to South Africa.

Christian Action was hardly a conformist organisation but it did operate within a concept of reasonable limits. These were wide by the standards of the Anglican Church, which was yet to efface its image as 'the Tory Party at prayer'. If Christian Action was not afraid to be controversial, it was reluctant to operate outside the consensus of enlightened liberal opinion. While the Treason Trial was running, Christian Action supported Collins in a campaign for the abolition of capital punishment, a commitment that caused no end of unpleasantness, including graffiti in large red letters on the Amen Court wall urging whomsoever to 'Hang Canon Collins'. But the council stood steadfastly by its leader despite national opinion poll evidence suggesting he was in a distinct minority. Collins and his friends were rewarded in 1964 when hanging was abolished on a free vote in the House of Commons.

All the same, a clear limit was reached in 1957 when Collins sounded out his council on its readiness to take on a brand new campaign, advocating the unilateral abandonment of Britain's nuclear arsenal as a contribution to world peace. Its members were concerned that the issue was too divisive to warrant its official endorsement. So Collins launched the campaign on his own account, with outside friends. Within a short time, the Campaign for Nuclear Disarmament (CND), like Defence and Aid, born in Amen Court, became one of the defining issues of British politics, arousing enormous sympathy and antipathy in equal measure. Denigrated by opponents as woolly-minded, defeatist and, of course, 'communistic', it captured the imagination of a large constituency in the universities, the churches and a substantial slice of the Labour Party. As chair, the greying Canon enjoyed his highest public profile, leading hordes of mainly youthful disarmers on Easter marches between Trafalgar Square and the atomic research installation at Aldermaston.

The 'thoughts of Chairman John' were reported far and wide. American television viewers were advised that, in the event of East–West conflict, it would be sensible for Britain to surrender, on the grounds that communism could be fought with the mind and it might be possible to convert the occupying Russians – or, as the *Daily Express* would have put it, 'Better Red than Dead'. To Western governments these assertions were sheer defeatism, but Collins saw them as a call to more militant Christian action on both sides of the Iron Curtain as a way of wrenching the course of history back from the nuclear brink. He was not blind to the implications of the Cold War but the battleground to him seemed as much spiritual as ideological. He once said: 'We have permitted the communists to capture the dove of peace, an essentially Christian symbol, to use as propaganda. If we are not careful, they will take the Cross as well' (Collins 1966: 138).

CND would become enormously time-consuming once its membership became fractious about the way ahead, but in its early days it ran smoothly enough, when it offered an emotional release for bottled-up fears about the arms race and Armageddon. The money rolled in and Collins delegated most of the administrative chores. He could still focus his energies on South Africa.

In September 1958, the Dutch-born Hendrik Verwoerd became South Africa's prime minister. He had a clearer vision than his predecessors of the road to the apartheid 'Eden'. While serving as Minister of Native Affairs under Johannes Strijdom he had perfected the concept of 'grand apartheid' or 'separate development'. In 1959, with the Promotion of Bantu Self-Government Act, he initiated a chain of tribal homelands where Africans could 'develop along their own lines'. Although National Party rhetoric made it appear as if something new was being granted to the African people, it was, in fact, the ratification of what had been stolen from them over many years. Now, two-thirds of the population would have citizenship in homelands or 'bantustans' that comprised the 13 per cent of the country's land mass least favoured in terms of resources. The white one-sixth would retain exclusive citizenship in the mineral-rich and largely fertile 87 per cent. The geographical imbalance was compounded by the fact that most blacks lived in 'white' areas where, for generations past, the only serious employment was available. Few whites lived in the bantustans.

These embryonic statelets offered opportunities for chiefs willing to go along with the government's plans. Those who refused were summarily deposed. But the puppeteer Verwoerd could not exercise complete control over his marionettes. In Sekhukhuneland, in the remote Eastern Transvaal mountains, a pro-government chief was assassinated following the deposing of the paramount chief in the course of a sustained peasant uprising. In the course of the rebellion, 14 tribesmen and women were sentenced to death, largely on the evidence of four women. As they waited on Death Row, a further 100 tribesmen were arraigned on related but less serious charges. To Collins this seemed a legal vengeance too far. The £2,000 he sent was an initiative of the fledgling Defence and Aid Fund. The four state witnesses told their story once again. Defence counsel David Soggot asked which of the accused had carried assegais. Each in turn repeated the names in identical order. Prompted by the police, they had learnt their evidence by heart. The magistrate had no alternative but to acquit. Collins had another card up his sleeve. Hearing that the new Governor-General of South Africa, 'Blackie' Swart, was in London, the Canon, his dog collar his *laissez-passer*, inveigled himself into Swart's suite at the Dorchester Hotel and subjected him to an impromptu lecture on the need for clemency towards the 14 condemned men. They were later reprieved.

Despite these initiatives, Collins was conscious that South Africa as an issue was going off the boil. By the end of the decade, the interminable phases of the Treason Trial had long since taken the gloss off its novelty appeal. After the 13-month preparatory examination, charges were dropped against 61 defendants, among them Chief Luthuli and Tambo. Further courtroom manoeuvres brought a late revision of the indictment, and a second group was discharged. By the summer of 1959 it appeared that only 30, which included Mandela, Sisulu and most of the ANC executive, would go to trial. Another year, even two, of droning courtroom rhetoric remained in prospect.

Meanwhile, with most of the ANC's leadership hunkered down with its lawyers, a potent new threat to its status emerged. In April 1959, the Pan-Africanist Congress (PAC) was launched at the Orlando Communal Hall in Soweto with a programme that specifically rejected multi-racialism. Its president, Robert Sobukwe, a university lecturer, and the national secretary, Potlako Leballo, had been in the ANC Youth League with Mandela and Tambo. They believed the ANC had lost its way by entering into an alliance with 'foreign minority groups' of Indians and white communists in the Congress Alliance that had fashioned the Freedom Charter. They aimed to put African nationalism back on track without benefit of communist or other 'alien' influences. Mandela denigrated the breakaway as 'a leadership in search of followers' but the PAC's 'Africa for the Africans' message quickly struck popular chords at home and abroad.

The PAC's anti-communism attracted the attention of Washington. Indeed, the ANC later suggested that the new rival was a Central Intelligence Agency (CIA) creation, its conception taking place in the Johannesburg offices of the United States Information Service where Leballo had been employed. The allegation has not been proved. But the split was not entirely displeasing to officialdom in Pretoria either. The new congress might weaken the ANC, whose non-racial demands could not possibly be appeased, but the message of 'Africa for the Africans' might, with skill, be blended into the dream of 'separate development'.

Chapter 5

SHARPEVILLE

In the early months of 1960 British shoppers were confronted by placard-wielding campaigners asking them not to buy Cape fruit, South African sherry and the Rothmans cigarettes produced by the Stellenbosch tobacco magnate, Anton Rupert. Many housewives, recently made aware of the links between the goods in the high street and the factories and farms of apartheid, were switching purchases. Sanctions would eventually prove of decisive importance in toppling white rule, though at the time they seemed to have the impact of a peashooter aimed at a rhinoceros.

The movement began as a response to the ANC's appeal for an international boycott of South African products. It went public in June 1959 at a meeting in Holborn, central London, called by the Committee of African Organisations, which represented students from African countries then in the throes of their own liberation struggles. In the autumn it was restructured into the South African Boycott Committee, with South Africans now to the fore: among them were Vella Pillay, an exiled economist; Collins's young friend, Abdul Minty, and Rosalynde Ainslie as the secretary. Tennyson Makiwane of the ANC joined the group, as did Patrick van Rensburg, who had moved to England after resigning as South African Vice-Consul in the Congo. He was fund-raising for Defence and Aid and briefly became director of the boycott movement.

The committee's limited objective was to spend a month pointing out connections between South African business and its political system. The Labour leader Hugh Gaitskell opened the campaign at a rally in Trafalgar Square. The boycott campaign quickly developed a life of its own. The organisation had a space in an overcrowded office of the

Committee of African Organisations in the basement of the surgery of the Grenada-born doctor, David Pitt, at 200 Gower Street. The appetite for consumer politicking, particularly among students, was greater than anyone had imagined. A network of committees was established in towns and on campuses across Britain. Collins, who was contributing financially, was impressed, though slightly alarmed by the thought that he might have helped create a monster. Indeed, this young group of articulate exiles suddenly appearing on the scene did cause tensions – pangs of jealousy, perhaps – with the Africa Bureau, the Movement for Colonial Freedom, as well as Defence and Aid.

Van Rensburg was paid £7 a week by Collins, but spent his spare time on boycott matters, which did not please his boss overmuch. A Christian Action council minute recorded his concern at the possibility of the boycott committee becoming a permanent organisation, 'but he (Collins) believed that the 130 committees set up throughout the country would greatly assist in raising money for the Defence and Aid Fund'. However, he was also well aware that they might retain the funds for their own campaigning purposes. Indeed, it was the more likely outcome. How then, Collins worried, would he keep up the payments to the lawyers in Pretoria? As Diana put it, 'If you can criticise John, it was that he was always afraid of someone else siphoning off money. He wanted to control everything, not for his personal aggrandisement, but because he feared that another organisation would deflect money from the trials' (Diana Collins interview 1996).

The boycott committee was due to terminate the public phase of its campaign at the end of March, at which point a collision seemed likely between the interests of Defence and Aid and the activists, who wanted to put the enterprise on a permanent footing. Then an event occurred that ensured the survival of the boycott campaign, refurbished as the Anti-Apartheid Movement (AAM), while simultaneously relieving Collins of his worries about money. That event was 'Sharpeville'.

In South Africa, on 21 March 1960, the Pan-Africanist Congress had launched a campaign against the pass laws, pre-empting the ANC, who were due to begin their protests at the end of the month. One demonstration site was Sharpeville – a 'location' near the Vaal River town of Vereeniging – where a large crowd of determined but good-tempered demonstrators converged on the police station. The panicky white policemen opened fire, killing 69 and wounding many more. Many had bullet entry wounds in the back, indicating that they had been shot as they ran away. It seemed like a firing squad at an execution. 'Remember Sharpeville', wrote the South African poet, Dennis Brutus, 'Remember bullet-in-the-back day' (Brutus 1978: 89).

As pitiless massacres go, Sharpeville was neither unprecedented nor the worst in South Africa's history. In 1921, an African religious sect squatted on land at Bulhoek near Queenstown in protest at the Land Act. In a one-sided battle with the police, 183 unarmed members of the sect were left for dead. A few years later, General Jan Smuts sent in the air force to chastise Bondelswart tribesmen in Namibia for their refusal to accept a dog tax. As with the poll tax in South Africa, the dog tax was a device to create an economic need among tribesmen to force them to become labourers in factories, mines and white-owned farms. But dogs were essential elements of their traditional economy, for hunting and the destruction of jackal. The Bondelswarts were brought into line by the first systematic aerial bombardment of a civilian population, preceding by ten years the *Luftwaffe's* decimation of the Basque town of Guernica. Pablo Picasso would immortalise 'Guernica', creating the most enduring image of the Spanish Civil War. The Namibian bombings inspired no one. The bodies of the dead were left for vultures to pick over.

What made Sharpeville so public an event was its accessibility. It was an easy drive for the Johannesburg press corps, so that photographs of the survivors crouching among the corpses were quickly wired overseas and splashed across the front pages. The images made those who saw them feel that they understood a little more what it was like to be black and South African. Western powers, normally loath to criticise a dependable Cold War friend, felt constrained to register disapproval. President Eisenhower's State Department issued its first serious rebuke of

Pretoria, expressing the hope that South Africa's black citizens would be able to 'obtain redress for legitimate grievances by peaceful means' (*The Times* 23.03 .60).

These were turbulent times in white South African politics. Two months before the massacre, Britain's Conservative Prime Minister, Harold Macmillan, had stunned the white Parliament in Cape Town with an epoch-making speech. In telling his silently disapproving audience that a 'wind of change' was blowing through the continent, Macmillan intimated, in his very English way, that it was becoming more difficult for South Africa's friends to shore her up in the changing political climate. At the time, no fewer than 17 African colonies were on the verge of independence. But with Sharpeville and its repressive aftermath, Verwoerd was able to demonstrate that however forceful the external currents, apartheid was not about to be blown off course, though it did wobble dizzily in the weeks after Sharpeville.

On 26 March, pressured by strikes at home and condemnation abroad, Verwoerd temporarily relaxed the pass laws. The next day Chief Luthuli, Mandela and others publicly burnt their passbooks. On March 30, the government counterattacked, declaring a State of Emergency, implementing South Africa's first exercise in mass detention without trial since the 'Boer War'. The thousands of 'big fish' and 'minnows' that were rounded up included the Treason Trialists past and present. That same day, a mile-long column of 30,000 black men and women wound along the national highway from the black township of Langa to police headquarters in the heart of Cape Town, almost within hailing distance of the Parliament building. A cabinet minister promised a sympathetic hearing of their grievances, but only if they dispersed. They did – and the march leaders were promptly arrested.

The Verwoerd government rushed an Unlawful Organisations Bill through Parliament, and on 8 April declared the ANC and PAC illegal. Henceforth the penalty for furthering the aims of either organisation was ten years' imprisonment. And still the tension rose. On 9 April, David Pratt, an English-speaking farmer, fired two bullets into Verwoerd's head. The Prime Minister survived. Miracle, said the faithful. Poor marksmanship, said his more numerous detractors. From his hospital bed the survivor announced that there was 'no reason to depart from the policy of separate development'. On 10 April, pass searches were restored, as the Commissioner of Police assured 'law-abiding Bantu' that there was nothing to fear from the police provided their passbooks were in order. The signs of a return to 'normality' were the queues to renew passbooks (lost or burnt) needed to make withdrawals from Post Office savings accounts or receive a pension.

Verwoerd provided further proof of his resolution by appointing Balthazar Johannes Vorster as his Minister of Justice. Vorster had been interned during the Second World War for his activities as a general in the *Ossewabrandwag* (Ox-wagon Guard), a para-military grouping sympathetic to Nazism. By 1960, he was seen as the up-coming strongman in the National Party. Meanwhile, word of the grim prison conditions experienced by detainees had reached Amen Court. An Indian detainee at the time compared the treatment of 'non-white' prisoners to that of cattle, and made the familiar point that whites were separated in jail, with better conditions, so that white murderers were treated better than the black philosophers.

The prolonged press coverage generated by Sharpeville – and an editorial in *The Times* of London uncharacteristically critical of the police – provided the necessary advertising for Collins's campaign. In the month following the massacre, donations of more than £40,000 were logged into Amen Court. At peak periods, nine volunteers were hard at work in the basement counting-house, opening the mail and drafting 'thank-you' letters. Along with the British contributions, donations arrived from Norway, Sweden, New Zealand, Canada, Jamaica, Tunisia and Nigeria. The operation became the international focus for anyone hoping that a personal donation would accelerate the end of apartheid. The accounts for the year ending June 1960 indicated that £65,000 had been sent for the Treason Trial defendants, with another £75,000 for welfare and other initiatives inside South Africa.

Now Collins took a step deeper into the morass of apartheid by agreeing to finance an independent commission of inquiry into the shootings. The Bishop of Johannesburg, Ambrose Reeves, had conceived the idea. He knew the State would do everything in its power to mount a cover-up and he saw the importance of gathering the facts and issuing an impartial report. But then the Bishop fled the country after he and his family had been threatened with violence. Dr Ellen Hellman took over the Treason Trial Defence Fund. The inquiry went ahead, led by the Treason Trial advocate, Sydney Kentridge. Some officials did consent to give evidence. Kentridge asked Lieutenant-Colonel Pienaar, the senior police officer at Sharpeville that day, whether he had learned 'any useful lesson from the evidence in Sharpeville'. 'Well, we may get better equipment', was his response (Herbstein 1979: 31).

The Collins welfare operation began with help for the families of the Sharpeville victims, but now, with the State of Emergency, it was extended to dozens of cities and towns. As detainees were usually heads of families, thousands of dependants faced destitution, uncertain when the emergency would end or if their breadwinner would be tried in court. In theory the government was by law responsible for the destitute, but its means-tested maintenance grants for dependants were hardly generous. A maximum of £11 a month was on offer for white adults; £3 for Asians and coloureds; and £1 for urban Africans. For rural Africans, who suffered dearly when a breadwinner was incarcerated, there was nothing. For those who could not produce a passbook, there was once again nothing.

The welfare problem was especially acute in Cape Town where, after the dispersal of the Langa marchers, the army instituted a reign of terror that left 400 township families homeless. Peter Hjul, a local Liberal Party leader, was among the first to become active on the welfare front. Membership of his State of Emergency Relief Fund (SERF) was at first white and middle-class, drawn from Liberals, Quakers and the Black Sash, an outspoken women's protest group that favoured liberalising the race laws. Several churches were involved, though the Catholics stayed away – Hjul found Archbishop (later Cardinal) Owen McCann 'very cautious'. Individual members included a brace of businessmen and Mary Stoy, the wife of the Astronomer Royal. Blacks, such as Imam Haron from the city's large Muslim community, were co-opted later. Liberals ran the show, mainly because those further to the left were banned or in prison. (The Liberal Party, of which Alan Paton was the most prominent member, was opposed to segregation but tried to operate within the confines of the system.)

Hjul quickly ran out of money. Then he was summoned to the palace of the Anglican Archbishop of Cape Town. 'How much do you want?' asked Joost de Blank. Hjul ventured £1,000. De Blank wrote him a cheque for £2,000, to be drawn on funds received from Collins in London. 'It was no secret,' Hjul recalls, 'but we did not make a public song and dance about it. Collins gave us over £10,000 during the emergency period. It enabled us to get down to business' (Hjul interview 1992). With the money, Hjul rented an office in central Cape Town and it was from there that families were helped to restore their homes and hold together the threads of their lives. Detainees were given pocket money, clothing, cigarettes and food. The white suburbs needed help too. Fred Carneson, a communist who represented Africans in the Cape Provincial Council, and his wife, Sarah, had both been detained, and they received their rent from SERF. One of SERF's more esoteric undertakings was to keep up payments to Bothner's music shop for saxophones and trombones being bought on hire purchase by volunteer bandsmen at the Simonstown Naval Base, 20 of whom had been detained. But to no avail. When the dockyard detainees were released, the Navy refused to take them back again.

With the end of the emergency in August 1960, SERF reconstituted itself as Defence and Aid in Cape Town, and offices bearing the name sprouted in Durban, Port Elizabeth and East London. In Johannesburg, it doubled with the Treason Trial fund. Although deliberately modelled on Collins's Defence and Aid and with similar terms of reference, they were organisationally distinct, with a national board of trustees who included Joost de Blank and Alan Paton. The prime connection with Collins, other than the name, was that they looked to Amen Court for most of their funds. So if the new offices brought a degree of cohesion to the relief efforts, they also gave Collins a new headache. The amount sent out for welfare during 1960 was a quantum leap from previous years, but it never seemed remotely enough, and regional rivalries compounded the difficulty. Cape Town and Johannesburg, a thousand miles apart, were each inclined to believe that the other was benefiting at its expense when Amen Court's funds were apportioned.

More worrying for Collins was the deepening bitterness between the Congress movements. While the events of Sharpeville might reasonably be seen as calling into question the wisdom of the PAC's leadership, the effect was to give the Pan-Africanists potent revolutionary credentials. It contributed to a widespread belief among the emergent black nations to the north that the PAC was not just a rival to the ANC, but was capable of superceding the older organisation as the number one vehicle of liberation. Collins himself was never shaken in his belief that the ANC represented the way ahead, but at the same time he could not afford to ignore the new organisation that had furnished so many martyrs to the cause. He was therefore determined that ANC and PAC claims on his funds should be treated on an impartial basis. But Sharpeville had so changed the atmosphere it was impossible for him to appear even-handed. While he could assist the ANC in the courts, discreetly paying the fines of Chief Luthuli and others for burning their passbooks, he could not so readily help the PAC, for the simple reason that he was not asked.

PAC activists coming before the courts were ordered to follow the example of their President, Robert Sobukwe, who argued at his trial for incitement that he was under no obligation to obey laws made by a white majority. 'Without wishing to impugn the personal honour and integrity of the magistrate, an unjust law cannot be applied justly', he said. 'It is not our intention to plead for mercy' (Benson 1976: 7). In refusing to recognise the legitimacy of the courts, PAC members would neither accept bail nor offer a defence. There was thus, in most cases, no call on Collins's resources.

Sobukwe did appeal, unsuccessfully, against his conviction

and three-year sentence, and Pan-Africanists did put up a courtroom defence in some instances. Regina *v* Mongi Tyahali was one such case. Mongi chose a crowded third-class carriage on a suburban train to 'exhort passengers to join the PAC and follow the leadership of Kgosana (the student leader of the march on Cape Town), Sobukwe, and Dr Nkrumah (of Ghana)'. The government, he explained, had 'come to the African people with weapons' (Barney Zackon [attorney] letter to SERF, Cape Town, 20.07.60). A fellow commuter just happened to be a detective. Without a lawyer, his conviction was certain, but one was found for him and, courtesy of Defence and Aid, he was acquitted.

The fund was relieved of a portion of the defence costs ahead of a serious incitement trial. Philip Kgosana was on bail for £125, and his co-defendants for lesser amounts, the money put up by the Society of Friends. According to Hjul, 'They were as guilty as hell, so a couple of them took off and crossed the border. I contacted the CIA man at the US embassy, Bob Cunningham, whose driver was a member of the PAC. "In all honour", I said, "I can't let the Quakers lose the money". Next day I picked up an envelope from Bob and handed it to George Barron, a Quaker on our committee. I said, "Sorry you lost the money, George, but here's the money". He did give me a quizzical look' (Hjul interview 1992).

With no chance of dealing with ANC and PAC defendants on an equal basis, Collins was all the more anxious to ensure that the welfare operation was handled equitably. When, in September 1960, allegations reached London that he was not being fair to the PAC, Collins wrote immediately to Archbishop de Blank asking him to check if there was substance in reports that the Johannesburg office was 'discriminating against Africanists in welfare'. De Blank wrote back saying that on the basis of his enquiries there was 'absolutely no substance in such a charge' (De Blank letter to Collins, 4.10.60). An affronted Johannesburg chairman, Alex Hepple, chipped in angrily with an indictment of what he called 'mischievous gossip circulating in London' about anti-PAC discrimination. 'Every appeal for assistance is treated on its merits, without reference to the applicant's race, religion or political beliefs', he wrote (Hepple letter to Collins, 14.11.60). And yet, despite all the aggravation, Collins accepted more and more calls on his resources. In a world short of water, he was seen as the man who controlled the bucket at the village pump. He allowed himself to be drawn into the festering problems of Southern Rhodesia, part of Britain's disintegrating colonial creation, the Federation of Rhodesia and Nyasaland.[1] Collins sent funds to lawyers in Bulawayo to challenge the 'preventative detention' of 500 African nationalists under the leadership of Joshua Nkomo. The extrovert Labour MP, John Stonehouse, was given £300 to go to Bulawayo as an 'observer'.

Collins also added Pretoria's fiefdom in South West Africa to his list of commitments, and found himself embarrassingly overextended. Three months before Sharpeville, in the 'Old Location' in the capital Windhoek, Pretoria-trained policemen shot dead six men and women for resisting their removal to Katatura, a new 'home' for blacks several miles out of town. Some of the survivors were charged with public violence. In the absence of willing local counsel, Johannesburg lawyers were flown in, but at crippling cost. The South African Liberal Party raised some money but Amen Court's inability to make up the difference led to an angry exchange of letters with the attorneys. Fortunately, all were acquitted and the lawyers received some financial satisfaction.

Collins's penchant for derring-do did not come cheap. During the 1960 State of Emergency, many political activists crossed the porous borders into Bechuanaland (Botswana), Basutoland (Lesotho) and Swaziland. None could feel entirely safe, as South African agents enjoyed a free run in this British-ruled periphery to the point where they at times abducted escapees and brought them back across the border into detention in South Africa.[2] Collins earmarked £10,000 to move higher-profile refugees, many of them white, to safer countries. He teamed up with a Mrs Bing, English wife of the Ghanaian Attorney-General, who chartered a plane under her maiden name, collected the refugees on a remote airstrip in Bechuanaland and flew them to Elizabethville in Katanga province, Congo, for onward transportation to Ghana, there to become guests of President Kwame Nkrumah. The London

Daily Mail (20.05.60) headlined the story: 'Canon Collins was behind plot'. Mrs Bing, it said, wore 'a neat blue print dress and a gay blue ribbon in her hair during the operation'.

Among those who went into exile via Bechuanaland was Oliver Tambo. On his arrival in England, Collins arranged for his wife and their three children to be flown to London. Tambo had been mandated by the ANC executive to keep its flag flying abroad by establishing an exile structure. Though lacking the charisma of Mandela and the down-to-earth directness of Sisulu, Tambo proved to be an extraordinarily capable diplomat – on both sides of the Iron Curtain. The ANC had no funds of its own, anywhere. Its leaders and members in England clamoured for cash and patronage, and Collins stuck with them through thick and thin. He put aside his distaste for communists and saboteurs. But the chemistry between the Canon and Tambo, the gentle freedom fighter whose first career choice was the priesthood, was not to be measured in terms of money alone. Tambo used to refer to himself as the Canon's 'eldest African son'. On a very personal level, by devoting his exceptional energies to the preservation of the ANC and its leader, Collins made an important, if largely unheralded, contribution to the struggle for freedom.

The emergency lasted five months, though the proscription of the ANC and PAC would endure for 30 years. With that behind him and having recovered from the attempt on his life, Prime Minister Verwoerd was now ready to deal with the old enemy, Britain. In October 1960, white South Africa voted by 850,000 to 775,000 to convert to a republican form of governance. For the Afrikaner, the dream of a Boer republic, where the white man was 'baas' and the 'kaffir' knew his place, was about to be realised.

The formal declaration of the Republic was scheduled for May 1961, but first the matter of South Africa's relationship with the Commonwealth needed to be clarified. The country's altered status required an application by Pretoria to remain within the Commonwealth. Verwoerd initially opted to stay within the grouping and enjoyed the support of Harold Macmillan. But the Commonwealth had by this time ceased to be a cosy club dominated by the white dominions; its principal forum, the Commonwealth Prime Ministers' Conference, now had an Afro-Asian majority. The Anti-Apartheid Movement plunged into its first great challenge.[3] Abdul Minty, helped by its Chairperson, the fiery Labour Party left-wing Member of Parliament, Barbara Castle, organised a three-day vigil of Labour and Liberal MPs outside the conference in Marlborough House. Wavering prime ministers were buttonholed. In the course of the conference, Julius Nyerere argued that if South Africa stayed in, Tanganyika, soon-to-be independent, would not join. Cause and effect are not easy to establish precisely, but it is certain that South Africa was blackballed by a combination of the new Commonwealth members and the Canadian, John Diefenbaker, a conservative who held no truck with racism. In the face of growing opposition, Verwoerd withdrew the application.

Verwoerd returned home to a hero's welcome, proclaiming to an airport crowd of supporters that 'a miracle' had ensued. For Collins, this 'miracle' sparked a brief upturn in contributions, but the general trend, after the Sharpeville high, was downward. There was, however, a buoyancy in the number of letters from South Africa referring to the Canon as 'a stinking, red negrophile', or worse. They were consigned to the anonymity of the 'hate file', although a persistent series of postcards assuring Mrs Collins that she was about to receive the sexual attentions of six 'buck niggers' was referred to New Scotland Yard.

Chapter 6

FIRE THE CANON!

The Treason Trial was finally dispatched into history on 29 March 1961. Nelson Mandela and the 29 others who remained of the 156 charged five years earlier were shepherded into Pretoria's Old Synagogue to hear their fate. 'On all the evidence presented to this court and on our finding of fact,' Mr Justice Rumpff told them, 'it is impossible to come to the conclusion that the African National Congress had acquired or adopted a policy to overthrow the state by violence, that is, in the sense that the masses had to be prepared or conditioned to commit direct acts of violence against the state' (Mandela 1994: 247). They were accordingly found not guilty and discharged. Chief Luthuli immediately cabled Collins with the thanks of the accused.

It was to be the last of the conventional political trials. The government had played according to western rules of procedure, and lost. Maisels recalled seeing Johannes Vorster, then a backbench MP, sitting in on the proceedings (Maisels interview 1992). The future Minister of Justice would have drawn his own conclusions. The gloves would come off. The rules would be changed to make conviction easier. Next time, there would be no mistake. And if there were, the rules would be changed again.

In this rare moment of triumph a powerful undertow of pessimism pervaded the camp. In legal terms, the trial had tidied up the agenda of the previous decade, a span characterised by the exercise of the politics of non-violence. But now they had to face the fact that they had reached a cul-de-sac. The Treason Trialists were free, but in a world where they were not free to practise politics. If anyone cherished the hope that the arrival of the Republic in May

1961 might bring a softening of the Afrikaner's demeanour, Verwoerd made it clear that the new constitution offered no dilution of 'separate development'. The ANC and PAC would remain outlaws. The shut-down of legitimate protest was forcing ever more activists to contemplate direct acts of violence against the state.

Collins was aware of these developments and of the threat to Christian Action and its commitment to non-violence. But through much of 1961 he had a larger worry on his mind. At one stage he even considered stopping fund-raising altogether because of the poison that had entered the relationship with his erstwhile inspiration, Michael Scott.

Why Scott and Collins, who shared the Anglican faith and discipline and the same broad aspirations for South Africa, came to such a pitch of animosity was not altogether clear, even to their intimates. But the fact of it was palpable. The *New Statesman* writer, Mervyn Jones, who knew both men, observed that Collins found Scott exasperating and 'distinctly a Savonarola type'[1], whereas Scott 'simply hated' Collins (Henderson 1976: 79).

Some found clues in the natural resentments that arise between a combat soldier and a staff officer who never leaves headquarters. Against Scott's record of those years in foreign fields sharing the causes of Indians and Africans and showing a readiness to go to jail for his beliefs, Collins's on-the-ground experience was confined to two months as a political tourist in South Africa. Both had been in the RAF during the war but it was Scott who enlisted for active service, as an aircrew rear-gunner, although he was invalided out before the completion of his training. Even in peace campaigning, his were the more impressive battle honours. While Collins led the CND marchers into Trafalgar Square, Scott journeyed with an audacious group of protestors to stymie a French nuclear test in the Sahara desert.

There were the differences of style and personality. Collins was a contented family man, with a wife in whom he could confide and the priceless security of a pulpit for life and the Amen Court tied cottage. His four boys wanted for little, unless boarding at Eton, England's most exclusive public school, could be considered a hardship. He was a *bon viveur*, with the ability to make friends across a wide social spectrum. A consummate political animal, radical sensitivities lurked behind his Toryesque mask. Most pertinently, Christian Action was his baby and his alone. He was a crafty committee man, extracting precisely what he needed from his followers. As a fund-raiser he could coax sovereigns out of an empty slot machine. John Grigg, writer for the *Observer*, admiringly perceived that, 'spiritually, John Collins belonged in the Stock Exchange' (Astor interview 1998). Love him or loathe him, no one could accuse him of being ineffectual.

For many, Scott was a saint – the celibate who immersed himself in the suffering of others without regard for personal wealth or possessions. A nomad more at home in a tent on the veld or a squatter-camp hovel, he never adjusted to the complexities of existence in the city. A friend spoke of 'a kind of innocence, a naïveté... if he saw something that wasn't right, he went for it. But he never understood politics' (Legum 1995). The ascetic monk had no permanent London base, no family life. At their first meeting Diana Collins thought he had been sleeping in his clothes. South African author Mary Benson, who was Scott's secretary for several years, remembered him as forever mislaying discarded overcoats given to him by David Astor, the *Observer* newspaper's owner-editor. He found fundraising distasteful and had no skill in handling committees, though, like Collins, he had an admiring band of helpers ever at hand.

Yet the reason for supposing that the bitterness between Scott and Collins turned on differences between an unworldly and a worldly priest is not convincing. Trevor Huddleston, whose record as a monastic activist in South Africa compared favourably with that of Scott's, maintained an excellent working relationship with Collins. Similarly, Ambrose Reeves, in the Johannesburg front line, regarded Collins as a reliable friend. When Reeves and his family fled South Africa, their first refuge was Amen Court.

David Astor has related that what Scott most disliked about Collins 'was the use of hatred in fighting apartheid. He thought it demeaned Christianity. Scott was always ready to talk to his enemies, to treat them as humans' (Astor interview 1998). Many, inside and outside the church, found the Canon's rhetoric off-putting. On topics with a moral dimension, such as capital punishment, nuclear arms and apartheid, Collins's idea of a Christian's duty was not so much to argue and debate but to denounce. There is no reason to suppose that he saw opponents as less than human. On the contrary, he regarded them as all too human. But his approach to evil was invariably the big stick.

Collins had at first been eager to bring Scott into the Christian Action orbit. He sat briefly on its race relations committee and Collins invited him to run the race relations programme. But Scott had ambitions of his own. His Africa Bureau became an effective vehicle for providing African nationalists with a voice in London's corridors of power, directly, rather than through well-meaning European intermediaries. He was a gifted propagandist, whether highlighting causes through the Bureau's publications, putting Africans in touch with useful people in Britain, or lobbying MPs. There was no conflict with Christian Action, as the Bureau's initial preoccupation was with Southern Rhodesia and its place in the Central African Federation.

According to Collins, as Huddleston cast around for a helping hand in the Defiance Campaign in 1952, he approached Scott first. This is not surprising, for the two priests knew each other in South Africa. Scott, 'in some distress', told Collins he had been unable to persuade his 'rather respectable executive' to sponsor the fund (Collins 1966: 187). Collins took it on and never looked back. According to the *Observer* journalist Colin Legum, the friendship might have soured in the very week that an Africa Bureau fund-raising campaign was to be launched. Collins posted a series of press advertisements for South African causes. Until then, says Legum, Collins had not been publicly identified with South Africa. 'Scott was convinced that Collins had learnt of the bureau's plans and had deliberately pre-empted them' (Legum letter 1996). But the two men were already at odds – over the Khama marriage, a headline issue in the British and South African press.

Born to rule the Bamangwato nation in the British protectorate of Bechuanaland (Botswana), Seretse Khama came to England in the 1940s to complete his education at Balliol College, Oxford, and fell in love with an Englishwoman, Ruth Williams, daughter of a retired army officer. The protectorate shared a long, exposed border with South Africa, and the white South African press was vocal in its opposition to this 'mixed' marriage. In this they were echoing the views of the ruling National Party, which was then preparing legislation to outlaw both inter-racial marriages, and also physical contact across racial lines. The Attlee government capitulated to this pressure from South Africa and its opposition was transmitted to the Anglican hierarchy, and the couple was obliged to marry in a registry office. They were also prohibited from returning to Bechuanaland. For Collins, it was a clear case of church and state kow-towing to South African objections to miscegenation, and he said so forcibly. Scott, for his part, shared the perspective of his old friend, Tshekedi Khama, Seretse's uncle, who had acted as Regent since his nephew's infancy. For him the marriage was a flouting of tribal values. During Seretse's exile, the Africa Bureau became centrally involved in brokering a deal between uncle, nephew and the British government, a process that was not, to Scott's mind, helped by Collins's oversimplification of the issues. Time would show that Collins's partisanship was not entirely misplaced. Allowed to return to Bechuanaland in 1956 on condition he renounce the chieftainship, within a few years Seretse became Bechuanaland's first Prime Minister, then President of the independent Botswana.

Scott's autobiography, *A Time to Speak*, published after Seretse's return home, contained oblique references to Collins, without mentioning his name. Christian Action was clearly the target in a less than flattering reference to 'the stage army of the good' which finds itself rendered less effectual by 'going off stage again and coming on again for different scenes'. Scott also wrote of the limitations of 'an organisation with a flag-wagging name or one dominated by an individualistic personality. This applies as much to the religious as the political sphere.' He complained of 'misunderstanding, petty jealousy and efforts on the part of other organisations to "co-ordinate" us, on the plea of unity in the common fight.' He named the Movement for Colonial Freedom (run by the MP and doughty anti-colonial campaigner, Fenner Brockway), and Christian Action as having made unwelcome overtures to the Africa Bureau.

From the mid-50s Scott and Collins confined their attentions to their own bailiwicks, both prospering in their own ways. With Britain forced into decolonising its African empire, the Bureau's range was extended to other parts of the continent – its reports were well respected by lobbyists, politicians and journalists, though few members of the public knew of its existence. It struggled to make ends meet. Scott's gifts as a communicator and persuader did not extend to fund-raising, which he found distasteful. The efforts of his supporters to raise money were impeded by a fastidious insistence that contributions should not be accepted from South African companies or British firms with connections in Africa. Scott relied heavily on philanthropists, foundations and charitable trusts, but this was no guarantee against contamination. A no-strings grant of £3,000 a year to the Africa Bureau came from Fairfield, an American foundation later exposed as a channel for the US Central Intelligence Agency (CIA) (*Guardian* 17.03.01).

While Scott wrestled with money worries, he could not help noticing the stream of cash flowing into Amen Court. Collins's appeals laid heavy emphasis on the role of Christians who had seen front-line service in Africa – Huddleston, Ambrose Reeves and, to be sure, Michael Scott. Scott felt his organisation had a moral claim on part of the money raised by Collins and believed he could make better use of it. He objected to Collins's readiness to dole out funds to exiles living in Britain, who did not, said Scott, contribute directly to the struggle. He was encouraged in this opinion by his influential patron, David Astor.

In the summer of 1960, shortly before Huddleston sailed from England to take up his post as Bishop of Masasi, Astor held a dinner party designed to iron out moral and monetary ambiguities in appeal funding. His guests were Scott, Collins and Huddleston. 'I invited Collins, Trevor and Michael in an attempt at rapprochement,' Astor recalled. 'I hoped then that Trevor would be a uniting factor between John and Michael. But it didn't happen. I asked Collins whether he would share decisions on the use of the large sums of money he was raising. He hummed and hawed. And yet the lives of both Scott and Huddleston had contributed in their way to the money that was coming in. Collins and Huddleston appeared to unite in excluding Scott' (Astor interview 1998).

Despite the high profiles of these clerics, no hint of the discord appeared in the press. Indeed, the first public evidence of a rift arose over CND. On one level, 1960 was CND's finest year. Its Easter march from London to Aldermaston had acquired an aura of near-respectability. Among the banners paraded in Trafalgar Square was one proclaiming 'Eton College detests the tests' – held aloft by young Andrew Collins. By the year's end, CND could boast the remarkable achievement of having persuaded the main opposition party to endorse its policy, as the Labour conference voted for the unilateral renunciation of Britain's nuclear arsenal. But if CND had moved into the political mainstream, it had laid itself open to a serious counter-attack. The Labour leadership under Hugh Gaitskell resolved to 'fight, fight, and fight again' to reverse the resolution, which it duly did at the next conference.

Now CND's less than cohesive ranks fragmented. Its President, the octogenarian philosopher, Bertrand Russell, founded the 'Committee of 100', which resorted to civil disobedience to achieve the objectives of disarmament. But Chairman Collins was dead against direct action. If he had no qualms about advocating civil disobedience in a shackled South Africa, he felt that a popular movement could only harm itself by deliberate law-breaking in a society that respected conventional forms of political protest. By 1961 the Russell committee had effectively broken away, though still preserving links with CND.

Scott sided with Russell, emerging as Vice-President of the Committee of 100, supplying the maxim that encompassed its aims – 'Radical means for moderate ends'. He also circulated

CND's executive and regional organisers with a seven-page document pointing out the inadequacies of the organisation under Collins's leadership. Collins believed Scott was the inspiration for the placards that sprouted at CND demonstrations exhorting members to 'Fire the Canon'.

Collins, as it happened, also had a run-in with the law. He was arrested at a demonstration in September 1961 and charged with 'wilful disregard' of the Commissioner of Police's regulations. The question whether Collins had called his arresting officer 'a bloody fool' evinced a piercing whistle from his wife in the public gallery of the magistrate's court. Never in 22 years of married life, Mrs Collins told the press afterwards, had she known her husband to use a like expression. Case dismissed (*Daily Express* 19.10.61). Like other CND supporters, Collins had taken to the streets to show solidarity with a Committee of 100 'sit-down' in Trafalgar Square that was being given short shrift by the police. The arrest gave him a glimmer of a credential with the activists. But Russell, at the age of 89, and Scott upstaged him. By refusing to be bound over to keep the peace for a year they were sentenced to two months' imprisonment (reduced in Russell's case to one week, on medical grounds). Although not the end of Collins's involvement with CND, it was the beginning of the end. He resigned the chairmanship in April 1964, never losing his conviction that the Committee of 100 had been a foolish mistake.

If the acrimony generated by the South African appeal funds was kept under wraps, the CND conflict was hung out to dry for all to see. But, inevitably, the two arguments became intertwined. With the Committee of 100 still in its incubation phase, Russell, who was a Defence and Aid sponsor, began to question the Canon's financial arrangements. Collins guessed this was instigated by Scott, who made no secret of his belief that Collins was favouring ANC welfare cases at the expense of the PAC. Indeed, this was the real reason why Collins had sent instructions to the South African committees to be sure no such discrimination took place (in 1961 the PAC's supporters received more Amen Court money than did the ANC's). Nevertheless, it appeared to Russell and Scott and, most importantly, to David Astor, whose newspaper was a favoured vehicle for Collins's campaigns, that the Canon was not happy to take them into his confidence over finances. This was hardly surprising, given that Collins was aware that Scott and Astor had their own plans for the money he was raising. But if there were no skeletons in his financial closet comparable to being in receipt of CIA largesse, there were aspects of his operation that he might not have wanted shouted from the rooftops.

Chapter 7

THE 'ODD BODIES' OF AMEN COURT

Amen Court was no place for the safari-suited white South Africans who hung out in the pubs of Earls Court, talking of rucksacks, rugger and bedsits. Collins was host to a politically and racially diverse clientele – Brits, Swedes, Indians, Americans, the southern African multi-hued, Congress and Africanist, Lib and Red, Moslem, Christian, Jew and pagan. Present too were Labour cabinet ministers-in-waiting, devoted women, and suspicious rivals. It was part alternative embassy, part vicarage. A *Church Times* columnist wrote of the variety of 'odd bodies' passing through Amen Court. They came to report the latest intelligence out of Africa, of friends and family in peril, of their despair in a harsh city. The parish priest distributed comfort, advice, and money to the needy, unrestrained by committees or rules. 'Even if he didn't solve your problem,' said Maud Henry, 30 years at Defence and Aid, 'you always left feeling better' (Henry interview 1991). Collins could be the difference between despair and survival, between survival and constructive work. He offered them the space in which to begin to think about the conquest of their country.

If Collins's judgements about money, and how to disburse it, were reckoned to be generally sound, it was his judgement of people that sometimes gave cause for concern. In this press of humanity, John Prevett, the actuary who served on Christian Action's council, could not help observing that 'John spent a lot of time talking to rogues' (Prevett interview 1993).

Not long after the first souring of relations with Michael Scott, Collins created the post of 'Director', with responsibility for international work. The first – and only – incumbent was

John Lang, Bishop Reeves's attorney in Johannesburg, who arrived in London after the Sharpeville shootings. While in the post at Amen Court, Lang's past caught up with him in the form of a R14,000 (£7,000) shortfall in a widow's trust fund, and he was struck off the roll as an attorney in the Transvaal. John Blundell in the Cape Town Defence and Aid office alerted Collins to the finding, and Lang's appointment was quietly terminated.

Some time before, Collins had signed up Solly Sachs, a legendary trade union campaigner in the South African garment industry, who had been expelled from the South African Communist Party, and then successfully sued a government minister for calling him a communist. On coming to England, Sachs showed up at Amen Court, where his resourcefulness and rough charm appealed to Collins, who appointed him Secretary of the Fund in the hope that his reputation would bring in money from the trade unions. When Sachs had the chutzpah to be adopted as Labour candidate for Sheffield Hallam in the 1959 general elections, Collins wrote a glowing endorsement calling on 'all who respect the Christian ethic' to vote for him. The Lithuanian-born, Jewish atheist, campaigned vigorously on the anti-apartheid issue, and lost.

There was rarely a dull moment with Sachs around. He promised Christian Action the profits of a book he had written on the Treason Trial with one of the defendants, Lionel Forman. When it produced zero profits he wrote to the publisher, John Calder, demanding that a representative of Christian Action be allowed to go through the accounts 'to make sure the figure is accurate' (Calder letter to Collins 11.04.62). Collins had to step in to restore gentlemanly relations with Calder. And when the actress Peggy Ashcroft, in despair over Sharpeville, contacted Amen Court and asked if there was anything she could do, Sachs acquainted her with a play by his brother, Benny. Perhaps she could get it staged?

If these were the rough edges that could be tucked back under the carpet, the Scott–Astor reform agenda, as Collins saw it, posed a deadly threat. They wanted power sharing in the name of the common cause. They were asking for the creation of a board of management to control all incoming money and on which the Africa Bureau would enjoy equal representation with Defence and Aid.

Collins was horrified. Not only would it require another level of bureaucracy when rapid decision making was of the essence, it would also give Scott a continuing say in Collins's area of management, without a reciprocal advantage. Collins had serious doubts about Scott's administrative capacity. He had no wish to shape or influence the Africa Bureau in any way – Scott, however, would certainly want to place restrictions on Collins in the matter of supporting the ANC and the exiles in Britain. As with the Committee of 100, Collins sensed he was being offered a recipe for disaster.

The spectre that had presented itself at the Astor dinner party had returned, much enlarged. Huddleston (now in Tanganyika) was not there to assist in the Collins corner, and the issues dividing Scott and Collins were given a harder edge by the larger considerations of the Cold War. One key difference between them was not so much in their contrasting styles, or their interpretations of how to deliver Christian charity, but in their attitudes to communism. Of the two men, Scott had much the closer acquaintance. While in India in the 1930s he had been, in David Astor's words, 'a fellow traveller of communism', working with the party, which he saw as the best protection against fascism. On his return to England, he helped establish communist cells among workers in munitions factories. Scott's fascination with communism did not long survive the Nazi–Soviet pact. Like many a disappointed left-wing idealist he came to see communism as a cynical, manipulative influence in world affairs.

Collins escaped disillusion by virtue of having no illusion in the first place. His pre-war political progress had been from Tory to mainstream Labour. Despite suggestions to the contrary – in the main, by publicists for the South African government – he never was, nor was he in the least bit tempted to become, a communist (although he confided to Walter Sisulu that he might have been, had he been born a white South African). He had a profound intellectual distrust of communism – as he did of 'Romans', whose allegiance, he said, was to a foreign master in the Vatican. But he had no qualms about entering into working relationships with individual communists whom he admired, and none more so than Bram Fischer. He was also influenced by the views of Oliver Tambo, certainly no communist, who told him: 'If you are drowning and someone throws you a rope, you don't stop to ask about his political beliefs' (Collins 1992: 207). None of this blinded Collins to the machinations of Soviet communism but he was prepared to view the activities of South African communists with a watchful trust. For Scott, it was very much a watchful distrust.

Scott was no enemy of the ANC as such. He was closer to Mandela than was Collins, had stayed at Mandela's Orlando home, and was described by him as 'a great fighter for African rights'. But he accused the ANC of becoming 'a harbourer of communists'. He welcomed the trenchantly anti-communist PAC and turned his wrath on Collins, misguidedly accusing Defence and Aid of discriminating against it. Under Astor's generalship, the *Observer* began to give space to the PAC.

The various elements in the simmering dispute over appeal funds came to the boil in the spring of 1961. Having been depicted as a man who hogged and misapplied funds, Collins was now characterised as 'flirting with communism' in a dangerous way. Peter Calvocoressi, who ran the Africa Bureau under Scott's direction, recalled a feeling among his group that Collins was 'not altogether straight' (Calvocoressi interview 1997). This did not imply that Collins had his finger in the till but that he had a power-seeking and devious way of going about his business.

Then Collins did something rash. He went on the offensive, announcing the launch of a fund for special political projects inside South Africa that fell outside the range of Defence and Aid's normal remit. Its aim, to help organisations pursuing 'non-violent and non-racial aims', sounded unexceptionable, but to seasoned Africa-watchers it was a divisive message. The PAC could not be classified as non-racial, certainly not as non-violent. But the ANC, only months away from its own armed struggle, fitted snugly into the twin criteria. His detractors perceived the fund as another ruse to favour the

ANC, which indeed it was. Years later, Diana Collins admitted that it was 'a big mistake', offering needless ammunition to the opposition.

The *Observer* broke cover, pointedly remarking that Pan-Africanists would feel discriminated against. There was also a very personal barb. The charge that Collins was 'so keen on championing various causes', wrote an anonymous columnist, 'that he sometimes takes actions which are hasty and perhaps injurious to those causes, is one that has often been heard in pro-African and anti-bomb circles' (*Observer* 28.05.61).

There could be no more disagreeable reading for Collins. And it did not stop there. Astor took it up with Defence and Aid's sponsors. This was serious, for his newspaper was the most influential Sunday broadsheet of its time. Its world view made its display columns an excellent window for fund-raising, with Colin Legum's championing of African decolonisation, and the contributions of Anthony Sampson and others who had worked in South Africa. Collins's bitterness overflowed at a special meeting of the Christian Action council in July 1961. The minutes record his 'grave concern at the public loss of confidence caused by Mr David Astor through the medium of the *Observer*' which was 'the culmination of a long period of hostility, not just an unfortunate isolated incident' (Defence and Aid Fund minutes, 18.07.61). Jock Campbell, the sugar magnate, chairman of the left-wing weekly *New Statesman*, and an Africa Bureau sponsor, was enlisted as peace-maker, but failed to head Collins off in his progress to Astor's office, where there ensued, the editor recalled, 'a gentlemanly slanging-match, with some laughter, but we didn't get anywhere' (Astor interview 1998).

Dispirited and angry, Collins talked with Diana about winding up Defence and Aid and going on to other things. A year of living in a miasma of rumour about money mismanagement and softness on communism had taken its toll. Rumours that the Canon was about to quit were by now circulating in South Africa. Among the letters he received begging him to continue was one from Albert Luthuli (Collins 1992: 284).

Against his better judgement, Collins decided to accept the Scott-Astor terms superimposing a Board of Management on the Africa Bureau and Defence and Aid. All parties were aware that a further outbreak of open conflict could sap public confidence, and then nobody would be able to raise funds. As it was, Defence and Aid's contributions had dwindled to a trickle after the *Observer* criticism. After the first Board meeting, Collins wrote to his friend Sir Kenneth Grubb of the Church Missionary Society that there was 'plenty of goodwill but very little direction or leadership and most of the time was wasted talking about irrelevancies introduced by Michael Scott'.

The very words 'Board of Management' stuck in Collins's gullet. It wasn't his style. He knew it couldn't work and it didn't. It limped along for a few months before the Chairman, Frank Pakenham (later Lord Longford), who enjoyed the confidence of both Scott and Collins, decided that all concerned would be better off without it. He found it difficult to adjudicate between an organisation that was expected to come up with the money and another that could only offer ideas on how it should be spent. This, as he saw it, served merely to demotivate the money-raiser while inspiring a lack of cost consciousness in the spender. No publicity attended the demise of the Board of Management, though Longford told Diana Collins, 'it wasn't John who was the difficult one' (Collins 1992: 284).

David Astor bore the scars of his roughing up by Collins into old age, remembering him as 'an operator who was not hindered by a sensitive conscience' and as a man 'who showed no respect for anyone who disagreed with him on anything'. He shared Scott's amusement at Collins's lack of personal dignity and at his 'Machiavellian style' of moving money around. Collins, he said, 'used his position as Canon of St Paul's in a fairly outrageous way' (Astor interview 1998). Perhaps, as an atheist, Astor entertained exalted standards as to what should be proper behaviour for a clergyman.

Yet years later Astor was able to offer a clear assessment of the respective contributions of Scott, Huddleston and Collins to the anti-apartheid cause. He observed:

> The impact of their three disparate styles made them an ac-
> cidental team of great power. Scott was always the servant of

the Africans, a man of action and a Gandhian revolutionary. Huddleston was their teacher, a great poetic orator and writer. Collins was their banker. Collins was a first-rate organiser and politician. He liked to use power. The other two were unable to do so and, in Scott's case, unwilling to do so. Neither Scott nor Huddleston could have raised all that money. I, personally, can recognise that Collins was much the most effective of the three men in hurting apartheid. (Astor interview 1998)

It could have been worse for Collins. In the last stages of the appeal fund row the degree of communist penetration of the ANC had increased beyond even Michael Scott's suspicions. This was a result of Mandela persuading his executive to establish an ANC army. *Umkhonto-we-Sizwe* (MK), unlike the ANC, could enlist whites, indeed needed their expertise, so that many senior recruits to the new undercover organisation were communists, including Arthur Goldreich, who had fought against the British in Palestine; Denis Goldberg, an engineer; and Jack Hodgson, a 'Desert Rat' in the South African Army in north Africa in the Second World War. Hodgson was MK's demolition expert. Mandela's most senior recruit from the SACP was Joe Slovo, who, in time, would become commander-in-chief of MK. If, up to the end of 1961, the ANC and the SACP could be regarded as separate but interacting entities, the armed struggle turned them into blood brothers. None of this was publicly known as Collins battled with Scott. MK's alliance with the ANC would not be acknowledged until late 1962.

Collins also managed to keep the lid on the 'Sachs Family Trust Fund', which could certainly have given colour to a charge of Christian Action funds being misrouted, if not actually misused. Collins appreciated its headline-making potential, for he told Dingle Foot, his legal adviser, that 'it would do great harm to the whole anti-apartheid cause if what had happened were to become public knowledge' (Collins letter to Foot 16.10.64).

The instrument of Solly Sachs's downfall was Rica Hodgson, a vivacious South African exile who had joined the Amen Court staff. Mrs Hodgson, like her husband, Jack, was a communist, but it was her fund-raising skills that impressed

Collins. In Johannesburg she had been an efficient money-raiser for the Treason Trial Fund. On starting work at Amen Court she was surprised to find Sachs occupying a position of trust. 'I knew him from the Garment Workers' Union days in Johannesburg', she recalled, 'when he took many people to court for calling him a communist but the money never went to his union' (Hodgson interview 1992).

Hodgson discovered that Sachs was sending appeals on Christian Action notepaper to the Canon's prized donors. They were couched in personal terms about himself and his lawyer son, Albie, then detained in a Cape Town prison. She noticed that cards had been removed from the index, which was the life-blood of the fund. One morning Sachs came in, put his briefcase down and went through to see Collins in his study. Hodgson emerged from the basement and opened Sachs' briefcase in front of his secretary. 'I did feel bad', she recalls, 'it's what the Special Branch used to do. But there were the missing cards. I confronted him and he told me to mind my own business. I told Collins that Solly was feathering his own nest. John called him in and he couldn't deny it. Solly called me a bloody Jewish communist bitch and resigned' (Hodgson interview 1992).

It was not quite the last of Solly Sachs. A year after his departure, he wrote to Collins: 'I shall not beat about the bush... I need your help.' He was buying a flat in Swiss Cottage, north London, thanks to a family trust that had raised £4,000. He asked whether the Canon could help out with the shortfall to close the deal and pay for a conversion. Collins obliged with a contribution that might charitably be construed as a belated redundancy payment or, less charitably, as hush money. After Sachs died intestate in the mid-1970s, his son Albie sold the property and settled the debt. Albie, later to become a Judge of the post-apartheid Constitutional Court, assured Collins that although his name had been used, he had never supported or benefited from the Sachs Family Trust Fund (Diana Collins interview 1997; Sachs interview 1996).

Sachs' departure was followed by the introduction of Phyllis Altman, another exile, to head Amen Court's administrative affairs. Initially, Collins had wanted Rica Hodgson for the job, but she turned it down, fearing that a high profile communist would damage the organisation. Altman, a communist but not a party member, possessed an intimate knowledge of the personalities involved in the struggle. She had a history degree and had written a convincing South African novel, *The Law of the Vultures* (1952, 1987). Her last post before being banned was Acting General-Secretary of the South African Congress of Trade Unions (SACTU). At Amen Court, Altman's security-consciousness could be stretched to maddening lengths, though in the fullness of time it would save Defence and Aid from destruction by the South African Security Police. But Rica Hodgson was correct about her image. She was the subject of a belligerent enquiry at a meeting in Central Hall. Why, the Chairman was asked, did an organisation calling itself Christian Action have a communist working for it? Without hesitation, Collins retorted: 'I don't ask my staff what their religion is or what their politics are as long as they do their work. Mrs Hodgson does a very good job' (Hodgson interview 1992).

With one exception, women were the main instruments for transmitting Collins's will at Amen Court, whether by accident or design. The one exception was George Hamilton, who won a Military Cross in the First World War, had started as the Christian Action Treasurer the day he retired from Hambro, the merchant banker. He would take no salary, not even luncheon vouchers. When he retired, Reg Gore, a retired bank manager, took over. While Hodgson and Altman were deployed on South African matters, Freda Nuell, the true-blue English secretary, handled Christian Action's other business, Maud Henry was the bookkeeper, and Diana edited Christian Action's *Quarterly Journal*, while standing in as her husband's sounding-board and adviser. In those pre-feminist days, Diana attributed John's preference for female employees to his secular taste in wine, women and song. But the women came cheap – Altman was paid £1,000 a year as Organising Secretary.

The Sharpeville effect ushered in the Swedish journalist Per Wästberg, who had come to London to research a blacklist for a boycott campaign. It was the beginning of a fruitful friendship – Collins called him his fifth son. With Wästberg working in the basement and Tambo a frequent caller, three key elements in the liberation struggle, Amen Court, Sweden and the ANC, came together. In time, all Swedish defence and aid funds would be channelled through Defence and Aid, one aspect of its benevolence that would make it the world's most generous underwriter of Africa's non-violent struggle.

Chapter 8

ARMED STRUGGLE AND RIVONIA

On 10 December 1961, in the presence of the great and the good of Norwegian society assembled in the hall of the University of Oslo, Albert Luthuli, dressed in the apparel of a Zulu chieftain, was presented with the Nobel Peace Prize. Although the first African laureate since the award for 'the furtherance of universal peace' was inaugurated in 1900, Luthuli was not its first black recipient. The American diplomat Ralph Bunche had won it the previous year. Luthuli accepted the honour as a tribute to half a century of non-violent political striving by an essentially Christian African National Congress.

After the ceremony, Canon Collins, who was in Oslo at Luthuli's invitation, offered him the chance to relocate to England, in the belief that his voice would be better heard there than in his native land. Collins received a gentle rebuff. Luthuli had given his word – he would return to live and die among his people (Collins 1992: 291). On his return home, this great man of Africa was immediately subjected to a new banning order confining him to the precincts of his farm in a remote corner of Natal. For the remaining six years of his life nothing he wrote or said could be quoted in his own country.

The Peace Prize ceremony was the final act of the non-violent ANC. Luthuli and Moses Kotane, the most influential communist on the ANC executive, had been among the last to relinquish the commitment, but they, like the others, were won over by the force of Mandela's argument that progress could no longer be achieved by turning the other cheek. Accordingly, on 16 December 1961, within days of Luthuli's return, bombs blasted the Bantu Administration Department buildings in Port Elizabeth, Durban and Johannesburg. Roneoed pamphlets heralding the arrival of *Umkhonto-we-Sizwe* (Spear of the Nation, 'MK' for short) proclaimed: 'The time comes in the life of any nation when there remain only two choices: submit or fight.' MK hoped to persuade the government to change its ways 'before matters reach the desperate stage of civil war'.

The significance of the date was not lost on Afrikanerdom. 16 December was the Day of the Covenant, the anniversary of the Battle of Blood River (1838), when the Boers routed the *impi* (warriors) of the Zulu state. It was the holiest date in the Afrikaner calendar, evidence that God was on their side.[1] More pertinently, it proved that powder and bullets were superior to assegais and knobkerries. The events of the Day of the Covenant in 1961 hardly rocked the foundations of the State, but they did demonstrate that black South Africans were finally preparing to improve their firepower.

In the ensuing weeks and months, acts of sabotage were directed at military installations, power plants, telephone lines and railway links. The on-the-ground saboteurs were drawn from all strands of the Congress Alliance, with trade unionists especially eager to join the fray. All the while the fiction was maintained that MK was something wholly distinct from the ANC, much as the ALN (National Liberation Army) and the FLN (National Liberation Front) had drawn a line between warriors and politicians in the independence war then reaching its climax in Algeria. The man who could clarify these matters was not about to give anything away. Mandela, MK's undercover commander-in-chief, had slipped out of the country to garner support in newly independent Africa. Interviewed in Addis Ababa, Ethiopia in February 1962 by the *Guardian* newspaper, Mandela disclaimed any personal connection with MK, though he did concede that it enjoyed his approval as an organisation that could hit back in reprisal for attacks on innocent people by the South African government.[2]

Collins had been obliged to face up to the contradictions in his position even before Mandela showed up at Amen Court.

The South Africa Defence and Aid committees were hinting nervously that it might be too risky to become involved in funding sabotage defences. And there was trouble at home. Raymond Andrews, a Quaker who served on Christian Action's council as well as the Defence and Aid committee, warned Collins of his unhappiness at being associated with a fund 'which underwrote violence'. Andrews said that up to December 1961 the anti-apartheid cause had been in harmony with the concerns of the Christians, Quakers and pacifists who were the backbone of Christian Action. Now they were placed in the position of having to support revolutionary ends backed by violent means – an altogether different ethical proposition. Andrews was not alone among the Canon's inner circle in having these reservations. But Collins won his council over with the argument that any man, even a saboteur, was entitled to a proper defence. He promised to ensure that the money raised would not go to arm saboteurs but to the relief of suffering and to the lawyers.

It was a thin line. Council members would certainly have understood that their aid made it easier for the saboteurs to continue their work. But Collins had a breathing space. There were no defections. 'I came to see,' Raymond Andrews was to say, 'that without confrontation South Africa would not change its ways' (Andrews interview 2004).

Mandela's visit to London strengthened Collins's position in his council, for he could now reassure its members that there was no likelihood of his transferring allegiance from the ANC to the more volatile PAC, and that there was no immediate prospect of MK switching targets from property to people. Another unexpected bonus of Mandela's visit was an easing in Collins's troubled relationship with David Astor, at least in policy terms. Mandela records in his biography, *Long Walk to Freedom*: 'I had been informed by numerous people that the *Observer* newspaper, run by David Astor, had been tilting towards the PAC in its coverage, its editorials implying that the ANC was a party of the past. Oliver (Tambo) arranged for me to meet Astor at his house, and we talked at length about the ANC. I do not know if I had any effect on him, but the coverage certainly changed' (Mandela 1994: 361).

In October 1962 the ANC finally acknowledged its connection with the bombing. Robbie Resha, the ANC's London representative and good friend of Collins, made the public disclosure. In the midst of a speech at a Defence and Aid rally in Central Hall, Resha admitted that MK was the military wing of the ANC. Few in the audience would have been surprised. But it was helpful to Collins to have the matter out in the open, as it made it easier to distinguish between ANC sabotage and the PAC's more brutal acts of terror. Collins's other featured speaker at Central Hall that night, the American civil rights activist, the Rev. Martin Luther King Jr, resolutely extolled the virtues of non-violent resistance.

The ANC and PAC were not alone in turning to armed struggle. Sharpeville was the end of innocence, and once the liberation movements were cast beyond the pale, outlawer and outlawed seemed to move forward according to a pre-ordained script. Neville Alexander, inspirational leader of a Cape Town underground group, the Yu Chi Chen Club, and who served ten years on Robben Island for its activities, once described how individuals in the early 1960s, irrespective of the organisations they belonged to, were drawn inexorably across the divide between a non-violent background and the armed struggle. When his group was caught in the plotting stage of insurrection, Amen Court covered a portion of the defence costs, and acted as a conduit for money raised in Oslo and at Tübingen University in Germany, where Alexander had acquired his doctorate. Five Club members were imprisoned for terms ranging from four to ten years. However, first in on the act of sabotage were the African Resistance Movement (ARM), a group of white liberal students and lecturers that had a brief foray with sabotage before being up-ended by the Security Police.

But it was *Poqo* (Xhosa for 'Our own' or 'Pure'), a militant PAC strain popular with disillusioned veterans of the march on Cape Town, which put the fear of God into whites of every description. *Poqo's* uprising was more ambitious, though less well conceived, than the ANC's – terror rather than sabotage. But its leadership was of the Light Brigade sort. With Pan-Africanism's towering figure, Robert Sobukwe, on Robben

Island, and his lieutenants out of the country, PAC–*Poqo*
dropped into the intemperate hands of Potlako Leballo, who
set it on a downward spiral from which Pan-Africanism would
not recover. From the British-run enclave of Basutoland,
Leballo plotted an 'African Socialist democratic state in which
only Africans would have any voice.' He conceived the idea of
each branch recruiting 1,000 members, and on one magical
day in April 1963 police and power stations and other strategic
targets would be set upon and as many whites – 'forces of
darkness' – as possible killed. The British police tipped off
their South African counterparts when two women crossed
into the Orange Free State to mail instructions to branches
around the country. One woman's handbag contained 70
addressed letters with Leballo's bloodcurdling instructions
to the network in South Africa. As a result, hundreds ended
up in prison and not a few on the scaffold. Poqo was not
immediately flushed out – in Paarl, a sleepy Western Cape
wine town, a rampaging group from the nearby location
killed two whites. But its end was imminent. Defence and Aid
financed the defence in the many Poqo trials that followed.

Unnerved by these events, in May 1963, Justice Minister
Vorster hustled through Parliament the most draconian
measure yet. The '90-day law' gave police officers the
power to arrest without warrant anyone suspected of having
committed, or having information about the committing
of, sabotage or other political crimes. Detainees could be
interrogated until their answers satisfied the Security Police.
Access to the detainee by lawyer, doctor, priest or family was
not allowed. The Police were under no obligation to inform
a detainee's family of the fact of the detention, let alone
of their whereabouts. Though the period of detention was
limited to 90 days, after it had expired the police could – and
often did – re-detain for a further 90 days, sometimes two
or more times. Vorster boasted that the clause allowed for
incarceration 'this side of eternity.'

The measure was partly aimed at stemming the flow of
ANC and PAC recruits who were leaving for military training
in Ethiopia, Algeria or the Soviet Union. But '90-days' would
soon have a devastating effect on the MK sabotage campaign

that had limped along with dwindling impact for a year. On 11 July 1963, the police swooped on Liliesleaf Farm, an isolated estate which was the MK headquarters in Rivonia, north of Johannesburg. They netted two of the ANC's most senior figures, Walter Sisulu and the trade unionist Govan Mbeki, as well as Denis Goldberg and Ahmed Kathrada. They were soon joined by Raymond Mhlaba, Andrew Mlangeni, Elias Motsoaledi and Rusty Bernstein, and in the heart of winter 'Bantu prisoner' Nelson Mandela was flown up from Cape Town in prison regulation shorts, khaki open-necked shirt and sandals – the previous November he had been sentenced to five years for incitement and leaving the country illegally.

The destruction of *Umkhonto-we-Sizwe* was inevitable, says Goldberg. 'We had to use people already known to the police, who simply rounded up everyone and subjected them to vicious interrogation' (Goldberg interview 1992). White South Africa was left in no doubt where it should stand on the issue even before proceedings commenced. Broadcasts on the state radio station, inspired by its Director-General, the former Nazi Piet Meyer, advised the defendants to begin making peace with their maker.

The Rivonia arrests stirred Amen Court into hyperactivity in much the same way as the Treason Trial had done seven years before, though now matters were more serious. After the first batch of Treason Trial releases there had been no real expectation that anyone would be hanged. This time round, the execution of at least some of those in the dock seemed probable. In his pursuit of funds, Collins at last got the Anglican hierarchy cautiously on side. A week after the arrests, an advertisement in the *Church Times* appealing for money for the defence cited a call by the Archbishops of Canterbury and York for a day of prayer for South Africa. On the secular side, Collins persuaded Christie's, the auctioneers, to make its showrooms available for a contemporary art fundraiser. The committee of honour featured legends of the 20th century – Pablo Picasso, Albert Schweitzer and Robert Frost. Jacob Epstein donated a Paul Robeson head, Henry Moore sent two magnificent bronzes, and from Stanley Spencer came a portrait of his wife in the garden. On the day, one invited guest paid £1,600 for a Picasso drawing: the top price of 4,000 guineas was for a Chagall gouache. The *Daily Telegraph*, ever wary of Collins, reported the day's takings as 'disappointing', though the amount, £36,000 (£438,000 in today's values) would cover the cost of the Rivonia Trial with something to spare. The auction was one of a host of financial opportunities that reflected the Canon's flair for publicity.

The painting of the 'Black Christ' made its appearance after Luthuli's Peace Prize award. The eight-foot high figure on the cross was unmistakably Luthuli, while the Roman soldiers bore a striking resemblance to Verwoerd and Vorster. The coloured artist, Ronald Harrison, was granted permission by Archbishop de Blank to hang it in his local church in Cape Town, where it enjoyed a brief celebrity in the local press before the police ordered its removal. In the ensuing furore the DRC called on Luthuli to denounce the picture as blasphemous. Luthuli replied (*sotto voce*, presumably) that his hands were tied as he could not, in terms of his banning order, comment publicly on any subject.

With the survival of the offending canvas under threat, at Collins's behest the painting was smuggled on a cargo flight to London in a roll of linoleum. Collins put it on show in the St Paul's crypt, then sold it to the *Sunday Citizen*, which took it on a provincial fund-raising tour and sent Defence and Aid a decent cheque.

There was symbolism of another sort in a single diamond and pearl brooch that arrived at Amen Court. The donor, the daughter of a general in the South African army, explained that she had received the gift as a child from her godfather, General Jan Smuts, the former prime minister. The jewels realised £350. Labour Party headquarters sent £1,400, a sign that the climate had changed and that sabotage now seemed inevitable to some elements of the left.

In parallel with these fund-raising efforts, the Anti-Apartheid Movement set about mobilising political opinion, establishing the World Campaign for the Release of Political Prisoners, with representatives from Defence and Aid and like-minded groupings. The Liberal MP, Jeremy Thorpe, was its active Chairman, and left-wing British MPs went on missions to western capitals with the message, 'Save their lives'. They were granted audiences by the Pope and the French President, Charles de Gaulle.

In line with Collins's belief in briefing the very best lawyers, Fischer assembled an exceptional team: Vernon Berrangé QC, the destructive Treason Trial cross-examiner known as 'the human lie detector'; George Bizos, an old hand at Defence and Aid rearguard actions; and Arthur Chaskalson, destined to preside over the Constitutional Court of the 'new South Africa'. Their fees were a fraction of what they could have commanded in a commercial case. This being the ultimate in political trials, their defence would not be restricted to the courtroom. In preparing their case they defied Security Police objections to prisoners of different races meeting in the same room for consultation. Once in court, they set about putting apartheid in the dock. They dispensed equal dignity. White or black, friendly or hostile, even the ANC turncoats battered into submission before being coached by the police for their performance in the witness stand, all were addressed as 'Mr'. State Prosecutor Percy Yutar and his team addressed blacks by surname only, while graciously prefixing white enemies of the State with 'Mr'.

Because of the menacing nature of the proceedings it was deemed too risky to attempt to raise funds through the local Defence and Aid committees, which were coming under increasingly oppressive police surveillance. The defence attorney, 'the general behind the scenes', was Joel Joffe, but Fischer was in charge of the cash from Amen Court. Joffe recalls him forever writing letters to Collins. 'There was a Bar rule that Counsel must be paid within three months and if they weren't, the attorney could not brief another advocate. The Bar was tougher than a trade union. At one point, with money running out, we had to ask Bram to move quickly. It arrived just in time.' Of course, the government knew all about it. 'Was the money from London used for sabotage?' Yutar asked Walter Sisulu, who naturally rejected the construction. But the slur had been planted for those who wished to take it further (Joffe 1995: 141). The men in the dock at Pretoria's Palace of Justice in 'The State against Nelson Mandela and others' were charged with sabotage and conspiracy to overthrow the government by force of arms. There was some surprise at their not being charged with High Treason. However, a treason charge required a long preparatory examination, which was reckoned to be beneficial to the defence. This had been the position in the earlier Treason Trial, but then the government had hoped, unavailingly, that drawn-out proceedings would keep black nationalism out of harm's way for the duration. Now, in 1963, the objective was simply to eliminate the opposition. The State needed to deliver swift and telling justice. Nevertheless, the defence was able to effect a number of delays through legal manoeuvring and disputes over the wording of the indictment. The final charge sheet listed 193 acts of sabotage.

The great dramatic passage in the trial was provided by Nelson Mandela, 'accused number one'. He surprised the prosecution by refusing to give sworn evidence, preferring to deliver his statement from the dock. While this did not carry the legal weight of sworn testimony, it freed him to deliver one of the most cogent political statements ever heard in a court of law. He admitted that he was indeed commander-in-chief of *Umkhonto-we-Sizwe*, and confirmed the strong communist connection, without naming names (five accused: Mhlaba, Mbeki, Kathrada, Goldberg and Bernstein were party members). It was true, he said, that there had often been close co-operation between the ANC and the SACP. He continued:

> But co-operation is merely proof of a common goal – in this case the removal of white supremacy – and it is not proof of a common community of interests. The history of the world is full of similar examples. Perhaps the most striking illustration is to be found in the co-operation between Great Britain, the United States of America and the Soviet Union in the fight against Hitler. Nobody but Hitler would have dared to suggest that such co-operation turned Churchill or Roosevelt into communists or communist tools, or that Britain and America were working to bring about a communist world. (Mandela 1973: 179/180)

Nor was the ANC, said Mandela, 'but at this stage in South Africa's history theoretical differences amongst those fighting oppression are a luxury we cannot afford.' His main point of departure from the communist ethic, he explained, was the respect he accorded democratic institutions – the Westminster Parliament and the American Congress. He concluded his affirmation of personal freedom with the words:

> During my life I have dedicated myself to this struggle of the African people. I have fought against white domination and I have fought against black domination. I have cherished the idea of a democratic and free society in which all persons live together in harmony, and with equal opportunities. It is an ideal which I hope to live for and achieve [– lowering his voice –] but if needs be it is an ideal for which I am prepared to die. (Mandela 1973: 189)

Bizos recalls the 'almost inaudible sound of people drawing in their breath, and hardly anything happened before Bram Fischer got up and said, "M'lord, I call our first witness, Mr Walter Sisulu".' Sisulu's appearance was no less heroic as he withstood the double-barrelled assault of Prosecutor and Bench. He refused to name names, unless the person was safely out of the country. In several *Poqo* and ANC trials, defendants had attempted to save their skins by implicating others, thus spreading persecution ever wider. Now Sisulu and his comrades established a precedent crucial to the *esprit de corps* of the struggle (Bizos interview 1992). From then on, a steady stream of witnesses refused to testify against their friends, and spent a year or more in prison for their principles.

Aside from the clear evidence of widespread sabotage, there was, among the papers seized at Rivonia, a document titled *Operation Mayibuye*, the authorship of which was attributed to Govan Mbeki and Joe Slovo. This outlined in detail a plan for nationwide guerrilla warfare assisted by foreign troops. The defence contended that it was no more than a discussion document, certainly not an approved policy position that was being acted upon. But the document's very existence appeared to tilt the case strongly in the prosecution's favour.

At an early stage, Mandela, Sisulu and Mbeki agreed that

whatever the sentence they would make no appeal for mercy. Their argument, opposed in vain by their legal advisers, was that in a political trial an appeal could only be an anti-climax when they needed to be firm about conveying the message that 'no sacrifice was too great in the struggle for freedom'. As the trial progressed their resolution came under extreme pressure. One day Mandela asked a friendly Afrikaner prison warder what he thought the judge would do. 'I said, "Agh, they are going to hang us?" I really did not mean it; I was asking for some support from him. I thought he would say, "Don't worry, that sort of thing would never happen to you." But he looked away from me and said, "Yes, I think you are right, they are going to hang you." It was not very pleasant to listen to' (Yule interview 1992).

After a three-week adjournment to consider his verdict, Judge Quartus de Wet returned to court on 11 June 1964. He was satisfied, he said, that the ANC was a 'communist-dominated' organisation, though accepting that *Operation Mayibuye* was not an authorised plan that could be said to have 'progressed beyond the preparation stage'. He found all but one of the accused guilty of sabotage. Rusty Bernstein was acquitted (and immediately re-arrested). De Wet confessed to having one residual uncertainty about the appropriate punishment. He would deliver sentence the following day. The Foreign Office warned its embassies in Africa to be on guard against the likelihood of 'concerted action and simultaneous demonstrations throughout the continent' if Mandela was executed (*The Times*, 02.01.95).

Joffe recalled his clients were 'calm, living now in the shadow of death... the strain almost unbearable, yet the only matter they wanted to discuss was how they should behave in court if the death sentence was passed' (Joffe 1995: 205). Sisulu was sure he would hang, along with Mandela, Mbeki and Goldberg, thought the others might conceivably escape with life imprisonment. 'The young boys of the PAC were being sentenced to 20 years, and we were doing something far more serious' (Sisulu interview 1992).

When Alan Paton had been asked to give evidence in mitigation of sentence he had posed just one question: 'Are their lives in danger?' He accepted, saying that the exercise of clemency 'is a thing which is very important for our future'. It was a canny ploy to have the crusty apostle of liberalism, and devout Christian, plead for the lives of those whose politics were out of harmony with his own pacifist instincts. Unusually for a witness pleading for men's lives, Yutar chose to cross-examine, and asked Paton about his association with Roley Arenstein, a communist attorney, whom he had met through Defence and Aid. Yutar asked whether 'that is another organisation with a high-sounding name which assists the saboteurs in this country?' No, said Paton, 'it assists in defending people who are brought before the courts so that they might get a fair and just trial' (Joffe 1995: 209).

There were no death sentences. In a curious statement Judge de Wet argued that the crime for which the accused had been convicted was essentially High Treason, carrying the maximum penalty of death, but as the State had decided to rely on the charge of sabotage, he felt he was permitted a small margin for leniency. He sentenced each of them to prison for life.

For Sisulu, a lifetime in prison 'sounded like a discharge when we were expecting death'. To this day, the defence attorney Joel (now Lord) Joffe remains astounded at the outcome. 'The Sabotage Act permitted the imposition of the death penalty on a person who threw a stone with a political motive through the window of a government building.' (Joffe 1995: 205). As agreed, none of the 'Rivonia Eight' lodged an appeal.

Why De Wet backed off from death sentences is not clear. It might have been that during the weeks of adjournment he came under pressure from a government that had decided that incarcerated icons were less of a threat to the state than dead martyrs. But this suggests a level of sophistication nowhere else apparent in the administration's thinking. On the contrary, it seems from other circumstances in the trial that De Wet, though an orthodox Afrikaner jurist, was not prepared to be a pliant tool of official policy. Indeed, his ruling that the ANC and MK should be regarded as separate legal entities was to have profound consequences. It meant that a rank-and-file ANC card-holder would face 'no more' than a maximum of ten years in prison and not – if treason or sabotage were carried out in the movement's name – hanging. The government, which insisted that ANC membership meant automatic responsibility for the acts of MK, would not have been grateful for this interpretation. Here was a vivid example of how the finest defence lawyers could establish the terms of engagement before an armed liberation struggle had moved into second gear.

Two factors combined to save them. Sisulu felt it was fear of an international outcry. Mbeki said: 'We had the best defence, thanks to D&A. Everything that could have been done for us, was done. On the question of hanging, I think it was more international pressures on the government' (Mbeki interview 1992). Mandela believes that 'anything could have happened if there was no defence. The prosecutor told our counsel that he would ask for the maximum sentence – which was death row' (Mandela interview 1992). What did count was the leisure of a protracted defence. George Bizos insisted from early on that it was essential for the judge to get to know these 'terrorists' as men. At first the atmosphere made it difficult for him to avoid imposing the death penalty. But the longer the trial went on, the less inclined would he be to take their lives. Sisulu's magnificent five days in the box opened a chink in the armoury of the Bench. Bizos remarked:

> I don't know what would have happened if the indictment that was first presented in October 1963 had not been quashed, if there had not been a high-powered legal defence led by Bram Fischer and the trial was done quickly, as was expected by the media supporting the National Party. And if it had not been for this period of six to eight months that the trial took, and the UN resolution, and the protests throughout the world by the trades union movement and human rights bodies. By mid-1964, although judges always deny that they are in any way influenced by what happens outside, it would be naïve to think it didn't happen in the Supreme Court. (Yule interview 1993)

Almost all the money for the trial defence, which preserved the lives, though not the liberty, of South Africa's first black

President and several of his closest advisers, was raised through Canon Collins in London. Shortly before he died, Oliver Tambo recalled how the Pretoria government had striven to make sure that there would be executions in the Rivonia trial. 'We worked very hard to prevent it. If our leadership had gone... Phew!' (Tambo interview 1992).

Chapter 9

ROUND ONE TO PRETORIA: THE ANC AND THE EASTERN CAPE

In these tumultuous times Defence and Aid's resources were stretched to the limit. The numbers of those detained, arraigned, imprisoned, banned, placed under 12- or 24-hour house arrest, or banished to unforgiving places, were unlike anything that had gone before. In June 1964, the Johannesburg office reported that for the first time it had to turn down appeals for defence assistance. In six months the Fund had spent twice the amount of the two preceding years. With 'Rivonia' out of the way, the cash drought had returned as part of the cyclical reaction of the British public to faraway cataclysms. Men and women facing long prison terms had not been defended or were forced to rely on *pro deo* counsel fresh out of law school and unlikely to be sympathetic to the aspirations of their clients. It goes without saying that the administrator of the parsimonious state legal aid fund did not look kindly on politicals.

The cash drought was all the more distressing because those who did have legal representation were manifestly more likely to have charges withdrawn before the trial began, or be acquitted. Sentences were invariably reduced when the Fund made an appeal possible. With no remission for good behaviour, every year knocked off was worth a full 12 months to a 'political'. A Defence & Aid newsletter reported on a man who came straight from a two-year prison term to the East London office to express his gratitude. 'He was of the firm opinion that had it not been for his defence paid for by the Fund his sentence would have been much higher' (*Defence and Aid Fund Newsletter*, No. 6, Johannesburg: January 1965). The impact of these interventions was illustrated by a profile of cases handled by the Johannesburg office between May and October 1963. Nearly all were for 'belonging to and furthering the aims of a banned organisation' or 'leaving the country illegally'. Charges were dropped in 122 cases, 15 were acquitted, and with four estreating bail, that left 49 convictions. In the rush of *Poqo* trials in Cape Town, the Defence and Aid effect was impressive – 537 defended, 235 acquitted, 213 gaoled, a few fined, the remainder awaiting trial or the outcome of an appeal. One sign of the times, as interrogation methods ran riot, was that 23 prisoners on the Fund's books were committed to mental institutions (*Defence and Aid Fund Newsletter*, No. 6, Johannesburg: January 1965).

The lawyers were instrumental in forcing the State to give ground on prisoners awaiting trial. Writing to Collins in late 1963, Alex Hepple reported on the fate of hundreds of *Poqo* detainees charged after long periods in detention and made to wait several months more in custody for their trial. Many were of school age. When lawyers applied for bail, the Security Branch opposed it in almost every case, on the grounds that their release was likely to endanger the safety of the state. Magistrates did what was expected of them and refused bail as a matter of course. Selected cases were then appealed to the Supreme Court, backed with descriptions of torture. 'A remarkable change came over the attitude of the State,' Hepple said. In nearly every case the Attorney-General instructed that bail be granted. 'Terrorists' deemed too bloodthirsty to walk the streets a short while before were being freed on their own recognizances.

If MK and the PAC were resorting to 'unlawful' methods to achieve their ends, the police counter-attack took no account of the UN Declaration of Human Rights. Two months after the Rivonia arrests, Looksmart Solwandle Ngudle was found hanged in his cell. A trade unionist from Cape Town's Langa location, he had been detained for suspected membership of Denis Goldberg's sabotage cell. The Cape Town District Surgeon certified that Ngudle had taken his own life. But his family claimed he had been brutally tortured, and a contentious inquest seemed likely. Four days after his death, Vorster formally banned Ngudle under the Suppression of Communism Act, ensuring that the dead man's tales were not told through the mouths of the living. Under the terms of the banning order nothing Ngudle had said or written during his lifetime could be quoted, except in a court of law or with the Minister of Justice's express permission. The family's QC, George Lowen (who was funded by Amen Court), made a tactical withdrawal from the proceedings, saying that as an inquest by a magistrate was not a court, 'he or his witnesses would have no protection if they quoted statements... made by Mr Ngudle' (*Survey of Race Relations* 1963: 51). Vorster was forced to relent, but warned that the production of statements by banned persons at inquests should not provide a platform for the expression of their views. Lowen and his team returned.

The finding, predictably, was that Ngudle had indeed hanged himself. It was the first in a long line of deaths in custody, made possible by physical and psychological torture techniques administered under the '90-day' law and the more draconian Terrorism Act that superseded it. In the coming years, magistrates would consistently ignore the evidence of torture and return findings of 'hanged himself' or 'fallen down the stairwell'.

Depending on the money available, Defence and Aid funded as many trials as it could but there were disastrous omissions. In June 1963, a group of Pretoria Pan-Africanists were charged with conspiracy to commit sabotage. All but two of the 14 were teenagers, bright and doing well at school. It was said that they had sat on a *koppie* (hill) outside Pretoria and plotted to capture the Union Buildings and shoot everyone inside. One defendant, Dikgang Moseneke, aged 15 at the time (now a Supreme Court judge), recalls: 'We'd been in solitary for over 100 days, and suddenly we were projected from the dark cells into the glare of the court.' Sydney Kentridge, hastily engaged as counsel, asked for time to prepare a defence. Judge Cillie refused. The next day, he again refused. Then, says Moseneke, 'Sydney went off to defend Helen Joseph (British-born social worker and one of the leaders in the Union Buildings demonstration) for contravening her house arrest, though we were facing a possible death sentence. Two more advocates tried and each was refused a postponement. The judge insisted: "We start tomorrow. Find counsel." Then he would postpone no longer, and our junior counsel withdrew on the Bar Council president's advice that in the circumstance he should not defend.' Cillie – for Kentridge 'the most evil of the government appointees to the Bench' – offered to look after the defendants' interests (Moseneke interview 1992).

For three months the defence was left to Jeff Masemola, an idiosyncratic sculptor, but no lawyer. He and John Nkosi spent 27 years on Robben Island, and the teenagers 10 years. As the trial was ending, the judge learnt that one of the boys had lost his hearing from a blow by a policeman and could have heard nothing of the evidence against him. After the verdict, an embarrassed Alex Hepple found something in the kitty for an appeal. But without a decent defence in the lower court there were no grounds on which to overturn the judgement or have the sentences reduced. Thirty years later, Moseneke said: 'Kentridge would not have wilted under pressure' (Moseneke interview 1992). Kentridge described the episode as 'perhaps the low-water mark of our jurisprudence' (Dugard 1978: 245). The episode added fuel to PAC suspicions of Defence and Aid.

Others were not even aware that help was on offer. While at school in East London, Hamilton Xolile Keke joined a PAC group gearing up to respond to Leballo's insurrection. They were arrested and charged with conspiracy to commit sabotage. 'Our parents raised the money selling cattle and goats or they borrowed from money-lenders in the Duncan Village location.' For each rand, they had to pay back 25c a week or forfeit a sewing machine or some other piece of furniture. They did not know that the city had a Defence and Aid office run by two retired women doctors and an Anglican clergyman. Keke was gaoled for 10 years. He later represented the PAC in London (Keke interview 1992).

•

The Xhosa-speaking Eastern Cape was where African nationalism first became a way of life, its membership cards inherited by sons and daughters from fathers, mothers and grandparents. Congress nationalism, Pan-Africanism, Steve Biko's yet-to-be-born Black Consciousness, all had their lead roots in the cities of Port Elizabeth and East London, and the expanse of location and kraal stretching from the Sundays River to the Natal border. Schools, teacher training colleges and the University College of Fort Hare inculcated dangerous notions of equality and no taxation without representation. So it was here that the police and the courts worked together to ensure, in a security policeman's prophetic phrasing, that 'we have peace and quiet in this area for the next 10 years' (Sparks, *Rand Daily Mail*, 1965).

The extent of the vendetta waged through the medium of the courts – and the role of Defence and Aid-funded lawyers in attempting to reverse it – was revealed by Allister Sparks in the *Rand Daily Mail* (22.07.65, 23.07.65). It was the first public indication that a grave and mass miscarriage of justice had been perpetrated. With the national leaders of the ANC on Robben Island, Sparks wrote, 'the political police are moving in against the rank and file members in the Eastern Cape stronghold... with thoroughness and ruthlessness.' The objective was to crush 'every individual member of it'. In the previous 18 months, 918 people in Port Elizabeth's townships had been tried for purely technical offences relating to the banned ANC and PAC. Trials were held before magistrates in *dorps* (small towns) a half-day's drive from Port Elizabeth, so that families were unable to be present. Hearings were held in camera, effectively secret. The cast of these farces included the Afrikaner magistrate, the Afrikaner prosecutor, the Afrikaner policemen and a hooded MK renegade who travelled the country like a medieval balladeer recounting tales of terror and murder against erstwhile comrades.

Every effort was made to allow the trials to pass unnoticed. But for Defence and Aid, wrote Sparks, 'these people would have been tried and sentenced, undefended and in silence'. Port Elizabeth lawyers, facing pressure from clients not to take on ANC cases, were not tempted to leave town. The rare friendly country attorney was vulnerable to pressure. So Dennis Scarr, the local Defence and Aid Chairman, imported advocates from Johannesburg and assigned one to defend every 'political' case coming before the court in the course of a month. They worked on a low tariff, with travel and hotel expenses. They might receive short notice of a case and be incompletely briefed. Or a prisoner would write to inform Scarr of his pending appearance, only for the letter to arrive after he had been tried and shipped to Robben Island. In all, 513 prisoners were sentenced to an aggregate of 2,586 years for these illegal but non-violent activities. In 12 months Defence and Aid spent £12,500 on the Eastern Cape trials.

It was only the beginning of the Eastern Cape's travails. Some years later a Robben Island prisoner wrote to the Cape Town attorney, Himie Bernadt, saying he had been re-tried and sentenced for the same offence. Could anything be done? Bernadt's firm uncovered a strategy of 'multiple jeopardy' aimed once again at the humble sword-carriers of African nationalism. Thus, Winnard Mati had first appeared in court in Graaff-Reinet, 150 miles north of his home in New Brighton, and had been gaoled for two and a half years for being an ANC member. A month before his scheduled release, Mati and three comrades from the first trial were brought from Robben Island to Humansdorp, 50 miles west of Port Elizabeth, to face further charges of 'soliciting subscriptions' and 'allowing his home to be used for meetings'. All related to the very ANC activity for which he had already been gaoled. In a normal judicial system, a defence lawyer would have pleaded *autrefois acquit* and expected his client not to be punished two or three times more. But the statute had been enacted to obviate such ethical niceties. A man going to a tea party to raise funds for the ANC, wearing its badges and distributing pamphlets, was open to four separate charges, each carrying a maximum three-year sentence. The prosecutor, JH Liebenberg, kept quiet – indeed, the record stated 'None' in the space reserved for Mati's previous convictions. The magistrate was thus not formally given the opportunity to impose a more lenient sentence, though the men were clearly serving prisoners. Mati returned to the Island for four and a half more years. Now, on appeal, the Supreme Court effectively reduced the second sentence by three years, and Mati was released within a month. The case sparked an unprecedented series of appeals, so successful that 158 men were saved 258 years in prison.

Dependants were wary of applying for the meagre welfare grant at the local Bantu Affairs Commissioner's, the very office that 'endorsed them out' (expelled them from urban areas) when their papers were not in order. They preferred the friendly face of private charity. Defence and Aid helped 700 'political widows' and 2,500 children. Dennis Scarr needed £230,000 a year in his region simply to maintain families on the £24 per month poverty-datum line. He could raise no more than a tenth of that. While Amen Court accounted for the bulk of the available money, other welfare organisations, Oxfam, the World Council of Churches and the Rowntree Trust, chipped in. But conviction, or even acquittal, was only the beginning of hardship. There followed the systematic expulsion of families of political prisoners from their home towns to dump settlements miles from anywhere. The search for the needy then switched to the countryside and arrangements were made for the delivery of food parcels. The office employed two full-time social workers and several volunteers to track down families. But after the government denounced the fund for giving assistance to saboteurs and communists, Scarr had difficulty finding people to work for Defence and Aid.

•

The idea that the law could be an ally of black aspirations was something of a novelty in South Africa. The 'whiteness' of the courts, and exclusion from the making of the laws that set them up as victims, combined to make blacks feel cheated by the legal process. Even when it seemed that a law offered no opportunity to dispense unequal justice, blacks received a raw deal. When breaches of the Immorality Act resulted in white men being acquitted while the black women with whom they had shared sexual favours were convicted, it was simply part of the natural order of things.

Before the advent of Defence and Aid very few blacks enjoyed the luxury of being represented by a personal lawyer. Now, to be consulted by your own attorney, to have your case argued in court by a committed advocate, offered a veneer of equality, if not before the white man's law, certainly in terms of one's own self-esteem. And it certainly improved the chances of a successful day in court. In all probability the sympathetic legal representative would be white, though that was gradually changing. There were Indian practices in Johannesburg and Durban, but rarely African (Johannesburg's first, Mandela and Tambo, was no longer in business), and coloured in the Cape, where a future Justice Minister, Dullah Omar, belonged to an informal pool of attorneys who took low fees in political matters. Not all practitioners had the necessary altruism. A white attorney was struck off the roll by the Cape Law Society for fiddling Defence and Aid trial money.

So Defence and Aid depended on non-African lawyers because few Africans were in practice. The profession evolved out of the political and racial pecking order of the nineteenth century Cape Colony. The earliest lawyers were English or Anglicised Dutchmen, followed by Afrikaners, Jews, and other 'Europeans' such as the Greek-born Bizos, then Indians and coloureds began to qualify. Africans came through a distant last, and then qualification did not guarantee mainstream practice. Duma Nokwe, the Treason Trialist and first black advocate at the Johannesburg Bar, was not allowed to rent chambers with white advocates in their city centre building opposite the Supreme Court. The Minister of Native Affairs, Verwoerd, citing the Group Areas Act, told him to set up shop in Soweto and work for the benefit of his 'own' people. On his rare appearances in the Rand Supreme Court, Nokwe had a robing room to himself 'to avoid contaminating white colleagues', as he put it (Maisels interview 1992).

Godfrey Pitje, an anthropologist turned attorney (in the firm Mandela and Tambo), was convicted of contempt of court for refusing to sit at a table in the Johannesburg Magistrate's Court reserved for blacks. On appeal, Chief

Justice LC Steyn said Pitje 'could not possibly have been hampered in the slightest in the conduct of his case by having to use a particular table.' No statute ordained these separate court facilities but Steyn reasoned that as Parliament had sanctioned separation in other walks of public life it was not unreasonable in a courtroom (Pitje interview 1992).

And yet judges saw themselves as fitting snugly into the orthodox western mould. Mr Justice Claassen of the Transvaal Bench claimed to have been told on good authority that the English judges, who were seen as the most eminent in the world, considered only South African judges as their equals. This rose-tinted perception (or dual misconception) rested on the stance of a handful of old-style Appellate Division judges who had resisted (unavailingly) attempts to remove Cape-based coloureds from the common voters' roll in the 1950s. By then, however, matters were well in hand. The first apartheid Justice Minister, CR Swart, adjusted the political balance of the Bench by appointing a series of Afrikaner placemen. If you were not ideologically attuned to apartheid, you were unlikely to get the call. These men held sway in political trials. Non-political or liberal judges were more often found working the commercial or purely criminal shift.

By the mid-1960s Vorster, the one-time country attorney, could ease up on political appointments. The courts were by then sufficiently reliable. But being English or Afrikaner, liberal or segregationist, was not always a reliable clue to behaviour on the Bench. Chief Justice Ogilvie Thompson, a pillar of the Cape liberal establishment, would sometimes hand down judgements deemed offensively pro-executive. In contrast, Afrikaner judges who had defended pro-German saboteurs and spies during the war came to display considerable independence of mind. Kobie Marais, himself a wartime detainee, spoke out publicly against a law that conferred wide powers on the executive to exclude evidence from court in the interests of security (Sachs 1973: 256).

The legal profession did attract radicals, even communists such as Bram Fischer and Roley Arenstein, but the great mass of its membership tended to be conservative and conformist.

The Law Society, a closed shop of all the country's attorneys, resolutely kept its head down, refusing to take up the cases of left-wing colleagues restricted by banning orders, and declining to be drawn on 'human rights issues' when 'security' was involved. The regional Bar Associations, representing the advocates, were somewhat bolder. Several emerged at the forefront of libertarian protests against what came to be regarded as the state's licence to torture, the 90-day law and its successor, the Terrorism Act.

It was upon this relatively small band of attorneys and advocates that Collins would lean in the barren years after Rivonia. Now other worries added to his cup of woe. Collins's copy of Paton's *Cry, the Beloved Country* was as well-thumbed as his Bible, but in the late summer of 1964 there were disquieting signs that the two men were singing from different hymn-sheets. Paton was concerned about how Collins was using the money he raised. Unlike Michael Scott, he was reluctant to embarrass Collins by going public.

Paton articulated his annoyance in a letter to Mary Benson, the South African author who had settled in London after working on the Treason Trial Defence Fund. Perhaps expecting her to pass his words on to the Canon, he wrote:

> For years my name has been used to collect money for people whose views are not the same as mine. Yet we have not been able to get anything for the non-violent Liberal Party. One of the aims of the Defence and Aid Fund is to support the establishment of a non-racial society, but in fact the Fund has given hardly a penny to liberals who work to this end. One does not establish a non-racial society by blowing up a train. (Paton letter 07.04.64)

Collins was accustomed to accusations of rendering assistance to terrorists at the expense of positive non-violent elements, but coming from Paton, so soon after his public disagreements with Scott, it had a special potency. To lose the support of one inspirational figure could be accounted bad luck; the loss of two might look like carelessness.

Funds were now so short that Collins could not have directed more money to the Liberal Party even had he so wished. The party that Paton led as National President had, in truth, never impressed Collins as being in the vanguard of progress against apartheid. When founded in 1953 it advocated a staged progression to universal franchise. By the urgent sixties this had become an unqualified vote for all. Liberals had at one stage been ready to join the Congress of the People – which produced the Freedom Charter – but had backed off, suspecting they were being lured into a communist-manipulated 'popular front.' In consequence, the Liberal Party found itself marginalised among whites (because of its anti-apartheid stance) and blacks (for not sharing their main political objective).

Frustration at the hopelessness of the non-violent struggle led a group of lecturers and journalists, many of them liberals, with a sprinkling of communists and Trotskyists, to launch the African Resistance Movement (ARM). They blew up railway lines and pylons, hoping to affect white thinking and raise black morale. Collins provided legal support when they came before the courts in Johannesburg, Pietermaritzburg and Cape Town. The only 'non-white' ARM member to be sent down, Eddy Daniels, a coloured photographer, received the harshest sentence – 15 years on Robben Island. The movement considered itself a 'no loss of life sabotage' operation, striking only at symbolic targets and communications facilities. But it did not always work that way. The tragic denouement came when John Harris, a teacher with a Politics, Philosophy and Economics degree from Oxford, planted an ARM bomb in the Johannesburg railway station in July 1965, killing a 77-year-old woman. He was hanged on 1 April 1965, the first and only white to be executed for a political offence in the apartheid era.

In the months after the Rivonia Trial, MK cadres carried out sporadic but largely ineffective actions. Among the last hopefuls to be caught was a group of cooks and waiters from Pretoria. In December 1964, a bomb in a telephone booth in a Cape Town suburb, Lakeside, marked the final gesture in round one of the ANC's liberation drama. Years later, Joe Slovo, Mandela's closest white lieutenant, said: 'Untimely inaction would have been worse than untimely action' (Slovo 1996: 192).

•

By early 1965 Defence and Aid was finding it increasingly hard to function inside South Africa. Most officials and employees, and many lawyers, were in the Liberal Party or in sympathy with its aims. Vorster, however, saw them as fair game under the flexible Suppression of Communism Act. Among the first to be banned were Barney Zackon, a Cape Town attorney, and David Craighead, Alex Hepple's successor as the Johannesburg chairman. Ruth Hayman, who liaised directly with Collins in the allocation of legal work in the main political cases, was put under 12-hour house arrest, then prohibited from leaving Johannesburg, communicating with banned persons or drafting any document except in her legal capacity. She was able to continue her practice, but the restrictions were a serious blow to her work with Collins. Sydney Kentridge described her as an attorney of 'great devotion, competence and undoubted integrity' whose banning was 'inexplicable save on the assumption that it was punishment for her professional work' (Dugard 1978: 244).

In his book *Inside BOSS*, Gordon Winter, an English-born petty criminal employed by South Africa's Republican Intelligence network, describes how the security services approached the task of combating Defence and Aid, which, he said, had become 'a massive thorn in Pretoria's side'. Winter's boss, General Hendrik van den Bergh, told him to recruit Andries Chamile, who worked in the Johannesburg office. Chamile, then aged 67, told Winter he 'would rather die than betray my people.' Winter reported his lack of success to his chief, who promptly had Chamile placed under house arrest and banned from all contact with the Defence and Aid office. Laura Hitchins, who ran the office, was then also banned. 'If Pretoria can't get you one way,' wrote Winter, 'they quickly find another' (Winter 1981: 65).

Pretoria's allies in Britain were also active. Harold Soref, a right-wing commentator (later a Conservative MP), alleged in his book, *The Puppeteers*, that 'many of the so-called refugees from South Africa (working in Amen Court) are actively engaged in plotting the overthrow by violence of the South African Government.' Collins initiated legal proceedings, then thought better of it. The rebellion was over; there was no point in raking over old ground.

As the process of dismembering South Africa's Defence and Aid network proceeded, Collins was not reduced to watching impotently from the sidelines, though this might have seemed to be the case to his followers in South Africa. By now he was hearing the hoofbeats of the cavalry, in the shape of the United Nations, and with it the prospect of an enlarged international Defence and Aid with the resources to take on the might of Pretoria.

Chapter 10

ENUGA REDDY AND THE UN TRUST FUND

After the Pan-Africanist Congress meltdown and the end of the Rivonia trial, the West breathed deeply, though quietly, so no one would notice. South Africa was moving into an era of unprecedented prosperity, heavily fuelled by investment from Britain, western Europe, the United States and the tiger economy, Japan. But if the struggle had entered its doldrum years, there was still a need to defend and to aid. It was clear that voluntary fund-raising could no longer cope. Collins was not blustering when he threatened to close down the operation for want of money. A junior official at United Nations' headquarters in New York heard the cry.

ES (Enuga) Reddy had a classical Indian Congress Party background. The British had gaoled his father for peacefully resisting their unwelcome presence, and the son was aware how Gandhi had fashioned the craft of *satyagraha* in South Africa. India's first Prime Minister, Pandit Nehru, had called on the Indians of South Africa to join with Africans in the common struggle. Reddy, by now a student in New York, was fired by newspaper reports of the Indian passive resistance campaign in Natal to organise a demonstration of Indian students outside the South African Consulate. He also heard about South Africa at first hand from the ANC President, Dr AB Xuma, leading a mission to the United Nations.

In 1949, Reddy abandoned his doctorate at Columbia University and joined the United Nations as a junior research officer, drawn by the idea that the successor to the League of Nations could make the world a better place. Behind the dispassionate façade was a man able to channel his horror of racism into realisable objectives. There was an early setback when he was taken off the South Africa desk by his Greek supervisor who was worried about his strong views on the treatment of Indians under apartheid. But Reddy was soon reinstated. The tireless organiser was adept at working and, when required, sidestepping the system. 'Over the years I took some personal risks,' he recalled from retirement. 'I could have been fired several times if all I was doing was known' (Reddy interview 2004).

There was a mountain to cross. The United Nations was, after all, the creation of the victors of the Second World War, with General Jan Smuts, South Africa's Prime Minister, a revered founding father, as he had been of the League of Nations a generation earlier. Then it was essentially a white man's club. Of the 51 members at its inaugural meeting in 1946, only Liberia, Ethiopia and Egypt were from Africa, apart from South Africa. Yet soon, to the indignation of Smuts, the Indian delegation saw to it that the plight of South Africa's relatively small Asian population was aired in the General Assembly.

For a decade and a half the West used its influence to protect South Africa from the mounting wrath. If the General Assembly reflected the world's conscience, the Security Council, where the big five powers could exercise their veto, set the agenda. If accusations of UN toothlessness were justified, it was Britain, France and the United States who drew the teeth. The status of the South West Africa mandate, which would dog South Africa for 40 years, sucked in Clement Attlee's Labour government, which for several years prevented Michael Scott and several Namibian petitioners from being heard at the UN. Through the 1950s the General Assembly repeatedly called on South Africa to bring its policies into line with the human rights sentiments of the UN Charter. Reddy recalled those days. 'Every year, around October, the South African question would be discussed, people would make speeches and go home and nothing would happen. Next year, they'd come and make speeches again' (Reddy interview 1992). But if the UN was to stand for something more than an arena for Cold War posturing, the issue of apartheid could not be ignored.

Sharpeville was the turning point, as apartheid at last received the full attention of the Security Council – although Britain and France were still able to abstain from the condemnatory resolution. Reddy, now more confident in his job, suggested the need for continuous reporting of events in South Africa. When, in November 1962, the Afro-Asian states pushed a sanctions resolution through the Assembly, appended to its coat-tails was a 'Special Committee against Apartheid' charged with keeping Pretoria's racial policies under review during the nine months of the year when the Assembly was not in session. Reddy recalls that 'fairly high officials in the Secretariat, my Director and others, were wishing to be the Secretary. I was asked whether I would be Deputy Secretary, but I said I would have differences of opinion and wasn't interested.' Then the western powers declined to join – the first committee to be boycotted by them – because it had been established in a resolution calling for sanctions. Suddenly, nobody wanted to be Secretary. It was offered to Reddy, who accepted gladly. 'You've given me a lifetime's job,' he told his head of department. 'The whole of Africa will need to be liberated before South Africa is liberated.' But he was under no illusion that he had got there because 'it was regarded as a committee which would prove worthless'.

Over the next 30 years Reddy's committee notched up one of the UN's few success stories. From his unrivalled seat of influence, he was the anonymous facilitator, the insider available to John Collins and to nationalist and anti-apartheid groups across the world. Reddy was effectively placed in charge of action against apartheid, with ready access to U Thant, the Burmese Secretary-General, who had chaired the non-aligned countries' sub-committee on South Africa. Eleven fairly low-key states made up the committee, with five from Africa, and Hungary alone from Europe. They decided there was 'no point in filling up the UN records with a lot of paper. So we should do whatever we can to promote sanctions and all kinds of action against apartheid. It became an action-oriented committee' (Reddy interview 1992). Reddy won the confidence of the Afro-Asian delegates. These were poor countries with small missions and no staff to do research so they asked him to draft most of the proposals and even write the speeches of the Chairman and other delegates.

The western powers had hoped the committee would be just another talking shop. However by staying away they were unable to neutralise it. Their absence gave it the space to establish an anti-apartheid culture at the United Nations. In its first year, it issued two interim reports and a final report, which led to increased pressure for an arms embargo and help for political prisoners. The West was now forced to take Reddy's committee seriously. The Americans offered the first sign of hope. President John Kennedy's UN Ambassador, Adlai Stevenson, assured Reddy that despite 'certain difficulties with sanctions, they would take action in their own ways.' Washington then announced an arms embargo and, when the issue reappeared at the Security Council, supported a voluntary ban on sales. France and Britain once again abstained.

In October 1963, Reddy heard on his radio that the Rivonia Trial was about to begin. He sprang into action, calling the Special Committee Chairman, Diallo Telli of Guinea, who by midday had convened a meeting of the Africa group and within half an hour had sent a delegation to U Thant. At 3 p.m. the debate was under way in the Special Political Committee (on which all member states were represented). Oliver Tambo and Bishop Reeves were in town and they were able to report on the significance of the trial. 'I was outside the room when the African delegates emerged… the Algerian delegate told me what they had decided and said they needed a resolution. I took it out of my pocket and gave it to him. But, critically, several western countries abstained in the resolution calling for the release of political prisoners.'

Reddy and Telli were determined not to allow them to kill off the initiative. 'It was a Thursday. It so happened there was a dinner the next night for all the delegates to the General Assembly, hosted by the Secretary-General. I was invited and with Diallo Telli, we talked to every one of the delegates who had abstained.' When the resolution came before the General Assembly on the Monday the Africans asked for a roll-call vote. Australia, Belgium, Canada, France, Netherlands, New

Zealand, Panama, United Kingdom, United States... 'As the names were called, each of these western delegates changed and voted for the resolution. There were big cheers. Portugal slipped out. Only South Africa voted against – the vote was 106 to one. For the first time, South Africa was totally isolated in the General Assembly.' Reddy heard later that Bram Fischer had told Mandela about the resolution. 'Mandela was very happy and very moved... it was one of the most satisfying things in my life' (Reddy, interview, 1992).

Reddy first became aware of John Collins through a speech reported in *The Times* in July 1963. With the mass arrests, the Canon said it was getting beyond his capacity to raise sufficient funds through public appeals. In New York, Tambo had discussed the question of humanitarian aid with Reddy. 'Oliver was at first rather hesitant... he thought it might divert the UN's attention from political action on sanctions and the Rivonia Trial.' Reddy understood that it was not politic to overplay the term 'human rights work'. For African delegates the real issue was national liberation, but they did appreciate that the humanitarian act of helping victims of apartheid had profound political implications.

Here, at last, was an opportunity for constructive action without fear of rejection by the West. On 16 December, two years to the day from when the ANC went to war, the General Assembly voted overwhelmingly for a resolution (drafted by Reddy) asking the Secretary-General to 'find ways and means of providing relief and assistance, through appropriate international agencies, to families of all persons persecuted by the Government of South Africa for opposition to the policies of apartheid'. Members were invited to 'contribute generously'. The move had the powerful backing of the Secretary-General. But U Thant, in a statement before the vote, did not envisage providing direct relief, since no funds had been made available for the purpose. Nor was there talk of money for trial defences. But what frightened Collins was the reference to 'international agencies'. It was perhaps why, after returning to London, Tambo wrote to Reddy saying 'people' (Collins being one of them) were enthusiastic about the resolution.

The Security Council had appointed a group of experts to examine how best to introduce human rights in South Africa. It was a delaying tactic, as Britain's Ambassador in Pretoria, Sir Hugh Stephenson, made clear in his annual review to Rab Butler, the Foreign Secretary: 'Adroit manoeuvrings by the United Kingdom and other delegations deflected pressure for sanctions and a respite was gained, which may last for some months, at the cost of agreeing to the setting up of a "committee of experts" to report on a possible solution for South Africa'.[1]

Reddy, as Secretary of this group of experts, came to London early in 1964 and was taken by Tambo and Robbie Resha to Amen Court. Here was a meeting of great moment. Reddy found Collins to be an improvisational genius. Collins saw Reddy as a quiet, self-effacing person who knew which ropes to pull on the confusing stage of the United Nations. Reddy explained that though the resolution by itself would not bring funding, it would give respectability to his operation. It was during this visit that Sir Hugh Foot, the committee's rapporteur, took Reddy to an archetypal Defence and Aid occasion, a 'Rivonia' full house at Central Hall featuring the ex-Archbishop of Cape Town, Joost de Blank, and a movie star introduced by chairman John as 'Brandon Marlow'.

Reddy wrote frequently to Collins, exploring ways of increasing donations. He noted:

> I was not very careful about drafting my letters to him, as they were personal. I believe one letter mentioned that international organisations with consultative status at the United Nations would try to get UN and government money and undercut Defence and Aid. I believe I mentioned Amnesty International and the World Council of Churches. I had no intention of alarming him, only to suggest that the unequivocal support of the liberation movements was crucial for D&A. I was sure I could handle the situation to his benefit. (Reddy interview 1992)

This letter jolted Collins into action. By now there were Defence and Aid committees in Scandinavia, Switzerland and Australia, though some were embryonic. He called a meeting of delegates from these countries at the Russell Hotel,

Bloomsbury on 20 June 1964 and founded Defence and Aid Fund (International)[2] 'a fund to safeguard freedom and human dignity in South Africa'. Collins was elected Chairman. The minutes were hurried off to the Special Committee in New York. So Reddy first heard of the new fund after it had come into being.

In November, the United Nations Special Committee gave Collins the stamp of approval he was so desperately seeking. Together with Amnesty International and the Joint Committee for High Commission Territories (which helped South African refugees), the Defence and Aid Fund was designated a body to which member states could contribute in terms of the Secretary-General's appeal. This was no act of favouritism. 'IDAF were doing a very good job,' says Reddy. 'No other organisation had done it, over a long period of time, so well, and raised such a lot of money. And we had a very strong recommendation, constantly, from the ANC and occasionally from the PAC, that we should support the D&A Fund. I had several letters from Oliver Tambo about it; many times he said we should strongly support the Fund' (Reddy interview 1992).

The formal recognition put paid to real and imagined rivals. The 'Scottites', David Astor, Dingle Foot and Martin Ennals, were rumoured to be planning an organisation with similar aims to Collins's fund. Collins now hastened to head off potential opposition in South Africa. In a letter to John Blundell in the Cape Town office (11.11.64), he described the UN's support as a 'tremendous breakthrough'. Now they would separate defence work from welfare work, with Christian Action and Defence and Aid continuing to raise money for trials (the UN was still only talking about welfare aid). It was more urgent than ever, he told Blundell, to have a national committee to receive the money, soon to be rolling in from governments and organisations worldwide.

In that same month, Reddy got the ball rolling at home with 25,000 rupees (*ca.* £1,875) from the Delhi government. It was Defence and Aid's first-ever state funding. Reddy wrote to Mrs Myrdal, Sweden's Ambassador, and her government sent US$100,000 each to Collins and the World Council of Churches. In the meantime, Collins seized on the UN's 'approval' to write to the 99 governments that had voted for the humanitarian resolution. In the first year there were helpful contributions from Denmark and the Netherlands, with smaller amounts from Greece, Hungary, Iraq, Malaysia, Nigeria, Pakistan and the Philippines. The Soviet Union's US$10,000 would have been noted in Pretoria.

Collins never took no for an answer. An exchange of letters with Canadian government officials illustrates his terrier-like qualities. At the Commonwealth Prime Ministers' Conference in London in June 1965, his opening appeal listed those countries which had responded so far. The need was greater than ever, he said. A gift would 'make concrete the rejection of apartheid policies expressed in the Resolution and would ensure a fair trial and the care of the families.' He received no reply, so a month later he wrote to the Canadian Prime Minister again, addressing the letter 'Dear Prime Minister'.

This time Collins's appeal was geared to the urgent situation in Southern Rhodesia:

> As you will no doubt remember, during the conference in London of Commonwealth Prime Ministers, we sent you a memorandum indicating that £10,000 was urgently required to provide legal defence in that country. The priorities are to finance appeals for those 24 men condemned to death under the mandatory hanging law, and to challenge in the courts the validity of the restriction orders served on so many of Mr. Smith's opponents. (Collins, letter to Prime Minister Lester Pearson 26.07.65, in IDAF files)

A secretary in the Prime Minister's office acknowledged the letter on 30 July, saying that a reply would be sent soon. On 2 September the reply declared that it was 'not appropriate for the Canadian Government to intervene in this matter by contributing to your fund.'

On 15 October, Collins wrote again to the Prime Minister, ignoring the 'no no' in the second letter, referring instead to the first acknowledgement note. 'We realise that in your letter of 30 July you stated that you were considering the matter, but the tragic and worsening situation in Southern Rhodesia makes it all the more urgent that the Defence and

Aid Fund (International) should be able to appeal effectively.' Changing tack, he reduced his range and asked for 'at least a token grant so that we might appeal to individuals in Britain and elsewhere on the basis that our work has the approval of your Government.' The Under-Secretary of State for External Affairs replied that 'as indicated in my letter of 2 September', it would not be appropriate to intervene. Collins wrote once again, 'deeply regretting' that the Canadian Government did not feel it appropriate to implement the United Nations resolution by contributing to the Defence and Aid Fund (Letter 12.11.65 in IDAF files). This marked the end of the correspondence. However, in time, the Ottawa government would make handsome amends for the snub.

In December 1965, the United Nations made specific its earlier, vague financial appeal by establishing a Trust Fund for South Africa. The idea was born in the Special Committee, and passed through the General Assembly, where the West had no veto power, with Pretoria alone opposing and only Portugal abstaining. The Portuguese delegate complained about interference in the internal affairs of a member state. He was right, of course. The appeal was no longer limited to the relief of dependants, education of prisoners and their families, and the refugees flooding into the neighbouring territories. In writing the rules, Reddy had prioritised 'legal assistance to persons charged under discriminatory and repressive legislation'. It was unprecedented for a UN fund to pay for the defence of freedom fighters charged with attempting to overthrow the government of one of its own member states.

Reddy's preparation was meticulous. In a note to U Thant, he named five countries best calculated to serve the aims of the Trust Fund. The permanent Chairman should be Swedish, 'so that it will be seen that if a western country is chairman, this money is not going to be used for armed struggle.' The Vice-Chairman should be Nigerian, with Morocco to represent Francophone Africa, and Pakistan and Chile providing a moderate continental spread. The effective actors would be Sweden, whose Ambassador, Sverker Astrom, was the Chairman, and Nigeria. Reddy had chosen to be the committee's Secretary so as to watch over its deliberations. Before the meetings his proposals would be finalised at an informal Swedish–Nigerian caucus, which were largely devoted to how much should be allotted to each organisation. The others simply 'got the papers we had to distribute for the meetings, but did not know much more'. The secrecy extended to the UN itself. The trustees took the 'extraordinary decision that the names of recipients of its grants would not be published in the annual report to the General Assembly'. When the marxist President Allende was overthrown, Chile, under Pretoria's friend General Pinochet, posed a serious threat to the security of the Trust Fund.

And yet Collins was not entirely in his seventh heaven. He worried that the Trust Fund would impede his own money-raising potential. Would it become a rival, or worse, fund rivals? Reddy had discussed it with him shortly before its adoption by the UN, but he remained suspicious. 'There was no conflict between the trust and IDAF,' says Reddy, 'though the Canon could never be satisfied until every penny and more went only to him.' The money, it had been made clear in the debates, was intended to supplement direct contributions to unnamed voluntary organisations unable to cope with increasing demands, and not to replace them. The formula made it possible to direct funds to Defence and Aid International, though at the time it had no special status with the UN. Amnesty International had consultative status with the influential Economic and Social Council (ECOSOC), and its founder, Peter Benenson, wanted to be the channel for the Trust Fund money. But central to Amnesty's ethos was the rule that it did not support victims who had employed violence. Hundreds of men and women would have been denied legal aid.

Once the Trust Fund was up and running, Reddy told Collins he should count on getting 50 per cent of the takings. In fact, over the years, it amounted to two thirds of what was on offer. Collins had forced the pace and got what he wanted. Resistance in South Africa was dropping away, and yet his idea of defending and aiding had been co-opted by the international community. No longer dependent on the purses inside the crocodile skin handbags, Amen Court Inc. was about to become the sorting house for undreamed of millions. It was as if a successful but under-capitalised business had been taken over by a multi-national corporation, with the founder staying on as MD of the new monolith. The first UN grants took a year to come through, but at least the Canon knew that IDAF had been properly launched.

The formation of the Trust Fund marked the end of an important stage in the Defence and Aid story. Reddy believes that the years 1952 to 1966 were John Collins's time of greatest achievement. 'People in the West did not care about Africans being jailed or even killed. They were massacred, but the world paid no attention because they were black. John did a tremendous job in sensitising opinion, involving people through their own contributions' (Reddy interview 1992).

Chapter 11

THE SWEDES

It is extraordinary that the Swedes, their spiritual influences seemingly in the austere hands of Martin Luther and August Strindberg, should feature so largely in Africa's emancipation. Yet without the Swedish connection, numerous nationalist movements would have been much less effective in their wars of liberation. And Defence and Aid would have remained a domestic do-good fund, raising money through appeals and art auctions, dependent on the goodwill of an impoverished Third World. Fortunately, by the end of the 1950s, Sweden, affluent and social democratic, was searching for a role in the wider world. It was in a suitable mood to have its conscience pricked by a journalist.

Per Wästberg was not a journalist by profession when he left on a Rotary travel scholarship to South Africa and Southern Rhodesia. Much of what he knew of southern Africa had been gleaned from articles written years before when Herbert Tingsten, editor of the country's influential medium of communication, *Dagens Nyheter*, focused for the first time on apartheid. As a result the newspaper's journalists were frozen out of South Africa. Wästberg made contact with a spread of ANC, Communist and Liberal party ideas, entering, as did John Collins five years previously, a world of sights and opinions beyond the range of ordinary whites. He had a precocious talent, having written a teenage novel. Now the reports he sent back were snapped up by *Dagens Nyheter* and appeared in newspapers across Scandinavia. Pretoria duly declared him a prohibited immigrant (Wästberg interview 1992).

Wästberg ended his series with a request: 'If you think you can help, contact this address'. The response revealed deep concern about the state of affairs in South Africa. He linked up with a Lutheran missionary, Gunnar Helander, who had known South Africa since before the Second World War. The two men set up a fund, and cheques poured in from school projects, church and street collections, and an avalanche of 'ordinary people'. The money went directly to South African refugees in Basutoland, to non-apartheid schools, and to black students by now trickling into a friendlier Sweden.

The two men had only a vague idea of the work of Canon Collins, but when Wästberg, 'an innocent Swede', came to London to work on a blacklist for a Swedish boycott campaign, he made his way to Amen Court. As a result of this visit, much of the private and state money raised in Sweden for southern Africa would henceforward be channelled through London.

Helander and Wästberg created a Swedish–South Africa boycott committee through the Swedish Youth Council, an umbrella for a sweep of tendencies: political, trade union, Christian, sporting, even teetotal. On the list of sponsors were Sweden's Prime Minister Tage Erlander; the man who would succeed him, Olof Palme; Tingsten, the editor; and a future Nobel literature laureate, Eyvind Johnson. Professor of Medicine and popular novelist Lars Gyllensten donated one per cent of his salary to African education funds for countering the effect of Bantu Education.

Sweden's trading links with South Africa were nothing like as extensive as Britain's, but exports such as 'worker's cognac' were popular. The campaigners persuaded the state wine monopoly to stop buying Cape wine and brandy. The Lutherans, Sweden's established church, ended the import of 'Sweet Constantia' after a Wästberg piece in *Dagens Nyheter* exposed 'the scandal' of its widespread use as a communion wine. Co-operative stores removed Koo marmalade and Cape apples from their shelves. The government ordered hospitals and the armed forces to stop using anything that was 'Made in SA'. The embargo remained in force for a long time. 'Sweden was ahead of most other countries in establishing an anti-apartheid culture,' says Wästberg. 'After 1966, you were unlikely to see South African goods anywhere, maybe the odd apple in a small shop inbetween seasons.'

Helander, one of the rare Swedes to have first-hand

experience of how the Christian Afrikaners mastered their blacks, made a powerful impact in church circles. He had gone to the Natal Midlands, an area evangelised by German Lutherans, in 1938 and at one stage lived in a house on the battlefield of Rorke's Drift, where Briton and Zulu once indulged in mutual slaughter. His ebullient spirit and fluency in the Zulu language made him friends across the colour line. While a student in Birmingham, he had befriended a wealthy Natal Moslem, Cassim Lakhi, who warned him that when they met in South Africa things would be different. Helander soon realised how right he was. On one occasion a shop-owner in Greytown questioned him about the 'coolie' waiting outside for him. Incensed, Helander replied that 'this man is superior to you in every way: education, wealth, upbringing. All you have is your white skin' (Helander interview 1992). In 1941, he was on a committee consisting largely of white missionaries, which, to the consternation of the church authorities, elected Albert Luthuli Chairman of the Natal Missionary Conference.

Helander offered articles to newspapers at home, but found that 'Sweden was totally cold to the question of apartheid. When war broke out people in Europe couldn't believe that South Africa, an ally of Britain in the war against the Nazis, had a kind of Nazism itself. They thought my articles were false, so they were refused.' His work was accepted more readily after the war, with the installation in Pretoria of a cabinet of ministers so recently sympathetic to Hitler. He also wrote books recounting parables from South African life. His *Endast för vita* (1955) was the first novel in any language to depict South African Indians as ordinary human beings. When the South African government media targeted his writings, Helander knew his South African days were numbered. His visa was not renewed after he returned home on leave in 1956.

Though of medium size, Sweden was once a dominant power in the Baltic, a considerable player in the second division of European history. Copper, lumber and especially iron-ore exports gave the economy a head start over its neighbours. At times Sweden needed to fight for national survival with guile and courage against Danes, Germans and

Russians, but it was the Finnish connection that left the most profound mark on the national character. 'We colonised Finland for practically five hundred years,' wrote broadcaster Bjorn Kumm, 'and long after Sweden lost Finland to the Czar in the Napoleonic Wars we kept looking down on them. So when the Finns were building their nation they remained more anti-Swedish than anti-Russian because our settlers were still running the country' (Kumm letter 14.05.96).

The Second World War was a terrifying test of Swedish neutrality. Those times are rarely, if ever, talked about, but they caused deep resentment elsewhere in Scandinavia. The Social Democrats headed a coalition on the lines of Winston Churchill's wartime government. Sweden furnished Finland with material and military volunteers in its war against Russia, but otherwise stayed carefully on the sidelines. Despite Finland's large Swedish-speaking minority, the Stockholm government rejected their neighbour's desperate call for Swedish regulars to come to its aid. The British and French request for their troops to pass through Sweden to Finland was turned down on the grounds that they would come from Norway, then at war with Germany, thus violating Swedish neutrality. For many, the Swedish rallying cry, 'Finland's cause is ours', had a hollow ring.

At first, Sweden was able to resist German demands for the transit of their troops and armaments across its territory. But with Norway finally subdued by Germany, and Denmark under sullen occupation, Sweden's isolation was complete. It caved in to the pressure; its railways moved in war supplies and moved out German soldiers on home leave. Elderly Swedes have painful memories of sealed German troop trains steaming through their countryside. At the outbreak of the second Russo–Finnish war, in the late summer of 1941, an armed German division was allowed to cross from Norway to Finland by train. In exchange for essential imports, 35 million tons of iron ore and ball bearings were sent to Germany, much of it by the giant company SKF. Churchill said Germany could not have sustained its war effort without Swedish ore. By the summer of 1943, with Hitler's armies rebuffed at Stalingrad and El Alamein, Sweden was able to act more independently, building up its own military strength, reducing exports to Germany, and even concluding trade agreements with Britain and the United States.

These events shamed many Swedes, but they were too intimidated to voice their protests in public. Documents released in Finland indicate that leaders of Swedish society, not excluding the Prime Minister, had their telephones bugged. Newspapers were, in theory, free to speak their minds, but only Torgny Segerstedt, editor of the Gothenburg (Göteborg) newspaper *GHT*, consistently attacked Nazi Germany and accused the government of cowardice. Local businessmen, alarmed at this outspokenness, withdrew their advertising and the paper never recovered. Swedes seemed to retreat into the security of home and hearth. In that war decade of the forties the population increased by a prodigious 10 per cent.

It is well to remember that this was not a case of willing collaboration with the German invader, as in Croatia or the Ukraine or by sections of French society. In spite of its exposed position, the government did avoid being sucked into the European 'New Order'. The small Jewish community was not deported to Auschwitz, and Finns, Danes, Norwegians and Balts on the run were granted exile status. The authorities managed to retain contact with the Allies, turning a blind eye to clandestine flights of Norwegian couriers to their military leaders in London. Thanks to her neutral status, Swedish diplomats in enemy capitals were a rare and trustworthy source of intelligence for London and Washington. They were able to perform acts of charity, even heroism. Raoul Wallenberg's negotiations with Adolf Eichmann saved 20,000 Hungarian Jews from the gas chambers. On the other hand, the Wallenberg family bank, Enskilda, traded in gold looted from Jews, and on one occasion bought securities seized from Dutch Jews, the proceeds of which were used by the Nazis to deport these same Jews to the death camps.

After the war, the Social Democrats returned gratefully to a non-aligned foreign policy. Sweden never joined NATO, but did become a late and grudging member of the European Community after the collapse of the neighbouring Soviet power bloc. Throughout those years, the serious outlet for international activity was through the United Nations and its associated organisations. Swedish diplomats were deployed in the world's trouble spots, and sometimes suffered the consequences, as when Count Folke Bernadotte, the UN emissary in Palestine, was shot by Zionist terrorists. Swedes sporting the UN's *casques bleus* kept the peace around the world, and in Katanga had to fight for it. When their UN Secretary-General, Dag Hammarskjold, died in an air crash on a mission during the post-independence anarchy in the Congo, Swedes saw it as a sacrificial killing.

Alongside this process of eschewing power blocs, the Social Democrats offered fulsome support to the struggle for colonial self-determination. Wästberg speaks of 'a kind of natural anti-colonialism embedded in the Swedish consciousness... not even a matter for discussion; simply part of what is.' And yet there were emotional hurdles to overcome in the shape of Sweden's western allies. When attitudes changed in the mid-fifties, South Africa played an inadvertent role. Sven Oste, *Dagens Nyheter*'s finest foreign correspondent, had applied for a South African visa, but was told by the Third Secretary at the embassy, one Pik Botha (later Foreign Minister), that no reporter from his newspaper had 'a hope in hell' of getting there. Oste went to Algeria instead. His reporting on that colonial war captured the imagination of Sweden's political class. For the first time, a Prime Minister, Tage Erlander, saw fit to criticise France, hitherto a beacon of liberty for so many Swedes. This falling-out was followed by a critical assault on America's war in Vietnam. And on Britain, for its feeble response to Rhodesian UDI – though the Swedes were reminded that their own behaviour during the German occupation was not beyond reproach. Whatever the carping, Sweden had moved smartly from benign neutrality to the forceful advocacy of decolonisation.

The changes initiated under Prime Minister Erlander would make Sweden the world's most generous purveyor of foreign aid in terms of population size. Sweden was the first western country to provide cash from state coffers to movements at war with a presumed ally – Portugal – starting with Mozambique, followed by Guinea-Bissau and Angola. Sweden's international mood was nurtured by young idealistic social democrats preparing to make their contribution to Africa's freedom struggle and its post-colonial development. Many became influential in public life. At the heart of this crusading group was the charismatic figure of Olof Palme. While on a student delegation to Prague, he had married a student desperate to quit Czechoslovakia, then divorced her in Sweden. His 'first political act' had been to initiate a student blood donor scheme to finance black scholarships to Johannesburg's University of the Witwatersrand. Eduardo Mondlane, a future leader of the Mozambique nationalist movement, Frelimo, was one beneficiary. But for the role of Sweden (and Norway, Denmark and Finland), it would have seemed to the oppressed of Africa and Latin America that only communist regimes were prepared to offer a helping hand.

As a cabinet minister in the 1970s, Palme helped develop a new judgemental foreign policy, though it was not universally popular at home.[1] Carl Tham, a friend of Palme, says his politics challenged a die-hard Swedish traditionalism, 'in a country where the view of worldwide conflicts has for so long been, and still is, dominated by the American perspective' (Tham 1987: 62). It seemed ironic to some that Sweden's commitment to African liberation and the hosting of a war-crimes tribunal on the Vietnam War should square with her neutral status. Palme argued that neutrality should not imply moral toothlessness. 'Between the exploiters and exploited,' he once said, 'there is no middle ground.' The policy was justified in terms of UN resolutions inviting member states to provide material support for liberation movements. This took the form of medical equipment, food, educational materials, and transportation, but never weaponry. Certainly, the aid freed the guerrillas from non-military worries and enhanced the fighting ability of the two most successful movements, Frelimo in Mozambique and Guinea-Bissau's PAIGC. It would have been a factor in the Portuguese Colonels' decision to throw in the towel sooner rather than later. In the six years prior to the 1974 Lisbon coup, £6.5 million was earmarked for the PAIGC alone.

The engine of the aid operation was the Swedish International Development Agency, SIDA, set up in 1962 to service Third World development and African liberation. Its first director, Ernst Michanek, was a meticulous Swedish civil servant well able to make real Palme's ambitious crusade, which involved direct funding to a number of southern African liberation movements. In time, Sweden would become one of the rare countries to live up to the UN call that one per cent of GDP be reserved for foreign aid. Unlike the Marshall Plan, it was done without fanfare, and without an intentional element of aid tied to boosting Sweden's own industries. Nor was it simply an exercise in doling out money to begging blacks. There was pride in the relationship. Freedom fighters were made welcome in Sweden. They enriched the political landscape. They were treated as men and women engaged in a just war. In Britain and the United States, prime ministers and presidents were terrified to be seen with the 'wrong' terrorist or guerrilla fighter. If they were seen with the 'right' one, a Tshombe, a Savimbi or a Buthelezi, they would be on the evening television news. But if they were the 'wrong' ones, their visits to the United States would be restricted to the neighbourhood of the UN headquarters in New York.

Swedes of all political hues seem agreed on the motives for this extraordinary national generosity. Bjorn Kumm believed that it had to do more with the opening up of the world than with national guilt, and wrote that 'the older generation had no idea what was going on outside Europe. And then suddenly we discovered colonialism' (Kumm letter 14.05.96). The daughter of the intrepid wartime Gothenburg editor, Ingrid Segerstedt Wiberg, believes that disappointment at American, and most of all of French, behaviour shaped their attitude. 'The Americans were responsible for the Hiroshima and Nagasaki bombs and the French government for the atrocities during the Algerian war. That resulted in a strong wish among young people in Sweden, intellectuals and others, to support the black peoples' fight for their human rights' (Wiberg letter 22.03.96).

There was an unspoken, perhaps unconscious, desire to make amends. The dilemma posed by the terrifying brush with Nazism does not seem to have been a matter for public debate, nor even for private soul-searching, for the Swedes admit to being not a greatly self-reflecting people. The Social Democrats, who were there during and after the war and for much of the time since, have preferred to keep the issue off limits. Potential debate has been hindered by the Swedish special branch's refusal to allow publication of contemporary archival records. But Ernst Michanek, who was at the heart of Sweden's political life for several decades, is sure 'the fact that we did not resist the Germans, as Norway and the Finns did, gave us guilt deep down' (Michanek interview 1992).

Neutrality was largely responsible for Sweden's prosperous emergence from the Second World War. In Europe, only the Swiss economy was in better shape. At least Sweden was able to offer generous credit to Norway and Denmark to make up the leeway. She was well placed to supply industrial goods to war-torn central Europe. In the decades before the oil price recession of the 1970s, Sweden enjoyed unprecedented economic growth. Industrial production grew six per cent annually in the second half of the sixties. This virtually seamless accumulation of wealth made possible Sweden's huge aid projects in the developing world. Wästberg has described a strong feeling, especially among students and the young, 'that the very advantages that Sweden enjoys, its relative affluence, its advanced welfare state, constitute in themselves an opportunity and an obligation to take a moral stand upon important international issues' (Wästberg interview 1992).

The Social Democrats were neither loony lefties nor Marxist fellow travellers. Their solid anti-communism was buoyed by the colonialism staring at them across the Baltic Sea from Latvia, Lithuania and Estonia. The Russians marching on Hungary and Czechoslovakia reinforced their fear and hatred of communism. Had any one of the Scandinavian governments been in the slightest degree pro-Marxist, Pretoria – not to mention London and Washington – would have been quick to denigrate its aid ambitions.

•

Oliver Tambo went to Sweden for the first time in 1962 to speak at a May Day rally in Gothenburg. After his meeting with Palme, the Social Democrats took the ANC under their wing. But Swedish society had adjustments to make. At that year's May Day rally in Stockholm, a trade unionist was prosecuted for displaying the slogan 'Verwoerd commits murder on African soil'. Collins, accompanied by Robert Resha of the London ANC, had been in Sweden the year before. He was allowed to put his case on national television, and thereafter was welcomed in the highest government circles. It was so different from his treatment at home. Soon, the Swedish fund began to channel money through Amen Court, starting a 30-year association from private and state sources. The Swedes took to Collins because he was the dependable agent they were looking for to carry out a delicate part of their programme. On a personal level, they probably liked the way he defied their preconceptions of how a posh English clergyman should behave. They knew his rejection of apartheid was absolute.

Chapter 12

ROCK BOTTOM: THE BANNING OF DEFENCE AND AID

With black nationalism behind bars, the whites of South Africa may have been tempted to believe they could cling to power forever. Certainly Verwoerd, cock-a-hoop, pressed ahead with his final solution to the 'Black Problem'. He uprooted coloureds and Asians from town centres and stitched up a Balkan patchwork of 'Bantu homelands', large, small and polka-dotted. Those who did not like it were by definition liberals, 'commies', *opstokers* (rabble-rousers) or terrorists. As with any social programme that needed to be force-fed to the masses, the race laws were backed up with the means of ensuring acceptance or punishing rejection. Vorster and his security chief, Hendrik van den Bergh, gaoled, banned, house-arrested, banished and executed. The 90-day clause was replaced by a 180-day clause, not because resistance had doubled, but so that the police could hold witnesses until they were ready to testify against comrades or loved ones.

South Africa's neighbours were powerless to influence events. Liberation wars were under way in Angola and Mozambique but these Portuguese colonies still acted as cushions against independent Africa. The Malawi of Dr Hastings Banda (Nyasaland until it achieved independence from Britain in 1964) was comfortably seduced by Pretoria's gold. Further north, above the *cordon sanitaire*, black Africa was finding its voice but there was little it could do beyond closing down South Africa's consulates and banishing South African Airways from the skies, forcing it into an expensive detour round the Dakar bulge to Europe.

The western business community had the power to hurt South Africa, but this was a far-fetched prospect. An impressive spread of African leaders and western academics gave the issue of economic sanctions a good airing at a conference in London in 1964. The papers covered international law; gold, arms and oil sanctions; the impact on Britain, the United States and on the British High Commission Territories south of the Zambezi. The conference showed that sanctions were 'necessary, urgent, legal and practical,' wrote the conference convener, Ronald Segal, in a Penguin Special book, 'but likely to succeed only with the full co-operation of Britain and the United States' (Segal 1964: 14).

It was a vain hope: western investors could not keep their snouts out of the trough. Their governments positively encouraged investment, rationalising that prosperity, not isolation, would persuade the whites to mend their ways. This was the aftermath of the Cuban missile crisis and the erection of the Berlin Wall, when left-of-centre liberation struggles were viewed as a red menace. The South Africa Foundation, a lobby of industrialists headed inevitably by Harry Oppenheimer, spread the good news about South Africa abroad. Its secretary, Sir Francis de Guingand, had been General Bernard Montgomery's wartime *aide-de-camp*. Monty, as a director of Tube Investments, toured South Africa to observe the spread of Raleigh cycles, a Tube subsidiary. After manifold photo opportunities with beaming '*piccanins*' (young African children), he pronounced South Africa a country with bright prospects. Within two years of the post-Sharpeville capital flight, South Africa's gold and foreign currency holdings were back to pre-massacre levels. It was no surprise that the boom coincided with the unprecedented assault on human rights and the steamroller enforcement of 'grand apartheid'. The flood of repressive measures was necessary to reassure the West that the era of the outrageous dividend would return.

So it was easier for Verwoerd, having crushed the enemies within, to square up aggressively to those without. Collins had emerged as the clear leader in the pack of clerical enemies of South Africa. Huddleston, now Archbishop of the Indian Ocean, resident in Mauritius, was a distant though no less authoritative voice. Reeves was President of the Anti-Apartheid Movement, but the Anglican authorities had exiled him to a parish in deepest Sussex after Prime Minister Macmillan refused to sanction his appointment as Bishop of Blackburn, fearing it might not be well received in Pretoria (Collins 1992: 279). Michael Scott busied himself with a new passion, the Naga struggle for independence from India.

The first annual conference of the International Defence and Aid Fund in March 1965 gives an idea of the speed with which Collins was off the mark in pursuit of worldwide opportunities. South Africa House would have noted the jaunty press statement that delegates from Norway, Sweden, Denmark, Britain, Switzerland and Australia 'greeted with acclaim the announcement by Canon Collins that two governments, India and Sweden, had made generous donations to the Fund.' National committees were in the process of formation in Ireland, Holland, Canada, the USA, New Zealand, France and Belgium – although the last two did not get off the ground (IDAF minutes, 26/27.03.65). Perhaps, after these events, the real mystery was why Vorster waited so long to deal with Defence and Aid inside South Africa. There were even those, fund supporters among them, who thought the Canon was visiting misfortune upon himself.

Collins had a reputation, not entirely ill-founded, for being occasionally reckless with the facts. In February 1965, appeals in British and Irish newspapers featured the plight of the widow of Wilson Khayinga, a trade unionist hanged for complicity in the killing of a police informer in the Eastern Cape. The South African embassy in London complained to the Advertising Standards Authority that it had been a 'cold-blooded murder of a potential prosecution witness in a sabotage trial [who] was never a police informer'. The widow, said Collins, had six children and had been forced to live cut off in a rural village. The embassy retorted that she had four children and lived in a community of 17,000 people linked to the city of Port Elizabeth by public transport. The South African press went to town. Dr Bill Hoffenberg, Defence and Aid's Cape Town chairman, sent word to Collins that 'such advertisements are doing the Fund's image great harm, and may even damage our continued existence' (Hoffenberg letter to his Johannesburg counterpart, David Craighead, 18.02.65).

Collins's debut appearance before the UN Special Committee on Apartheid in June 1965 set a new standard of bravura utterance. His words, widely reported in South Africa, infuriated Vorster, incensed the local committees and pole-axed his already strained friendship with Alan Paton, while Enuga Reddy, shown the speech in advance, pleaded with him to tone down certain passages. Collins refused (Reddy interview 1992).

'To put matters right in South Africa,' he began, 'requires political action on a big scale.' And '...it seems probable that only external pressures and the threat or execution of internal revolution will bring about the desired result.' The contribution of Defence and Aid

> fosters the morale of the internal resistance for, if the necessary political changes are to be brought about with the minimum of violence – and no sane person could wish otherwise – it is the resistance movement inside South Africa, the front line of the struggle for freedom, which alone can give to South Africa the ability to become a non-racial society based upon a free and democratic way of life. (Collins 1980: 6)

He instanced those not hanged in the Rivonia Trial, and a Cape case that ended after a 21-month fight with 31 acquittals and 13 convictions: 'without the Fund to provide proper defence, all 44 would have gone to gaol'.

Collins then spoke of

> the necessity to provide for the families and dependants of the underground resistance. Because of the tyrannical legis-lation of the present South African government, no political organisation, which seeks to change South Africa's racial poli-cies, can function properly in the open; the black political organisations are banned. Those who wish to continue the struggle have to go underground. But what man or woman can... undertake such dangerous work if he or she knows that, by doing so, the well-being of their children and other dependants is at stake. (Collins 1980: 10/11)

At a conservative estimate there were between 15,000 and 20,000 wives and children with breadwinners in gaol, he said. 'The conscience of the world is so easily aroused when there is an earthquake or a flood; but this vast disaster which is forced upon the opponents of apartheid gets so little publicity' (Collins 1980: 9/10).

Reddy objected not to the sentiments but to the emphases. He fully supported the humanitarian aims of IDAF but for political reasons both at the UN and inside South Africa he wanted them played down.

> We were trying to say that the main action we needed for changing the situation in South Africa was sanctions. Canon Collins didn't like it because it seemed to downgrade the importance of the work of his Fund. That was not our intention but we wanted to do that deliberately so it would not divert attention from the sanctions campaign. But he had talked about support for the liberation movements and this was fully publicised in South Africa. We knew that some bad would come in due course. (Yule interview 1993)

Diana Collins later rejected the idea that it was yet another example of canonical recklessness. Her husband had considered that a passionate speech was required to convince doubting nations of the need to put a UN Trust Fund for southern Africa in place. But the words 'underground' and 'resistance' were manna to Vorster, who had long accused the fund of assisting saboteurs. A story in the Johannesburg *Sunday Times* (20.06.65), headlined 'Defence Aid repudiates Canon Collins', had the local committee disassociating itself from 'remarks by Canon Collins concerning "underground resistance"'. Collins asserted, a shade disingenuously, that the South African fund was not connected in any way with any political body, lawful or banned. The newspaper quoted Alan Paton and Helen Suzman, the lone Progressive Party MP, as strongly supporting the fund, though privately they cursed Collins's unerring ability to put his foot in it.

As if this was not enough, the same newspaper's front page splash screamed out the headline: 'Dutch embassy invaded'. The Dutch government had announced a donation of

$20,000 to Collins's fund 'for the victims of apartheid', a fund, said foreign minister Helgard Muller, that helped 'knowingly or unknowingly, communist ambitions in South Africa'. Once South African radio's vitriolic early evening commentary, 'Survey of Current Affairs', had got to work on Defence and Aid, a throng of 2,000 protestors, many recent Dutch settlers, burst through the gates of the embassy in Pretoria and festooned the walls with rotten eggs. The police stood idly by. Who in South Africa could now claim not to have heard of the Canon of St Paul's Cathedral and his 'terrorist' Fund?

Alan Paton wrote to Collins directly this time (03.08.65), describing his UN speech as 'incomprehensible in its folly'. Apart from his anger at what he saw as its unnecessary provocation, Paton was aggrieved on other matters, and repeated several points from his earlier indirect letter to Mary Benson. One of Defence and Aid's stated aims, he wrote, was the achievement of a non-racial society in South Africa, yet his party, the Liberals, which shared that aim, had received hardly any money. Paton did approve of legal help for political offences, 'even when serious crimes such as murder have been involved. Yet are saboteurs in your eyes the only kind of resisters worth sustaining?... Did you know that the overwhelming burden of the work of Defence and Aid (in South Africa) was being done by people (Liberal Party members) whose own causes you did not, or perhaps would not, support?' He urged Collins to answer these questions, 'for your answers are vital to our friendship'.

Collins might have pointed out that several saboteurs were drawn from the ranks of Paton's own party, and that Defence and Aid's bankrolling of John Harris's trial must have displeased the government as much as its role in Rivonia. He could also claim to have sent money, and quite a lot of it, to the Liberal Party for overt political purposes in the past, before the pressure of trial defences had built up. In 1960 Collins made at least two transfers, totalling over £5,000, and had been thanked by Susan Spence, the party's national secretary, for 'the most generous gift' in a letter on Liberal Party of SA notepaper (14.10.60).

Collins sensed, however, that this was no time to indulge

in a fractious, point-scoring correspondence with an old and trusted friend. What was needed, in response to the demand for 'answers', was a healing personal touch. But as his arrival at Jan Smuts Airport would certainly have ended at the re-embarkation desk, he dispatched his wife to patch up the quarrel and do what she could to revive the sagging morale of Defence and Aid in South Africa (Collins 1992: 315–321).

'Collins' being a common name, and with 'holiday' given as the reason for her visit, suspicions were not aroused at first. Then, as now, Britons entered South Africa without a visa. But the trip was clandestine and its purpose was political. The police might have cottoned on had they seen Diana Collins calling at Ruth Hayman's office in Johannesburg, which acted as a clearing-house for political cases; or visiting the former treason trialist Helen Joseph, restricted to her cottage in the north of the city; or Helen Suzman; or the radical Afrikaner clergyman, Beyers Naudé, who ran the Christian Institute along lines openly defiant of the regime and the Dutch Reformed Church to which he belonged. Diana also made efforts to contact Bram Fischer, by then on the run from the police. He sent a message thanking her for the 'phenomenal work' of her husband's organisation, but sensibly did not meet with her.[1]

If the police were still unaware, they might have caught up with her during her days as a guest of the Patons in Botha's Hill, near Durban. She got on well with Paton, who admired her intellect and no doubt saw her as a counterweight to her husband. She assured him that no matter what the government might say, IDAF was not, and never would be, used surreptitiously to arm the ANC or the communists. 'Defence' remained the operative word. Pacified to some degree, Paton resumed co-operation with Amen Court. His biographer, Peter Alexander, has him saying that he felt he could not resign 'because who then would have done our work' (Alexander 1994: 338).

Diana stayed with Defence and Aid office bearer Peggy Levey in Port Elizabeth and with Bill Hoffenberg in Cape Town, where she noted one beneficial consequence of Collins's UN speech. The outrage it caused had made the long-simmering regional rivalry between the Cape and the Rand seem of little consequence. Out of the new sense of shared aggravation and danger, a national committee had been formed with headquarters in Cape Town. It was a reform Collins had long been urging.[2]

After her return to Johannesburg, the police served on Diana the documentation requiring her prompt departure from South Africa. She was a prohibited immigrant. Vorster explained that Diana Collins was visiting the country under false pretences. Collins said Vorster was piling up excuses to ban Defence and Aid. They were both right.

•

When the news came through in the late afternoon of 18 March 1966, it seemed to John Collins that the great work of his life had been stopped in its tracks. Johannes Vorster had banned 'the British-based Defence and Aid Fund of Christian Action' as an 'unlawful organisation' under the Suppression of Communism Act. It was, explained the minister, 'part of a network of extremist and loosely connected organisations in Britain noted for the vehemence of their hostility towards South Africa.' The order was counter-signed by Collins's old adversary, CR Swart, now the State President.[3] The banning did no harm to the government's popularity. When the electorate (1,800,000 whites and 351 enfranchised 'coloured' males in Natal) went to the polls 12 days later, it handed the National Party 35 extra seats.

The manner in which Vorster prepared the ground for the banning is revealed in official files that survived the post-apartheid destruction of so many of the records of the period. They provide a revealing insight into the motives for the banning, official concerns about the consequences and how the government tried to win over neutral opinion at home and, more especially, abroad.

The Suppression of Communism Act required a preliminary procedure before an organisation could be proscribed. Accordingly, one month before the banning, a committee was set up under the Act, made up of the 'liquidator', DP Wilcocks, a magistrate, and Swart and van Dam, two white

Afrikaners. They duly presented their 'factual report' on Defence and Aid to Vorster. The procedure was one-sided, secret and hardly a fair hearing.

The Wilcocks report made various 'specific findings of fact', which were detailed in a 14-page appendix. Boiled down, they were that:

• The SA Defence and Aid Fund was merely a local committee of the Defence and Aid Fund of Christian Action, with its head office in England;

• Christian Action was affiliated to the Movement for Colonial Freedom, a British organisation which works very closely with the Africa Bureau and the Anti-Apartheid Movement;

• The Movement for Colonial Freedom and the Anti-Apartheid Movement both 'enjoy the support of the British Communist Party';

• The Defence and Aid Fund 'enjoys the support of the Communist Party';

• The Defence and Aid Fund was an active supporter of the 'so-called freedom struggle in South Africa', aimed at 'political, social and economic change in South Africa', which advocates change by force.

Dr Raymond ('Bill') Hoffenberg and the South African fund appealed against the banning on the grounds that the fund was independent of London. They cited the decision of the meeting of all branches of the fund in Cape Town in August 1965 that 'because the aims of the Defence and Aid Fund in South Africa differ from the aims of Defence and Aid in London, the former will henceforward be named "The South African Defence and Aid Fund"'. To no avail. The appeal was lost, albeit with the judges divided.

The appendix to the Wilcocks Report offers a graphic illustration of the mendacious, wish-fulfilment, guilt-by-association quality of its research into what Defence and Aid in London represented. By the mid-1960s, the Movement for Colonial Freedom was a spent force. Collins had no need for it, and one sees virtually no mention of it in the IDAF files. That this organisation should be linked with the Africa Bureau and the Anti-Apartheid Movement (AAM) is laughable – and ignorant on the part of the informants in the London embassy. As for the Africa Bureau – as we have shown, Collins already loved and loathed Michael Scott.

The Wilcocks Report cites the book *The Puppeteers*, a notorious work co-authored by the far-right Tory MP Harold Soref, as proof that the Bureau was organising opposition to South Africa, the Central African Federation and the Portuguese territories. It did not fail to mention that Scott himself had been in the Communist Party. The journalist Colin Legum and his wife Margaret Roberts, who were active in the Bureau and calling for sanctions against apartheid, were exiled liberals, and if anything, anti-communist.

It was no secret that Collins was close to the AAM, and he boasted that it had begun life in the Amen Court basement. The report named the AAM's communists – Ros Ainslie, Leon Levy, Sonia Bunting, but missed its founder and most influential office-bearer, Vella Pillay, who had left South Africa before communism was outlawed.

The paragraphs on Defence and Aid in South Africa make no allegations of local communist association or control, but the report then goes on to link it to the communists by asserting that the mother body, the Defence and Aid Fund of Christian Action… enjoys the support of the Communist Party' (Press statement by John Vorster, Minister of Justice, 18.03.66).

> It was one Bartholomew Mory Hlapane, a member of the South African Communist Party, who on 1 October 1964 made a sworn statement as follows: The Defence and Aid Fund, which was at this junction [sic] already in existence, was extensively used for the purposes of the SACP. In turn, cash advances to the fund were made by the SACP. Who the persons were that served on this fund's committee, I do not know, except that Rica Hodgson, who was in fact a member of the CP, was serving on this fund's committee. (Press statement by John Vorster, Minister of Justice, 18.03.66)

What is not mentioned is that at the time this statement was made Hlapane was in security police detention and had agreed to collaborate with the police by giving evidence for the state in political trials.

Explaining his reasons for banning Defence and Aid, Vorster quoted Hlapane as 'a self-confessed member of the South African Communist Party [who] during August 1964 took charge of the funds of Defence and Aid in SA. Since that time a small portion of these funds was actually used for dependants of prisoners. The largest slice has been employed for the political activities of the outlawed ANC and the Communist Party. Salaries of officials of the Communist Party have also been paid from these funds.' The 'self-confessed' communist was Laura Hithins, who ran the Johannesburg office until she was banned.

In the days immediately following the banning, the security police raided the offices and homes of Defence and Aid operatives. In Cape Town, these were Stephanie Urdang, the local secretary; Leo Marquard, founder of the Liberal Party; and Mary Stoy, wife of Dr RH Stoy, head of the Royal Observatory. The Port Elizabeth Defence and Aid office was 'completely cleared' and the Christian Council for Social Action, an inter-church body that helped dependants of detainees, was also raided. Herbert Lovemore, a Methodist minister, and John Arderne, Defence and Aid's legal adviser, received home visits, as did Paton and other fund officials in Durban. The chairperson in East London, Daphne Curry, was taken from her home to her office where police removed 23 items, including six letters from Robben Island prisoners asking for financial help with their further education.

Five months after the banning, the liquidator produced a list of 'office holders, officials, members or active supporters' of the fund. It was largely a roll call of white, liberal, Judeo-Christian South Africa. Cape Town had 35 names, of whom perhaps only Albie Sachs and Caroline de Crespigny could be termed far left, and they were by then living in England. They included Peter Hjul, Dot Cleminshaw of the Black Sash, even Adrian Leftwich, a former student leader who had given evidence against his fellow ARM saboteurs. The report noted that Donald Molteno QC and Barbara Wilks had resigned from the committee when the Soviet Union made a donation to the British fund – a reaction from which the government would have drawn some comfort. Johannesburg's 36 names included Jack Unterhalter, Issie Maisels QC, Max Borkum (later chairman of the stock exchange), Jean Sinclair of the Black Sash, Margaret Smith (a journalist on the *Rand Daily Mail*), with Julius First, Ruth First's father, the only recognisable communist. In Durban, the lawyers Ismail Meer and JN Singh were party members. Clive van Ryneveld, a former Springbok cricket captain and married to the daughter of a bishop, was one of eight people named in East London, while in Port Elizabeth, JE Laredo of ARM was by then in prison.

The *Rand Daily Mail*, a thorn in apartheid's side, asked pointedly in an editorial signed by the Editor-in-Chief Lawrence Gandar: 'If communists give money to famine relief, is it wrong for others to furnish help as well?' (19.03.66). The *Daily Telegraph*, on whom white South Africa could normally depend, ran a damning editorial. 'The purposes of the fund are to finance the defence of persons accused of political crimes, and to relieve distress among their dependants while they are in custody… The first of these is pure justice and the second pure charity; no government could dare to object to them. If the administrators have exceeded these purposes and spent money in aid of political intrigue, they are guilty, first of an offence against the 25,000 subscribers, who are not predominantly Communist, even in the South African sense in which the term can be applied to any opponent of the regime. (They include the Russian Government, but also that of the Netherlands)' (*Daily Telegraph* 19.03.66). Collins could almost have written it himself.

The editorial was sent by the Trafalgar Square embassy to the Secretary for Foreign Affairs in Pretoria. Perhaps as a result of this harsh judgement as well as Dutch government criticism, Vorster issued a statement in an attempt to clear the air. He made three points:

His first point, that 'The Defence and Aid Fund was not banned because it collected money for defences but because it was found that the organisation was promoting communism' has been shown to be a bogus claim.

The second point was that 'a fund financed by the state was available for the defence of people charged with all offences.' This was an attempt to rebut the *Telegraph*'s charge that there would now be no defence for people charged with political crimes. But there was no such fund, certainly no state legal aid as such, except in capital cases such as rape and murder, in which an ill-equipped *pro deo* advocate appeared.

The *Cape Times* reported (19.3.66) that at all centres where there were attorneys willing to help, a Legal Aid Bureau had been established, each with a state-appointed legal aid officer. The legal aid officer interrogated applicants for free legal aid to ascertain the problem involved. But a Cape Town attorney complained that the officer, a magistrate, did not have the time to spare for the job. Moreover, people were scared to go to him. One lawyer said in the three to four years his firm had been part of the scheme, not one case had been referred to them. And those were probably non-political cases. The Legal Aid Bureau Chairman, D Reichman, was quoted as saying:

> If a person has a prima facie defence and falls within the means test, we should proceed according to our normal rule, namely to take the case and try to get legal representation free of charge. It will be a big problem, however, to get legal representation for long trials as the Legal Aid Bureau does not pay any legal fees – we simply arrange for legal practitioners to give their services free of charge.

Very few lawyers could afford the time and expense involved in giving their services free for a lengthy trial (*Rand Daily Mail* 25.3.66).

Vorster's third point was that 'the liquidator would honour monies owed by lawyers engaged by the fund if there were sufficient assets'. The liquidator was left with a balance of R4,000 once he had paid off those Defence and Aid-financed lawyers whose trials were on the go at the time of the banning. They were allowed to complete their cases, though, in the worsening security climate, it is possible that some were nervous about applying for a payout.

The R4,000 went to the Association of Law Societies 'to assist poor people who needed legal assistance' (*Rand Daily Mail* 24.08.67). The government later announced that people accused of political offences would in future qualify for free legal defence at state expense in the same way as people accused of capital offences. The local bar council or law society would appoint lawyers (*Star* 04.08.66).

By then, thanks to Collins and Neville Rubin, it was irrelevant.

Chapter 13

Cut-outs and Noble Lords

Collins had a model tortoise on the mantelpiece of his study, and he used to tell visitors that it offered a lesson in how one should proceed: steadily, without stopping, confident of outstripping the hare. Those who hardly knew him, indeed, even those who knew him well, might have considered that the metaphor did not reflect the Canon's way of doing things. And now, faced with the very real prospect of the collapse of his Defence and Aid network, hare-like celerity was called for.

Every aspect of the organisation was under threat. The safety net that he had promised to those on trial seemed doomed. Lawyers in South Africa who were found receiving IDAF funds faced 10 years in prison under the Unlawful Organisations Act. The supply side was equally worrying. The fund was raising £40,000 a year but there was no guarantee that the faithful on the Christian Action mailing list would still cough up when they could not be sure their pound notes were being put to good use. And some of the more earnest souls might have hesitated about breaking the law, even in unlawful South Africa. More serious, however, was the effect on his new-found benefactors. Having battled for years to gain the ascendancy in the channelling of aid, Collins now faced the prospect of his sponsors having second thoughts about his ability to get their money through the apartheid curtain. The Dutch government's decision to divert the controversial $20,000 from Amen Court to the UN Trust Fund was an indication of the changing climate. The question was whether there would be a come-back from Amnesty International, the World Council of Churches, the Michael Scotts, or rivals whom he had seen off so smartly. Equally important was the support of the new 'kid on the block', the Washington

Committee, President John Kennedy's initiative for change in South Africa, which Pretoria loathed but could not conceive of banning. He needed the support too of the Swedes, and of Reddy in New York.

The Canon displayed signs of panic. His first response was to tell South African journalists that he would distribute money through the churches, even churches in South Africa. Two days later, a correction appeared: 'We have no specific churches in mind, either inside or outside South Africa.' Within days of the banning, a Christian Action council meeting gave him *carte blanche* to act as he deemed necessary for the next four months, with the proviso that whatever he did should be legal under both British and South African law. This is the final mention of Defence and Aid in the minutes. IDAF's third annual conference, at the Russell Hotel, Bloomsbury, took place at the end of the banning month. Collins promised that Defence and Aid would be carrying on. No details were offered, but Reddy was present with a reassuring message – don't worry about gaining the confidence of the UN Trust Fund, 'you have that already'. The chief concern should be the methods of carrying on the work. Reddy went on to Stockholm where he asked Sverker Astrom, the fund chairman, for a confidential Swedish rescue package 'while we sort out the problem'. The next day, Reddy met the international assistance minister, Ulla Lindstrom, who donated $25,000 to tide IDAF over.

The question was how to secrete money into South Africa. The lifeline was thrown out by Neville Rubin, a South African student activist of the 1950s, and latterly wanted at home for his role in ARM sabotage. He contacted Collins, who knew his father Lesley, a former Liberal Party member and Native Representative member of the South African Senate. They lunched at the Wig & Pen, the watering hole for lawyers and journalists across the road from the Royal Courts of Justice. Rubin found Collins very despondent. 'He had given up, more or less. He said, "If you can show me the way in which I can keep saying that we exist, then you'll be doing the most marvellous thing."' Rubin had recently completed a stint as legal adviser in a lengthy hearing at the International Court of Justice at The Hague, where South Africa's claim to its South West Africa (Namibia) mandate was in dispute. Here was a question of extra-territoriality in which South Africa was dealing with a matter technically outside its control. When Collins said, 'What can we do, we're banned?', Rubin said: 'No you're not, Pretoria's writ does not run beyond its own borders. It has banned something inside South Africa. It hasn't banned you. It may be making it more difficult for you to work inside South Africa – that's a different matter. But don't let yourself or anybody else be bluffed into believing that you've been banned.' Rubin outlined his plan, and the Canon suddenly became 'wonderfully responsive'. He asked for a diagram of how it would work. Rubin went away to flesh out a plan that would cleanse 'tainted' money en route to South Africa (Neville Rubin interview 1991).

Rubin devised a system of barriers that concealed the link between Amen Court and the South African lawyers. The system worked in the following way: Collins decides to assist in a political trial, instructs a firm of solicitors in London, which in turn briefs solicitors from a second, unrelated English firm, which then gives a Johannesburg attorney the go-ahead. The double *cordon sanitaire* allows the defence lawyer in South Africa to say, 'honest to God', he had no idea the money had been anywhere near St Paul's Cathedral. A snooper would always be two sniffs off the scent. This system of 'need-to-know' was, and still is, a device utilised by intelligence services and communist cells. Its success depended crucially on the trust between Collins and this first-rank solicitor, the conduit for all legal matters. The candidate would of course have to be committed to the aims of the plan and, Rubin suggested, he should be at home in the English and South African legal systems. Several South African solicitors were practising in London and Rubin suggested Martin Bayer, a partner at Birkbeck Montagu's, which was handily placed at Ludgate Circus, three minutes' walk up Ludgate Hill to Amen Court.

Collins checked Bayer out and found he was the solicitor to several of his South African acquaintances. He probably was not told that Bayer had advised Michael Scott's Africa Bureau and had set up the legal framework of the Bertrand

Russell Peace Foundation. Bayer was given the nod. The two lawyers, Bayer and Rubin, met over lunch, this time further along the Strand at Simpson's. They were from similar liberal, Jewish backgrounds, both graduates of the University of Cape Town (UCT), though Bayer had gone on to Cambridge. 'He turned out to be a very fortunate choice,' recalls Rubin. 'We were on the same wavelength and it didn't require lengthy explanations nor did I have to tell him who Collins was.' Bayer, for his part, was bowled over. 'Guess what?' he said to Bill Frankel, a South African articled clerk, back at the office; 'Canon Collins is going to be a client.' Bayer met Collins at Amen Court and discussed the plan, as well as welfare for the dependants and relief for refugees fleeing South Africa. Bayer accepted the assurance that the money would not be used to buy weapons. When they met a fortnight later in the Cathedral, they were joined by Phyllis Altman, Rubin and Frankel. For the next 15 years the secret of how IDAF funds made their way into South Africa would be confined to these five, and to no other. At Amen Court and outside, Birkbeck Montagu's lawyer was never mentioned by name. He was simply 'Mr X' (Bayer interview 1991).

Collins and Bayer then devised an ingenious second leg to the legal operation in which the British aristocracy and the Swiss banking system, moribund lords and capitalist devils, would come to the aid of the struggle. Collins rounded up reliable friends from the left-wing establishment to stand in as apparent paymasters for the South African funds. It was a smoke-screen. They were not bogus, but little of the money came from their own pockets: Lord (Jock) Campbell, the Booker sugar baron and chairman of the *New Statesman*; the archaeologist Jacquetta Hawkes, with her husband, the author JB Priestley, intimates of the Collins; the Labour peers, Harry Walston and Gilbert Mitchison, and the latter's wife, the prodigious authoress and Tswana tribal mother, Dame Naomi Mitchison; her fellow novelist, Lord (CP) Snow, and the international lawyer Professor Norman Bentwich. They trusted Collins enough to allow their names to be attached to fine-sounding but vaguely framed trusts, operated through a network of numbered accounts at the Zurich branch of Lloyds Bank, and later the Union Bank of Switzerland. Frankel recalls sitting round a table thinking up names and 'John chortling over such a mouthful' as the 'Freedom from Fear International Charitable Foundation', which funded the legal defence programme (Frankel interview 1992). Lord Campbell was its chairman. The trustees knew little about the provenance of the money in their charge, though they understood it was being used secretly against apartheid.

The deed setting up the trusts gave little away. 'Freedom from Fear's' primary object was 'to provide for the legal defence of poor persons accused of or charged with offences under discriminatory or repressive laws of a racial and/or religious nature or character which bring about fear and poverty in those parts of the world where such laws are in operation', could have been aimed at any one of several nasty regimes, not least communist. Diana Collins recalls that 'we managed to get these very public, respectable people to perjure themselves in a good cause by saying they had sent money' (Diana Collins interview 1992). Her husband chose well. None of his friends let him down. One of them would even save his bacon.

Birkbeck Montagu's South African clients had not always been of a liberal persuasion. Cecil John Rhodes's personal solicitor was an early partner, and its biggest client, the Rand mining giant, Consolidated Goldfields, would have been dismayed to learn that the firm was in league with the troublesome Canon Collins of St Paul's. But the connection may have helped Bayer when he sounded out the solicitor friends who would correspond directly with the trial lawyers in South Africa and transmit funds to them. Delicate political reasons precluded his firm from handling these matters, he told them. They were not radicals, simply lawyers disturbed by the turn of events in South Africa and pleased to be able to do what their humane beliefs demanded and conservative profession permitted. After a while, the work was concentrated in three or four English firms. A Cambridge friend, Nick Garrett, was at the old-established City shipping lawyers Ingledew Brown. Paul Finnemore at Cole & Cole in Oxford was a contemporary at law school in Cape Town, though fairly soon his firm got cold feet because of its mainstream South African clients and pulled out. In Cambridge, Rosemary Sands at Miller & Co, wife of a South African don, Ken Pollack, would later have the lion's share of the work. Collins brought in another City firm, Fox & Gibbons.

But in the early days it was the Tory-voting David Futerman who shouldered the bulk of the work. The very name of his firm, Carruthers & Co., conjured up thoughts of Bertie Wooster and deceased estates in Sussex. But to begin with Bayer trawled widely, so Pretoria might be less inclined to point a finger at a single funder. The foreign lawyers were intended as a smokescreen to draw Pretoria's suspicions away from England. In the early days there were friendly firms in Canada, New York, France, West Germany and Zurich. Frankel recruited a lawyer sitting next to him at a dinner party in Sydney – Paul Lander handled several IDAF cases, and later became the New South Wales Attorney-General. The firms, including Birkbeck Montagu's, were paid at a reduced rate for the job, though soon after the system was inaugurated Collins noted that more money was needed to achieve the same amount of assistance as before the banning because 'the methods of distribution were more expensive and also lawyers were now forced to charge top fees'.

When Birkbeck Montagu's came through with a case, the go-between lawyer would send a letter to a South African legal firm couched in sparing forensic language: 'We understand that you are acting for clients in the Pretoria Terrorism Act case. We act for clients who are prepared to provide finance...' They might be more specific: 'Lord Mitchison is concerned about this trial. Please let us know whether you are handling the matter and whether you are prepared to receive legal costs from him.' There was no fixed style. The scattergun approach might have suggested that these were genuine individuals around the world coughing up money to assuage their consciences. They acquired legendary status in unlikely circles. Henry Brown was a young attorney handling much of the political work at Frank, Bernadt & Joffe in Cape Town. Many of the 400 people on their books were funded through Fox & Gibbons in London. An attorney in a remote Eastern

Cape *dorp* (small town) was once heard to complain that he did not have the resources to defend a group of men facing serious political charges. The public prosecutor offered a solution: 'Go to Brown, man. He can get money from Lord Mitchison' (Brown interview 1996).

Rubin's construct meant that the South African lawyer knew nothing of Birkbeck Montagu's, while the channelling lawyer was in touch with Birkbeck Montagu's but not with Amen Court. But, with the best-intentioned of arrangements liable to spring leaks through human error or undetected design faults, every stage needed to be secure in itself. Access to Birkbeck Montagu's offices at 7 St Bride Street was by a lift that rose gently from a closely observed reception area. The upper floors had the feel of a terraced house, with selections from Bayer's art collection adorning the walls. No air of mystery here, no clue that it housed something of interest to the government of a foreign country. The IDAF files were held in a safe to which only the two lawyers and their secretaries had access. Each file listed 'Client's name: St Paul's School Choir' on the cover, and British intelligence or a BOSS plant would have been delighted to find the name of the defendant listed below. There was no such intrusion. As Bayer climbed the firm's hierarchy to become the senior partner, the running of the secret operation moved to the newly qualified Frankel. It helped that the new Mr X (he was at first referred to as 'Mr Y') was in charge of the firm's finances for 20 years. The dozen Birkbeck Montagu's partners, Britons and South Africans, understanding the need to keep off the territory, were content to leave matters in his hands. 'They knew we were handling very secret and confidential work in South Africa, and that substantial funds were passing through our client accounts, but they didn't feel any need to ask further questions,' Frankel recalled. The books were audited in the normal way by accountants on behalf of the Law Society, though the IDAF trust funds were independently audited.

It was at Amen Court that a self-respecting spy might start prying. All employed there were sworn to secrecy, even if only two people knew how the obstacle course operated, or indeed, that it existed at all. Diana was not in on the secret. 'I heard John talking about Mr. X and Mr. Y, but I didn't know who they were. Didn't want to know' (Diana Collins interview 1992). The files were in the basement and Altman had the key. Visitors never got down there, and those whom Collins saw in his office were expected to mind their tongue. Rubin recalls the radio on Collins's desk and his explaining that the way to block out electronic eavesdroppers was to switch the gadget on, 'followed by squawking and crackling and then he would walk to the other side of his study and talk'. If there was something very sensitive to discuss and it was getting on for lunch they would decamp to the 'Wig & Pen', or the 'Good Friends' Chinese restaurant off Ludgate Hill.

Messrs X and Y never set foot in Amen Court. The special IDAF phone on Frankel's desk rang and, without introduction, a voice would intone: 'The boss wants to see you'. It was David Floyd Ewin, the St Paul's registrar, the lay official in charge of cathedral finances, the Canon's utterly discreet go-between. They would meet in the Chapter House or, on a quiet morning, in the cathedral itself. Frankel recalls passing through the busy concourse in earnest discussion with Collins when, alongside the choir stalls at the effigy of John Donne in funeral shroud, the Canon pushed at the wall that opened onto a flight of stairs. No outsider could have suspected that it led to the dean's vestry, a Narnia-type alcove where the canons robed before the services. There they sat and talked trials.

But St Paul's was also a tourist attraction, and there was a risk that the well-known features of the Canon might be photographed with a South African lawyer. So for much of the time Altman was Frankel's contact. He would stroll up Ludgate Hill, amble through the west door and see her upright back in a pew. Neither was in a hurry. He studied the Duke of Wellington on his high horse, peered up at the heavenly dome, until, moved by the need for pious reflection, he seated himself in the row in front of her. They meditated a while. She leant forward, he swayed back and whispered – 'two Jews praying'. in Altman's words. Someone sat down nearby and one of them would get up and the wandering and settling, cats in search of a haven, began again. A check that no one was watching. Altman whispered again; go ahead with this case; the trial lawyer is no good in that one, get someone else. She stood up, took in more of the statuary, wandered out. 'Mr X' stayed a while, walked through the west door and down the hill, soul refreshed (Altman interview 1992).

There were not many trials in the weeks after the banning of Defence and Aid, but Oliver Tambo was concerned enough to inform Collins that his followers were being gaoled without benefit of legal defence. In June, Bayer flew to South Africa to make contact with the remnants of the Defence and Aid committees. It was a fraught visit, for he had to see men and women who loomed large in the sights of the security police. He called on Ruth Hayman on the pretext of discussing family matters. At lunch in a Johannesburg department store she nodded at the two gentlemen at the adjoining table – they were from the Special Branch. Bayer told her that there was cash for whoever needed it. In Cape Town he saw Henry Brown's boss, Himie Bernadt, and called on Dr Hoffenberg, then engaged in the doomed appeal to the courts (through Bernadt's firm) to have the Defence and Aid ban lifted. 'I was very careful and simply told them money was available from wealthy sponsors for individual cases.' In Johannesburg, returning to his hotel, the desk clerk warned him: 'If I were the police, Mr Bayer, I'd be very interested in your movements.' The files in his wardrobe had been moved around. He returned to London the same day, glad to have given the green light to the small group of human rights lawyers who would carry on Defence and Aid's work. Years later, Tambo said: 'We knew large sums of money were sent through, but we didn't know the means' (Tambo interview 1992).

The strategy involved having to tell the world that it was business as usual without showing how the trick was done, or making so much of it that Pretoria and friends might be goaded into breaking into the secret channel. The opportunity presented itself at a UN human rights seminar in Brasilia. Collins was brimful of confidence. He gave 'a categorical assurance that the banning of the committees in South Africa, though it has created difficulties, has in no way stopped the Defence and Aid Fund from functioning... and equally categorically let me add an assurance that we still function through channels that are legal not only outside but also inside South Africa.' He half-apologised for having embarrassed South African friends in that speech in June 1965, but he remained unrepentant. It was so easy 'for a white man, with all his privileges, to call for patience and restraint on the part of those who have no such privileges.' Warming to his theme, he went on: 'By what right do we of the West or the East, with our arms races, our persistent dependence upon the force of arms to achieve our ends and to preserve our respective ways of life, counsel the oppressed of South Africa to use nothing but non-violence to gain for themselves the basic rights incorporated in the UN Charter and the Universal Declaration of Human Rights?' (Collins 1980: 12–19). Collins was irritated when the UN Trust Fund's first post-ban contribution was posted to the 'International Freedom from Fear Trust'. It seemed like a capitulation to South Africa, he complained. He suggested to Reddy and Astrom that the world be told that the United Nations still supported IDAF. Thenceforward the grants went to IDAF. From Sweden, there were comforting words from Dean Helander. He had held discussions with the department of foreign affairs 'and it appeared that his government had taken on the task of caring for IDAF.'

Bayer remembered the year as 'nightmarish, with worries about leaks and constant arguments about publicity as John wanted South African blacks to know he was still interested in them.' He talked with Collins about the moral dilemma of terrorism and his concern about helping in trials involving violence. The lawyer, so correct in his professional conduct and political upbringing, was troubled by the Canon's 'indiscretions... what made me raise my eyebrows,' he recalled with a smile, 'was that his son Richard was at the Bolshoi ballet school in Moscow'.

Bayer might not have known it but Pretoria's spies had already been active in Britain. In February 1961, The *Observer*'s respected South African correspondent, Stanley Uys, reported from Cape Town that Security Branch detectives from South Africa were in London investigating the activities of the South African United Front[1] before Prime Minister Verwoerd arrived in London for the Commonwealth conference, which ended in South Africa's departure from the club. Uys said detectives were working with local agents, who were said to have infiltrated the organisation, 'which includes many South Africans, whites and non-whites, living in exile.' It is not known if the 'local agents' were British intelligence or private individuals.

At Amen Court, vetting procedures were offhand and the wrong people were sometimes hired. The South African spy, Gordon Winter, said his girlfriend, Jean Lagrange, a voluntary worker in Christian Action's Christmas card department, was a BOSS agent. It seems she uncovered nothing revealing, although Winter claimed in his often unreliable memoir that while helping in the publications department Lagrange copied the Defence and Aid subscribers' list, providing Pretoria 'with many vital clues about enemies of apartheid all over Britain' (Winter 1981: 294).

The security-conscious Rica Hodgson recalled that a man taken on as a packer of Christian Action Christmas cards had mailed the minutes of a meeting on Rhodesia to a contact in South Africa House, but as the person had left it had been returned to Amen Court. His appointment was terminated (Hodgson interview 1992). Hodgson helped uncover yet another infiltration. In the early 1970s, Chris Evelyn White, son of a priest recommended through the Collins network, was given a job working on files. He went on holiday and a series of postcards from various resorts in the south of England arrived at the office. But the young man had been spotted in Salisbury, Rhodesia. On his return, Hodgson and Altman called him in and asked what he was doing in Ian Smith's illegal domain. He denied he had been there but when presented with the evidence pleaded with the two women that 'I am on your side'. 'We threw him out there and then,' said Hodgson. 'But I don't think he did any damage.' Altman said: 'It was the only time my guard slipped' (Hodgson interview 1992). The episode brought to an end the epoch of the voluntary worker (Cook interview 2003).

•

So the new system was put in place. Bill Frankel said they talked in terms of keeping it going for a couple of years, no more. They never dreamed it would go on for 25 years, before the tortoise finally outstripped the hare. There was an added reason why the survival of Defence and Aid delighted Collins and Altman. While awaiting trial in Pretoria Central prison, Bram Fischer sent a chatty letter to Phyllis, which ended with an innocent 'PS' of 'love to John and his wife. I will think about them very often. I'm sure he will find a solution to his problems.' Altman signalled back; 'Sorry for the delay, I have been very busy'.

Chapter 14

THE 'WHITE LIE'

From the start, the plan worked with an efficiency that surprised both Collins and Mr X. But the early trials were relatively minor ones that did not seem to invite attention. Or perhaps the authorities were biding their time. The two men wondered how the scam would hold up in the glare of a show trial in an apartheid courtroom. They did not have long to wait.

On 13 August 1967 the front page of *Beeld*, an Afrikaans-language Sunday newspaper, proclaimed '*Defence and Aid stuur R4,000 vir terroriste*' ('Defence and Aid sends R4,000' – then £2,000 – 'for terrorists'). The story was neatly timed to surface as lawyers finalised the defence of 37 'Bantu terrorists' who would go on trial the following day for fighting for the independence of South West Africa (Namibia).

One year earlier, at Omgulumbashe in the remote north of Namibia, the South West African People's Organisation (SWAPO) liberation movement had launched its armed struggle against South Africa's occupation of its country. Some freedom fighters had been trained in China and Egypt, but most of them had received only rudimentary instruction in the bush of Ovamboland. It was a brave but hopeless skirmish, as tribesmen fired arrows at police helicopters. They were rounded up and spirited away to Pretoria, into the oblivion of 180-day detention, even though the law was not in force in Namibia. The uprising had been put down easily enough but it still dismayed the government, which had hoped that the Rivonia sentences would see off all internal opposition for a generation. It also marked a new low in South Africa's relations with the United Nations, where its management of Namibia was under intense scrutiny. In October 1966 the General Assembly revoked South Africa's mandate to administer the territory. The vote was 102 to two; South Africa and Portugal were against; Britain's Labour government and De Gaulle's France abstained, along with Malawi.

Following the assassination of Verwoerd, stabbed to death in September 1966 in the House of Assembly by a parliamentary messenger, Demetrio Tsafendas, Vorster became prime minister. The Namibia problem was an early test of his leadership and he met the challenge head on. The UN vote was effectively ignored, though South Africa would formally challenge its legality at the Hague International Court of Justice. Leaving nothing to chance, Vorster rushed a terrorism law through Parliament, with retroactive effect to 1962, thus covering the earliest preparations for SWAPO's uprising. He twisted the knot by putting the onus on the defence to prove SWAPO's innocence. The minimum sentence was five years; the maximum, death.

The Terrorism Act became law on 21 July 1967. The next day the Namibians were brought out of solitary confinement and charged. It would be the Treason Trial and Rivonia rolled into one, in what Pretoria intended would be a knockout blow for the aspirations of the sparsely populated colony. These men, God-fearing and, in normal times, law-abiding, and demoralised by long imprisonment in a country hundreds of miles from home, were not expected to tax the prosecution unduly. Then the IDAF network linked up with one of South Africa's more flamboyant attorneys. When Joel Carlson arrived at the prison, the defendants viewed him with suspicion. But he soon won them over. Unlike other political lawyers, who were schooled in the English tradition of phlegmatic distancing, Carlson was an American-style defender, brave, sometimes to the extent of foolhardiness. The trial would be long and costly, but a firm of solicitors in London had written offering support from a 'concerned person'. Carlson had never heard of Carruthers & Co., but Ruth Hayman would have told him that overseas money was still on tap.

After that first brief court appearance, Carlson was a marked man, a 'terrorist lawyer' armed with 'Moscow gold' to defend bloodthirsty revolutionaries. Newspapers reported that banned organisations were financing the case using cover names. The police fired bullets into his house and, unnerved by the threatening atmosphere, Carlson wrote to David Futerman at Carruthers asking for the source of the funding. Lord Campbell of Eskan, was the reply. The security police would have read the letters and tapped the phones, for *Beeld* had stated that it was not clear whether the lawyers knew the identity of the original funder, 'seeing that the Defence and Aid Fund's role in the money is hidden behind a frontman'. If the security police established that Defence and Aid was the real funder, the paper warned, the next tranche of money could be seized. The police leak to *Beeld*, of which the Defence Minister PW Botha and other cabinet insiders were directors, was intended to frighten, and it had just that effect.

John Dugard, the University of the Witwatersrand professor who advised on international law issues at the trial, recalls the fraught atmosphere when the defence team met later in the day to finalise preparations. In charge was an anxious Namie Philips, the senior – and only – defence counsel named in the article. 'We had to provide a public explanation of where the money came from,' says Dugard. 'Carlson told us about Campbell, how he had made his money from sugar in the West Indies. And as Carruthers said the money was Campbell's, that was that'(Dugard interview 1992).

Fortunately for the fiction, Jock Campbell seemed to be a man of considerable means, and mildly eccentric to boot. The source of the money was the sugar plantations of Demerara (later Guyana). Though the slaves had long since been freed, working conditions on the estates where he learned the trade had invested him with a reforming zeal. The family firm amalgamated with Booker, and on becoming managing director, Campbell sold off the company's small merchant bank in South Africa. He liked to 'preach socialism to the shareholders' and was pleased to describe himself as a traitor to his class. When Collins asked him to lend his name to 'Freedom from Fear' he at first refused because he did not consider himself rich enough for the role of bogus benefactor. 'But John was very persuasive,' he recalled, ' and there were very few people willing to do it.' Campbell was assured that he would only have to discharge a background role; his name was all that was required. As it turned out, the main threat to the secret funding arose not in South Africa but in London, where Campbell found himself suddenly exposed in the front-line.

Events in the Pretoria courtroom had aroused the curiosity of Michael Scott, who knew Campbell well, since he had served on the board of Scott's Africa Bureau. Scott's understanding was that Campbell, though rich, was not that rich. He asked Campbell directly who was behind the SWAPO trial money. Campbell stuck to his story: from his own pocket. It was the end of their friendship. 'Scott said I didn't have that amount of money and wrote me a very rude letter. He never spoke to me again. Had I told him the real story, I felt he would have come out with it publicly. Michael would always speak his mind, especially if he felt Collins was doing something wrong' (Campbell interview 1992).

Scott was not alone in playing the game of 'find-the-funder'. David Futerman of Carruthers & Co. had agreed to be a go-between on the understanding that he would be no more than a conduit, essentially a passer of messages from 'Mr X' to the South African attorneys. Returning to his office in Shaftesbury Avenue one day he discovered that Joel Carlson was in town and had called, wanting to see him. Carlson, still not convinced about the source of the defence money, was determined to find out more. He was perfectly entitled to assurances on these points – indeed, it was his duty as a professional to be sure – but there was no way that he could be led to the door of 'Mr X', much less of Canon Collins, without causing a grievous breach of security. Futerman rang Bayer: 'What the hell do I do?' (Futerman interview 1992).

Putting Carlson in touch with Jock Campbell averted the crisis. He promised the attorney that, if necessary, he would testify in court that he was the sole funder of the SWAPO defence (Carlson 1973: 204). Mollified, Carlson returned to the courtroom battle. Campbell did donate £1,000 to the trial from his own resources, but was not called upon to lie on oath. 'If ever there was a white lie, this was it,' he said in old age. 'I didn't have any qualms about it. The end justified the means. I would certainly have done it again. We saved lives' (Campbell interview 1993).

In fact, Collins was not the only funder of the trial. Carlson had gone on to New York where he met Reddy at the UN and told him 'D&A is full of spies'. Reddy spoke to Arthur Goldberg, the American ambassador, who arranged for $5,000 to be transferred by the Lawyers' Committee for Civil Rights under Law to one of the Swiss trust funds. It went through the Defence and Aid books (Reddy interview 1993). Carlson would have shown more understanding had he known that the obtuseness in London was for his own protection.

After Carlson's disruptive visit to London, Bayer asked Futerman to deepen his involvement by going to South Africa as a 'low profile' observer when the trial resumed. The appearance of a pin-striped London solicitor, the personal representative of Lord Campbell, might convince doubters on both sides of the courtroom. Futerman read the papers passing through his office and acquainted himself with the facts. But he was not prepared for Joel Carlson's buccaneering style.

On the Sunday afternoon of his arrival, Carlson drove him into Soweto, without the permit that was mandatory for non-Africans entering a black township. 'Joel's attitude,' Futerman recalls, 'was, to hell with them, I'm not interested in their regulations, I'll do it my way.' On his return from Soweto, Futerman found that the contents of his hotel room had been gone over. The day the trial resumed at the Old Synagogue in Pretoria, Carlson walked his English guest past Sten guns and police dogs into an iron shed to introduce him to each of the waiting prisoners. 'They were amazed that anyone should take the trouble to come from England to see them,' Futerman recalled. 'They were aware of the financial help coming from there and I'm sure it boosted their morale' (Futerman interview 1992).

Before Futerman returned to London, Carlson invited a reporter to interview the man from Carruthers & Co., and an article under his picture appeared in the *Rand Daily Mail*. This was one last favour Futerman could have done without. The feeling intensified when, on his return to London, an express delivery from the ministry of the interior in Pretoria prohibited his return to South Africa. 'Here in England I was a socially aware Conservative,' says Futerman. 'In South Africa I was a communist.'

In court, the defence team exposed the 'bloodthirsty communists' in the dock for what they were – a fervently religious group of men whose conversion by Finnish Lutheran missionaries had sharpened their awareness of injustice. In his eloquent statement of defiance, their leader, Andimba Toivo ja Toivo, told Judge Ludorf:

> We find ourselves here in a foreign country, convicted under laws made by people whom we have always considered as foreigners. We find ourselves tried by a judge who is not our countryman and who has not shared our background... Had we been tried by our equals, it would not have been necessary to have any discussion of our grievances. They would have been known to those who judge us... Violence is truly fearsome, but who would not defend his property and himself against a robber? And we believe that South Africa has robbed us of our country. (Benson 1976: 49–52)

As in the Rivonia trial, the hangman's noose loomed over the proceedings. But, thanks to concerted international pressure, no one was sentenced to death. Twenty were gaoled for life, nine for 20 years, with shorter terms for the others. Most were dispatched to Robben Island. On appeal – still funded by IDAF – their lawyers were able to establish a slightly less drastic application of the law. Judge Ludorf had emphasised that imprisonment 'for life' should be interpreted as 'for the rest of their natural lives' but the Appellate Division declared that the state, and not the courts, retained the power to release a lifer. That would not happen unless the political climate improved, but it was something. Less helpfully, the appeal court rejected the argument that the Terrorism Act, passed after the UN's revocation of South Africa's mandate, did not apply in Namibia. The UN, hampered by the West's reluctance to endorse positive action, lacked the muscle to enforce its writ. In the short term at least, Vorster could claim to have won the day. But then, in terms of international publicity and the preservation of human life, so could Canon

Collins. Most relevant of all, the secret channel had survived its first big test, with all links in the chain intact.

By early 1968, IDAF had outgrown the Amen Court basement. The section handling trial defences, code-named 'Clause One,' moved into the upper floor of a building in Newgate Street, to the north of the Cathedral. Phyllis Altman, steady and discreet, was in charge there – though at times she regretted not being on hand at Amen Court to regulate the Canon's rushes of blood. But anyone breaking into her office hoping for tell-tale evidence would have been disappointed. A colleague, Al Cook, recalled the 'Clause One' meetings. 'We would talk quite normally until we got to a name and Phyllis would write it on a piece of paper and hold it up and whisper, "This person", then scratch the name out and rip the paper up.' It did not matter if sophisticated listening devices picked up talk of 'subversives' so long as the named were not identified in connection with a particular action (Cook interview 1993).

The IDAF legal work was tedious, as the linking solicitors copied and exchanged every scrap of communication passing into and out of South Africa. The payment out of the trust funds was a cumbersome business, with exchange control permission needed to export money from an account in Britain. On the alternative offshore route, Swedish money was deposited in an IDAF account at Lloyds Bank, Zurich; transferred to Birkbeck Montagu's Swiss bank; to the trust fund account; then, without the need for Treasury permission, to a go-between solicitor in France or Australia. Once a year, Collins and Per Wästberg paid a quiet visit to Switzerland to tinker with the dozens of accounts, constantly changing codes and account numbers. Fearing South African infiltration, they moved from Lloyds to the Union Bank of Switzerland. They were not rumbled, thanks to the Swiss banking system's three-monkeys philosophy. In the event of Collins's death or incapacity Diana and Wästberg would take over, though neither knew the identity of Mr X.

Other trusts were set up. 'The Freedom from Persecution (later changed to 'Hardship') International Trust for Southern Africa' catered for family welfare needs, while union leaders on the trades union international trust featured Jack Jones, the Spanish civil war veteran and leader of Britain's biggest union, the Transport and General Workers' Union; Tom Jackson, the postmen's leader, and a Labour MP, Bob Edwards. 'The International Christian Fund for Justice and Goodwill in South Africa' came later, with the Bishop of London, Gerald Ellison, and the Bishop of Stockholm, Ingmar Strom, listed as trustees.

Although the trustees had no control over the movement of money, the norms of legal stewardship were preserved as far as possible. They met formally once a year in St Paul's Chapter House, taking care to enter the building unobtrusively – some thought Jacquetta Hawkes's large black hats were too eye-catching. Altman checked out the room before the meeting, peered under tables and ascertained that no one was hanging around outside. It struck Bill Frankel as 'amateurish' but it did instil the habit of secrecy. The trust accounts were audited by Martin Miller, yet another South African expatriate. He was not told that IDAF was the source of the money. 'He never asked,' said Frankel. 'If he had, I would have lied.'

The end of the Namibian trial ushered in a quiet period for Amen Court. Internal resistance was at its nadir. Indeed, it seemed as if there was more anti-apartheid activity in Britain than in South Africa as the spotlight on Pretoria's racial policies came to focus more and more on its sporting life.

•

When the classified 'coloured' Basil d'Oliveira left South Africa for England in the mid-1960s to play county cricket, he unwittingly set off a sporting revolution. Once established as a regular member of the English national team, controversy was thrust upon 'Dolly' when the cricket authorities first omitted him, then in the face of public outrage, picked him for the 1968 tour to South Africa. Vorster retaliated by calling off the tour, saying he would not play host to a team chosen by Bishop Ambrose Reeves and the Anti-Apartheid Movement. The Marylebone Cricket Council (MCC) cancelled the tour. Apartheid, after several quiet years, was back on international centre stage. The following year an all-white rugby tour of Britain was disrupted by scenes of social disorder not seen since the Mosleyite marches of the 1930s. While establishment opinion condemned the excesses of the demonstrators, it was compelled to lament the South African practice of fielding whites-only national teams and putting pressure on their opponents to do likewise.

These demonstrations were organised by a group known as 'Stop the Seventies Tour' and spearheaded by the teenage son of exile, Peter Hain, who had delivered the funeral address at the graveside of John Harris, the ARM bomber.[1] Their aim was to stop the Springbok cricket tour of England scheduled for the coming summer. The Anti-Apartheid Movement (AAM), though more restrained, stoked things up with a dramatic poster picturing a white South African policeman batoning cowering blacks, captioned: 'If you could see their national sport you might be less keen to see their cricket.' The violence in and around Britain's rugby grounds led to more than 4,000 arrests. When the Labour Home Secretary, Jim Callaghan, called off the cricket tour, Hain was accorded much of the credit. Collins did not play a conspicuous part in these events, other than to provide financial support for three members of Hain's executive. But he had been one of the originators of the idea of a sports boycott.

From the earliest days of Christian Action, Collins understood that nothing would hurt South Africa so much as exclusion from international competition, where its teams displayed what the government imagined was the God-given superiority of the white race. Laws criminalising mixed sport were reinforced by regulations specifically restricting halls and arenas for the exclusive use of one or other race. So playing sport at any level that required decent facilities necessarily involved a tacit acceptance of apartheid. Collins organised one of the earliest boycotts. Among his eclectic circle of friends was the fine West Indian cricketer, Learie Constantine, who had returned to Trinidad to become a government minister. In March 1958, Collins had alerted him to plans for a West Indies side to play black teams in South Africa. The source of the rumour was Alan Paton. 'Alan's point,' wrote Collins, 'is that to accept the idea of playing against an all-black team, however attractive on the surface it might seem, is in fact to play straight into the hands of those who are out for Apartheid.' Collins hoped Constantine 'could do something about it'. Constantine replied by return, sending a fiver for the Treason Trial fund and telling Collins to write to the West Indies' captain, Frank Worrell, then based in Manchester. Constantine also wrote to Worrell. The tour idea was quietly scotched.[2]

Collins was also a keen student of the sports-related political actions of Dennis Brutus, a Port Elizabeth poet and activist of mixed Afrikaner and African parentage. Through the 1950s – an era of disproportionate British sporting influence – Brutus made a nuisance of himself by repeatedly writing to Oscar State, British president of the International Weightlifting Federation, objecting to the exclusion of black South African lifters from the Olympic Games. These letters made little impact, despite his citing the Olympic Charter – 'no discrimination is allowed against any country or person on grounds of colour, religion or politics'. In 1958 Brutus broadened his scope, launching the South African Sports Association, which brought together a number of non-racial sports bodies into an organisation representing 70,000 sportsmen and women. Already loathed by the white sporting establishment, Brutus had more plans up his sleeve.

In 1962 he established the South African Non-racial Olympic Committee (SANROC), which aimed to have South Africa expelled from the Olympic Games unless it mended its ways. Brutus was then banned as a communist, though he was close to the Liberal Party; Alan Paton was a SANROC patron. In 1963 Brutus was arrested just as he was about to put his case to a visiting Olympic official. While out on bail, he tried to leave the country, crossing into Swaziland and then Mozambique, en route to Baden Baden to plead, before the International Olympic Committee, for the suspension of South Africa from the next Olympic Games in Tokyo. A SANROC colleague, the station-bomber John Harris, had obtained a Southern Rhodesian passport for him (Brutus was born there) and a visa from the Portuguese embassy in Pretoria. Unimpressed with this documentation, the Mozambican police handed him back to their South African colleagues. On the drive back to Pretoria, Brutus broke free from his captors, and one of them, an expert marksman, shot him in the back. White sports lovers would curse the constable for not finishing him off. Brutus spent 18 months on Robben Island for 'furthering the aims of communism'. His real aims, however, found much favour with Canon Collins.

Brutus topped the agenda at the September 1963 Christian Action council meeting. It resolved to 'place such assistance as it is able at the disposal of SANROC in order to ensure that its views are heard by the International Olympic Committee'. For many years, Collins kept the exiled SANROC organisation in London in pocket with an annual subsidy of, eventually, £12,000. It was money well spent – the Olympic Committee barred the Springboks from the 1964 Tokyo games and the green and gold was not readmitted to the Olympic fold until 1992. Brutus had beaten his gaolers, game, set and match.

Chapter 15

THE IMAM AND THE DEAN

When they met for the first time the rapport was spontaneous. A colleague who was present at the secret assignation in a London hotel room in 1966 wrote that 'the erect, greying Canon of Christendom and the Islamic Imam embraced like long-lost friends' (Desai and Marney 1978: 28). Amen Court was out of bounds, for Collins was setting up a pipeline for destitute families in Cape Town. As for Abdullah Haron, he was a marked man at home and abroad. When they had settled their business, Collins bade him farewell with the words, 'Take care, Imam, we can't afford to lose you' (Desai and Marney 1978: 29).

Abdullah Haron was 32 years old when the congregation of the Al Jaamia mosque in Cape Town chose him as its Imam. A friend recalls that he was 'a dapper little man who wore his black fez perched at altogether too-fashionable an angle upon his controversially clean-shaven head' (Desai and Marney 1978: 3). Some of the elders thought him insufficiently learned in theology to lead the prayers in the mosque and mend the broken spirits of his flock.

They were wrong on the score of learning and piety. Haron had a deep knowledge of the Koran and was fluent in Arabic, following lengthy stay-overs in Egypt and Saudi Arabia, during which he had made three pilgrimages to Mecca. The congregation could not pay him a stipend, and he continued working in his father's small grocery shop. Haron could not avoid being sucked into the political ferment. By the late fifties the apartheid plan for Cape Town was up and running. Its centre piece was the Group Areas Act, and coloureds and Malays were being pushed out of the suburbs at the foot of Table Mountain – 'District Six' – to the sandy infertility of the Cape Flats. The Harons lost their comfortable three-bedroomed house to a white family.

The cultural influences went far beyond his own upbringing. After seeing the film *Judgment at Nuremberg* Haron related the Nazi war crimes to events in his country. The removals left mosques high and dry in what were now all-white suburbs. Haron argued at the Muslim Judicial Council that the precincts of the mosque were inviolable and none should be sold or destroyed. It seemed like a declaration of holy war. The state relented and the mosques survived. On Fridays, expelled congregants had to travel across the Cape Peninsula to pray in their now isolated mosques. According to Haron's biographers Barney Desai and Cardiff Marney, 'his religious and political concerns began to come together in the struggle for liberation' (Desai and Marney 1978: 20). There was widespread disgust with Christianity among young Africans, and they seemed ripe for Islam. As editor of *Muslim News* he sharpened the paper's social viewpoint. By 1965, Haron's Friday sermons, delivered in his home language of Afrikaans, were keenly anticipated and widely discussed. Police agents in the congregation noted down the passionate pronouncements on poverty and oppression. Haron was by now a salesman for the English chocolate firm Rowntree, and so could work legally in the black townships. It was a good opportunity for mission work, political and religious. He also raised funds for the Coloured People's Congress. When it broke with the Congress Alliance to ally itself with the Pan Africanist Congress, Haron found himself immersed in a movement dedicated to the overthrow of apartheid by all means at its disposal, including violence (Desai and Marney 1978: 22).[1]

On a visit to Mecca in 1966, he linked up with an exiled friend, Ibrahim Desai, and produced a leaflet aimed at South African *hadjis* (pilgrims), which described the destruction wrought by the Group Areas removals and the persecution of Moslems by the Christian government. Though warned of spies among the pilgrims, he would not be silenced. He lobbied the Islamic World Council, pleading with Moslem states to intercede against apartheid. King Faisal granted him an audience and he was interviewed on Saudi radio and television. In Cairo the exiled PAC leader, Potlako Leballo, gave him the 'old-comrades' treatment (Desai and Marney 1978: 27). That too would have been noted.

By the time he and Collins worked out their plans for the transmission of money to the families of prisoners, Haron had stepped into more perilous waters, as he was now recruiting young men for the PAC to train as guerrillas while on the *hadj* or at college abroad. It is uncertain whether he actually sent anyone overseas but he was now very much in the front line, engaged in two dangerous underground operations. The police raided his mosque and combed through his library. They called regularly at his home. His bank account was perused.

In 1968 he again undertook a three-point overseas journey to Cairo, Mecca and London. In England, Collins suggested he come into exile and, like Luthuli before him, he declined. He was arrested on the Prophet's birthday, 28 May 1969, held under the Terrorism Act, and placed in the charge of a psychopathic security police captain with a well-known reputation for brutality, *Spyker* ('Nail') van Wyk.[2] Under interrogation, he denied, at first, meeting Collins or Leballo. He was then shown a bank account with R4,000 from the London Muslim Welfare Association. They had checked and this association did not exist. It was Collins's invention. According to his biographers, they then 'shattered him by giving an account of everything that was discussed at a meeting he had attended in London. They [also] showed him reports of his meeting with Canon Collins. They further showed him that certain associates of his had in fact been passing information on to them. They had a complete list of his code names' (Desai and Marney 1978: 82). His biographers say that IDAF was not the source of the spy's information.

The Imam's treatment under Van Wyk was characteristically brutal, featuring a *donnering* (beating) by a posse of constables. Word got out and questions were asked in Parliament. The district surgeon in Bellville, Dr Viviers, diagnosed 'muscle' trouble. More beatings followed, and this time Cape Town's district surgeon, Charles d'Arcy Gosling, prescribed pills for 'an influenza-like illness'. For those who took the Hippocratic Oath seriously, it was a fractured rib (Desai and Marney 1978: 131).

One of his guards at the Maitland police station turned a blind eye to lavatory paper messages from Haron. One was smuggled out in dirty clothes, another in a biscuit tin. His wife sent them on to London. The first said: 'They told me yesterday I must supply the names of those working with me, then I can go home! I am negative. No sir...' In the second, he told Collins: 'If you hear that I have died in prison by accident, you will know that it will not have been an accident' (Collins 1992: 335). Collins was frantic. He tried without success to have the Archbishop of Canterbury intervene with Pretoria. Rowntree was no help. On the day of Haron's arrest, the company sent him a letter of dismissal.

Haron's time was running out. Stripped naked and softened up with electric shocks, he finally admitted that the money was Defence and Aid's. He had told Collins that 'I will give my life but never will I divulge any of my companions.' He confessed to working for the PAC but the names he offered were beyond the reach of the police. Afterwards, Van Wyk and his superior, Major Genis, remembered that Haron was 'quite cheerful' (Desai and Marney 1978: 135), had no complaints, when they saw him for the last time. He died 133 days into his detention and 30,000 mourners followed his coffin to the Moslem cemetery in Salt River.

The inquest magistrate, SJ Kuhn, untroubled by compelling forensic evidence that the Imam had been used as a human punch bag, found that 'a substantial part of the said trauma was caused by an accidental fall down a flight of stone stairs' (Desai and Marney 1978: 139). Two years later the minister of police made an *ex gratia* payment of R5,000 to his widow, Galiema Haron.

Collins held a memorial service in the St Paul's crypt and spoke of the imam's devotion to the cause of families of victims of persecution and his preparedness to die rather than betray those who worked with him. It was the first time the Cathedral had commemorated a Moslem. Security precluded a public reference to IDAF but Collins knew he was anointing its first martyr (Collins 1992: 335).

Three centuries earlier Shaik Yusuf, a Javanese prince in revolt against the Dutch occupation of his island, was banished to the infidel refreshment station on the edge of the earth – the Dutch East India Company's settlement at the Cape of Good Hope. The descendants of his retinue became the craftsmen who made the Cape a stylish place, their religion, language and cuisine, a cosmopolitan African city. Now the Imam's martyrdom stirred that rebellious tradition. Within a decade of his death, the apolitical Cape Malay community would become a small but potent force in the final push to liberation. But had he been a fair-complexioned, foreign-born minister of the Church of England, rather than an olive-skinned *gamatjie* (little Malay, short for Mogamat) from the wrong side of the tracks, Abdullah Haron would have survived to tell the tale, as the fortunes of the Anglican Dean of Johannesburg, the Very Reverend Gonville Aubie ffrench-Beytagh, seem to indicate.

•

On leave in England, shortly after the Defence and Aid banning in 1965, the Dean visited Amen Court with a plan for smuggling welfare funds into Johannesburg. He introduced Collins to the linchpin of the enterprise, a resolute Christian, Alison Norman. She was a mental-health social worker in the East End of London but, as the daughter of a major-general and a cousin of a former governor of the Bank of England, it was reasonable to suppose that she had substantial assets of her own. Her bank account was therefore of the kind that could be credibly inflated from time to time without attracting attention. It was agreed that IDAF money should be channelled through Norman's private account at Martin's Bank branch in Maidstone and thence to the dean's fund in Johannesburg. Wealthy friends of Norman agreed to say, if called upon, that they were giving money to the cause through her. But all the money involved would come from the IDAF coffers (Norman interview 1997). Back in Johannesburg, the dean was soon aiding the needy on a wide and increasing scale, making him the largest single dispenser of private welfare in the Transvaal.

At first sight, Gonville ffrench-Beytagh was not the sort of person one would select to carry out undercover work in South Africa, or anywhere else. But he was a man of passionate conviction and, as with Collins's other favourites, *un homme d'action.* He was born in Shanghai of Irish parents, brought up by an aunt, expelled from Bristol grammar school, and somehow became a shepherd in New Zealand – in sermons he would wryly reflect on his qualification to speak on the subject of the Good Shepherd. He then followed his half brothers to South Africa. It was Alan Paton, he would say, visiting him in hospital as he recovered from the effects of an iron bar smashed over his head at a riotous party, who led him to Christianity and ordination. After his death a (female) obituarist spoke of 'the kindly priest who brought me home from the agnostic jungle... here was a truly saintly man despite his penchant for gin, whisky and cigarettes' (*Guardian* 14.05.91).

Unfortunately for ffrench-Beytagh, the security police were already closely monitoring his activities. John Davies, the Anglican chaplain at the University of the Witwatersrand, which fell within ffrench-Beytagh's diocese, had employed Nelson Mandela's wife, Winnie, as a social worker to check out needy African families and, where necessary, to distribute cash. Beyond Robben Island, there was no more conspicuous figure in the nationalist movement than the feisty Winnie Mandela. With her 'Mother Teresa' status in the townships, you could almost hear Afrikaner MPs spluttering that all would be quiet in the land if only that *kaffer meid* (kaffir girl) was out of the way. And they had tried. She had been detained in 1958 while pregnant, for participating in a demonstration against passes for African women; banned three times as a communist, confined to the Soweto suburb of Orlando and obliged to give up her job with the Child Welfare Society; charged twice in 1967 for breaking her banning order and sentenced to a year in prison, all but four days suspended.

The Dean understood that the IDAF funding initiative would not benefit from a close association with so controversial a figure. Though friendly with her, he stopped using her as a cash distributor and allocated the work to

African priests and Quakers. Where possible, money was paid direct – to school or outfitter or municipal rent collector or, in one instance, to a building contractor who raised a garden wall to blot out the view of a police officer living next door to the house-arrested Helen Joseph. The dean's debt to Winnie Mandela was limited to inheriting the list of families she had been aiding, and which, somewhat amended, became part of his own distribution network. Mrs Mandela did receive R500 (£250), via Alison Norman and the dean, towards the cost of a car (ffrench-Beytagh 1973: 206).

This relatively tenuous connection might not have excited the security services over much, but for the arrest of Winnie Mandela and 22 others in May 1969. Charged under the Suppression of Communism Act for attempting to revive the ANC, they spent 17 months in detention and were tried twice in court. In October 1970, all were acquitted. The lawyers' fees were paid through Mr X. Harrowing accounts of their ill-treatment identified a Colonel Swanepoel[3] as the torturer-in-chief. The dean ensured that the report found its way to London where Collins published it in a damning pamphlet, 'Trial by Torture'. But a Cathedral insider, in the shape of Louis Jordaan, ostensibly a faithful member of the congregation, relayed snippets of Cathedral life to the police. On one occasion the dean had declared that Swanepoel was 'a sadist who should be shot' – though he later disarmed a prosecuting advocate by explaining that he had recommended much the same treatment for several Anglican bishops. Having silenced the Liberals who once ran the Defence and Aid committees, the police were not about to let it operate under another guise. And there was the bonus of being able to discredit another busy-body Anglican slanderer of Afrikanerdom.

The Dean's arrest on 20 January 1971 was conducted in tough but gentlemanly style by Colonel Johan Coetzee[4], the state's chief spy-handler. The search of the dean's flat took longer than expected, and he was allowed his usual sundowner, pouring himself 'one of the biggest brandies I have ever had in my life.' But his experience of detention was a world away from the Imam's lonely cell. The British ambassador sent a representative to ascertain that all was well.

Not quite... the Dean disliked his breakfast of dried bread, hard-boiled egg and 'horribly sweet' coffee. A doctor called to give him a check-up. Swanepoel, the interrogator, was unable to lay a finger on him. Within eight days the Dean was charged and out on bail.

In August 1971, attired in clerical black and collar, voice clipped and clear, the Dean pleaded not guilty in the Pretoria supreme court to ten charges of terrorism. The tenor of the prosecution case was that he had given moral support to sabotage and the violent overthrow of the state. The device he used was to pass on R51,000 (then £30,000) sent from London by the ANC and Defence and Aid to the relatives of detainees, 130 of whom were named as co-conspirators. The wording is worth noting – 'to further the aims of the ANC by relieving its members of the anxiety about the welfare of their families.' In London, *Anti-Apartheid News* (September 1971) ran a front-page charge sheet, '...that he paid C Masondo £237 to cover the cost of an artificial leg and her fare to Robben Island so that she might visit her son, convicted of sabotage and jailed for 12 years.' To those white South Africans who were aware of such things, IDAF was synonymous with the ANC. But efforts to show that Alison Norman's money was not just IDAF's but that of the ANC-in-exile as well were never credible. It begged the question whether the ANC had any money of its own to speak of. Besides, the Dean's fund was helping families of all political persuasions and of none. His advocate, Sydney Kentridge, pointed out that the ANC would hardly countenance the use of its funds for a PAC wife to visit her imprisoned husband.

A meticulous church bookkeeper saved ffrench-Beytagh's skin. She had recorded every cent paid out by the dean, collecting a signed voucher for the most modest acts of charity. Nothing had been intentionally allocated to the ANC or showed that the dean and Winnie Mandela were 'in cahoots'. They were not helped by the Church's accountants, Alex Aitken and Carter, refusing a request by the dean's attorney, Raymond Tucker, to audit the books for the defence evidence. Another firm, Peat Marwick, stepped in and reported that everything was in order.

The appearance on day one of the police agent, Louis Jordaan, as a state witness took the defence by surprise for he had been named as a co-conspirator. But his impressionistic account of life at the deanery was not enough to substantiate the charge that ffrench-Beytagh had become the Nelson Mandela of the Anglican Church. Who could credit his report that the dean had incited the bourgeois ladies of the Black Sash to 'prepare for violent revolution'? Or his description of a meeting in London, presumably with an emissary from Amen Court, that began in a jeweller's shop in Soho and was then forced to move to a toilet?

Alison Norman was not in the dock but she was to all intents and purposes a co-accused. Coetzee had impounded her letters to the dean, and gone through them with great interest. Every friend the gregarious Norman had chatted about became an object of suspicion. There was a Thai girl from boarding school days; an Anglican contemplative nun; and, in particular, Diana King, the Dean's secretary in Salisbury, Southern Rhodesia, who was named as a co-conspirator. Both her father and her brother-in-law were Conservative MPs.

The tension of the proceedings was relieved, if not for the dean, certainly for followers of the trial, by a sub-plot with the texture of a Peter Sellers farce. While on holiday in South Africa in 1970, Alison Norman had paid a visit to a cousin in a Transkei convent. The journey began at the Johannesburg railway station where the only passenger in her compartment was a woman who introduced herself as 'June'. It was the start of a chain of orchestrated happenings. With the train barely out of the station, 'June' left her seat and returned with a friend, a 'Mr Morley', whom she claimed she had not seen for many years. Did Miss Norman mind if he joined them? 'Mr Morley' – in real life, Major Zwart of the security police – was tall and well-built and an affable travelling companion. A car awaited him at Pietermaritzburg station. He was, he explained, in the herb business and would be passing quite near the nunnery en route to a herb farm in which he was interested. Would Miss Norman care for a lift? A better prospect, surely, than eight hours in a bus in blistering January. She accepted.

There would, naturally, be two accounts of the journey to Sister Phoebe Margaret at the Community of St Mary the Virgin in Tsolo (ffrench-Beytagh 1973: 210–213). 'Mr Morley' (Major Zwart) claimed in court that during 'very serious political discussions' he convinced his passenger of his dedication to the Liberal Party and of his opposition to the prevailing system in South Africa. She was not expected at the convent until later in the day so she agreed to take lunch with him at the Tsolo Hotel. Zwart testified that Norman downed several beers and two brandies, after which she attempted to enlist him as an agent for the banned Defence and Aid organisation. There were, she allegedly assured him, 'several prominent clergymen in Johannesburg' who could protect him if he ever found himself in trouble.

Alison Norman's cousin, Sister Phoebe Margaret, was called by the defence to give rebuttal evidence in court. The *Rand Daily Mail* (ffrench-Beytagh 1973: 213) headlined its report: 'Nun: Alison did not smell of brandy'. Norman gave evidence on commission at a formal hearing in London. She denied she had attempted to recruit 'Mr Morley' as an agent for Defence and Aid and, moreover, had never in her life drunk brandy in the middle of the day. Years later, with the heat off, Miss Norman was able to admit that though she preferred gin she had probably drunk a brandy because it was cheaper for 'Mr Morley'.

Her more substantial untruth under oath was to declare that all the funds channelled to the dean through her English account came from wealthy friends – not IDAF. Years later she admitted that she had been troubled about committing perjury and had sought the advice of Trevor Huddleston, then Bishop of Stepney. He had counselled her to 'go ahead'. 'I was,' she now says, 'lying through my head about the source of the money' (Norman interview 1997).

As presiding judge, Mr Justice Cillié was the Judge President of the Transvaal and a dependable government appointee, of whom it was said that he had never been known to disbelieve the word of a senior police officer. He came up trumps again. He was satisfied beyond reasonable doubt that the devout English lady did tell Zwart she was an IDAF agent. And he believed Jordaan's story that the Dean had advocated the violent overthrow of the State. The sentence of five years' imprisonment caused consternation at Amen Court. Collins hurried to Lambeth Palace hoping for a tough statement. Instead, the Archbishop asked him to pray. Diana recalled her 'raging' husband on his return to Amen Court, 'swaying up and down' in a demonstration of the Archbishop of Canterbury at prayer. He had better luck with the Bishop of London, Gerald Ellison, who offered to help with funds for the dean's appeal. Some money was raised, but most of it came from IDAF.

The Appellate Division was no liberal touch, but the lower court's decision was too much for even the ultra-orthodox (and Anglican) chief justice, Ogilvie Thompson, who thought it 'inherently improbable' that if Norman were a Defence and Aid agent she would have communicated the fact to a chance acquaintance. The chief justice also took the opportunity to place a limit on the vague definition of what constituted an act of terror. The Terrorism Act was the plinth of the police state, its terms so widely framed that you were presumed guilty of terrorism if, 'with the intent to endanger law and order in the Republic', you took part in any act 'likely' to 'embarrass the administration of the affairs of the state'. Paying money to the loved ones of terrorists was just the sort of thing Vorster and General van den Bergh had in mind when they framed the statute. Ogilvie Thompson's words are worth recounting: 'Knowledge that his family is receiving some assistance while he is serving a prison sentence (or while he is outside the Republic's borders engaged in terrorist activities) is no doubt some solace to the individual concerned, but that can hardly be regarded as an intended boosting of morale in such a degree as to qualify as promotion of the activities of the African National Congress.' It was, he added, 'too remote a contingency' to be 'likely' to fall within the terms of the Act (ffrench-Beytagh 1973: 224).

When the Dean returned to St Mary's Cathedral there was, literally, dancing in the aisles. The success of the appeal was to have immense consequences. Since his conviction six months earlier, volunteers had distanced themselves from charities working with families of political prisoners in the belief that their activities were illegal. Now the narrower definition of terrorism handed down by the Bloemfontein court offered a pale green light. It did not unban Defence and Aid, but welfare work was no longer as dangerous as it had been. The Dependants' Conference, having come into existence after the banning and funded by churches in Europe and America, reasserted itself, so that over the years the refuge it provided to families on prison visits would complement the work of Amen Court.

But even with the successful appeal, it might have seemed that IDAF had suffered a knockout blow. The State had destroyed Haron's operation in the Cape, and in Johannesburg, though ffrench-Beytagh had come through his ordeal physically intact, there was no way in which his scheme could be reassembled in its old form or under the old management. Indeed, no effort was made to revive it and, even so, the Dean was immediately on a plane to England, to the anonymity of a parish priest in the city of London. For many, his departure signified the end of IDAF's welfare activity in South Africa. In reality it was no more than a mild hitch.

Collins had by now evolved a more elaborate system for delivering welfare payments to the families of detainees. It was more secure than the Dean's operation, for both giver and receiver of money. The system was working well elsewhere in South Africa even before the Dean went on trial.

Chapter 16

WELFARE LE CARRÉ STYLE

The state did not rest on its laurels. Success in the courts and the executive measures that neutralised its opponents were by no means the end of the story. It was engaged in destroying the very culture of African liberation. Vorster and his security chief, General Hendrik van den Bergh, trained their sights on the support mechanisms of those left behind. Security police eyes and ears – and tongues – were everywhere, persuading a township administrator to terminate a tenant's lease or a factory owner to sack a 'communist'. They barged into homes, terrifying mothers and children. You did not murmur 'ANC' or 'Mandela' or 'Robben Island' without looking about to see who was in earshot. Banishment to Dimbaza, Ilingwe and the other 'no-hope' dumping grounds in the Eastern Cape bantustans was stepped up. The counterpoint to this notion of liberation as heresy was the big sell of a segregationist political culture. Bantu education, ethnic elections, the lively phone-ins on the Bantu language radio programmes, set the mood for separate nationhood.

Collins understood that for the morale of prisoners and activists alike he needed to protect the daily lives of the families left behind. But the banning posed an awful dilemma, for now aid recipients faced ten years in prison if an Amen Court connection were proved. A second rabbit needed to appear out of the hat. It was produced by Phyllis Altman. For several years she had been sending small amounts of money to a score or so of banned trade unionists. The funds were donated by the British seamen's and fire brigades' unions and the Prague-based World Federation of Trades Unions, and distributed in Johannesburg from the Defence and Aid office. This was the seed corn for what was to become a multi-million-pound pen-pal operation. As a welfare scheme it owed more to John le Carré than to Lord Beveridge.

This stratagem also worked through a system of cut-outs aimed at keeping sender and receiver in healthy ignorance of the others along the chain. If it ran smoothly, a prying intelligence service should be kept at bay. Defence and Aid recruited (at its height) 700 letter writers to send money to South Africa. All but a handful had no idea they were being orchestrated by IDAF, indeed most had never heard of the organisation. A covering letter and cash arrived at their homes in a bulky registered package from 'Rev. Williams' – the Reverend Austin Williams of St Martins-in-the-Fields, Trafalgar Square, across the road from South Africa House. That was the first cut-out. They in turn mailed a money order to a family in South Africa, who believed it to be a personal gift from the sender. The family wrote back a thank you letter, which served as a receipt. The British letter writer, now acting purely as a conduit, mailed the letter to another clerical go-between at an address in London. This priest was the welfare equivalent of 'Mr X'. He was the second cut-out. Amen Court then collected the letters from the church or priory. The cycle was reactivated every two months with another bag of cash and fresh directions for the letter writer from Amen Court, via 'Rev. Williams'.

Much depended on the quality of the recruits. Rica Hodgson, who was in charge of welfare, or 'Programme Two' (the legal defence programme was 'Programme One'), sought writers 'free of political microbes.' She was reluctant to use exiles, especially if they worked at Amen Court. 'Some of us had had our fingerprints taken by the police back home. And there was the danger that they might want to get involved in political polemic'. The first batch was recruited by word of mouth by the Amen Court inner circle and Collins found a ready response from his Christian Action following. They, in turn, were asked to recommend names, or an existing writer took on more cases, and so the net spread (Hodgson interview 1992).

As each link in the chain had good reason to keep silent, so the operation had a built-in security system. If some early writers were aware of a Collins connection, they in turn drew in others without disclosing what they knew. They were happy to go along with the fiction, for it was a constructive way of registering distaste for apartheid. One of the earliest, if not the first, recruits, Vera Morgans, was recommended by her sister, the South African writer, Hilda Bernstein. This single source netted succeeding waves of writers. Rhoda Pulling and her husband Bob were both in the Communist Party but had dropped out of politics, apart from 'a tithe of CND activity'. Bob Pulling sometimes wondered about the air of cloak and dagger. 'Did all the money go on "bread and butter" – or did some pay for Semtex? Were they really priests or cardboard front characters?' (Pulling letter 26.02.92).

But how to track down those in need? Many lived in the Eastern Cape, but Amen Court had no direct dealings with them. In Dimbaza, most notorious of the dumping grounds, ANC and PAC ex-prisoners were to be found in every street. Walter Cola was dispatched there straight from Robben Island to an unviable R18-a-month job as a carpenter. Three years later, hearing from a friend about the 'fairy godmother', he wrote asking to enrol and in turn sent the good news along the grapevine. Jean Schurer corresponded with him for 18 years (Cola interview 23.01.92). The liberation movements in London also produced names. 'Phyllis and I [Hodgson] became known as persons who, if you put a name in our hands, something was done.' Nancy Dick, yet another exile to arrive on an exit permit (having given up her right to return), was taken on as a researcher at IDAF's Newgate Street office. She scoured half a dozen South African daily newspapers for names in trials, banishments or house arrests. The *Government Gazette* listed addresses of the banned. All were followed up. Hodgson was not joking when she said: 'We were looking for business; the more names we could find the more money we got' (Hodgson interview 1992).

So Amen Court passed the name of a needy family to a correspondent. The opening gambit was carefully played. 'Dear Mrs Mpetla, as a concerned member of the public, I've been told (by church, women's organisation, friend) that you are in trouble. My friends would like to help you.' A £10 money order was enclosed, with a promise of more to come. A positive reply, and the cycle was activated. Every two months Nancy Dick went to a nearby Barclays Bank to withdraw thousands of pounds in cash. The next day the correspondent received a bulky registered parcel with cash for South Africa. It arrived as regular as clockwork – postmen knew the time of month by it.

Writers were guided by a 12-point list of instructions ranging from how to send an international money order to what should *not* be talked about in a letter. 'We do not think it is a good idea to discuss South African politics as this may endanger the recipients, but you may otherwise extend your letters as you wish to cover such subjects as family news, cost of living, weather.' They were not to write on letterheads bearing a telephone number as 'there have been instances of reverse charge calls made from South Africa.' Hodgson wanted it 'vague as hell'. Vera Morgans recalls using language so cagey that a woman mistook her for an old employer and referred to her as 'Madam'.

The letter-writer bought the postal orders at her local post office. Filling in dozens of small denomination postal orders – with muddles over the spelling of an African name, mutters from the waiting queue, the irritated eye of the post office clerk – added up to a nervy outing.

Across South Africa, in squatter hovel and township tenement, mine 'bachelor' dormitory and one-goat farm, recipients puzzled over these generous foreigners who had taken them under their wings – so unlike the 'Europeans' at home. 'Friend', one wrote, 'I don't know what I should do for you, so that you will see how essential are you in our lives.' A wife who used to push her sick husband 15 miles in a wheelbarrow to the nearest hospital now indulged in a taxi.

With the ex-Robben Islanders in Dimbaza cashing their IMOs (international money orders) on the same few days every two months, the small Debe Nek post office was not able to cope. The unlucky ones made the half-day's walk to King William's Town where the post office was near the police station and its attendant security policemen. The white woman at the counter would cloak her jealousy behind a front of suspicion. One day she boiled over, warning Walter Cola that the money would get him into trouble. Angered, he told her that if she wanted money, she should go to the Royal Hotel and 'find a boyfriend to send you money'. He was reprimanded by the postmaster for being cheeky. A PAC veteran, Elias Mzamo, was once warned by Charles Sebe, who ran security in brother Lennox's Ciskei police statelet, that he had a mind to stop this money 'from your Russian brothers' (Mzamo interview 1992). A postal clerk turned away a woman because her name on the money order was written with an 'a' instead of an 'o'. The R500 was for a funeral.

The £40 was a great help, but the strength of the rand made for an unfavourable conversion for the recipient. The post-Sharpeville resurgence of the economy and the devaluation of sterling held the rand at under two to the pound until well into the seventies. Only in the eighties did the buying power of the money orders shoot up, El Dorado-style. More often than not, the money had been spent before it arrived. It was owed to school or shop or undertaker, or had been borrowed from a neighbour or a moneylender. Wives and teenage children were given money to travel twice a year to Robben Island or the Barberton women's prison or wherever a father or sister was incarcerated – a special boon for those living 1,500 miles away on the Zimbabwe border. A mother passed on a message that her son, aged 13, who could read and write English, was going to write a sweet and detailed letter very soon to the generous donor.

Thank you letters were unadventurous, omitting mention of politics or police, though it eventually dawned on one lady in the Home Counties that a recurring reference to 'my church' was a code word for the ANC. The recipient might be illiterate or find writing difficult in a language not her own. A grandchild replied with schoolroom formality or the local schoolmistress wrote for others in her neighbourhood. Margaret Rich, who read thousands of letters as part of the IDAF welfare group, found that despite the absence of a writing tradition, Africans had a way of putting words together 'which is like music or poetry. These were banal, ordinary descriptions of the horrible things that happened to them but most of the letters you could set to music' (Rich, interview, 1992). A lively correspondence still left the door open for cultural disparities. Rhoda Pulling's recipe instructed Dorothy Zhilangu to 'place in oven for one hour'. Dorothy replied 'but Rhoda, we don't have ovens.' It worked both ways. Elias Mzamo's picture of the Middlesbrough football team torn from a magazine and stuck on the wall of his prison cell featured the English player, David Armstrong. Not me, I'm afraid, wrote the London architect, David Armstrong. The correspondence continued nonetheless (Armstrong, interview, 1991).

Hodgson read every letter. This was social work through the mail. There might be a request for an exceptional payment, granny's funeral, a bout of July bronchitis. The onset of the school year was especially fraught, for in addition to the fees, principals would insist on school uniforms. She read between the lines and threw in an extra tenner postal order. A Solomonic solution quietened a wife who complained that she was seeing none of the money from her ex-Robben Island husband – Hodgson divided it between the two. Her comments, penned on the letters, guided the office typists on what to tell the correspondents about how they, in their turn, should couch their replies.

The mix of social and political rehabilitation inherent in IDAF's work is illustrated by the life of Elias Mzamo. He was born in Paarl, in the lush wine country close to Cape Town. Gaoled for five years in 1965 for PAC activities, he endured terrible maltreatment at the hands of the police before being worked over by common-law prisoners on Robben Island. On his release, he was sent to Dimbaza, though he had no connections with the Ciskei. The police then called on his parents, who had settled in Paarl in 1906 and had never been active in politics, and persuaded them to give up their home and join their son in his 'nice home' in King William's Town. The house was of concrete slabs, four rooms shared with an ANC man, an outside bucket toilet, no light or water. And it was far from the town. 'The SP (security police) used to visit us and ask how we liked it here.' Mzamo was not 'banned', but had to report to the police if he moved or found a new job. This was meaningless, for prisoners were not allowed to take jobs in Port Elizabeth. He heard from a Robben Islander about the English money, and was told to write to 'Humphrey'. Two months later he received his first money order and bought clothes and schoolbooks for his dead brother's children who lived with him. David Armstrong later inherited the correspondence. IDAF helped Mzamo's own family as well as his brother's family through periodic unemployment, a nervous breakdown and a second spell in prison.

Alan Sapper, radical leader of the film and television technicians' union ACTT wrote to Ruth Mini, widow of the executed Vuyisile Mini.[1] Ruth worked for the Council of Churches in Port Elizabeth, and received £240 each year for much of the seventies, which helped with the schooling of her four children. 'Through your help I can see the light after a still dark night,' she told Sapper. By the late eighties she was addressing him as 'My Brother in Christ'.

Sometimes Hodgson forgot about the fingerprints. The poet Barry Feinberg took on the Port Elizabeth artist, George Pemba, when his brother joined Umkhonto we Sizwe, leaving George to bring up his brother's 12 children in addition to his own eight. As Feinberg worked at IDAF, he used an alias. Jenny Maimane, an Englishwoman married to a South African journalist, Arthur Maimane, began to write for Hodgson after giving up work. Maimane wrote under the name of the actress Constance Cummings – she and her husband, the architect Benn Levy, were friends of John and Diana. 'Constance Levy would send me a wodge of headed notepaper and I would send out the letters in her name,' Jenny Maimane recalled.

The Rivonia families received special treatment. In 1967, Govan Mbeki's wife, Epainette ('Piny'), was granted £300 to stock her trading store in Idutywa, in the Transkei, in the expectation that she would help the five children of another Rivonia prisoner, Raymond Mhlaba. It did not work out. Eighteen months later she told Sonia Bunting that she was disposing of her business – and complained of the 'red tape' of having 'to refer practically every move to Govan for his signature'. In an SOS to London, Mrs Mbeki said two Mhlaba children were living with an aunt in Port Elizabeth who had lost her job when her employers took exception to her receiving Christmas cards from overseas. She was sent a bi-monthly £40 for the children until they left school. Another letter, sent to Mrs Bunting's London house, asked her to contact her son Thabo, then a student at Sussex University, and 'let him know his father needs some financial assistance for his studies.' The message was intended for Collins, as Bunting worked at IDAF. The outcome was a cheque for £100 for his study fees, with more following when required. In October 1968, Amen Court arranged for Govan Mbeki to be fitted with glasses. IDAF also covered the cost of tuition and boarding at the University of Lesotho for another Mbeki son.

The first collection point for the returned letters, St Dominic's Priory in Kentish Town, north London, was set up by Fr Simon Blake, a member of the Christian Action council. The priory was near Rica Hodgson's flat and every few days she would collect letters addressed to 'Fr John Dominic'. After a while, the venue was changed to St Margaret's Church, Lothbury, across the road from the Bank of England. But parking was a problem and the priest was not always there. In the mid-seventies, Collins switched to St James's Vestry, on Garlick Hill, running up to Mansion House.

The rector, Donald Mossman, was an old friend of Collins, and an honorary canon at St Paul's. Considering himself too well known, he asked an elderly churchwarden, Leslie Smith, to be the addressee. Mossman did not tell him the reason for secrecy. It was one of those City churches where nobody lived in the parish, so he reasoned that 'South African agents might not have tracked Leslie to his home.' Mossman could tell from the way a letter was addressed whether it was personal or for Amen Court. The clue lay in the writing of the name 'Leslie' in full. Playing it safer, the forwarding address was given as St James's Vestry and not St James's Church. Mossman left the mail under a mat in the deserted lobby. Margaret Rich, the letter collector, called on her way to the office. She would 'grovel on the floor in the murky light', then stroll nonchalantly out of the front door like an early morning worshipper.

The young ladies' employment agency, Stella Fisher, recruited for Collins. Thus Lydia Percival was taken on as a typist, and in turn persuaded Margaret Rich, her neighbour, to come in to the office a few days a week. Rich, a housewife living with three daughters and an engineer husband in Orpington, was intrigued when Lydia said: 'I can't tell you what you'll be doing.' From their humdrum existence in the commuter belt the two women were thrust into a cloak and dagger world. 'It was quite extraordinary that I should end up at a place like this,' Rich recalls. 'I was conscious of the enormous importance of the work, and that I dare not put a foot wrong. If anyone asked me what I did, I said "secretary" and, as nobody is interested in what a secretary does, it was a good cover' (Rich interview 1992). They worked in the basement where the windows were half above the paving, and wrote down a name on a scrap of paper in case they were being bugged.

'These girls weren't political, they weren't even in the Anti-Apartheid Movement,' said Hodgson. 'When they arrived, South Africa for them meant sunshine and oranges. They weren't well-paid, but they got so involved when they read the letters.' Later, Rich wrote under a pseudonym (to the family of the Black Consciousness prisoner Saths Cooper). Her daughters also wrote under *noms-de-plume* from addresses scattered about politically innocuous Sussex – Judith was 'Caroline Johnson' in Haywards Heath and Christine was 'Fiona McKenzie' in Three Bridges. Margaret chose 'Clare Owen' of Beckenham. 'We did our best to make it difficult for the South Africans.' Her husband drove round the countryside collecting the replies.

The beauty of this silent network was its personal touch. This was not a vast charity showering cash on an anonymous peasantry, but an international crusade based on helper and persecuted, housewife (in most cases) writing to housewife. The manner of its giving seemed as important as its buying power, restoring both material comfort and faith in humanity. The first reply might start with a 'Dear madam', the next with a 'Dear Mrs Smith', and in a few months they were into 'Dear Mary'. But some correspondents were troubled by the flaw in the scam that relied on the recipient's belief that the money came out of the new-found friend's own pocket.

However well researched the operation, it was not possible to be sure that every case was deserving or that the money was landing in the right hands. The observant letterwriter might be alerted by a nuance in a reply, a change of handwriting or a misspelling. Twenty-five years on, Bob Pulling recalled the 'talkative' John Ndzunga, 'his banana and fruit trees, struggles with ill health and poverty conveyed movingly in a small clerkly hand.' Then, suddenly, Ndzunga was 'less articulate, scarcely literate... we went on sending cash, but where was, who was, the "real" John?' They might voice their doubts to Amen Court, which would attempt to fathom the relevance of the change, or cause discreet inquiries to be made in South Africa. Hodgson admitted she 'couldn't be absolutely sure every letter went to the right place – we just had to take it on trust. We once discovered someone in Soweto was cashing other people's money.' But the donors seemed happy. Scandinavian and United Nations' officials called to inspect the books and leaf through the thank-you letters. Altman said the first time the Danes came 'they were very suspicious, till I showed them a letter-card with a Robben Island stamp on it, and then they understood we were doing what we said we were doing' (Altman interview 1993).

Throughout the entire period the money arrived seemingly unimpeded. To a large degree, IDAF's welfare programme, 'Programme Two', depended on the efficiency of the South African postal service. Hodgson thinks it had something to do with the Calvinist mentality that permeated the country. 'You just didn't interfere with the post. It was a matter of Dutch Reformed Church pride that letters got through.'

Years later, General Johan Coetzee, head of the security police, paid an inadvertent tribute to the effectiveness of the campaign:

> This was the big problem that we objected to in South Africa... if you come to me and say if you are arrested we'll see that you've got the best defence, we'll see that your wife is looked after whilst you are in prison, you've got a prison education

scheme running for you and once you are through all this we'll see that there is work for you. Isn't this removing the inhibitions which are operative among ordinary societies? (Coetzee interview 1992)

Chapter 17

STEPHANUS AND EILEEN

Eileen Wainwright, a middle-class, *Guardian*-reading, underemployed housewife, was ready-made for writing letters. She met her husband Ted at the tail-end of the Second World War in a government laboratory where her job was to test the resistance of paint to mustard gas. They settled into a Georgian house in the Home Counties, near London. She was politically engaged enough to join the Campaign for Nuclear Disarmament (CND) although she never actually marched behind a banner in Trafalgar Square. Her ordained role was to bring up three sons. They grew up, they began to manage on their own, and she thought about what to do next (Wainwright interview 1991).

The eldest son was dating a girl in Hemel Hempstead. Her mother asked Eileen if she would care to send money to needy South Africans on behalf of well-wishers in England who wanted to conceal their identities. It sounded like the interest she was looking for. But it needed to be low-key, as Ted was by now a production manager with Dickenson Robinson, which, among its varied activities, made Basildon Bond notepaper in South Africa.

The 'Rev. Williams' sent her five names, with the usual injunctions: 'Tell them the money is yours or comes from friends. Do not discuss controversial matters nor encourage them to talk politics.' Mrs Wainwright wrote off the introductory letters – 'Friends tell me you are in need... we would like to help' – and soon established a regular correspondence with several South African families. Rica Hodgson came to deliver a pep talk to local housewives and asked them to recruit more writers but Eileen still had no inkling of the John Collins connection. In time, she would be writing to 12 African families – to six as Mrs Wainwright, and another six under her maiden name, Beldon. Over the years one correspondent became a bit special.

In October 1973, Abulon Bafana Duma, a former trade union official from Durban, wrote from exile in Swaziland to the ANC office in Algiers: 'My family needs help, especially my youngest of 8 years who lives away from his mother and brothers and sisters. Will you care for him and help pay for his school? He is with my grandparents who are Mr and Mrs Stephanus Mpanza. They should not know it is me.' The request was passed to Amen Court, then to 'Mrs Beldon', who wrote directly to Stephanus Mpanza. In January 1974 she received a reply:

Khethokuhle B.C. School
P.O. Greenvale
Donnybrook, Natal.

Dear Mrs Beldon,

Your letter came to me as a surprise, which is a proof that God provides. Whoever told you that I am in need of assistance is a sincere friend indeed. All my children are married but I have a small boy who is my great-grandchild solely dependent on me. I am 81 years old and this little boy Philippus by name was born in 1966.

I am a minister in the Bantu Hervormde Kerk. Although I am still employed my salary is inadequate to cover my daily living and provide for this little boy's future to give him sound education. At the moment this is a great worry to me.

'A friend in need is a friend indeed.' 'Cast thy bread upon the water and thy shall find it after many days.' I sincerely thank you for your kind promising letter.

Thank you madame,
Yours obediently,

S. P. Mpanza

Over the next eight years the correspondence between 'Eileen Beldon' and Stephanus Mpanza, from his mission settlement in the foothills of the Drakensberg, would enrich each other's lives. Her letters to Stephanus have not been found and might have been destroyed for reasons of security. But his have survived. If he did know why he, in the wilds of Natal, had been singled out for IDAF munificence, it is nowhere hinted at in the 55 letters addressed to Hop Cottage, Malting Lane, Dagnall, Herts. True to the conventions of the correspondence, Stephanus seldom touched on contemporary politics but he was rarely at a loss for words, as his third letter demonstrates: [1]

> Dear *Inkosikazi*,
>
> I would like to explain the Zulu word I like to use when address-ing you. It is a high honour to a married lady to address her as *Inkosikazi*. The word comes from *inkosi* – king – and *kazi* is a suf-fix to denote the king's female. The word is now used to honour a special group of females with dignity. As a Zulu it gives me pleasure to address you *Inkosikazi* better than madam or Mrs. In other words *Inkosikazi* means she is bigger than a king.

Stephanus's wife is a shadowy figure. Stephanus wrote that she and the boy Philippus

> are not very good friends … because she was a very strict teacher and still has that tendency and discipline. [But she was] one of the best teachers in Natal during her time. All English admire her for her good English and ask her where she was educated or whether she has some degree but she only passed T2. I remember at one place we came to there was no school of any kind, children were roaming about. Without my knowledge she had organised the children and formed a Class A. Today that school is a high school. Of course she is now old and hardly has time to teach Philippus his homework.

Stephanus Mpanza and his wife were among the first aspiring blacks for whom the ministry, teaching or nursing was a step out of tribal society into the professional classes. Their four children were also teachers. He was born near Vryheid in 1892, son of 'a preaching elder under the first missionaries'. Northern Natal was settled by the Voortrekkers, which accounted for his adherence to a sect of the Dutch Reformed Church. His was a *dogter kerk* or 'daughter church', as the segregated African, Indian and coloured sections were officially described. (Unofficially, Afrikaners called it *kaffer kerk*, 'kaffir church'.) His mother was 'a pure Swazi woman who spoke to us in Zulu', so it is likely that for Stephanus, English was a third language, after isiZulu and Afrikaans.

He admired Britain – 'a country well advanced in good manners and the source of all good habits in the world – no exaggeration' – and had a soft spot for its royal family. Early in the correspondence he wrote:

> London is the capital, the glory and the brilliance of the world. I remember one incident while a small boy. I had some trouble somehow, when I decided to write to King Edward VII whom I have heard that in his kingdom the sun never sets. He might be merciful and have pity on me and help me out of my trouble. My letter was discovered by my teacher who laughed till he could laugh no more. To my great disappointment he destroyed my letter.

The Queen's Silver Jubilee in 1977 stirred another memory:

> I was fortunate to see the Prince of Wales in 1925 at Eshowe... my birthplace. It happened that I was in the choir that would sing for the Prince. The Prince sat in the pavilion built for the occasion. The choir stood facing the pavilion which gave us a good view to see the Prince: Prince Edward who was to be King Edward VIII. That scene was an indelible impression. The second fortune was when King George VI & Queen visited Eshowe again [1947]. There we stood... and the King and his family drove round the Oval to let us look and see them but this was not so close as that of Prince of Wales, and the number of people there were far more in number. Eshowe was the capital of Zululand before it became a province in the Union of South Africa in 1910, the year King Edward VII died. So I know of the events pertaining to the United Kingdom. I beg your pardon for my long uninteresting letter...

He was full of curiosity about Eileen's world. 'Is baas working at sea?' Stephanus inquired, wondering at her husband's temporary absence, possibly in South Africa, which he visited once for his company. 'Toboggan is a new word to me and have to look it up in English dictionary. It is a sport we are not accustomed to, but still am glad to know the word.' And 'old Darby & Joan, is it a story or something else?' He asks for more detailed information about 'the wonderful bird Cuckoo' which reminds him of the *Phezu-kom-Khono* bird whose song 'tells people to get their hoes in the ground.' Stephanus had hunted it, without success, 'creeping towards where it is singing it soon ceases to sing and to my great surprise it sings behind me.'

There was a reference in one letter to a family tragedy in Hertfordshire: 'Stillborn is a new English word to me and had to find an assistance to its meaning.' He continued: '*Nkosikazi* in all our griefs we condone ourselves through the word of God. "To everything there is a season, and a time to every purpose under the heaven. A time to be born and a time to die; a time to plant and a time to pluck up that which is planted." *Ecclesiastes* 3(1–2). This is God's timetable that no one can alter. Yes they are young they will have other children.'

He was perplexed as to why *Inkosikazi's* eldest son, Adam, should work with emotionally deprived children. 'We Zulus have no school of that kind. All orphans, needy, poor were adopted by the well to do people and make them part of their family.' And why, he asked, did Angus (her youngest, doing his 'A' levels) 'like to study French, while he is in England and he is English? How will he benefit by this French language?' The second son David was finishing a science degree with a view to beekeeping. 'Your sons all select difficult subjects to study. I congratulate David to prefer to live a simple life from all town or city strenuous living with its numerous worries. I envy David for keeping bees. I wish I would. I am very fond of honey but South Africa has wild bees and hard to rear. I wish I could learn to rear bees.'

David must have told his mother to ask about snakes. They occupy two lengthy replies, not all herpetologically well-founded.

> The biggest snake is python. It is large, long, catches its prey by coiling itself around its victim's body crushes & squeezes it to death. But before it kills its prey, it puts its double tongue in the nostrils of its prey in order to suck out his brain. When its prey is dead, then starts its great task. It applies its slippery saliva on the whole body of its dead victim... It takes time to swallow...

> When its prey is in its mouth she will not defend herself. She is
> utterly helpless at this stage. When its prey has been completely
> swallowed in you can see the shape of the prey are jutting out
> in the stomach. Now she will not move at all till its food is rot-
> ten. Some say that the under part of her body rots too to let out
> all the rotten stuff inside it. Then she moves away again leaving
> the bones of its prey.

These replies usually closed with a self-mocking flourish. 'I
beg your pardon Nkosikazi for I have raked all my rubbish
and piled it on you to keep you occupied before you do your
kooking [sic]. Best wishes to your loving family.' One day he
wrote: 'Is it impolite *Nkosikazi* for one to ask for a family snap?'
No reply. Next letter: 'There is one point in my letter which
Nkosikazi ignore. If that was your purpose, please ignore it
again. I shall understand.' IDAF letter-writers were instructed
not to send photographs of themselves to deny Pretoria's
official letter-snoopers any snapshots of those deemed to be
helping the families of terrorists.

As Philippus grows and passes exams, the boy looms larger
in the correspondence. 'Philippus is now a great help to the
house, he fetches water from the well (we have no pipes) and
I am teaching him to milk our cows'. Philippus, he says, 'is
getting taller every day. He is very fond of shoes.'

While books, clothes and money orders went south,
Stephanus sent northwards what offerings he could. For
Christmas 1975 he announced a 'hearty gift that I have
decided to present my lovely family overseas.' By separate
post arrived 'one picture in a plastic frame being the Zulu
Royal Family as it was founded by Shaka'. The founder of the
Zulu nation featured again as Eileen described the swallows
gathering outside her house, perhaps to fly to southern Natal.
It reminded Stephanus of 'Shaka's last word when his brothers
murdered him. He said, although you kill me you shall not
rule this country, but will be ruled by the white swallows who
build their houses with mud. Meaning white men.'

They had been writing for three years when Eileen
suggested they get on to first name terms. 'Dear Ellen', (it
took him a while to get the hang of 'Eileen') 'you always give
me a surprise even if I did not expect one. Thank you Ellen

although I nearly said *Nkosikazi*. I think it is goodbye to my old famous name to make room for its new friend "Ellen". Thank you so much for our friendship.'

When Eileen/Ellen reveals she has been mildly out of sorts for a few days Stephanus responds with a display of sympathy: 'Our thoughts were as the flooded river carrying with it all sorts of things, including rubbish down to its mouth. It was even hard to fancy you lying in bed with fever, just like one in a dream. Our wave of shock has not yet passed away. But there is always wish and hope to sustain us from staggering.'

It must have seemed strange to Stephanus that the only whites he was able to befriend were 6,000 miles away. The Mpanzas lived in an overwhelmingly African ambience, where white people rarely intruded and the mail travelled the 15 miles from Donnybrook once or twice a week. When '2 fat beasts' were slaughtered for those who 'gathered from far and near' at the mission for the Easter weekend (Passover, he called it), only one white minister was there. The mission was 'an isolated place', the nearest clinic 45 miles away and the general hospital 100 miles off in Pietermaritzburg. 'Doctors refuse to visit our place because of bad roads or non roads. On wet days we can't move an inch. We pay a lot of money to take our sick to the hospital. Some die on the way. We are now trying to collect money to build a clinic.' The white magistrate visits to hear the Clinic Committee (Stephanus is chairman, his wife secretary) give a progress report and 'let him have the money we have collected'.

The letters are a calendar of the passing seasons, the havoc of flood and 'lightening' and hail on crops, cold seeping into ageing bones of a winter's morn, the joyous sunshine ripening his favourite food, maize. 'Winter is now gone and summer is in. We are happy now for we shall eat green mealies which is a great treat for us Zulus. We often grind the fresh mealies & boil the dough to make some kind of bread. Summer is the time when our hunger is driven away because we kook different varieties of dishes from these summer stock.'

He visits relatives in faraway Eshowe, the Zulu heartland where Shaka had his kraal, and his family return the visits. 'My eldest daughter is coming... She is Mrs. Handsome Mbule &

has 5 girls and 4 boys. The last born is taking matric. Most of her family is clever. There are BAs – teachers & nurses.' Despite the pride in being Zulu, he can be dismissive of their perceived backwardness. 'We do not know how to keep and use money... I remember during the Zulu War at Isandlwane 1879 when the Zulu warriors hammered 2/6 to produce 2 separate shillings and a sixpence and drank paraffin for liquor.'

Bantu education is 'not pleasing', he writes on another occasion. 'Many children leave school because their parents are unable to pay for their school books and education. Whites, Indians and coloureds have their schooling free.'

When Ted and Eileen went on holiday with friends in Cornwall, Stephanus was prompted to write: 'We Africans rarely have holiday, perhaps it is the financial side that do not allow us to do so. I have never been in a steam engine although it has long been my desire to visit Cape Town [1,000 miles away] travelling by sea... I once visited the City, I think it was 1912.'

The interplay between Grace, the family tabby cat and Chloe, Eileen's talkative three-year-old granddaughter, provides Stephanus with a series of fade-out lines. 'My family laughed till their sides ached when I told them about peaceful Grace, that Grace does not like the noise in the house made by active Chatterbox. Therefore Grace steals away to the garden whenever Chatterbox is busy in the house.' And again: 'Before winding up my letter... you forgot to say something about my two friends – Chatterbox and Grace. One who likes noise and the other graceful and peaceful.'

He is charmed by Eileen's maxim 'stick to your bush' to describe her son's persistence in the precarious world of beekeeping. Stephanus again ruminates about setting up in a similar line of business himself. Would David send a manual? In reference to the industrial unrest during Britain's 'winter of discontent', he wrote: 'We have read... with regret about the drivers' strike when everything on wheels stood still. It has been a severe blow for England.'

In July 1979, Eileen received a short letter: 'Tryphena Lilian Mpanza my wife passed away peacefully at the Christ Hospital on 30th June, a diabetes patient. But she died of a fall & broke one of her head veins. Her funeral on Saturday the 7... summoned all the district in spite of the bitter cold. There is only one way to leave this earth & that is by death. I have not yet received my booklet for bees. But will soon arrive. Stephanus.'

By now Stephanus is 87 years old and the handwriting on the letters belongs to Philippus though they are still couched in the man's imperishable style. 'Thank you for the joy & niceties,' he writes in response to one letter. And later, 'your letters are a joy & comfort for us: Philippus and I. I long for them now & I miss them if they do not come.' In 1980 the money was raised to £50, converting to about R90 in the still buoyant currency. 'Philippus paid his school fees with R10, & with R5 paid for his toilet materials. His Zulu Bible cost him R2, plus toothbrush & new socks. Now you can see it yourself what this gift does.'

On the occasion of Prince Charles's wedding to Diana he gently chides Eileen. 'Were I a well-to-do man I should have attended the Royal Wedding. I can see that you were not interested.'

Soon there are hints that the end is near. Stephanus's doctor tells him that his blood is weak and there is 'a lump in my womb'. The doctor discharges him from hospital, a hopeless case. 'I know that you are very busy in the garden', he writes, 'but where did your milk come from because you never said you own a cow?' In his penultimate letter he says he can walk around the yard. His memory is very poor, as is his hearing, 'but my eyes are wonderfully strong... I can read a holy Bible with small types without spectacles... I hope to write more sensibly next time. Where is your husband now? Still helping you at home? You busy bee.'

Then Eileen received a letter dated June 2, 1982:

Thank you for your letter which I received on June 2... and thank you very much since we have met. It is a very long time. As from today I have difficult words to write. All your letters have shown me pleasure which I have none at all. I am afraid I am not as you think. My body is declining. Today I feel very bad to catch postal orders in such a way that I can't catch them but Philippus must catch them and I distribute them accordingly.

I think it will be last time. God bless you all, you Eileen; Ned, Adams, David, Angus as well as Chloe I repeat, God bless you. Yours Stephanus.

The death of Stephanus was not quite the end of the story. The support for Philippus continued until he had completed his studies and become a Dutch Reformed Church pastor, like his great-grandfather (Mpanza interview 1992). Abulon Duma, the ANC activist whose letter requesting help brought Philippus to the attention of IDAF, never saw the boy as a grown man. In 1977 Duma lost his arm in a letter bomb explosion in Manzini, Swaziland, in an assassination attempt undertaken by members of the security police based in Ermelo, a South African border town. The operation was authorised by the then Major (later General) Nic van Rensburg[2]. After treatment in East Germany, Duma was re-deployed by the ANC to Zimbabwe where he died in the mid-1980s.

Chapter 18

AN OLD MAN IN A HURRY

It was an article of faith among white South Africans that their country's tribulations, at home and abroad, were rooted in a heavy tonnage of Kremlin gold. Certainly the ANC depended on the Soviet bloc for weaponry and training. Collins, however, was the recipient of nothing more than token roubles. But in the autumn of 1969, he was invited to the Soviet embassy in London to discuss a bid to rescue political prisoners from Robben Island. The island's location, eight miles off Cape Town, was thought to make it accessible to ambush from the sea. The diplomat said his country was prepared to provide a submarine and incidental hardware. What he wanted from Collins, as an expert on the island's political population, was advice on how to make contact with the prisoners, and a map, as detailed as possible, showing the location of the prison buildings.

At the time, perhaps not entirely by coincidence, Collins had developed a soft spot for Moscow. To the surprise of the family, Richard, his third son, had become an accomplished ballet dancer and was on a scholarship at the Moscow conservatoire. However, it is probable that even without the Bolshoi connection, Collins would have been tempted by the rescue offer. Not long before, he had been in contact with a Johannesburg businessman, Gordon Bruce, mulling over another plan to get Mandela off the island in a lobster boat as a preliminary to his being flown out of South Africa by the aviatrix, Sheila Scott. MI5 got wind of that idea and it was aborted (Bruce interview 1992; Winter 1981: 282).

The Canon decided to cultivate the Soviet connection. More cloak and dagger meetings followed, to the mounting alarm of Diana, who did not think the project politically wise, and even so was sure there was no chance of preserving security – not from BOSS, but from MI5 which, given the informal alliances in the world of espionage, amounted to much the same thing. Her husband, she knew, found it painfully hard to keep tales of derring-do to himself. And she had it on the best authority that their phones were bugged. Gerald Gardiner, the Labour Lord Chancellor, had once called for a chat with Collins, when the telephone rang. After Collins replaced the receiver, Gardiner remarked: 'By the way, John, I hope you don't trust that machine' (Collins 1992: 336).

The submarine scheme foundered, largely over disagreements about who were to be sprung. The Russians, it transpired, were largely interested in effecting the escape of communist prisoners. Mandela, not being a communist, was not even on the original list of target escapees. Collins backed off, saying he could not accept the selectivity. But in 1971 he was involved in yet another plan, this time to effect the escape of Mandela and his close prison friend, Eddie Daniels.[1] There would be an ambush while the two men were under escort in Cape Town to receive medical treatment. The Canon was enthusiastic but the ANC doubted it could work. This, too, came to nothing. 'In every man,' Diana Collins mused, 'there is a little Scarlet Pimpernel waiting to get out' (Diana Collins interview 1992).

In some ways, Collins was an old man in a hurry. By the time the Russians approached him to talk submarines he was already a pensioner. He must have despaired of seeing the end of apartheid in his lifetime. Small wonder that he sometimes looked for short cuts.

In England, he suffered from a lop-sided public image. He was famous for having been chairman of CND – a post long since vacated – and his maverick comments on the issues of the day served simply to remind the public of his appetite for controversy. It was marginal activity but it was the margin that created the public reputation. To journalists he was the eccentric cleric ever ready with a quote from his own book of rules. He told the Board of Film Censors that Stanley Kubrick's 'Lolita' was 'a provocation to rape and murder' and should be banned. How unchristian to condemn a film you haven't seen, rejoined Peter Sellers, one of its stars. Collins resurrected the Campaign for the Abolition of Capital Punishment as a precautionary measure in case Edward Heath's Conservative government was of a mind to turn back the clock (it was not). He won feminist applause by speaking up for the ordination of women, and abuse from organised labour by calling striking electricity workers 'hijackers'. His graphic description of the effect of napalm and fragmentation bombing by the Americans in Vietnam, delivered from the pulpit of St Paul's, caused several queasy worshippers to walk out, complaining of political sermonising. He crossed swords with the Duke of Edinburgh, who appeared to have the Canon in mind when declaring that moral considerations were secondary to self-interest in matters of trade. Collins mounted his pulpit to denounce the Duke's view as inconsistent with the Christian gospel (*Cape Argus* 03.07.67).

Collins did admit to an 'adolescent streak' that led to his 'indiscretions', though he rejected the frequently levelled description of himself as being irresponsible or self-indulgent. 'I resisted authority', he would say, 'when, in the course of what I deemed to be my work as a priest, it seemed necessary to do so and any enjoyment was only incidental.' The enjoyment of a good row, however, came over strongly. Donald Woods, the South African journalist who knew Collins well, spoke of a priest 'whose benign smile masks a relish for rough political infighting' (*The Times* 31.10.92).

So the idea of Collins as a hyperactive, dog-collared 'loony' was not confined to white South Africa. It may well have contributed to his being passed over for the post of Dean of St Paul's when the office became vacant. He coveted the job. But Diana Collins recalled Mervyn Stockwood, the radical Bishop of Southwark and old friend of the Collinses, telling her not to entertain any hopes. 'He won't get it,' said Stockwood, 'too many enemies.' She believed there were fears that donations from industry and the finance houses would dry up if the spokesman for the City of London's great cathedral advocated sanctions against a friendly trading partner (Collins 1992: 328).

He was more respected abroad, particularly in Scandinavia, with its subtle understanding of what IDAF was trying to achieve. By the end of the 1960s the Stockholm government had become IDAF's largest direct contributor. The British government, in contrast, had not made a single direct contribution. Sweden, Norway, Denmark, Finland and Holland knew that however bizarre the public image, he was efficiently carrying out difficult and dangerous work. One measure of the esteem in which the Canon was held was his nomination for the Nobel Peace Prize in 1971 but as the award went to the German, Willy Brandt, motivator of Ost-Politik, he could hardly complain. Then, in 1974, Sean MacBride won it, and that did hurt, for the one-time Irish freedom fighter was Chairman of rival Amnesty International (though his roles as President of the International Peace Bureau and UN Commissioner for Namibia were also cited). MacBride had the additional 'brownie points' of three stretches in a British prison.

The IDAF council met twice yearly, usually in London but occasionally in Dublin or Stockholm. For much of the seventies its members were the Swede, Dean Helander, Gilbert Rist of the Swiss committee and Kader Asmal, a South African who taught law at Trinity College, Dublin and later became a cabinet minister. Collins managed the council in benignly despotic style. 'It was all decided by John,' recalled Helander. 'Sometimes he did the opposite of what we decided. Once he asked for about £10,000 to buy a house for an exile but as the Swedes wanted their money used directly for the fight against apartheid, the council said "No". But he did it all the same, wrote a cheque. We took it up at the next meeting, and he said, "Oh, did you, I'll look into it." We heard no more about it' (Helander interview 1992).

The identity of the recipient is not clear, but Collins did dip into the IDAF coffers to help Oliver and Adelaide Tambo buy their home in Muswell Hill. Collins believed that the ANC President-General was entitled to the dignity of living in a respectable north London suburb. 'We did not give money to political organizations, but the ANC had no money,' Diana Collins recalled later. 'It was expensive because of the need for security. We paid the mortgage. The mortgage was finally paid off in 1991' (Diana Collins interview 1992).

The annual meetings of the Fund – held in a London hotel or, again, in Dublin or Stockholm – offered some idea of the Fund's work, without giving away the secret paths. Meetings were by invitation only – representatives of overseas committees and donor embassies, invited guests and the liberation movements. Collins liked to have witnesses of the situation on the ground so that donors had an idea of what their money was doing. Reading between the lines of the minutes one senses the strong emotions of an Angolan or a SWAPO freedom fighter in a faraway country put in touch with a sympathetic audience. The feelings were reciprocal. Louise Asmal recalled 'the impression made by representatives of the liberation movements who were given a platform, especially in countries outside the UK, where in the beginning we had not had an opportunity of listening to many of those who spoke' (Louise Asmal letter to author 09.08.99).

In 1972, the delegates heard from Colin Winter, the exiled Anglican Bishop of Damaraland in Namibia – 'the SWAPO bishop' was the whites' epithet for him – on the benefits of an IDAF-funded defence. Twelve men charged with organising a migrant workers' strike were 'resigned to a mock trial and sentences of five to 10 years'. But the Windhoek magistrate hearing the case became concerned when Bryan O'Linn, the territory's leading advocate, took over the defence. With good reason. Each accused wore a number so that a police officer could easily identify number 5 as the man he said had incited the workers and threatened those who tried to leave the compound. O'Linn asked his clients to leave the courtroom, then switched the numbers round, with the result that the policeman was unable to identify the alleged ringleader. Four of the 12 were acquitted and the remainder given small fines and suspended sentences.

The one IDAF section that was allowed to push its nose above the parapet was Research and Information ('Clause 3'), charged with producing objective, factual information about South Africa. The department began in the late 1960s with the arrival in London of Alex Hepple, who had run the

Johannesburg Defence and Aid office, and been an outspoken Labour MP in South Africa. Collins installed him and his wife, Girley, in an office in suburban Finchley and asked them to produce a digest of South African events. The Hepples recruited a team of local housewives who pasted up reports of torture and sabotage and other apartheid matters cut from a range of publications. The Swedes footed the bill. When the Hepples retired, their sucessor, Alan Brooks, replaced the loose-leaf format with *Focus*, a tightly edited bi-monthly.

Although its circulation never rose above 4,000, *Focus* was a mine of information for those who needed to know about political prisoners and trials. Another South African exile, Al Cook, who worked in Research and Information from 1973, recalled producing 'devastating indictments of apartheid by taking the government's own information and putting it together in a way that demonstrated the truth.' The magazine went to embassies, UN agencies, non-governmental organisations, liberation movements, selected journalists, Africa-watchers, even into South Africa. IDAF publications were routinely banned in the Republic's *Government Gazette* but might still be available to research students at the Pretoria and Cape Town public libraries and on university campuses. The magazine was in time supplemented by a flow of books of which Mandela's *The Struggle is my Life*, which Cook edited, was the most successful, selling more than 50,000 copies in several languages.

Hugh Lewin, as director of information, ran Clause 3 from 1972, and was able to launch a photo library with the work of *Observer* photographer Tony McGrath, who had been despatched to South Africa by Lewin to record the quirks and horrors of daily life. The photographer John Seymour contibuted photographs for a calendar that made a 'fairly handsome profit'. Gilbert Spilker, IDAF's contact man in West Germany, persuaded all the members of the Bundestag (West German Parliament) to take a copy. The collection was boosted from inside South Africa by Jurgen Schadeberg's photographs for *Drum* magazine, and by Eli Weinberg, apartheid's defiant chronicler, who bequeathed to IDAF his entire portfolio going back to the 1940s.[2] Under Barry

Feinberg, Lewin's successor, the library acquired a collection of 100,000 images. It was a matter of pride that it constituted the most comprehensive collection anywhere of still pictures on apartheid.

Feinberg also produced a series of TV documentaries. One of them, *The Anvil and the Hammer*, won awards at film festivals in Leipzig and London. But the work of his department – by 1990 it had a staff of 17 – was rarely shown on mainstream British television. Feinberg saw IDAF as a victim of a strange irony, that 'we were avoided by the media in the same way as was South African government material, but for opposite reasons... too radical' (Feinberg interview 1993). Feinberg's enterprise included mailing IDAF publications 'blind' to people inside South Africa. It is not known how many arrived safely.

Clause 3's style was low key. Collins was wary of causing friction with the Anti-Apartheid Movement (AAM), the main vehicle for public campaigning. In the division of labour it was understood that IDAF produced information while the AAM dealt in propaganda – though often making use of IDAF's material. IDAF employees were discouraged from drawing attention to themselves in public. Altman frowned on fraternisation, even with comrades in the cause. And if there were fundraising events, they were in the name of British Defence and Aid or the AAM. 'Come Back Africa', a concert to mark UN Human Rights Year and South African Freedom Day 1968, attracted a quality mix to the Albert Hall, all performing *gratis*. Dankworth and orchestra were there once again, with his wife Cleo Laine, Julie Felix, Annie Ross, John Williams, Igor Oistrakh, though Brando and Dick Gregory 'no-showed'. Dusty Springfield, who had abandoned a South African tour in midstream rather than play hard rock in segregated halls, sent best wishes in a half-page of the programme. Thabo Mbeki, a student at Sussex University, performed the miners' gumboot dance together with a group of exiles.

The staff in the Newgate Street office working under Altman (trials), Rica Hodgson (welfare) and Lewin (information) were keenly motivated and modestly recompensed. As an employer, Collins occupied the close-fisted end of the spectrum. He disliked straight all-round pay rises. In July 1970, the minutes reported that Phyllis Altman's request for a raise was turned down, though the Council 'would be glad to give sympathetic consideration to an application from her as an exiled victim of apartheid for an eleemosynary[3] grant from the Fund'. When the office establishment rose above 20 there were murmurings about the need for union representation. Collins would have none of it, saying he was prepared to shut down the operation if unionisation was forced on him. A charitable view would be that Collins economised on pay in order to have more money for the trials. But one employee, Jan Marsh, complained that Collins 'traded on the fact that most of us were doing it for our beliefs.'

The office had a wide political spread and there seemed no ideological design behind the appointments, many of whom were exiles. Lewin, a vicar's son, had spent seven years in prison for sabotage. He and Al Cook had Liberal Party beginnings. Sonia Bunting, as with Rica Hodgson with whom she worked closely, was a communist. Her husband, Brian, worked in the London office of the Soviet TASS news agency. The poet Barry Feinberg, who joined from the Bertrand Russell Foundation, belonged to one of the several London cells of the South African Communist Party. Edna Wilcox, in the welfare unit, was in the Trotskyite Unity Movement. Neville Rubin, recalled Collins 'forever dancing on eggs' in his efforts to harmonise the contending factions but there was no basic disagreement about the tune. If communists played a hugely influential role in the exiled ANC, Collins and Altman, for reasons that had nothing to do with Moscow, gave it their unstinting support. Disharmonies, when they did occur, tended to be more about tactics than overall political strategy.

While at IDAF, Lewin played a prominent role in launching 'South Africa, the Imprisoned Society' (SATIS), a joint project with the AAM and the trade unions that highlighted the cases of men and women in prison. It was a successful propaganda venture and would later be transmuted into the 'Release Mandela' campaign. But the security-conscious Altman was not altogether happy. She banned the copying of SATIS documents in the office. She was even less pleased when

Lewin became involved in efforts to form alliances between IDAF and other international agencies working in the anti-apartheid field. This kind of activity enraged Altman, who felt that it needlessly involved outsiders and increased the threat to the core enterprises of IDAF – trials and welfare – that had to remain as secretive as possible. Peace broke out when Lewin moved to *Drum* magazine (and later to *The Guardian* newspaper). Lewin's departure was seen as the loss of a creative information chief. Altman remained dry-eyed.

Altman was sure that BOSS had a firm grasp of how the trial defences were financed, if only because the same small group of advocates, led by George Bizos and Sydney Kentridge, cropped up regularly in security cases. Bizos admits they were felicitously placed, being 'a little distant in relation to where our instructing solicitors got their money. We didn't ask many questions. A fiction was created that was comfortable for us. But I think most of us knew it was Defence and Aid money through other channels' (Bizos interview 1992). If the advocates could figure it out, then, logically, so could BOSS. But as long as the cut-out system preserved secrecy on the detail of individual cases, it was difficult for the authorities to act. For the moment, South Africa's keenness to show that it remained respectful of western criminal law and procedure worked to IDAF's advantage. But there were blunders.

Alex Moumbaris – an Australian of Greek origin, raised in Paris, living in London where he worked for Reuters – was arrested along with his wife while in South Africa reconnoitring sea-borne guerrilla landing stages for MK. His wife, who was pregnant, was released following the intervention of President Charles de Gaulle. An Irish national, Sean Hosey, was also charged. Frankel engaged a French legal firm to find a lawyer, which produced an apolitical Johannesburg attorney, Richard Wilson, who retained Bizos as counsel. At the initial consultation the lawyer did not realise that four blacks would also be named in the indictment. 'Alex and Sean were happy for me to represent the others,' says Bizos, 'but Wilson said it would compromise him and his clients if there were joint representation.' So the four ended up with *pro deo* advocates whom Theo Cholo, a senior ANC intelligence operative, recalled as being 'not to my taste'. Bizos believes it made no difference – they were sent down for the 'usual' 15 years (Bizos interview 1992; Cholo interview 1992). But in London, Slovo, mastermind of the doomed mission, had a 'huge row' with Altman. 'Joe was only excited because three of them were members of the (Communist) party,' she said mischievously. 'It was the only big mistake we made.'

The stakes involved in IDAF's welfare operation were not quite so high, but there were still delicate problems to negotiate, not all of them in South Africa. Among the keen letter-writers recruited by the welfare department was Elinor, wife of Sir Robert Birley, retired headmaster of Eton College ('Red Robert' to his boys), and later a visiting professor of education at the University of the Witwatersrand in Johannesburg. The couple made a substantial contribution to the fees of the Mandela daughters, Zenani and Zinzi, at Waterford School in Swaziland. Back in England, Elinor continued the good work for the girls and other children through the medium of IDAF. She took security so seriously that her attempts at obfuscation defeated even the intermediaries at Amen Court. 'We are somewhat confused with various pseudonyms you use for the children,' Rica Hodgson wrote to her, 'and would be very grateful if you could tell us who is who' (IDAF files 13.06.77).

There was one internal battle that would not be resolved – between Collins, a man who found it hard to say 'no', and Altman, a woman for whom it was relatively easy. A summons to Amen Court for high-level discussions with the boss, Altman maintained, was excellent preparation for a career on the stage. 'I became the best heel-tapper in London. He would send for me and an hour later I would still be hanging around.' The office theory was that no deliberate discourtesy was intended, but that Collins was clearing his study of any visible paperwork on initiatives that would not meet with Altman's approval.

Altman was rigorously observant of the terms attached to the UN Trust money, particularly Enuga Reddy's insistence that none of it be used to help indigent exiles or for the families of guerrillas killed in action. The money donated directly from Sweden could be flexibly deployed but not, she was inclined to think, as flexibly as Collins had in mind. Their areas of potential friction were increased by Altman's steadfast belief that the ANC, as the liberation organisation most likely to succeed, merited most of the cash. Collins, on the other hand, was sensitive to criticism that he discriminated against the PAC.

For exiles of all factions, the Canon was known as a soft touch for 'loans', for anything from buying a pair of spectacles to doing up a house. Mathew Nkoana, a PAC dissident who was unable to make ends meet as a journalist in London, was put on a monthly retainer. Barney Desai, the PAC's official representative in London, received a rent grant. When the sons of Potlako Leballo, the exiled PAC leader, started boarding at Shoreham grammar school in 1970, Collins sent them £120 to kit themselves out at Messrs Kinch and Lock of Victoria, London (Hodgson letter to Sibeko 10.08.70). Collins's closest PAC friend, David Sibeko,[4] received a prompt £5,000 to fund a PAC initiative in New York (Sibeko letter to Collins 15.10.78). Hamilton Keke found Altman unsympathetic to a request for funds to run the PAC's London office. 'She wanted to know all the other donors to the PAC, but I refused. She was ANC. Why should I tell the ANC who our donors were? But if we asked John for help, he just got out his cheque book' (Keke interview 1992).

David Mason, who worked with Collins in Amen Court, says donations of a discreet nature came out of a 'number 2' account. 'He joked about it. People would come and see us and John would say, "for God's sake, don't let Phyllis know"' (Mason interview 1992). Collins's room for manoeuvre was enhanced by the fact that Altman could not possibly monitor all the money coming in. In the flow of contributions some would be made out to Collins personally. The cash raised by British Defence and Aid, through newspaper appeals and the occasional fund-raising spectaculars, was not normally tied to specific activities, as was money from overseas donors. So Collins was able to maintain a 'slush fund' dedicated to the cause of doing good, as he saw it, by stealth.

Through the many years of PAC complaints of favouritism towards the ANC, Collins's role in helping the movement's one indisputably great figure, Robert Sobukwe, could not be disclosed. It had begun when Sobukwe was restricted to an isolated cottage on Robben Island after serving his sentence,[5] and continued during his internal exile in Kimberley. When Sobukwe was offered a teaching fellowship at the University of Wisconsin, Collins promised to cover the family's air fares but Pretoria would not let him go. Support for Sobukwe's school-age children continued after his death from cancer in 1978.

Collins's own intimation of mortality came in September 1974 when he suffered a coronary and was out of action for several months. But he was back on the beat by the New Year, and was restored to good health by his seventieth birthday on 23 March 1975. Resplendent in a luminous green smoking jacket, he presided over a celebration dinner at Stationer's Hall, close by Amen Court. JB Priestley, Lord Longford and Adelaide Tambo were among those who spoke in his honour. They contributed to *Man of Christian Action*, a collection of essays on the several aspects of the man (Henderson 1976). The King of Sweden (who was not present) made him a Commander of the Northern Star for his work for IDAF.

Despite the grim news from inside South Africa, where resistance seemed to have all but expired, there were encouraging portents in the region. The collapse of Portugal's colonial empire and the resulting liberation of Angola and Mozambique had immediate implications for Pretoria. (IDAF's welfare grants to anti-Lisbon liberation movements included medical aid to the MPLA in Angola and help for a publication in London.) Pretoria feared that the new socialist republics on their borders would become ANC springboards for assaults on South Africa and Namibia. For a brief period Vorster fumbled with the idea of a policy of *rapprochement* with the African states to the north but he and his successor, PW Botha, chose the bloodier option, fomenting destructive civil wars in Angola and Mozambique.

And, at last, came the sound of marching Christian soldiers. In the Anglican hierarchy, Collins and Huddleston had made the running on South Africa, and if Collins's speaking engagements were largely limited to the pulpit of St Paul's, Huddleston's passionate oratory was to be heard in London, now that he was Bishop of Stepney (and vice-president of the Anti-Apartheid Movement) – though he took off once again in 1978, to become Archbishop of the Indian Ocean, based on Mauritius. But their voices were finding echoes down the line and abroad. In the early 1970s the World Council of Churches emerged as an important player with its 'Programme to Combat Racism' providing grants for social projects in South Africa and then, increasingly, to liberation movements for non-military needs in the refugee camps.

In Britain the pace was set by Christian Concern for Southern Africa (CCSA), which dodged the conservative church hierarchies by inviting Catholics, Quakers and missionary agencies to belong in their individual capacities. Investment in apartheid was a prime target, with British churches, and the Church of England in particular, holding large stocks in GEC, ICI, Rio-Tinto Zinc and other British heavyweights operating in southern Africa.

Another strand of clerical protest was directed at the banks. David Haslam, a Methodist minister in the north London borough of Brent, learned that Midland Bank was a member of a European consortium lending money to the illegal Rhodesian regime, which was forbidden under British law. Shareholders at the bank's 1974 AGM were taken aback by demonstrators holding aloft placards denouncing the loan. Influenced perhaps by the God-fearing nature of the protesters – Haslam and Pauline Webb, later vice-moderator of the World Council of Churches – the Midland promised to reform its ways. The group turned itself into 'End Loans to South Africa' (ELTSA), teaming up with the AAM to target another bank, Barclays, and its entrenched interests in South Africa. Barclays proved a tougher nut to crack but ELTSA shook up a number of boardrooms over the years by deploying a new, ethical version of insider trading. The group would buy a block of a company's shares, then split them so that a half dozen or more acquired the right to attend AGMs, where they posed prickly questions about collaboration with Pretoria. Just as the rugby protesters had run onto the pitch at Cardiff Arms Park, these Christians collared company chairmen on their home ground (Haslam interview ca.1996).

Meanwhile, Collins's friendship with Alan Paton had moved to a calmer plane. Paton had lobbied on Collins's behalf for the Nobel Peace Prize, though he rumbled on privately about the incongruity of 'recommending a man for a peace prize who encourages guerrilla fighting.' Money may not have been responsible for the full restoration of the friendship, but it helped. It may also have helped that one conduit for Paton's IDAF funds was the Afrikaner novelist Laurens van der Post, a dinner-party friend of the Collinses.

Van der Post had a system that he detailed in a letter to Collins, enclosing a copy of a letter he had sent to Paton:

> I am sorry this reads as if your contribution to our needs in Africa is a gift from me. The fact is that Alan knows where the money comes from but both he and I are breaking the law and are compelled to give ourselves some legal cover. We can only do this by pretending that the money he receives is a gift from me out of my earnings in the United States (but) instead of having my dollar earnings sent to me from America I send a portion of them to South Africa to pay into my account an equivalent of the sum of money you give me in London. No money in London is sent by me to Alan and although we know that the South African Secret Police are aware of the fact that for some years now I have been passing on money to Alan they have no means of telling, or even suspecting, it is not a straight-forward gift from me, which of course is not illegal. (Church of England archives)

On Van der Post's regular visits to South Africa, Paton gave him an account of what he had done with the funds and 'I of course again make it clear to him that, apart from a small annual contribution I myself make to his fund, the great bulk comes from you.' Van der Post assured Collins that Paton was 'eternally grateful'. The money went on trial defences. But the Liberal Party, of which Paton had been president, had been forced by the Prohibition of Political Interference Act, which outlawed multiracial political parties, to disband in 1968.

There was however, to be no *rapprochement* with Michael Scott. If anything, the animus towards Collins became more pronounced over the years. He never overcame his suspicion of the Canon's communist affiliations nor did he give up trying to crack open the IDAF system. When the SWAPO trial attorney, Joel Carlson, published his autobiography,[6] Scott wrote to Lord Campbell asking for an explanation of his role as the presumed defence funder in the case. Campbell sought Collins's advice: 'What on earth am I to say? I would not want to hurt or mislead him: presumably I cannot tell him the truth?' Collins advised him to avoid anything linking him with Defence and Aid – and not tell the truth. Some time later, Donald Woods was cross-examined on the subject by Scott at David Astor's London home. 'Scott appealed to me to blow the lid on John,' Wood recalls. 'I said I admired him, and even if there was undue communist influence, I was not going to do anything to please Vorster and Botha' (Woods interview 1997).

The doldrum years ended abruptly on 16 June 1976. The Soweto uprising was the next irreversible tightening of the ratchet after Sharpeville. The immediate objective of the 15,000 marching schoolchildren was to overturn a government ruling that half the subjects in secondary schools should be taught through the medium of Afrikaans, the language of their oppressor. The police opened fire, killing and wounding hundreds in the ensuing chaos. The recurrent resistance and school boycotts across the country shattered the myth that blacks had acquiesced in their inferior status. The wave of aggression had grown out of the 'bush colleges' created by Verwoerd to instil an education that would prepare them for their lowly place in the social order. The theory backfired, giving birth to the Black Consciousness Movement under the charismatic leadership of Steve Biko.

The Soweto uprising caught Collins unawares. From being on cruise control as far as trial defences were concerned, IDAF was suddenly besieged with requests to help defend a new generation of young black militants with names that Phyllis Altman had never heard of. Nonetheless, she and 'Mr X' managed to finance a flow of competent lawyers to the trouble areas. In the meantime, Biko's widow Ntzikie, left with two young children to bring up, was added to the letter-writers' list. She would receive her first IDAF grant, through an English correspondent, Rod Prince, within two months of her husband's murder by the Port Elizabeth security police.

IDAF helped ensure that the grim circumstances of Biko's death received maximum publicity by paying for Sydney Kentridge to represent the dead man's family at the inquest. In custody in Port Elizabeth, Biko had been chained to a wall, naked save for leg irons and handcuffs, and in no condition to do himself damage. However, one morning he was deemed to be so ill as to require immediate transfer to Pretoria. He was loaded naked into the back of a police Land Rover and driven the 700 miles, but died of brain injuries within hours of his arrival. The callous evidence of police witnesses, under Kentridge's exacting cross-examination, caused an international outcry. The pathologist, Professor Jonathan Gluckman, and Professor Neville Proctor at the Institute for Medical Research at the University of the Witwatersrand, exposed the crucial evidence of brain damage. Pretoria's Department of Information complained that Biko's 'extremely damaging' death had received greater in-depth coverage in the world's media than any South African story since Dr Christiaan Barnard's heart transplant operation.

It brought about a sea-change in medical politics. The British Medical Association (BMA), the staid doctors' trade union, pressed its counterpart in South Africa, through the World Medical Association, to take effective disciplinary action against the doctors charged with responsibility for Biko's health while in custody. When the initiative failed, the BMA instituted a boycott of its own by quitting the world body. All in all, reports of the inquest – and the Afrikaner magistrate's predictable exoneration of all the guilty men – broke through United States' apathy towards apartheid, leading to a progressive breakdown in relations between the Washington and Pretoria governments.

Collins, as usual, headed the list of hate figures. In 1978, Justice Minister Jimmy Kruger complained to Parliament that 'a few advocates and attorneys repeatedly appear in security cases.' He cited Collins's words to the United Nations about Defence and Aid fostering the morale of the internal resistance. It was, he warned, 'a deliberate subversion of our democratic legal system.' Stern measures, he indicated, were required to deal with the situation, though he omitted to mention that his government was already hard at work on the subversion of Canon Collins.[7]

Chapter 19

A FAILED COUP: CRAIG WILLIAMSON AND THE IUEF

The see-saw shuddered and the high plank of white rule began, imperceptibly, to descend, and the voteless masses edged skyward. But if there was a sense that the political landscape had been rearranged, few could have foreseen that 'Soweto' was the beginning of the end. As the world expressed alarm at the continued shooting of young, feebly-armed people, the government was jolted into action. The Ministry of Information beefed up a worldwide programme of infiltration of the organs of public opinion that would end ignominiously in the scandal of 'Muldergate'.[1] More directly, Pretoria took on its perceived enemies, the foreign organisations that were spreading 'lies' about apartheid and giving succour to those waging the internal struggle.

The man chosen to lead the counter-attack was Colonel (later General) Johan Coetzee. By South African standards, Coetzee was an old-style cop. He cherished the occasion when, as a teenage mounted policeman on duty during the 1947 royal tour of South Africa, Princess Margaret Rose requisitioned his horse, Monty, for an early morning canter. Coetzee's career break came about through his ability to take Pitman's shorthand at 200 words a minute. He was put to monitoring political meetings, so that from the 1950s he was in contact with the country's radical leadership. 'You learnt a lot about them,' he said, 'by listening to the rhythm of their speeches.' It was Coetzee who reported the speeches at the Freedom Charter convention in Kliptown that would become evidence in the Treason Trial. A studious man, he gained an honours degree on the Palestinian question.

Coetzee knew better than most that trial and welfare aid boosted the morale of the resistance and was an integral part of the struggle. And yet Defence and Aid had been banned for a decade and still the money poured in. But as long as the links in the chain remained secret, IDAF's role was secure from scrutiny in the courts. 'We knew the so-called sponsors on the letterheads didn't have the funds to send these millions,' he said. 'Many were in impecunious circumstances.' Coetzee's sense of the appropriate was outraged. He explained: 'The normal laws operative in a society were counter-balanced by this input [of IDAF defence funds]. If you commit a murder in South Africa, and you've got no money, you're defended *pro deo.* But if you commit a technical breach of the security laws, then three or four advocates would appear for you in court. These things were defended *ad nauseam*, then fought on appeal, keeping a whole portion of the justice department and the police force occupied, a drain on manpower, energy, finances' (Coetzee interview 1992).

Coetzee's particular skill was orchestrating infiltration into communist cells. An early protégé, Gerard Ludi, travelled to Moscow in a Communist Party delegation and had a part in securing Bram Fischer's life sentence. A plant in a communist cell in Durban led to the jailing and removal from the roll of attorneys of Roley Arenstein, an IDAF defender. Coetzee, however, was aware that the strategy of picking off individual lawyers in the pay of IDAF was of limited value. What was required was a man or mechanism, or both, capable of penetrating the decision-making process in London. But if, from afar, IDAF seemed too difficult to break into, there was another option.

Craig Williamson combined membership of the students' representative council at the University of the Witwatersrand with being a police agent. The son of a Johannesburg businessman, he was large, bearded and never at a loss for words. He served two years in the police service before going to university. Williamson would explain to radical acquaintances that the police experience had helped him appreciate the true awfulness of the system from the inside.

In fact, he retained his police rank while under cover as a student 'radical', in which capacity he rose to become full-time vice-president of the National Union of South African Students (NUSAS). NUSAS was a non-racial students' organisation, which in the 1960s was one of the few lawful anti-apartheid groups operating inside South Africa. In 1974, the government declared NUSAS an 'affected organisation', prohibiting it from receiving money from abroad. This did no harm to Williamson's radical aura.

Williamson's handler was Coetzee, who set about toning up his left-wing credentials. Williamson, the concerned student leader, accompanied the Progressive Party MP, Helen Suzman, on a mission to Justice Minister Kruger to complain about legal abuses. Williamson, the underground activist, ran an escape route into Botswana for students on the run from the police – the group was composed entirely of undercover policemen. Then, with faultless timing, the International University Exchange Fund (IUEF) in Geneva offered an opening.

The IUEF had much in common with IDAF – Scandinavian backers, a culture of secrecy, the unorthodox transfer of funds into South Africa, and a driving ambition to become the biggest of the anti-apartheid relief agencies. Under the vigorous leadership of Lars-Gunnar Eriksson, a former Swedish student leader and trade unionist, the IUEF established itself as an organisation respected by the liberation movements it served. In addition to supplying 3,000 scholarships and bursaries to refugees, mainly southern African but also from Latin America, it was covertly funding a range of publications, arts projects and training schemes inside South Africa. The Black Consciousness Movement ran many of these.

Eriksson made little secret of his desire to absorb IDAF into his operation – with Collins not long past his first coronary and without an obvious successor, this seemed a plausible possibility. At times, Collins did not appear averse to the prospect. He and Eriksson got on well enough, even committing themselves to a joint venture, the Foundation for the Relief and Education of Exiles, or FREE. Collins saw it as a means of helping those in need who might slip between the provision of IDAF and IUEF. Neville Rubin was once again the fixer, with Hugh Lewin the link between London and Geneva. Altman knew nothing about it – until one morning she opened 'a fat letter' addressed to Lewin from Eriksson containing the minutes of the first meeting of FREE, naming Collins and the Swede as joint chairmen. She 'went off her head with rage'. She saw it as a prelude to an Eriksson take-over. Besides, she said, any organisation with the word 'free' in its name must be anti-communist. FREE was not heard of again at Amen Court (Altman interview 1992; Lewin interview 1993).

The IUEF was more effectively tuned in to Europe's political establishment than was Collins. Dame Judith Hart, Overseas Development Minister to Prime Minister Jim Callaghan, had previously served on IUEF's London committee – Collins was also a member at the time. Now she incurred Collins's wrath by refusing government aid to IDAF while putting in place a handsome annual grant of £250,000 to the IUEF, most of it earmarked for Rhodesia. The Geneva fund was considered to have greater practical experience in these matters. And, she added for good measure, its accounting procedures were superior to IDAF's (Beer interview 1992; Collins 1992: 358; Altman interview 1992).

In reality, the shambolic state of IUEF's accounting was one reason why Coetzee and Williamson were about to find it a pushover. In South Africa, BOSS had already achieved a comprehensive penetration of IUEF's internal covert funding system. It had fewer cut-outs than IDAF, so that much of its accounting was actually in police hands. One IUEF conduit was 'Southern Futures Anstalt', a company registered in Vaduz, Liechtenstein. Once again it was the idea of Eriksson's confidant, Neville Rubin. But disbursements to South African front organisations were largely in the hands of Coetzee's army of student agents, among them Williamson's sister, Lisa, and Karl Edwards, who headed up an IUEF front organisation in Port Elizabeth, the Environment Development Agency (EDA). Edwards, like Williamson, was an officer in the security police. By now Williamson himself had embarked on a programme of ingratiation with Lars-Gunnar Eriksson.

By the time NUSAS had been prohibited from receiving overseas funds, Williamson was felicitously placed as the union's finance officer in its Cape Town headquarters. He won plaudits by ensuring that important IUEF projects survived the ban. This he did by setting up a funding channel through Swaziland using a bank account of John Daniel, a former NUSAS president in exile in that country. Eriksson was able to thank Williamson in person when the spy came to Europe in October 1975 on a NUSAS delegation. He took Williamson to London and made him known in the exile scene. This included meeting a group of young ANC members in London.

Eriksson and Williamson met again in Botswana in July 1976, when Eriksson was on a tour of inspection in the region. Williamson emerged from the encounter with 'a three-quarters promise' of a job. Now a piece of pantomime was required. With Coetzee's assistance, a suitably theatrical departure was arranged. When the police raided his flat and seized his passport, Williamson 'escaped' across the border in the company of a harassed student, Eric Abraham, who could bear witness to the terrifying ordeal he had gone through. By January 1977, Craig Williamson, aged 31, captain in the South African security police, was installed as Eriksson's information officer with special responsibility for IUEF's internal South African programmes (Williamson interviews 1992 and 1993).

Williamson quickly made himself part of the furniture. He was an easy-going colonial, he had a personable wife (Ingrid, a Danish-South African), and he talked cogently about 'the struggle' back home. Casting around at his good fortune, he must have felt like a gold prospector deciding which glinting seam to work: ANC, PAC, Black Consciousness, IDAF, churches, students, United Nations funds based in Switzerland. He prepared to conduct a 'reasonably intelligent destabilisation operation of this international community', playing organisations and individuals off against one another. 'You can't go in as one person and destabilise the whole thing, but you do know who hates who, who is jealous of who, who is gambling or sleeping with whom, who is trying to get money from the same source, and then you start to play and let the momentum cause whatever happens.' The 'game' is a favourite Williamson word. There was a fine line between under-cover information gatherer and *agent provocateur*.

From the early 1970s, Eriksson had been happy to establish clear water between the IUEF and the ANC and place more of its funds at the disposal of black consciousness students and projects. The South African police had been caught off balance by these articulate young blacks filling the vacuum left by the seemingly dormant ANC. One of its brightest stars, Okgopontse Tiro, had fled to Botswana after upheavals at the Turfloop black ('bush') college in the northern Transvaal. IUEF gave him a job in Gaborone. But mail to Botswana was still routed through Johannesburg. In 1974 Tiro was blown up as he opened a parcel that carried the markings of the IUEF in Geneva. The Botswana government noted that Tiro had 'incurred the displeasure of certain powerful circles in South Africa'. It is the earliest known case of Pretoria's successful use of a letter bomb.[2]

Once Williamson had copied the key to Eriksson's filing cabinet, he bombarded his handler with sheaves of photocopies on IUEF activities. Couriers carried back the lists of 2,000 South African, Namibian and Zimbabwean scholarship holders, and, as a bonus, the students who had fled Chile, Argentina or Nicaragua. These were of no special interest to Williamson but his superiors might have circulated the names of young dissidents to the obnoxious regimes from which they had fled. They were the small change of the intelligence market. 'Intelligence is like a business,' said Williamson, 'and information is its currency. We tell the Argentinians something if they tell the Israelis something who tell us something.' One piece of information seems to have been used with lethal effect.

In the summer of 1977 it was known in restricted exile circles that Steve Biko, father of black consciousness and public enemy number one, was planning to leave South Africa for a meeting with Oliver Tambo and other exiled nationalist leaders, in west Africa, though possibly in Botswana. The IUEF, having funded Biko's projects for several years, was party to that knowledge. Coetzee recalled Williamson writing in one of his reports that Biko would take part in an attempt to form a united front of the three major movements. Williamson, more cagey, did not recall tipping Pretoria off, though he admitted 'we knew about it the whole time. I just kept telling them what was going on.' So when the Port Elizabeth police arrested Biko at a roadblock was it to prevent him going abroad? Or was it carried out on their own initiative, for some routine purpose? The two men believe he was arrested on other grounds. But Biko's death did nip in the bud any attempt to bring the liberation movements closer. On the other hand, Biko's assassination raised the world's awareness of apartheid. A martyr, caused for whatever reason, mused General Coetzee, 'is a nail in your coffin'.

After Soweto, IUEF became the largest funder of Black Consciousness. Eriksson, like many Swedish Social Democrats, was alarmed by the ANC's heavy military dependence on Moscow. But from the summer of 1978 Williamson, now elevated to deputy-director, pursued a more adventurous course, manipulating events rather than simply monitoring them. He contrived to steer Eriksson back to favouring the ANC on the grounds that, whatever its imperfections, it still seemed to be the one nationalist organisation with real stamina. Eriksson was persuaded that his protégé enjoyed 'the full confidence of the ANC'. This may have been stretching it a bit, but Williamson was undeniably friendly with some influential ANC officials.

The ANC had good reason to be grateful for Williamson's supportive role in the about-turn. Here was an exiled liberation movement down on its luck suddenly granted the capacity to deliver bursaries to many hundreds of sometimes politically uncommitted refugees. They knew the red-bashing Eriksson was not responsible, and Williamson was not one to hide his light under a bushel. To Abdul Minty, visiting Geneva after the policy change, Williamson appeared 'jubilant, as if he was the ANC rep in the office'. Other IDAF visitors were surprised at the Release Mandela and *Umkhonto-we-Sizwe* posters on his office wall (Michanek interview 1992). Williamson's currency within the ANC rose enormously. Thomas Nkobi, the ANC treasurer-general, was by all accounts charmed by him (Michanek interview 1992), and Aziz Pahad, who ran ANC security in London, came to know him, as did the up-and-coming Thabo Mbeki. Indeed, Mbeki's wife Zanele was employed by the IUEF, running its office in Lusaka, Zambia (Nkobi interview 1993). On frequent visits to London, the spy mingled with ANC acquaintances.

But Williamson had already worked with the ANC while in South Africa. Ronnie Kasrils was a member of the London committee (with Joe Slovo, Yusuf Dadoo, head of the SA Communist Party, and Rica Hodgson's husband, Jack) which from 1967 ran underground operations inside the Republic. Williamson, on his earlier visit to London, was passed on to the committee by the ANC local committee chief UK representative, Reg September. 'We did not trust him, he seemed to be under such tight self-control. He was clearly a guy with tremendous nerve, but no emotion and that really put me off.' But, Kasrils recalled, he had 'terrific contacts'. Kasrils set up a means of secret communications. 'I taught him how to use leaflet bombs. It was at the Russell Hotel. It was simple schoolboy stuff, a couple of teaspoons of black powder – potassium permanganate with charcoal and sulphur – taught me by Jack Hodgson. It was an invention of Jack's. You put it in the bottom of a bucket and it blows up leaflets. Williamson was terrified. Karl Edwards was there too and he took back to South Africa ANC leaflets and comic books, to be reproduced there.'

Kasrils said Williamson, by now in Geneva, sent cuttings from the Johannesburg *Sunday Express* reporting that hundreds of leaflets had circulated in townships. 'I showed them to Slovo and we laughed because comics had been distributed for many years and had never been commented on. It made us more suspicious (Kasrils interview 1993).

But Williamson did not entirely escape suspicion in other quarters. Horst Kleinschmidt, an exile who was about to join IDAF, harboured reservations from their university days. He had no hard evidence of Williamson's involvement with the security police but he voiced his suspicions to Frene Ginwala in the ANC London office. 'Stop maligning this Williamson guy,' he was told. Word got back to Eriksson, who warned Kleinschmidt to quit spreading rumours about his deputy. 'He said he could make life difficult for me,' Kleinschmidt recalled.

In retrospect, Williamson cherished his role in the switching of IUEF support to the ANC, thus 'knee-haltering the Black Consciousness Movement'. But even if he did write a persuasive memorandum, he most certainly exaggerated his influence. When he left South Africa, black consciousness was on the crest of a wave. By mid-1978 it was running out of steam and Eriksson knew (in the words of the commission of inquiry report into the IUEF) that the ANC had begun to assume 'a greater paramountcy' in the struggle. The decision to make the ANC the primary beneficiary of the exchange fund was taken by the donors, who in turn were influenced by national student bodies, governments, the United Nations, as well as the IUEF. A year earlier, Tambo had been given red-carpet treatment in Stockholm with an unprecedented £1 million in extra funding for the ANC.

As Williamson set out on 'Operation Daisy', his spymaster had called for 'very close co-operation' between IDAF and the exchange fund in an effort to discover how the money came and went. But Williamson found that IDAF was run like a communist cell. 'For the same reason that we never had great success against the internal structures of the Communist Party, we found IDAF difficult to penetrate. It's a family. How do you infiltrate a family?' The answer seemed to be, marry into it. Eriksson hoped at one stage that he would succeed the Canon as head of IDAF and so bring about a merger of the two funds. He had powerful friends among the Social Democrats at home, and he played on the Scandinavian fear of communism. In 1975, he had written to the trade unionist and future General-Secretary of Socialist International, Bernt Carlsson, warning that IDAF was about to fall to 'the enemy' (his term), namely Altman, Hodgson, Barry Feinberg and Abdul Minty – though the latter was not a communist and had recently been appointed by Collins as his liaison to foreign governments, funded by a Swedish grant.

But the Canon was not one for forced marriages. If he

seemed 'naïve' to Eriksson, it was simply his courteous way of giving the brush off. 'Please believe that I am not in the least worried about our relationship with each other', he wrote to Eriksson, 'at worst... there may be misimpressions from time to time, particularly as it is no doubt to the interest of too many people to keep us apart' (Collins letter to Eriksson 14.02.76). Tensions were simmering before Williamson's arrival. Now the spy stoked the fire. He would whisper to Nkobi and other visiting ANC officials: 'Who is this bloody Canon who controls all the money? You guys should control it.' The commission of inquiry found that Williamson had been manoeuvring the IUEF into a competitive position with IDAF in the area of legal aid, 'although it was not an area in which the IUEF properly had a role to play.' On one occasion, the IUEF sent to South Africa some of the defence funds in a NUSAS student trial, and was then paid back by IDAF. Egged on by his assistant, Eriksson was able to complain to the donors that IDAF's secrecy led to double funding, the curse of aid agencies. The essence of the Williamson strategy was to put IDAF on the defensive with its donors and with the ANC. Then Collins would be forced to appease his critics by agreeing to joint meetings and information sharing with IUEF, thus avoiding wasteful duplication of effort. Coetzee liked the sound of it. But how could Collins be persuaded to see this inescapable logic?

Confident of his persuasive charm, Williamson decided to take the direct route, not to Collins, but to the toughest nut at IDAF, Phyllis Altman. One day she received a call from the ANC office in London suggesting she meet Williamson, a good friend of the struggle, who was passing through London with his wife en route to Spain. Altman, who had already taken a number of 'rather fishy' calls from Williamson in Geneva in which he had made ostensibly helpful suggestions about trial defences that IDAF might be interested in, responded with a 'sorry, too busy.' Williamson tried again when the couple were on their way back from Spain. Altman, seeming to relent, said OK, make it the steps of St Paul's. Instead, she sent Kleinschmidt, by now working as a fundraiser at IDAF, to say she was unable to keep the appointment. 'Williamson was furious,' Altman later recalled. 'He phoned me from Geneva to say he had come especially to meet me. I said, "send the bill and we'll pay it." He didn't' (Altman interview 1992).

Eriksson wrote to Collins complaining that Altman had been rude to his deputy. Collins showed the letter to Altman, hoping to smooth matters. Altman said she was not prepared to discuss IDAF's business with Williamson, but if it was a problem, 'OK, dismiss me.' Altman did not know that Williamson was a spy but she had gleaned enough from Kleinschmidt and others to sense something odd about his background. She saw no reason to give him the time of day, much less discuss IDAF's inner mechanisms.

In the autumn of 1979, a meeting was arranged under the auspices of the Danish International Development Agency (DANIDA). Eriksson and Williamson, Collins and Altman were present and their hosts hoped they would put an end to the damaging rivalry. Collins was asked to enter into the new co-operative spirit by opening his files to ensure there was no double funding. The Canon might originally have been slow to pick up on the Williamson threat, but now he was rock solid. 'We do trials and welfare,' he declared, 'you chaps do bursaries.' There was no good reason why either organisation should compromise its confidentiality. Collins was the soul of amiability but it was obvious there would be no marriage ceremony. Williamson, however, derived some encouragement from the Danes, who threatened to review their grants to IDAF if co-operation did not improve. If the Swedes could be persuaded to make a similar threat, Williamson felt he might still be in business.

The end was not as the mastermind in Pretoria had planned. In December 1979 Williamson was in London, en route to Moscow for a connecting Aeroflot flight to Angola. On the following Sunday, the *Observer* newspaper ran a double-page exposé of BOSS by a defecting operative, Arthur McGiven. When, says Williamson, the 'counter intelligence guys learnt McGiven was living with a man, they went bananas. He was abused, told he was a security risk, so that, unable to stomach any more, he packed a suitcase of documents – including stuff relating to our operations – and took the overnight plane to

London.' Williamson and McGiven had been fellow spies on the University of the Witwatersrand students' representative council before McGiven moved to the BOSS overseas communications section. The *Observer* made no mention of Williamson, but the following week an oblique reference to the IUEF hinted at more disclosures in the pipeline.

Back in Geneva, Williamson, fearing that exposure was only days away, cleared his desk and packed his bags. Now Coetzee arrived in Geneva with a last-ditch plan. Although Williamson's erratic behaviour had aroused suspicions in the office, Coetzee was of the opinion that all was not lost. He instructed his man to set up a meeting with Eriksson at a hotel in Zurich. There Williamson confirmed Eriksson's worst fears by acknowledging that he was indeed an apartheid spy. He invited Eriksson to discuss the situation with his superior – and on cue the demon spymaster walked into the room.

'Mr Eriksson,' Coetzee intoned, by way of introduction, 'you and we are both fighting communism,' then proceeded to outline a possible course of action. He hoped that with the Swede's continued support Williamson might still ride out any doubts about him. The 'deal' he proposed was to keep Williamson on at IUEF for another six months, long enough for his man to progress his ANC contacts to the desired level, after which, Coetzee promised, Williamson would discreetly depart. In the course of their conversation Eriksson discovered that Coetzee knew a lot about his drinking habits, his rocky marriage, money lent to the Polish representative of the World Peace Council for a disarmament seminar but gambled away in a casino, and the creative book-keeping to mislead Swedish and Danish auditors. 'The word is blackmail', Coetzee said later, 'but this is the world of intelligence.' Eriksson claimed that death threats were made against him, though Coetzee and Williamson have no recollection of this aspect of the encounter.

To his credit, Eriksson chose disclosure as the least bad way out of his dilemma. He rang Hugh Lewin, then on the *Guardian* in London. In a state of advanced agitation, Eriksson drove through the night to meet up with Lewin and Walter Schwarz, the paper's French correspondent, at Charles de

Gaulle Airport in Paris. Their story 'How the Spy was "Blown"' appeared in the newspaper on 23 January 1980.

So Williamson came in from the anti-apartheid cold, to be elevated to the rank of major and hailed as a hero by white South Africa. For a while the standard agency picture of him tweaking his hat in a manner reminiscent of Orson Welles in *The Third Man* appeared in newspapers around the world. He made one starring appearance in court, giving the evidence that secured the conviction of Dr Renfrew Christie, a university lecturer, for supplying information about nuclear installations to Frene Ginwala in London. Puzzlingly, there were few further courtroom appearances, prompting some to wonder whether Coetzee was protecting other implants operating abroad. In the wash of publicity about evil deeds in the world of BOSS, Phyllis Altman's cousin rang to plead with her to watch her step, promising she would call every morning. Altman said not to worry. 'Either I'll answer the phone or I'll be dead.'

Although it had been no part of their original intention, Coetzee and Williamson did destroy the IUEF. It was wound up in 1981 after a thumbs-down by the high level commission of inquiry, funded by its donors and chaired by a former Canadian communications minister, David MacDonald. In a wide-ranging indictment of IUEF, it found that the Southern Futures link designed to fund 'inside' programmes in South Africa had been used 'to mask improper use of funds by the organisation'. One of IUEF's loans, the commission confirmed, had been 'spent in casinos'. There could scarcely have been more uncomfortable reading for Dame Judith Hart. Out of a job after the 1979 British general election, she had asked Eriksson for a grant of £12,000 to continue her work on Third World development. She pestered the IUEF London director, Chris Beer, who discussed it with Williamson. Dr Beer wrote to Eriksson suggesting £3,000, 'to be in strict confidence'. He added a PS: 'I'm going to be in the s... if we can't do this.' It was done (Craig Williamson files). The correspondence was duly sent to Pretoria.

IDAF refused to give evidence to the inquiry. 'We understand,' noted the report, 'that not much was given away to

Williamson that was confidential about IDAF's activities.' Had the inquiry heard from Boudewijn Sjollema, a senior official at the World Council of Churches, it would have learnt that plans were afoot for the IUEF to make a room available to the ANC in its Geneva offices. 'I was asked by Ruth Mompati [ANC representative] if the WCC would support the ANC in paying the rent,' said Sjollema, who later became an IDAF trustee (Sjollema e-mail to author 2004).

Looking back, Williamson said it was his intention to monitor IDAF, not destroy it – 'because they would just have created another structure.' This was disingenuous. Had the security services pierced the barriers of secrecy and the more committed lawyers been convicted and stripped of their right to practise, only the foolhardy would have been willing to appear in political trials again, even if a new funding route could have been devised.

There is no doubt Williamson had the degree of ruthlessness required to destroy IDAF. Two years later, and a further rung up the police ladder, he became involved in security police operations to eliminate certain of its opponents. Years later he applied to the Truth and Reconciliation Commission for amnesty for his role in the killing of Ruth First, wife of the MK leader Joe Slovo, in her office in Maputo; and the attempt on the life of the ANC's Marius Schoon in Angola – in whose house in South Africa he had once been a guest. Schoon was not at home but his wife, Jeanette, and six-year-old daughter, Katryn, died in the blast. A former henchman later claimed that Williamson was the brains behind the assassination of the Swedish Prime Minister, Olof Palme, in February 1986. The allegation remains unproven.

Chapter 20

AROUND THE WORLD

Acquaintances of the Collins family walking along Ave Maria Lane in the spring of 1979 might have been excused a double take at the sight of a Conservative Party election poster in a window at 2 Amen Court. Collins, weary of Labour's broken promises on South Africa, had decided to teach his old party a lesson. 'I'm not a Tory,' he told a reporter, 'but I thought, let's see what a woman can do.' There came the inevitable let-down but, he admitted, at least Margaret Thatcher never promised anything different (*Evening Standard* 5.11.81).

Labour had governed Britain for all but four of IDAF's first 15 years. Many Labour back-benchers, and several who became ministers, had enjoyed comradely associations with Collins through CND marches and fund-raisers for South Africa. So he had good reason to expect that Defence and Aid would benefit materially from an administration led by Harold Wilson, a man he considered a friend. But he was soon marvelling at Labour's capacity for promising the moon in opposition, only to imitate the Tories when in government.

Even before the final count in the October 1964 general election, as Labour returned to power after 12 years, Collins sent a hand-written letter to Wilson: 'A little note, before the result is clear, to congratulate you…' He followed up with a package containing a lengthy statement of IDAF's achievements and an LP (long-playing gramophone record) of Mandela's speech from the dock. Wilson replied with a 'Dear John'. He was 'most grateful for the copy of "Why I am ready to die"; this is clearly one of the classic speeches of all time. I look forward to an opportunity of some peace and quiet to hear it at leisure.' If that was a subtle put-down,

Collins did not give up. After Christmas he was granted ten minutes of the PM's time, only to be told that the government was unable to contribute to an 'unofficial fund'. Furthermore, Barbara Castle and Lord Caradon, now ministers, would have to resign from the Defence and Aid committee.

No doubt, once Wilson had encountered the complexities of office he found the Canon's plangent certainties less congenial. The prime minister needed to take account of a Foreign Office that refused to smile on unelected clerics such as Collins, Scott and Huddleston challenging orthodox policy and, at times, setting the agenda in sensitive areas. Anguished debates in the House of Commons pointed up the equation of cancelled arms sales set against jobs lost to Labour-voting trade unionists. There would be some reduction in the flow of weapons to South Africa but it did not add up to the sanctions Wilson had conjured up in the election campaign when he condemned 'this bloody trade in arms'. Once in Downing Street, he would not have been pleased to be reminded of the pledge.

But there were other, unstated, reasons why Collins did not find favour. A confidential Foreign Office (FO) memo (21.12.64; FO371/177072) to Oliver Wright, the prime minister's private secretary, offered the lowdown that was included in the briefing to Wilson for his meeting with Collins. It reported that a Defence and Aid committee in South Africa had just appointed as its secretary 'the wife of a man recently sentenced to seven years' imprisonment for sabotage activities'. At the same time, the London organisation was closely linked to the African National Congress and the Anti-Apartheid Movement, 'in both of which known Communists are active.' Furthermore, South African communist sympathisers had 'succeeded in working their way into the administrative office'. The briefing named 'Mrs Rica Hodgson and Mrs Phyllis Altman'. There was also a mention for John Lang, the Johannesburg attorney, 'who, as we and the South Africans know, embezzled £7,000 out of a Widows' Trust Fund and is smuggling explosives into South Africa'. This was a reference to an African Resistance Movement trial in South Africa in which Lang was said to have sent explosives on a passenger liner to Cape Town that were used in sabotage attacks (Stephenson letter 14.12.66).

The details of the FO memo had been lifted from a briefing by Sir Hugh Stephenson, Britain's man in Pretoria. Stephenson had also quoted a former South African ambassador to London as saying that the funds would to go the ANC, 'who openly advocated violence'. The briefing incensed the new Lord Chancellor, Gerald Gardiner. As a former sponsor of the Defence and Aid Fund, he told the FO, the allegations in Pretoria telegram no. 485 should not be allowed to circulate in London and New York without Canon Collins being given an opportunity to refute them. But the FO was adamant, calling in Lord Walston, one of its junior ministers – and, incidentally, a trustee of one of Collins's secret trusts – to placate and persuade the Lord Chancellor. So Collins never heard of this very real objection to his organisation.

The Christian Action committee discussed 'at some length' whether the refusal to help should be made public, presumably in the hope of shaming Wilson. 'Council notes,' the minutes reported ominously, 'in connection with the letter from HMG, that in an extreme position the Chairman might have to recommend publication of a letter and the Council is prepared for such a situation.' It didn't happen.

South Africa's banning of Defence and Aid 18 months later brought on another flurry of Foreign Office messaging. Ambassador Stephenson had mellowed slightly. He reported that the Fund was 'still doing important work in the defence field', notably in the magistrates' courts, 'where arbitrary decisions influenced by political considerations were more likely to be reached than they were in the Supreme Court'. He pondered why Vorster had not given leaders of Defence and Aid the chance to defend themselves in court. He had heard that the South Africans 'did not wish to waste informers by blowing them in court.' But then he returned to his familiar theme of communist infiltration and to reports that funds made available to Defence and Aid in Johannesburg were being used for 'purposes other than aid to families of persons detained'. Again, Collins was not given the chance to refute the allegations (Stephenson letter 26.03.66; FO371/188131).

There was a bright spot in the shape of a 'Dear John' letter from the new Foreign Secretary, George Brown, with news that the government proposed to contribute £25,000 to the UN Trust Fund. Collins, aware that Enuga Reddy would ensure at least half came to IDAF's coffers, was delighted. An initial commitment usually presaged regular annual contributions. But this was Britain. A grudging second – and final – British contribution to the New York fund was another dozen years off.

Collins found that the trade unions, which provided the bulk of Labour's finances, also flattered to deceive. While a few individual unions practised what they preached on South Africa, these tended to be of the minuscule variety. Tobacco workers, some at Anton Rupert's Rothmans factory, urged a boycott. Musicians and actors – many of whom were 'resting' and could have done with the money – turned down offers to perform in South Africa's segregated theatres. Alan Sapper's television and cinema technicians' refusal to work on films destined for South Africa caused some cultural deprivation in white circles – though when American actors later had 'Dallas' and 'Cagney and Lacey' banned, black and white alike experienced withdrawal symptoms.

The artistic world had long been a source of hope for Collins, going back to the sixties when Yehudi Menuhin, Dusty Springfield, Adam Faith and other international artists stopped performing for apartheid. Actresses of the distinction of Dame Peggy Ashcroft and Dame Sybil Thorndike contributed to Defence and Aid campaigns. It helped with the public profile but was no substitute for the political shove of union muscle. The Technical, Administrative and Supervisory Section (TASS) was a middle-weight union that had some success in dissuading its engineer and technician members from emigrating to work in South Africa's infant arms and nuclear industries. But in international matters the big battalions tended to follow the lead of the Trades Union Congress, which in turn kept in line with the Foreign Office. In 1970, largely as a consequence of vigorous lobbying by Ethel de Keyser at the AAM, the unions and constituency activists got together at the Labour conference to push through a motion supporting the liberation struggle. Then the dust settled and it was pretty much business as usual.

When Wilson returned to Downing Street in 1974, Collins once more allowed himself to hope for state acknowledgement of his work. British foreign policy in the 1970s was dominated by Rhodesia, milestoned by Wilson's very public attempts to outsmart the rebel leader, Ian Smith. But having Smith as the enemy did not persuade Labour to look kindly on Collins, despite IDAF's wide-scale trial defence and welfare support inside that country. When Lord Caradon, a former Labour ambassador to the UN, told Collins that the government could hardly be expected to contribute to a fund that supported violence, Collins was outraged. It was, he said, like accusing the Red Cross of supporting war. It was a measure of Collins's frustration that in January 1978 he called in the *Sunday Times* diplomatic correspondent, Nicholas Carroll, to voice his bafflement. Under the headline, 'Rebuff for race victim fund', Collins argued that the plight of black Rhodesians in the courts and in the proliferating prison camps was 'a British responsibility... yet it is left to other countries to find the money to help these unhappy Africans.'

His efforts eventually netted a quite small fish. From the opposition benches, the younger Jim Callaghan used to deliver lacerating perorations on misrule in South West Africa. As foreign secretary and, from 1976, prime minister, the tone was more measured. Indeed, Callaghan's foreign secretary, David Owen, though on the right of the party, was viewed as more responsive on African issues. It was Owen who set up the Bingham inquiry that exposed Britain's role in hindering the enforcement of oil sanctions against the Rhodesian regime after UDI. Collins, accompanied by Phyllis Altman and the Liberal leader Jeremy Thorpe, did meet Callaghan in his office. The prime minister pointedly manoeuvred his chair to avoid eye contact with Collins and spoke, 'rather defensively', to Phyllis Altman: 'He said he hadn't had a direct appeal from us, though we had sent one,' she recalled. 'But he would consider the UN Trust Fund if we sent a memo, which we did' (Altman interview 1992). In 1979, the government announced a £50,000 donation to the UN fund earmarked for Rhodesia. Provision was made – and delivered – in the summer supplementary estimates, by which time Margaret Thatcher had become the unlikely benefactor.

Other initiatives at this time were given a better airing. A group of Labour MPs, prompted by an Enuga Reddy reminder to Mike Terry, new secretary of the Anti-Apartheid Movement, signed a card for Nelson Mandela's birthday on 18 July 1978. When the South African embassy refused to pass it on, Callaghan sent his good wishes from the floor of the House of Commons, the first British statesman to publicly acknowledge the forgotten leader on Robben Island. Students and academics followed up by nominating Mandela for the vacant post of chancellor of the University of London. Though outvoted by loyalist supporters of Princess Anne, the Queen's daughter, it was a reminder of Mandela's rising esteem in the West. He was made a freeman of Glasgow and other British cities. Camden Borough Council renamed the street where the AAM had its London office Mandela Street.

•

Elsewhere, governments held a more generous view of John Collins. In 1977, the UN fund received a total of $1,300,000 from 45 countries. It would have been bigger had Enuga Reddy not asked Stockholm to send more of the cash direct to IDAF so the input would not appear 'too Swedish'. It has been suggested that the British government could not contribute to Collins's organisation, either directly or through the UN, because the Cold War parrot perching on its shoulder precluded any truck with the ANC, a movement armed by the Soviet bloc. But the roster of UN fund contributors included states with similar strategic concerns, notably France, Japan, Austria, the Federal Republic of Germany and, from 1978, the United States. They presumably understood that some of the money would be used to defend nationalists, among them communists, bent on the overthrow of apartheid.

Of the donor countries, Collins's natural preference was for Sweden, which over the years would contribute more than the entire UN Trust Fund combined. But it was not simply the money. He enjoyed the blend of acceptance that

Stockholm had to offer. His host and 'fifth son', Per Wästberg, had emerged as one of Sweden's most respected personalities, editor of *Dagens Nyheter* and, later, president of the writers' union, International PEN. He was the go-between for Collins in negotiations with Ernst Michanek, who ran overseas aid. Though conservative by instinct, Michanek once said: 'We knew pretty well that the British government was not in sympathy with our "subversive activities" in South Africa. But it is difficult to understand how getting legal defence for a man when there is no public defender can be called subversive' (Michanek interview 1992).

To be anti-apartheid was popular, almost fashionable, among ordinary Swedes – the country's 3,500 Lutheran churches held an annual collection for the cause – but, with the Soviet-occupied Baltic states across the sea, they, too, were touchy about communism. When the Soviet Union invaded Czechoslovakia in 1968, the ANC's Secretary-General, Duma Nokwe, sent Moscow a message of fraternal solidarity. It was the official line of the South African Communist Party (SACP), to which Nokwe belonged. Tambo was horrified. After all, Olof Palme had cut his political teeth in Prague. 'We did understand they needed friends wherever they could find them,' said Michanek, 'but the connections between the ANC and the Soviet Union were matters of some concern to us, and to me in particular.' The Social Democrats suspended aid to the ANC. Nokwe lost his job and his position on the ANC executive. It took four years and much diplomacy by Tambo – 'the embodiment of all that was good in the liberation struggle,' said Michanek – before funding was restored (Michanek interview 1992).

Few Swedes had any notion of their country's deeper connection with Collins. A brief press scare about a Swiss bank account with ties to IDAF came to nothing: otherwise, not a whisper. Michanek buried the balance sheets in a larger budget. He reported verbally to the Parliament's foreign relations committee, which accepted that it could not be told everything. When fielding MPs' questions at the budget board, 'my answer would have been very short if anyone had asked deeper questions, like technicalities on the transfer of money. No one did. They realised that receiving this money might have been dangerous.' As did his own Swedish International Development Agency (SIDA) board, whose directors included farmers, industrialists and conservative politicians, as well as those friendlier to African liberation. The SIDA committee for refugees and liberation movements – its 18 members drawn from youth and women's groups, the unions, churches, temperance groups and politicians – knew more about the funding, though not the routes it went by. 'As far as I knew,' Michanek said, 'they kept the secret.'

The Nordics worked hard at a united front, adopting, in 1978, a programme of action against South Africa with the focus on economic sanctions. The Danes later became the first, and only, country to enforce full sanctions. Norway was second to Sweden in its aggregate aid to IDAF, but its *per capita* contribution was larger. Norwegians could be forgiven for being irked by the limelight enjoyed by their larger neighbour. It was not simply their resistance to Nazi occupation, though the experience heightened their sympathy for victims of Africa's own racist ideologues. In the matter of private contributions to the world's poor, Norwegians were in the premier league, a product of their Christian and socialist make-up. In 1974, after a fraught national debate, Norway decided not to buy the French Crotal rocket system with its 85 per cent South African input. That year the Lutheran synod offered support to the ANC, with the justification that an oppressed people had the right to resort to sabotage. In time, as North Sea oil revenues delivered hefty foreign exchange surpluses, the 'Kuwait of Scandinavia's' contributions increased substantially.

In Holland, 'kith and kin' played its part, though differently from the British experience. The theological debate had begun in the fifties, as Reformed Church clergy wondered at the predilection of the South African *dominees* for the fundamentalist interpretation of the scriptural 'hewers-of-wood, drawers-of-water'. Half a dozen anti-apartheid groups, of varied church, communist and liberal strains, kept the debate livelier than anywhere else in mainland Europe, and drove the Afrikaners to distraction. The Defence and

Aid Fund Nederland, DAFN, was founded in 1965, after the government had supported Collins with the grant that so angered Pretoria. Conservative groups questioned the decision, but DAFN presented itself as a non-political relief organisation and did not campaign openly. It attracted church-goers, slightly conservative people who were wary of declaring open support for the ANC. A Dutch delegate, the war heroine Professor Gisella van der Molen, told a sceptical IDAF annual conference that they should love not only 'non-whites', but also whites, 'whom we hope to enlighten and to show that their basic premises are wrong'. Collins went to Holland to meet Queen Juliana. He was advised not to mention money, and did not, and afterwards regretted it. It hardly mattered; by 1980, the Dutch committee was raising £153,000 a year.

The Swiss committee complained habitually about poor communications with London. Ironically, for a nation that revered secrecy in its banking sector, the Swiss could not stomach Phyllis Altman's veiled reporting on the use of their funds. The committee chairman, Gilbert Rist, asked how they could be expected to raise money year after year 'and all we have is a receipt?' In 1983 the Swiss made a final payment of £20,000 to IDAF, then went off to do their own thing; effectively, by all accounts. Their *Commission de Parrainage Scolaire*, a programme to adopt South African families and help their children through school, was praised by Altman.

West Germany was an unrealised Collins' goal, partly because over the years its governments were as ambivalent about apartheid as those in Britain. Initially the prospects had seemed good. The Federal Republic made its first Trust Fund grant in 1974. A Defence and Aid committee was on the verge of being formed in Bonn, when the civil servant involved was accused of spying for East Germany and the project was killed off.

The German churches were, however, the backbone of the World Council of Churches Programme to Combat Racism, which funded the liberation movements from the early 1970s. Collins invited Boudewijn Sjollema, the programme's first director, to Amen Court to discuss 'mutual problems'. As the elder statesman, Collins felt he should warn Sjollema that a respectable organisation like the WCC faced the risk of entanglement in unseemly conflicts with other agencies in the field. Better, he suggested, that the WCC funnel its money through IDAF with the assurance that it would be spent creatively. Sjollema heard him out, then reminded him that one reason for raising the money was for the churches to be publicly seen to be taking a stand. 'If we put our money where our mouth is,' Sjollema told him, 'people might begin to hear what we're trying to say.' There were no hard feelings – Collins might not have been convinced of his own argument. (Sjollema interview 1998).

Apartheid firmly entered the Irish national consciousness with a lengthy strike at a Dublin branch of Dunnes supermarket after employees were suspended for refusing to handle Cape fruit. The Irish Government, though not yet enriched by the European Community, funded IDAF directly from 1985. Kader Asmal, exiled lawyer and Dean of Law at Trinity College, Dublin, was a persuasive figure, in both the AAM and, with his Irish wife Louise, on the Defence and Aid committee. Asmal talked of setting up a Japanese committee; the Swedes tried in Italy; and in 1967, Brutus had plans for Mexico, his eyes on the following year's Olympic Games.

France was not a success. After a great deal of effort, Collins persuaded Jean-Paul Sartre to address a gathering in Paris. The philosopher made a long speech introducing the Canon but when he sat down most of the audience left. They had only come to hear a famous Frenchman. Collins said he never wanted to go back to France again (Cook interview 1997).

Two oceans away, New Zealand Defence and Aid (D&A NZ), founded in 1967 following a speaking tour by Robbie Resha, one of Collins's dearest ANC friends, exerted significant influence on public opinion. For ordinary New Zealanders, the 'South African question' tended to be more about playing rugby than about racial justice. It would be years before they understood that by excluding Maoris from sporting tours to South Africa they were insulting their own citizens. Led by Jack Shallcross, D&A NZ was establishment rather than populist – the Maori queen was a sponsor, as were former prime minister Walter Nash, all the Anglican bishops and the writer Dame Ngaio Marsh – preferring to make its point through high-level political contacts and leaving the playing-field activism to others. But it had no qualms about bringing in conscience-stirring speakers of the likes of Dennis Brutus, Phyllis Altman, Donald Woods and Trevor Huddleston. Collins praised its newsletter for 'clarity, economy and quality'.

Nigeria was another Commonwealth country that seemed to offer prospects, and Collins decided to establish a regional office in Lagos. Its government, despite civil war and constitutional decay, was a consistent supporter of IDAF at the United Nations. Plans for the office were at an advanced stage when the Lagos lawyer negotiating on behalf of IDAF demanded an immediate payment of £50,000, warning that 'time is of the essence and delay is dangerous'. As the unexpected demand was being pondered in Amen Court, Collins received another communication, this time from the Nigerian government, warning that 'the substantial sum' it had earmarked for the project could only be delivered after the office had actually been set up. It explained that 'many charitable organisations have collected money from the Federal government with the intention of setting up an office but have made away with the money.' In November 1982 the plans for the Lagos office were quietly interred.

Collins had a soft spot for India, his earliest benefactor. Each year he would make a pilgrimage to the Indian High Commission in Aldwych, a mile along Fleet Street from Amen Court, to collect the cheque. John and Diana had been entertained by Indira Gandhi at her residence in Delhi. Afterwards, the Prime Minister wrote to Collins to say that though India's contribution 'may not be very substantial... it is nevertheless symbolic of our deep commitment to fight man's injustice to man based on the colour of his skin'.

No country or donation was too small. Mongolia (the People's Republic of Mongolia) was told that their £206 went towards a Namibian floggings appeal, a trial of strikers at Metal Box in Durban, and for the family of a man imprisoned for planning armed insurrection. From the embattled kingdom of Lesotho, where South African exiles sought sanctuary and schooling for their children, Prime Minister Leabua Jonathan sent R2,000 (£1,195 in 1977). In January 1973, Colonel Moamer Kadhafi [sic] of Libya was thanked for his $3,000. The buying power of these dollar donations fluctuated with the exchange rate – in 1973, $1,000 was worth £393, while a year later it was worth, £429.

The German Democratic Republic was informed that its contribution had been allocated to the extraordinary affair of two SWAPO men sentenced to death for the murder of a Namibian bantustan leader. When it became known that JA Smit, a partner of the otherwise liberal Windhoek defence solicitors, Lorentz & Bone, had, with the help of a woman clerk, passed trial information to the security police, the appeal, argued by Issy Maisels, was a formality. IDAF, working with the Namibian Council of Churches, contributed £74,000 to the case.

Most years, usually in autumn, Collins went to New York. At the UN he addressed the Special Committee, lunched with Swedes and Nigerians and the usual diplomatic wire-pullers and, most important, indulged in strategy sessions with his host, Enuga Reddy. Between the Rivonia trial of 1964 and the Soweto student uprising of 1976, when there seemed no sign of revolutionary progress inside South Africa, the two men did their best to inject life into the apartheid debate. In this they were assisted by the former African colonies now swelling the ranks of the General Assembly, where Pretoria's influence was dwindling like sand in an hour glass. Between 1963 and 1970 there were 14 General Assembly resolutions on South Africa; in the next six years there were 60.

If these resolutions sometimes had the air of empty posturing, they were important in the process of isolating South Africa, the essential prelude to action that would begin to bite. In 1972 the Assembly accepted the principle of armed struggle, then recognised both liberation movements, the ANC and the PAC, as authentic representatives of the majority of the South African people. In 1974 the Assembly effectively suspended South Africa from the United Nations. Then, in 1977, came real teeth with the Security Council's mandatory arms embargo.

Through it all Reddy kept a crafty lid on his Trust Fund. 'All our papers were confidential', he recalled. 'Only two people had access, and we took the necessary precautions so that the South African security people could not actually prove that UN money went to IDAF. And if they could, so what, they couldn't put me or Canon Collins in jail. Their interest was more to find out how the money was getting into South Africa.' The fund's annual statement to the General Assembly was a minimalist document, though Reddy never kidded himself that BOSS did not know what was going on. 'They would have been stupid not to know,' he said. 'At one time they *were* stupid, but their intelligence eventually got quite smart' (Reddy interview 1992).

Withholding risky information from the General Assembly was one thing. Keeping the five trustees of the Fund sweet was more of a worry. These countries had been selected for their non-controversial, not to say malleable, qualities. Sweden, Nigeria and Pakistan were still safe. But Chile and Morocco had become unreliable. Chile was once a haven of stability in a fiery continent. Overnight, the election of the socialist Salvador Allende as president gave it a dangerous profile, though safe enough for Reddy's purposes. Allende naturally supported any initiative against apartheid. Until, in the Latin American order of things, there was a Washington-instigated coup. The new man, General August Pinochet, shared military secrets, torture techniques and naval exercises with Vorster. His permanent representative at the UN, Ishmael Huerta, was cold-shouldered by the trustees. Reddy recalled him at his first committee meeting trying to make friends. 'He went up to Olaf Rydbeck, the Swedish chairman, and was ignored. When the meeting started, he made some innocuous comments and asked innocuous questions. Once again Rydbeck ignored his statement, didn't thank him and called the next speaker. Rydbeck never recognised him properly as the representative of Chile, addressing him as "You". After a few meetings he was silent.' So, said Reddy, 'he was not a serious problem.' Morocco was the other potential security concern. Its king had befriended friends of Pretoria – Jonas Savimbi, the rebel backed by South Africa as a spoiling operation in independent Angola, and later the KwaZulu bantustan leader, Gatsha Buthelezi. Reddy could also function without Morocco. With the Swede and the Nigerian, he had it stitched up. Much like a John Collins committee.

Collins, having entertained hopes of developing a transatlantic anti-apartheid axis, came to be wary of serious entanglement. The United States had a small anti-apartheid constituency. George Houser's American Committee on Africa (ACOA), the oldest and most efficient of the American pressure groups, was well dug in with the churches and trade unions and maintained excellent contacts in Washington and Hollywood. Collins was impressed by Houser's 'We Say "No" to Apartheid' campaign that brought Hollywood into the front-line. At an Actor's Equity party, Henry Fonda read the pledge and the names of the 65 celebrities who had signed their approval, among them Harry Belafonte, Leonard Bernstein, Sammy Davis Jr, Sidney Poitier and Paul Robeson – who was recruited by Collins to sing spirituals at St Paul's Cathedral.

Houser was a fundraiser in the early Collins's tradition. On hearing Houser and Enuga Reddy speak at a meeting in Harlem in 1966, a member of the audience cashed in $50,000 of General Motors' stock and sent it to ACOA earmarked for the UN Trust Fund. A Philadelphia couple donated their holdings in Chase Manhattan Bank. These donations were made against the background of a Congressional inquiry into investment in South Africa, where Walter Reuther, the influential Autoworkers' Union President, called for a total trade ban as the only practical way to end apartheid. South Africa was an issue that made black Americans more conscious of their African heritage. In 1971, Charles Diggs Jr, chair of the Congressional subcommittee on Africa, founded the Black Caucus.

There was a degree of co-operation between Houser and Collins and some mutual admiration. But the association languished. 'I liked him,' Houser recalled, 'we got on very well, but he was very jealous, territorial. He wanted to move in here, but I'm afraid it wasn't his territory' (Houser letter 09.01.99).

After the break with Houser, the ex-senator, Leslie Rubin, then teaching at Howard University, Washington DC, started a Defence and Aid committee and tried to raise money from, among others, the Kennedy family. But the churches and unions were already on ACOA's 25,000-name mailing list. A South African Methodist lay preacher, Ken Carstens, took over the committee on the recommendation of Reddy and the exiled black academic, Professor ZK Matthews. When Dennis Brutus arrived to teach at Northwestern University he was due to assist IDAF locally and at the United Nations, but he quarrelled with Carstens before throwing in his lot with the 'Black Power' movement. It made no real difference. Reddy talked of 'all kinds of constraints. If Rubin and Carstens ever got big, Americans would have asked about this organisation, then Collins and CND – for some Americans it was communist – would have come out.' And potential donors would have to be told that the money went to London. Reddy saw Carstens as 'a presence, not to raise money, as I knew the Canon would not raise money in the US.' And yet Carstens was full of ideas for raising funds and profile, and tried several schemes, including mail shots. But, Horst Kleinschmidt recalled, 'it would cost more than we got in. In 20 years American Defence and Aid never made real money.' In 1983, the new IDAF administration in London closed the operation.

In the meantime, Jimmy Carter made the United States a player in Collins's secret world. Horrified by the death of Steve Biko, the Democrat president authorised a $300,000 grant to the UN Trust Fund. It followed an approach by Reddy to Andrew Young, the black Secretary of State for Africa. Sweden's UN ambassador persuaded his American counterpart, Arthur Goldberg, to drop the need for reporting on how the money was spent. It may have been as a *quid pro quo* that the full Congress grant went to the Washington-based Lawyers' Committee for Civil Rights under the Law. Collins was not pleased but Reddy says the arrangement worked well. Gaye McDougall, the committee's efficient administrator, became the Trust Fund's lobbyist in Congress.

The Carter administration did smooth matters by donating $25,000 direct to IDAF, but the shine was taken off the gesture by the requirement that every last cent be accounted for. It did not matter, for Reddy assured Collins that IDAF would continue to receive the lion's share from the Trust Fund. He was as good as his word: through the 1980s, 60 per cent came to IDAF, and 30 per cent to the Washington Committee. The Canon was ever suspicious. In 1981 he saw fit to 'alert' IDAF's representative at the United Nations, Wilfrid Grenville-Grey, that Gaye McDougall was nosing around Europe speaking to IDAF-friendly governments and organisations. 'I would be very grateful,' he wrote, 'if you would, as discreetly as possible, get as much information as you can about her tour and the purpose of it.' Collins was 76 years old but the habit of a lifetime never withered (Collins memo 30.11.81).

When Pretoria said the communists were keeping Defence and Aid afloat there was a smidgen of truth to the charge. The Bulgarians sent their wine, the Yugoslavs their slivovitz and the Russians their vodka, all of which Collins auctioned at a bonded warehouse in London's docklands. He went to some lengths to win goodwill across the Iron Curtain, where governments, in the absence of national committees, pretended to represent the feelings of ordinary people. He always wrote directly to the Soviet Foreign Minister, Andrei Gromyko, outlining how the USSR's $10,000 had played its role in the struggle.

If this constituted supping with the devil, the actual transaction was carried off in style. Each year, at an appointed time, Collins repaired to the Russian embassy in Kensington Palace Gardens, where first secretary Pavel Filatov would intone a formal speech in support of the victims of racism, before handing over the cash. Collins provided an instant receipt and tea was taken from the house samovar. A less formal Soviet contact was effected in 1980 at a diplomatic reception at the UNESCO office in Paris. The Canon thought he had spotted an old acquaintance. 'You're the man who promised us a submarine to free Nelson Mandela from Robben Island,' he said, by way of cheery introduction. 'We Russians,' came the reply, 'do not engage in political adventurism.'

Chapter 21

LETTERS FROM ELSEWHERE

If **Pretoria did understand** that IDAF was master-minding trial and welfare payments, that was all the more reason for creative obfuscation. 'Mr X' had tried to scatter the scent but found it unwieldy working through lawyers in France, the United States or Australia. So he settled on three or four English dependables who spoke the language and practised the same system of law. The letter writers were different. As long as they wrote a reasonable English in a legible hand and were able to deliver like well-oiled links in a chain, there was no reason why they should not sit in Outer Mongolia and ply their trade. It never came to that; *Sersant* (Sergeant) van der Merwe of 'Letters Interception', a security police unit that operated within the postal service and which was located adjacent to Jan Smuts Airport in Johannesburg, must surely have cottoned on. But the network was gradually extended to countries with IDAF affiliates. They did not add up in numbers to all those writing from Britain but they made the system more efficient and therefore more secure.

Who would have thought, after Ottawa's initial brush-off of Collins, that Canada would run the largest and most efficient Defence and Aid operation outside Britain? From early in the 1960s isolated groups across Canada's time zones were raising consciousness. A Belgian professor of German and his wife were active in Fredericton, New Brunswick. Toronto had its southern African liberation committee and there was a French-run information centre for Mozambique and southern Africa. It was a progressive conservative, John Diefenbaker, who chiselled out an ethical benchmark as the only white prime minister to insist that there was no place for South Africa in the Commonwealth. His country's defining stance on apartheid made the cause acceptable to those on the right. The downside may have been to anchor successive Ottawa governments in complacency. Pierre Trudeau criticised, but his words were rarely translated into action, either political or financial.

That a coherent Canadian effort was slow to get off the ground was partly the fault of John Collins. Clyde Sanger, a journalist on *The Globe and Mail* in Toronto and long-standing anti-apartheid activist, recalled that he 'seemed to treat the Canadian government like a milch cow and headed straight for the teat on arrival in Ottawa. We took him to a well-attended public meeting where he performed OK, but he seemed to think it an unnecessary bother. It took him a long time to understand that our government judged non-governmental organisations by the size and liveliness of their Canadian constituency. You got clout not because you had a few impressive names but because you had lots of supporters who wrote cheques and then you could expect some matching funds [from the government]' (Sanger letter 1996).

The triggers, as elsewhere, were the Soweto schoolchildren, and then the murder of Biko. In the light of the United Nations' mandatory arms embargo (in 1977), a church taskforce on corporate responsibility had exchanged views with the Ottawa government. The Jesuit chairman of its southern Africa sub-committee, James Webb, voiced doubts about the toothless business code of conduct as Canadian firms continued to trade in arms or make bank loans to South Africa's strategic industries. A group of clerics and trade unionists received a sympathetic hearing from the external affairs minister, Flora MacDonald. North American rivalry played its part. Sanger recalls that 'some of us had seen our names on the letterhead of the IDAF branch in Boston and we said, "Why are we being add-ons to an American thing?" ' (Sanger letter 1996).

IDAFSA Canada began in 1980. The driving force was Andrew Brewin, an esteemed civil liberties lawyer who had recently retired as a New Democratic Party MP. Brewin chaired the core of four, with John Harker, international director of the Canadian Labour Congress, Doug Anglin, political scientist at Carlton College in Ottawa, and first Vice-Chancellor of the University of Zambia, and Sanger. After Brewin's death from cancer, he was replaced by the Anglican Archbishop, Edward Scott. The United Church of Canada put in C$5,000 and the Anglican Church C$2,000, which was matched by Collins. Sanger recommended Anne Mitchell to be the executive director. Scots by birth, Mitchell had been a barmaid in the rough-and-tumble North West Territories, then worked with disadvantaged children in Quebec and was now freshly back in Canada after a spell in Swaziland with its bird's-eye view of apartheid at work. Her attitude was: 'Just get on with it'. And she did, turning her living room into an office and within a year had a 100-donor network willing to fund trials and welfare. A year later it was 300.

Mitchell's knack of cultivating special advisers and ministerial assistants brought an early breakthrough. The government was looking for a channel through which to send a tranche of aid to newly-independent Zimbabwe. But the aid agency, Canadian University Students' Organisation (CUSO), was based in Zambia where its links were with Joshua Nkomo's Zimbabwe African People's Union (ZAPU), not with the election victors, Robert Mugabe's Zimbabwe African National Union (ZANU). Amen Court had irons in both fires and provided the way in, which added to its stock with Ottawa. Still the government baulked at playing its hand inside South Africa proper, though it made small grants to the UN Trust Fund. The tide turned again as the mid-eighties township rebellion was seen nightly on television newscasts. Brian Mulroney, a prime minister in the Diefenbaker tradition of progressive conservatism, was keen to respond, without actually aiding the liberation movements directly. IDAFSA Canada had raised C$20,000 for the rehabilitation of released Namibian political prisoners but more was needed. Now, five years of intense negotiations bore fruit as the state development agency, CIDA, added C$30,000, the cheque going directly to IDAF in London. Announcing the grant in the Ottawa House of Commons, external affairs minister Joe Clark said he was setting up a fund for the victims of apartheid and that IDAF was to be the main channel. This was, as he must have hoped, widely covered in the press – a far cry from the secrecy that shrouded IDAF elsewhere. The money was a godsend, for, with the persecution of SWAPO and the expulsion of churchmen from Namibia, London had been unable to find reliable outlets for the distribution of family aid. The South African authorities could not be seen to hinder the hand-over of Canadian government cash to men who had served their time on Robben Island.

In the absence of an Anti-Apartheid Movement, the Canadian IDAF filled that role as well. Whenever a storm blew up in South Africa, the media turned to IDAF as a reliable source of information, and so raised its profile.

The 'big brother' factor was a spur to Ottawa's higher profile. After Jimmy Carter had injected a refreshing dose of human rights into his foreign policy, a transatlantic axis of Ronald Reagan and Margaret Thatcher sympathetic to white South Africa moved into the White House and Downing Street. Mulroney wanted to distance Canada from 'constructive engagement', the discredited Reaganite diplomacy of sweet-talking Pretoria into making concessions to the black have-nots. So the two leading figures in Canadian society, Mulroney and Clark, climbed tentatively onto an anti-apartheid platform. Clark's objective was 'to bring South Africa to its senses, not to its knees'. In one initiative in 1987, with a whites-only election in the offing, he sent a three-page letter to 30,000 Canadian households inviting them to sign up to an Anti-Apartheid Register.

If this amounted to unprecedented behaviour towards an ostensibly friendly state, there was more of the same in South Africa proper as embassies indulged in the practice of 'witnessing'. Some members of the European and Commonwealth diplomatic corps attended rallies, funerals and political trials, out in the open, for all the world to see. It served the dual purpose of offering a degree of protection to those on trial, while telegraphing a thumbs-down message to the host country. In the same spirit, Canada's 'Dialogue Fund' doled out money for projects within South Africa; supporting conferences and workshops; strengthening the alternative media; giving technical support on social matters, and assistance to marginalised youth. Students received study grants for Canadian colleges after they had been cleared by IDAF or the ANC or, at home, by the United Democratic Front (UDF). Canada and other western governments hoped in this way to deflect critics calling for a complete break with Pretoria. If President PW Botha was unamused, he could not afford to increase the isolation by expelling diplomats for openly associating with the 'enemy'.

There were other reasons, apparent and subliminal, why Canada was ready to turn the screws on apartheid, which Archbishop Scott described as 'perhaps the most important human rights struggle of the twentieth century'. Anne Mitchell explained that 'Canadians have come from other nations, often to avoid persecution and felt strongly about persecution elsewhere. We remembered the war and the Nazis and abhorred the idea of what apartheid was.' It is a Eurocentric view skirting the question, as in Australia and New Zealand, of white settler relations with the indigenous inhabitants. Mitchell admitted that 'we felt guilty about the way our native people have been treated but found it easier to do something about the situation in South Africa.' In time the Canadian government would apologise to the Inuit (native Canadian 'Eskimos') for their 'historic mistreatment' and grant them a form of self-government over a vast tract of northern tundra (Mitchell memo 1992, interviews and letters).

All the while Kleinschmidt and Huddleston, from London, and the committee in Ottawa kept close to Joe Clark. From 1986, Canadian Defence and Aid received so much revenue from the government that its situation was comparable to that of Collins 20 years earlier when Sweden and the United Nations had taken over his budget. But from her office opposite the war memorial on Ottawa's Confederation Square, Mitchell raised ever larger amounts. By the end of the decade she had 10,000 donors, a jump of 3,000 in a single year, helped by middle-class awareness of the benefits of charitable status, which had been achieved after exhaustive deliberations with Canadian Inland Revenue. Even the Dr Scholl Foundation of Chicago enquired about a grant, but it came to nothing – a case of itchy feet, no doubt. In 1989, with the state subvention at C$1.6m, IDAF raised C$263,000 from the public and an equal amount in grants from private institutions. Annual reports made no mention of the ultimate use of the money, a moral parallel of the arms dealers who evaded sanctions by inventing a benign end user. Accounts were approved at the annual meeting but were not revealed to the public. The auditor conceded that 'the donations by their nature are not susceptible to complete verification by audit procedures'. There were, to be sure, many who were suspicious of this use of public money. Mitchell and the government received letters accusing them of supporting terrorism. Several MPs challenged IDAF's right to charitable status.

Deeper behind the scenes, Mitchell launched the letter-writing programme. The earliest recruits were from her church, old school and social network, women, invariably, middle-aged, middle-class Canadians, working in isolation. In this vast country, Hercules Poirot-like detection skills would have been needed to break into the homely drawing rooms. At its close, 375 South African families were receiving 'gifts' from 115 correspondents who ranged from British Columbia to Nova Scotia. The writer's sole contact was with a pseudonymous provincial co-ordinator, who in turn answered to one of three assumed names at post office addresses in Ottawa. Barbara Evans was all three of these, the coping stone of the pyramid, managing the programme from the basement of her home.

The replies from South Africa were sent on to London. There had been a wrangle about this, but given his wariness of double-funding the Collins' view prevailed over the Canadian desire for autonomy. Overseas aid was now widespread enough for sharp operators to milk the system. In May 1985, Bamvana Witness Biko (no relation of Steve) wrote to a Mr Hayes in Canada saying he had not had a stable job since coming off Robben Island 14 years before. Could he help? The letter landed on a desk at IDAF's Essex Road office, where Biko was identified as an existing receiver of 'gifts'. It was not the only case of an appeal from someone who did not realise there was a master list in London.

On 3 September 1984, a mob at the end of its tether attacked the house of a township councillor, stoned and burnt him inside his house. It happened in Sharpeville, which for a generation had sustained the legend of the white man's cruelty. Five men and a woman were condemned to death for the murder of a local councillor. There was evidence that two of them had thrown stones, though it was disputed whether the victim had died from brain damage or burns. Not that it mattered, for under South Africa's rule of common purpose each one of the dozens present outside the house could have been charged with being a party to an act committed by just one of them. Once five judges of appeal were unable to find a reason to reverse the decision, and President Botha had rejected a petition to spare their lives, the case of the 'Sharpeville Six' landed on the world stage. Mrs Thatcher met a wife and a sister of two of those on Death Row, and was said to have been impressed by the justice of their case. Chancellor Helmut Kohl and President Ronald Reagan likewise intervened with Pretoria. The European Community threatened to toughen up sanctions.

Throughout these times, Lynda Muir was exchanging letters with Regina Morathi, common law wife of Reginald Sefatsa, one of the Sharpeville Six. Muir, a divorcee, lived in Ottawa with two small sons, working as an editor at the National Gallery of Canada. Having taught in Botswana, she was better placed than most to read between the lines of the letters she was receiving. Sisterhood was one reason for the success of the programme. It is hard, as you well know, she wrote to Regina, 'raising children without the presence of their father. We women do our best.' Regina's daughter, Masefatsa, was two months' old when Reginald was arrested. Her letters are a catalogue of woe, about losing her home, building a shack in her sister's yard, problems with a drunk brother-in-law, her child's illness, her desire to make more of her life, learning to speak and writing better English, and her wish to marry the imprisoned Reginald. There were awful strains with his family when they made off with her furniture. 'These people want me six feet down for what, I don't know. I am out of their house and I don't cause any problems for them.' Was it jealousy brought on by the R420 every other month? The 'in-laws' wrote to Lynda, and then a letter arrived from Death Row. 'Please sister, don't accept their funny stories,' Reginald wrote of his parents. 'Not one among them wrote to me or even just to send me a card. They don't know whether I'm in or not. Regina is the only one who care for me and I feel her nearness... since my absence, you are the only one who give us moral support.'

Muir had accepted with some misgivings Mitchell's invitation to become a correspondent. Would she be able to keep her emotional distance, 'was I strong enough to help without being swamped by their very real troubles?' she asked herself. She read parts of the letters to her sons and showed them photos of Regina and her family – Nicky was two months younger than Masefatsa. Muir sent the girl a 'beautiful brown-skinned doll in Canadian Indian costume'; and when Reginald was told, he said it was just the one he wanted to give his daughter. One Wednesday morning in mid-March 1988, she heard on the radio that the 'Sharpeville Six' faced imminent execution. 'There were other stresses in my life at that point, but I almost went under with the sense of powerlessness and despair in the face of this injustice.' But Botha, relenting to the outside pressure, reprieved the 'Six', saving necks already measured by the prison hangman. [1]

And there were rewarding moments for Muir. The clerk at her post office said how kind she was to her 'people over there'. She was three years into the correspondence before she met other letter-writers, at a party at Anne Mitchell's home. 'I sustained my commitment by telling myself that a few hours every other month was a very small demand on me, and it was a lifeline to the families at the other end.' Reginald, a 'self-employed fruit vendor', wrote once more, after his reprieve but before his release. The letter is headed 'Hearty Greetings'. He wants to compose a perfect letter. He has just the one sheet of paper, but he scratches out lines. 'Writing is silence in conversation, but speaking with some-body face to face or soul to soul is easy to see someone's feelings. As you know that life can't be smooth at all times. There are all ways ups and down. I left Regina with problems alone... since my arrest the only person who is always by my side is her. You won't believe if I tell you that no one at home knows my whereabouts. Dear Sister, Regina is a brave woman. I won't forget her patience. She's my tower. So wonderful. There's only one of her...' He thanks the silent listener for her assistance, 'affectionately' (Muir letter 15.07.92).

•

We have seen how the success of a writing operation might depend on the energy of a single person, invariably, though not by definition, female. Rica Hodgson's first extra-territorial expansion, into Ireland, was an 'inside job'. The motivator was Louise, wife of Kader Asmal, the ANC's legal adviser. He was also secretary of the Irish Anti-Apartheid Movement, which Louise mined for 22 writers in Dublin, Cork and Galway – having checked each for 'financial reliability' and an ability to pen a decent letter. She found that 'if you wanted to be certain, women were best.' Ireland's writers were drawn from across class lines. There were Asmal's faculty colleagues, but also Lily O'Rourke, who had left school in Donegal at 13 and in the thirties had been active in *Cumann na mBan*, the Republican women's movement. From their home in the Dublin working-class suburb of Walkinstown she and her electrician husband, Sean, wrote letters to a dozen families. Nora Harkin, a founder of the Ireland–USSR Friendship society, was recruited at an AAM meeting in the basement of Dublin's Powers Hotel. 'The older I get,' she said, 'the more I believe there is enough wealth in the world for all of us. Our letters kept people ticking over. It was a small gesture, but when they are down it gave a feeling of brotherhood. Besides, we have apartheid in Ireland.' Nora began with two families, and inherited another six from a friend with arthritis. By the time it was over, she was in her eighties, and *her* arthritis was playing up (Harkin interview 1992).

The Asmals' friendship with the governor of the Irish Central Bank, Louden Ryan, helped cut through exchange control red tape. Normally, with money going abroad, the sender had to furnish details of the receiver and the reasons for its being sent. With Professor Ryan's intercession, Mrs

Asmal was allowed to fill in blanket forms that simply declared that the money was for charitable purposes. 'I can't imagine the Governor of the Bank of England doing that,' she said (Louise Asmal interview 1992).

In the case of the Norwegian writing network, once again the energy of a woman with South African connections was what mattered. Abdul Minty, who had known Norway since the time of Luthuli's Nobel Peace Prize, met (and later married) Kari Storhaug through her chairmanship of Norwegian Amnesty. A community dentist in Oslo, Dr Storhaug recruited most of her 50 writers from the confines of oral health care. Though they were colleagues, none discussed the letters. She roped in doctors and nurses, the editor of a dental magazine, a physiotherapist, the cashier and caretaker of the Frambu health centre in Oslo. Nearly all were women. They were reliable, says Storhaug. 'I recruited several men who never followed it up' (Storhaug interview 1992).

An exception was Dr Jan Ziesler, specialist in children's diseases at the health centre. He and his wife Anne-Liese, a laboratory assistant, had good reason to find the work satisfying, having lived dangerously in the underground during the German occupation of their country. The couple had been engaged for two days when Jan, under orders from the Resistance, skied into Sweden and was flown to England to join Norway's government-in-exile. Anne-Liese was a courier, carrying 'important messages between our leader at headquarters and outlying villages'. Only when they married did they learn the other's real name. Anne-Liese's family tradition helped prepare her for IDAF. Her father, Alf Sommerfelt, professor of comparative languages in Oslo, had lectured on the nature of Nazi ideology and escaped (to Britain) in time to avoid the Germans arriving at his home to arrest him. He was later a founder of the United Nations Educational, Scientific and Cultural Organisation (UNESCO). Before the war, Anne-Liese's mother, Aimée, a popular author of children's books, sent food parcels to the families of German political prisoners. A family friend was shot in reprisal for the killing of a Norwegian quisling, Martinsen. Anne-Liese says Norway's own situation during the war 'made us sympathetic to what black South Africans must have felt, occupied in a way like us.' They wrote their first letters in 1979, and for a time had 15 families. Anne-Liese checked her English spelling in the dictionary and, hearing of 'the terrible things that were happening there', ended her letters with the words, 'take care of yourself' (Anne-Liese Ziesler interview 1992).

Kari Seglem, who had been taught dental hygiene by Dr Storhaug, was the world's most northerly IDAF corres-pondent. Living in Tromso, inside the Arctic Circle at 70°N, where the sun goes down on November 21 and is not seen again until late January, provided ample time to write to six mothers. One of these was Monica Godolozi, wife of a South African *desaparecido*. As Mrs Godolozi did not herself know the true story until years later, it is not surprising that Seglem had only a sketchy notion of her plight. Her husband Qaqawuli was president of Port Elizabeth Black Civic Organisation (PEBCO), the black civics network that had sprung up in response to a need for humane housing, transport and quality of life. A strike called by PEBCO in 1984 had brought the city of Port Elizabeth to a standstill. Godolozi was also recruiting for MK training abroad. The Godolozis had named their son Mkhonto-we-sizwe, MK for short, which did not endear them to the police. One day in 1985, he and two other PEBCO officials were lured by a bogus caller to meet a 'British consular official' at the airport. They were detained by the police, murdered and their bodies dismembered. The wives lived in hope because the police had offered a R10,000 reward for information about their whereabouts, a cynical gesture in keeping with the men who had previously killed Steve Biko. Monica was given Seglem's name by her mother-in-law. With the first cheque she bought clothes for 'MK', a dining room table, then paid off her debts (Godolozi interview 1992). The PEBCO wives and mothers finally learnt the truth when the perpetrators pleaded for mercy before the Truth and Reconciliation Commission.

Holland's correspondents operated in a network separate from and largely unknown to its IDAF branch. The recruiter, for a change, was male. In 1979 Berend Meijer, a religious education lecturer at a college south of Amsterdam, was invited by one of the Dutch Defence and Aid leaders, Bert

Musschenga, who taught social ethics at the Free University in Amsterdam, to set up the operation. Rica Hodgson met him in Holland, and in time he co-ordinated 34 writers: his wife, friends and teachers, most of them practising Christians, in Amsterdam and in the countryside, each looking after three families. 'I did tell them that the work was for Defence and Aid but asked them not to say so, as I believe BOSS were aware of our operation, but it was a diffuse network.' The money was transmitted from London to Meijer's private account at the Hollandse Koopmansbank in Amsterdam, then transferred by giro to each writer's account for conversion to international postal orders. 'The workers were free, costs were low, and in 12 years I did not need more than 800 guilders (£300) in expenses' (Meijer letters and interview 2004).

Do Stuyfzand, a grandmother in the seaside town of Zandvoort in the Netherlands, worked in public relations in the flower industry. Her three wards were the mothers of defendants in the Delmas treason trial.[2] As the gallows loomed for all of them, grandma Do's warm words helped the peace of mind of parents and sons. She followed the romance of Gcinumuze Malinde, the son of a labourer, when he married his attorney, Caroline Heaton-Nicholls, before being jailed for five years.

As with Ireland and Norway, Sweden's 'Programme Two' controller, Anne-Lena Wästberg, was the wife of a member of the Collins's inner circle. After her divorce from Per Wästberg, she moved to Denmark, still in charge but not expanding her network. At the close, the programme was helping 47 families. Two members of her group wrote to Harry Gwala, school teacher and indomitable MK warrior. Gwala's experiences might explain why he chose to place his family in the front line. Thrown out of their home in central Pietermaritzburg, he bought a 'solid brick house' at Ockerts Kraal, but was on the move once more when the area was proclaimed a 'white Group Area' and renamed Hayfields. Mrs Gwala, four children and several relatives moved into a mud hut. Her husband was by now separately accommodated on Robben Island. The family next rented a single room, before moving, in 1972, to a house bought with the R500 compensation from the

Ockerts Kraal house – and help from IDAF. Just in time, for
on Gwala's release from prison he was house-arrested, until
returning to prison for 'life' three years later. His daughter
Lulu was detained for a year, and her baby was brought into
her cell to be breastfed. Lulu took over the letter-writing when
her mother died. In the State of Emergency she was detained,
held for a few days, freed, detained again; at home her sleep
would be interrupted by constant banging on the door. She
remembers as a young girl being 'so scared of the Boers...
maybe they would come and kill us in our homes... and we got
so lonely without our dad. We envied our neighbour, a schoolteacher, when he took his children on holiday.' Gwala claimed
he knew the money came from IDAF in London. 'When my
wife and daughters visited me on Robben Island, it took three
days by train through Bloemfontein.' Lulu reels off the names
of those who wrote to her: Rosemary Ramsay, then Violetta
Thompson in London and Catherine Kennington who sent
clothes, Margaret Timmer in Holland also sent clothes and
was very kind and, from Sweden, Michael Salzer and Annika
Hedstrom (Lulu and Harry Gwala interview 1992).

As thousands were detained in the 1980's States of
Emergency, IDAF sought further countries in which to
expand. Finland and Germany were about to join, followed
by Australia and New Zealand. But time ran out. A group got
off the ground in France, but fell through, largely because of
the language gulf. Their 21 families were incorporated into
the British list.

Denmark was the last of the national post offices. It worked
so well that the IDAF Essex Road office must have regretted
not enlisting their aid sooner. Kleinschmidt and Stevenson,
the Programme Two co-ordinator, met an Englishman, Edward
Broadbridge, at an Amnesty International meeting in Copenhagen. Having taught English at a sixth form college in
Randers for 25 years, he was looking for something extra
in his life. He went to South Africa to see for himself, then
did the rounds on the island of Jutland, and was inundated
with recruits, especially teachers. The Danes were thrust into
the legalistic madness that preceded the end of apartheid,
as the Upington 26,[3] (who were bystanders at a fracas in

which a policeman died) awaited mass execution in Pretoria. Broadbridge and his Danish wife, Hannah, wrote to one of the 26, a grandmother, Evelyn de Bruin, convicted of murder by 'common purpose'. IDAF-funded lawyers saved them all. At the close of the trail, 24 Danish writers, including a group from Danish Church Aid, were helping 183 families.

Chapter 22

KITH AND KIN

For John Collins the invitation to be a guest of honour at
the birth in 1980 of Zimbabwe (formerly Rhodesia) was
tantamount to a silver medal. If South Africa was the focus
of his life of service, Britain's last African colony ran it a close
second. But days before their departure, Diana went into
hospital with a heart ailment. She insisted her husband go on
his own, to show solidarity with old comrades. Collins arrived
in the Zimbabwean capital, Salisbury (soon to be renamed
Harare), expecting to be lodged in Meikles Hotel together with
the other VIPs. But there was a muddle over accommodation
and he was re-routed to a dispiritingly anonymous room on
the university campus. He was feeling his 75 years.

Joshua Nkomo, who was about to become Home Affairs
Minister in Robert Mugabe's first cabinet, took him home.
The friendship went back 20 years to when Nkomo had
arrived at Amen Court seeking support for his incarcerated
followers. The Canon and the father figure of Zimbabwean
nationalism were in a mood for reminiscing. Nkomo
recalled Collins 'reflecting on what he had done not only
for Zimbabwe but for all the parts of southern Africa that
required help' (Nkomo interview 1992). But then, tired and
anxious about Diana, Collins flew back to London before
Independence Day. His work, it could be said, was done.

•

In the last decade of the nineteenth century, Cecil John
Rhodes from Bishops Stortford seized the belly of Africa,
turned it into a chartered company and gave his name to it.
Rhodesia was a black man's country devoted to the wellbeing
of its whites, who were forever beckoning to those of like

mind, English-speakers preferably, to come and settle and so make the place appear a little less black. It was one of Africa's more handsome lands, the pleasant climate belying the tropical latitude, and with labour and land on sale more cheaply than in the dour *laager* to the south, it attracted in the years after the Second World War substantial numbers from Britain, South Africa and Europe. There they lived in an Edwardian golden age.

The British South Africa Company, Cecil Rhodes's personal fiefdom, ran the territory until 1922, when London granted the territory 'responsible government'. The whites' power was now unlimited, except for a British veto over colonial legislation if African interests were threatened. The veto was not once used. Rhodesia was thus akin to South Africa and South West Africa, places where Westminster had likewise abandoned the indigenous people.

In the 1950s, as west and central Africa emerged from colonialism, the behaviour of the split-level societies to the south became ever more illiberal. Rhodesia aped Pretoria, while offering a veneer of non-racialism. The British government's Central African Federation (Southern Rhodesia, Northern Rhodesia and Nyasaland) was an effort to keep up with the times. But its architect and first prime minister, Sir Godfrey Huggins, put the catchword of the Federation, 'partnership', in perspective – it meant a pairing of 'horse and rider'. he explained. Whites were keen on 'civilised standards'. But if too many Africans threatened to qualify for the vote under the constitution, the 'standards' were simply raised. By 1956, as Africans geared up for the long haul to liberation, a mere 560 of them were on an electoral roll of 52,000. They were obstructed from proceeding to secondary education by the simple device of not building sufficient schools; their first secondary school had opened only in 1946. The Land Apportionment Act handed their traditional acreage to white farmers much as the Land Act had done in South Africa. Rhodesia had 'parallel development' in 1930, well before Dr Verwoerd devised 'separate development' in South Africa. 'Passes' controlled movement and employment in 'white' areas. The peasant farmer might not be welcome in town, but his labour was. If he preferred to stay at home, he was persuaded to enter the white economy by a poll tax, a device contrived in the Kimberley diamond diggings by Rhodes.

By 1959, the federation was falling apart under pressure from black nationalists in the three territories. Southern Rhodesia enacted a preventive detention law, banned Joshua Nkomo's African National Congress (ANC), and detained 500 supporters. In response, a group of Salisbury whites set up the Legal Aid and Welfare Fund. Their spiritual father was Guy Clutton-Brock, the sole white to be detained. Amnesty International, the Africa Bureau and a local Indian businessman, Suman Mehta, helped with funds. John Collins sent £2,000. The ANC detainees, in Khami maximum security prison outside Bulawayo, contacted Charles Lazarus, a local attorney prepared to work for African politicals. After meeting James Chikerema, Joseph Msika and George Nyandoro, he put together a legal team to represent the detainees at the review tribunal. Among them were Herbert Chitepo, the first black at the Rhodesian Bar, and Anthony Gubbay, a future chief justice. But police evidence was heard in camera, with detainees and their lawyers excluded, ostensibly to protect witnesses. Detainees were given 'grounds for detention' drawn up by the special branch. Thus, James Mzila was 'an extreme racialist' who promoted hostility against the Europeans; his crime, committed at an ANC meeting, was to have called 'on God to free the Africans from the bondage of their enemies who hated them because of their colour.' After a score of fruitless hearings, it was clear that simple membership of Congress was enough to keep them in detention. Lazarus told his clients the money would be better spent on their families (Lazarus interview 1992).

Terence Ranger, a history lecturer and member of the legal aid fund, reminded Collins that Defence and Aid was virtually the sole source of British funding. Britain, he argued, had a greater responsibility in Southern Rhodesia than in South Africa. But the British seemed more concerned about the clear-cut horror of apartheid than the behaviour of their Rhodesian 'kith and kin'. Joshua Nkomo, finding himself in Cairo at the time of the detentions, had hotfooted it to London and set up an office in Golders Green. He was a frequent caller at Amen Court, seeking help for the trials that followed disturbances in Salisbury in 1960. Collins funded the lengthy battle for Michael Mawema, a lieutenant of Nkomo, who had shared a platform in England with the Tory MP, Christopher Chataway. Mawema's four-year sentence for belonging to an unlawful organisation was overturned on appeal.

The Khami detainees launched the National Democratic Party as a successor to Nkomo's ANC. It in turn was outlawed, to be replaced by the Zimbabwe African People's Union (ZAPU). A rose by another name to the government, it went the way of earlier movements, to the habitual fanfare of arrest, prosecution and detention. The British press, suspicious of black emancipation and petrol bombers, were happy to accept the explanation of a 'communist-inspired plot', though this was far from the truth. The charges were mostly for trivial offences, such as holding ZAPU cards or shouting out '*Kwacha!*' ('Freedom!'). By 1962, however, 12 ZAPU volunteers were in Egypt receiving training from Soviet instructors.

Collins now got into deep water with an advertising appeal in *The Observer*. Headed 'Fair Trial in Southern Rhodesia', it highlighted the arrests, the lack of bail money, six men in detention since 1959, distressed breadwinners, and in particular, the plight of a sick detainee who, 'unable to get satisfactory treatment, was refused permission to seek treatment available elsewhere.' At worst it was a marginal error, but the Federal high commissioner in London wrote to each of Collins's 150 named sponsors pointing out the 'false picture of the situation in Southern Rhodesia'. The detainee, the flamboyant George Nyandoro, had refused medical treatment for a slipped disc in a Bulawayo hospital on 'political and other grounds', insisting on an operation in England. Some donors swallowed the bait. Collins's friend, the publisher Victor Gollancz, threatened to resign as a sponsor. Lady Violet Bonham-Carter called Collins 'a holy crook', while the Jesuit priest Thomas Corbishley appeared to place the inaccuracies on the same level of horror as detention itself.

The last thing Collins wanted was a moral victory for white Rhodesia, followed by a collapse in funding. He cabled an SOS to Ranger, who was able to refute the high commissioner point-by-point, bar Nyandoro's story, on which the Canon had not been put entirely in the picture. *The Observer* ran the high commissioner's letter, but not Amen Court's rejoinder. Collins was forced to agree to forward details of cases to the high commission before they were aired and so give its government a chance to take action, if any (Freda Nuell letter to Ranger 17.12.62). When Nyandoro was released a year later, the Salisbury fund sent him to England for treatment for a tubercular spine. He was in plaster for eight months.

The tenor of the struggle changed dramatically in the early years of the 1960s, aggravated by the mandatory hanging clause in the 1960 Law and Order (Maintenance) Act – which Chief Justice Sir Robert Tredgold considered authoritarian enough to require his resignation. One night a burning bottle of petrol was tossed into the living room of a house in 'European' Salisbury, leaving a small hole in the carpet. Richard Mapolisa, a Zimbabwe National Party (ZNP) member, was arrested, but the court was not sure if he had even thrown the 'bomb', which had been made by one Cyprian, recently expelled from the ZNP on suspicion of being a police informer. Cyprian fled and was not charged, yet even if Mapolisa were not the thrower he had a 'common purpose' to commit the crime. With Defence and Aid's help, he appealed to the Supreme Court, then to the Privy Council in London, *in forma pauperis*.[1] The Law Lords rejected the appeal, referring to the death penalty's supposed deterrent effect in finding, ironically, that 'the purpose of providing sentence of death... was clearly to preserve human life' (*Weekly Law Reports* 05.02.65). Mapolisa wrote to Defence and Aid from his death cell: 'I am very glad to hear a great peace work which you have been doing to my family... Robert, 9 years old is in std 2; Benjamin 7 years old in Sub A; Terinha, 5 years old; Kufatrunescu, 2 years old... I am waiting for the gallows, so it's up to you to decide if my family can still get a help from you... May God bless you for your kindly work, in the name of God thanks on your hospitality.' After his execution, IDAF continued to support his family.

Discontent over Nkomo's leadership led in 1963 to a rancorous breakaway by the Zimbabwe African National Union (ZANU), led by a Congregationalist cleric, Rev. Ndabaningi Sithole. The new Rhodesian Front government was elated at the avalanche of inter-party stonings and arson as supporters of the two sides turned on each other. It led to another Privy Council appeal. Simon Runyowa and three others had 'cased out' the house of a Sithole 'sell-out' in Harare township. Runyowa had been given sixpence (about 10 cents in South Africa today) to buy paraffin, which he then handed to the others, who went off to make a bottle bomb, which one of them threw into the house, damaging a windowpane. Runyowa was sentenced to death. The Privy Council heard the arguments – by Morris Finer QC and Louis Blom-Cooper – in December 1965, a month after Rhodesia's Unilateral Declaration of Independence (UDI), and though the appeal was dismissed, Prime Minister Ian Smith was inhibited by the uncertain constitutional position. Three years later the Rhodesian Appeal Court, ignoring the Privy Council, ruled that UDI was legal. Smith set about clearing the backlog on death row. In an urgent application to the High Court for a stay of Runyowa's execution, Sydney Kentridge, citing the UDI constitution, argued that it was inhuman to execute a man after five years, when the delay was not of his own making. It failed; Runyowa was hanged and Kentridge, disgusted, gave up appearing in criminal trials in Rhodesia (*Weekly Law Reports* 06.05.66; Kentridge interview 1992).

Cases were forwarded to Amen Court by the legal aid centre or sympathetic attorneys, most prominently Anthony Eastwood at the Salisbury firm Scanlen & Holderness. Defence and Aid's London link with Rhodesia was the solicitor Bernard Sheridan, who had challenged Whitehall in a number of colonial human rights matters. Collins forwarded cases to his office in Red Lion Square, whence Sheridan, or his partner, Cyril Glasser, would instruct attorneys in Rhodesia. This worked well, but when Defence and Aid was banned in South Africa, Sheridan was seen as too prominent to become the Mr X of the secret work.

After UDI, Desmond Lardner-Burke, Minister of Justice, Law and Order, fashioned a police state along South African lines. He made the possession of 'weapons of war' a mandatory capital offence, with the onus on the accused to prove they did not intend using the weapons to endanger law and order. Police interrogation methods rivalled those of their neighbours for brutishness. South Africa was going through a quiet period in terms of trials, and IDAF took on a larger role in Rhodesia. A week before UDI, in November 1965, one of 14 senior 'restrictees', Daniel Madzimbamuto[2] asked to see Eileen and Michael Haddon of the legal fund. During his interview, he held up a packet of *Life* cigarettes that had scratched on it: 'Would like to test legality of regime.' His fellow prisoners contributed £10 each to start the ball rolling. Madzimbamuto's wife, Stella, a hospital sister, was chosen as the plaintiff to sue Lardner-Burke.

The nub of the case, argued by Maisels and Kentridge, was that the government, being illegal, did not have the right to detain. But the judges decided that the government had a *de facto* power to issue a detention order. Madzimbamuto's appeal to the Privy Council was heard three years later. Kentridge and Louis Blom-Cooper cited more than 100 cases in the ten-day hearing, which would have been longer had the respondents bothered to show up. Four of the five Law Lords decided that UDI, and therefore the detention order, was illegal. Once again Smith ignored them. Back on the ground in Salisbury, the registrar of the high court refused to release Madzimbamuto. His several more years in detention were alleviated by the knowledge that 'Stella Madzimbamuto and Desmond Lardner-Burke' had become a teasing international law exam question (Stella and Daniel Madzimbamuto interview 1992).

IDAF settled the legal bill, since *in forma pauperis* appeals were available in criminal cases only. At the behest of the Lord Chancellor, Gerald Gardiner, the costs of this and several other trials and Privy Council appeals were underwritten by Whitehall (Altman note 06.10.77). Britain sent £25,000 for the test case hearing, the sole occasion on which Collins was granted recognition by his own Government. The money was donated on the understanding that it remain a secret. Anthony Eastwood later found an appreciable sum left over in his firm's trust account. After consulting Altman, it was shared with local firms for further trial work (Eastwood interview 1992).

•

UDI precipitated an unholy family row. Diana was convinced that only the threat of British military force could keep the rebel regime in check. After all, the Archbishop of Canterbury, Michael Ramsey, had said publicly that it would be right for Christians to support military action. Collins issued a statement repudiating his Archbishop. It was, Diana said, 'one of our more serious disagreements.'

But Collins was soon in his element on this changed frontier. A new organisation, Christian Care, the welfare arm of the Protestant churches, had been set up in Bulawayo in 1967 to sidestep a legislative ban on relief work by the Christian Council of Rhodesia. Then Christian Care's first director, Terence Finley, was expelled – any foreign churchman respected by Africans was by definition mistrusted by the settlers. The churches turned to a Methodist minister, Stephen Manguni, who could not be threatened with deportation. IDAF and Manguni were to become the comforters of the Zimbabwe resistance.

In the aftermath of UDI, thousands languished in detention and restriction camps. In the summer of 1967 an inmate at Gwelo prison persuaded a guard to post a letter to London, for forwarding to IDAF. In due course, a parcel of books arrived for Cephas Msipa. 'What are they for?' Superintendent Paisley asked his prisoner, to be told that he and 23 fellow detainees were now students of a correspondence college in England. The smuggled letter marked the start of an extraordinary phenomenon in the liberation struggle: the campus behind bars. 'They knew detention would be less painful if we were bettering ourselves,' said Msipa, then president of the Rhodesian Teachers' Association. 'But it was too late. The publicity overseas would have been bad.' On receiving the letter, Phyllis Altman had arranged for the Gwelo detainees to be taken on by Wolsey Hall College in Oxford. There were no exchange control worries. The colleges were in Britain or South Africa, while fees for the two schools in Salisbury were settled through their London offices (Msipa interview 1992).

The enforced routine, the exam deadlines and the absence of domestic responsibilities produced results beyond the ability of a free man. 'We took the attitude,' said Msipa, 'let's make the best use of our time and prepare for a free Zimbabwe. The guards were jealous; they didn't want blacks to better themselves. Detention was meant to break you, and we showed we were not broken.' One day, Superintendent Paisley gave Msipa a clock and told him to invigilate the exams.

Amen Court was soon processing 100 applications a week. Altman was concerned that too many were doing public relations and such like 'phoney courses'. She asked the London ZAPU and ZANU representatives to pass on the word that detained teachers should assess each applicant. Nkomo, from his isolation in Gonakudzingwa Camp 5, directed that everyone should seize the opportunity to obtain a junior certificate or matriculation, the equivalent of 'O' levels (today's GCSE). He asked Joseph Msika to take charge. Those with a Form 4 pass were appointed teachers, though this was not even a sufficient qualification to teach in primary school. The 'illiterates' asked Msika to write to their wives. 'I said yes, but only for a few months. Why should I know all their intimate details?' The restrictees were a vertical cross-section of black society; schoolteachers, trade unionists, graduates from Fort Hare in South Africa, party officials, chiefs and headmen, Tribal Trust Land farmers, labourers. Some signed up for practical courses; bookkeeping, motor mechanics, radio and TV servicing, poultry and piggery. One man left prison as a qualified watch repairer, armed with a British Horological Institute diploma. Writing his University of London law exams, Daniel Madzimbamuto took the easy option and chose a question on his own case. He passed.

Gonakudzingwa was a gulag in the tropics, its several camps enclosed in 400 square miles of malarial game forest. This area of the 'lowveld' lined the border where the railway crossed into Moçambique, still an overseas province of Portugal. No one lived in 'Gona' by choice other than policemen, game wardens, customs officers and railway workers. Restrictees minded to escape were warned of lions, rhinos and hyenas lurking on the long walk to the nearest town. By 1969, IDAF was running 400 courses, among them four for the women at Wha Wha, east of Gwelo. 'Gona' restrictees lived 24 to a galvanised iron barrack, with virtually no furniture, and slept on the floor on sisal mats. The barracks had no electricity and three oil lamps provided a quivering light at night. They sat in the prison yard reading their textbooks and making notes, though even in winter the heat was oppressive. But whatever the hardship, the courses were a godsend. For most, learning to read and write, to pass exams, aim for a degree, was an unrealisable dream in the 'white' world outside. Study boosted self-esteem and helped them survive. It was almost an incentive to get yourself detained. Billy Hlongwane, a rare ZAPU activist still free in the late 1960s, recalls the relief at being sent to detention. 'It was now the best place for the struggle. Rhodesia was a police state. There was no life, no liberty, and no chance of finding a job outside. I could grow and take a breath in detention, as a step on the way towards more effective organisation.' On his release in 1970, Hlongwane was asked by a white policeman what he had achieved in detention. Several 'O' levels, he said, including Logic, 'a subject which they did not appear to know existed' (Ling interview 1986).

From the detainee section of Salisbury Remand Prison, the ZANU Secretary-General, Robert Mugabe, conducted a meticulous correspondence with Altman on matters great and small. Customs were insisting on R\$233 (£134) duty for 19 parcels of second-hand clothing collected by Zimbabwe students in Britain for the families of detainees. Mugabe thought it a bit much for unsolicited gifts. The attorneys were put on to it and the demand was dropped. The future president was concerned about the plight of his Ghanaian wife, Sally, who was having difficulty getting a work permit in England. The Home Office had told Altman there was no proof that she was the wife of Robert Mugabe. 'Let him come here to prove it,' she said. A barrister won her the right to stay. Mugabe then got down to discussing the most suitable social studies degree course for his wife. As with the wives of other leading exiles waiting in Britain, she received a monthly Amen Court stipend. Even before his detention, Mugabe, with three degrees, was among the best educated of Rhodesians, white or black. Enforced idleness and a penchant for academic achievement brought three more. It was not all plain sailing. In December 1971, there was bad news about his University of London LLM. He had failed African law 'rather badly' and 'just failed' Commonwealth constitutional law. Yet the more difficult jurisprudence and law of international institutions posed few problems. 'The reasons are obvious,' he said. He did not have statutes and reports of commissions on the law of marriage, succession and property in other African countries. Next time round there was no mistake. 'With all the material you were able to get me,' he told Altman, 'all that was left for me to do was to apply myself, and this I managed to do.' By then he was reading for the Bar, and getting to grips with Latin (IDAF files).

Convicted 'politicals' were at first refused study rights. But in 1969, IDAF was allowed to service prisoners in Salisbury, then elsewhere. Captured guerrillas at Khami, harshest of the penal institutions, had only a brief period of study before the privilege was withdrawn. Sly Masuku, who arrived after the commutation of his death sentence, held primitive classes behind the warders' backs. 'We had study groups for an hour outside in the sunshine, sitting like children around a teacher and writing in the dust.'

As with the Robben Islanders, Rhodesian undergraduate prisoners prepared for independence courtesy of the correspondence courses offered by the University of South Africa (UNISA) in Pretoria. Though some alumni had been captured by Vorster's police, the Afrikaner lecturers assessed the work without bias, says Cephas Msipa. He felt free to describe the bantustans as 'stupid' in a public administration essay. Josiah Chinamano, once a lecturer at Selly Oak College in Birmingham, and a 'Gona' veteran from opening day in 1964, was in charge of UNISA library books, packing them in large sacks and rarely missing a date-stamp deadline.

By the early seventies, IDAF's Rhodesia section had become a huge undertaking, with Altman and Joan Darling supervising letter-writers and book donors. A trust in the name of Eva Reckitt, proprietor of Collett's, the left-wing bookshop in Charing Cross Road, London, provided textbooks free. Quakers and nuclear disarmers in St Albans sent friendship letters and parcels of used clothes, which explains why a freed detainee was seen stepping out in a suit discarded by the Bishop of St Albans, Robert Runcie. Bales of second-hand clothes arrived from Sweden for distribution by Christian Care. IDAF was blamed when a detainee's wife metamorphosed into the best-dressed woman in her village, and then fell pregnant.

Educating detainees' children was another serious undertaking. In 1968 there were no secondary school places for 26,000 of the 34,000 successful black primary school-leavers. Even if a school was willing to take them, parents were landed with tuition fees of £20 a term. IDAF did its best to educate disappointed scholars through correspondence courses. By 1969, the fees of 900 primary and some secondary schoolchildren were being paid by Christian Care and IDAF. Another 50 children from devastated homes were sent to boarding school.

Altman insisted that each family welfare grant undergo quality checks. Manguni, the go-between for detainees, families and IDAF, criss-crossed the country – his peregrinations wore out three cars – to interview dependants and confirm that there was no help from other sources. Every March he went on a long drive to assess the extent of the rains, then estimated the incoming harvests and bags of millet that might be needed in each area. Joshua Nkomo, a Kalanga from the south-western town of Plumtree, passed on complaints from Ndebele detainees that their farms were getting too little assistance. In other words, Manguni's allocations were 'tribalistic', favouring the Shona majority. Manguni convinced him of his impartiality, and there the matter rested. The knottiest parent was Maurice Nyagumbo, ZANU's organising secretary, who spent 11 years in detention and refused to have his five daughters 'indoctrinated by the regime'. Mrs Victoria Nyagumbo wanted her children at school, but not against her husband's wishes. Manguni told her that she also had a say over her children, and she took the matter to the district commissioner. Mr Nyagumbo arrived under police guard, not knowing that his wife had instigated the hearing. The decision, to no one's surprise, favoured his wife (Manguni interview 1992).

Christian Care sent Nkomo the *Complete Guide to Gardening in South Africa* and packets of seeds for his herb garden. Letters were exchanged on the properties of mint, which the bulky freedom fighter had heard improved the taste of meat. Collins funded Nkomo's two sisters and a nephew, while the ZAPU leader's own children were educated out of the general Christian Care fund. The Bulawayo office settled Mrs Nkomo's clothes bill at Tee Vee Bazaars. But when, in 1973, Nkomo asked for R$200 from the IDAF Christmas welfare fund, Manguni sent half, promising that 'should any welfare of this nature creep our way as we glide along in our work, it will be our greatest pleasure to grant further assistance to you.'

Christian Care closed its Salisbury office in 1971. Most detainees were in 'Gona' or Wha Wha (Gwelo), and their affairs were more easily handled from Bulawayo. Manguni has his own explanation: the Salisbury office was run by women, and political detainees did not like discussing family problems with women. The Salisbury office re-opened in 1975, when Melphy Sakupwanya moved there from Bulawayo.

•

In 1967 a combined ZAPU–South African ANC force crossed the Zambezi and moved south along game trails, with the MK guerrillas heading for the Limpopo. Vorster sent paramilitary police to help counter the invasion. The guerrillas took them on, but perished from gunfire, hunger or wild animals. The survivors sought asylum in Botswana or were captured. Instead of recognition as prisoners of war under the Geneva Convention, those captured faced the Law and Order (Maintenance) Act. In the Salisbury high court the defendants had the distinct feeling that their *pro deo* counsel lacked the stomach to defend 'terrs' (white Rhodesian slang for 'terrorists'). The Bar, with few exceptions, was lily-white, and in this closed community were liable to put patriotism before professional duty. With all 32 sentenced to death, Altman insisted IDAF fund an appeal, and when that failed, a reprieve petition was sent to 'President' Clifford Dupont, which he turned down. But the intervention provided a breathing space. International pressure forced Lardner-Burke, the man with real power, to reprieve them[3] (Mcube interview 1992).

For most other matters, white Rhodesia was let off the hook. Ian Smith harped on 'kith and kin'. Had he not flown Spitfires against Nazi tyranny? And were the relatives of Brits not facing slaughter by 'commie terrorists'? British Labour ministers, who were in government for ten of the 15 UDI years, viewed the guerrillas as rebels against the established order. No wonder blacks saw Britain as being on Salisbury's side. Collins once stormed out of a meeting when a Treasury official remarked: 'But we all support Smithy, don't we?' After Labour's failure to reach agreement with Smith, in November 1971 the Tory Foreign Secretary, Sir Alec Douglas-Home, signed an agreement with the rebel leader designed to restore Rhodesia to the international fold. There was one proviso – the proposals should be acceptable to 'the people of Rhodesia as a whole'. A commission, headed by Lord Pearce (the sole dissenting judge in the 'Madzimbamuto' Privy Council hearing), and backed by a posse of Foreign Office desk-men, was set to test the true nature of this opinion. Smith, believing in the innate conservatism of rural Africa, was confident of approval. The countryside was to exhibit an unexpected level of sophistication.

At the request of the newly-formed African National Council, Collins dispatched IDAF's solicitor, Bernard Sheridan, his partner, Cyril Glasser, and his own son, Andrew Collins, by now a barrister – his first choice, the human rights QC Dingle Foot, had been refused entry. On arrival in Salisbury, not a single white lawyer would assist Sheridan, who then set up office in the Methodist mission, headquarters of the African National Council leader, Bishop Abel Muzorewa. There had never been a situation quite like it, as the British officials of the Pearce commission waded through an African political quagmire trying to discern whether a majority was in favour of permanent powerlessness. 'Typically English, they felt more comfortable talking to me than to Africans,' said Glasser. He used the nationalist network to collect statements, discover who was being detained or which employer was making it difficult for workers to express their views. Glasser inundated the commission with paperwork. Newspapers accused the cockney lawyer of manipulating black dissent. 'Nonsense. We were simply giving African opinion an airing' (Eastwood and Glasser interviews 1992).

In his report to Collins, Sheridan said the commission had not appreciated that to give evidence was in itself an offence. The legal team had drawn up a document on immunity that led to an undertaking by the regime's Attorney-General that no one who gave evidence would be prosecuted – though Sheridan still feared repression after Pearce returned home. The legal team also persuaded the commission that instead of saying 'no' in the traditional tribal way at open meetings, people should give evidence in private so that the Smith government could not blame the rejection of the settlement on 'whipped-up frenzy'.

With the men from the FO desperate for a settlement, it is possible that the guiding hand of IDAF tipped the balance against Smith and Home. Pearce's report was able to observe that the rural and urban areas were 'alive with political activity at the grassroots'. The commission's report that the proposals were not acceptable to the people scuttled the initiative. It was back to square one.

Mugabe was released in 1975 and, en route to Dar-es-Salaam for an Organisation of African Unity (OAU) foreign ministers' meeting, was detained by the Front for the Liberation of Mozambique (FRELIMO). It was a benign custody, for by now he was the leader in whom the ZANU guerrillas had confidence. And he was ready for another degree, a London MSc in economics. But in April he told Altman that due to his 'present circumstances, it is practically impossible to write my exams in May'. The prompt arrival of that letter depended on 'travel from one point to another by men on foot'. A year later, having visited London, he wrote to Altman of his pleasure in 'holding a little discussion with one whose name has become a household word amongst all our leading politicians at home.' Meanwhile the out-of-favour Rev. Ndabaningi Sithole, on a visit to London, asked IDAF to settle his hotel bill. Altman complained that 'he smoked cigars and drank brandies', and 'made John furious by leaving an enormous bill'. She passed this intelligence to the abstemious Mugabe (IDAF files).

By 1975, *Chimurenga*, a fully-fledged war of liberation, was under way, largely in the east of Zimbabwe, but on the western front as well. ZANU operated in the most accessible theatre of the war, the Eastern Highlands. Children barely into their teens were joining the frenzied exodus, to Mozambique in the east or Botswana in the west, to become fighting men and women. There were trials of those who encouraged youngsters to join the guerrillas. A schoolteacher was gaoled for 25 years for recruiting five boys under the age of fourteen. Ten years into UDI, the military tide turned decisively against the diminishing white Rhodesian base. Vorster and US Secretary of State Henry Kissinger forced Smith to accept the principle of majority rule. As he wavered, the guerrilla offensive intensified, with Mugabe's army emerging as the more effective fighting machine.

There was simply not enough money to defend every trial, nor was the legal profession large or progressive enough to take on such cases as those of guerrillas charged with killing white farmers. As in South Africa, the Rhodesian Bench was white and conservative. Once Judge Davies had ruled that the rebel government was legal, judges felt free to validate ever more bloody defences of an untenable way of life. 'If anarchy is not to prevail,' said Judge Beck, 'justice demands that every manifestation of the terrorist curse must be brutally deterred' (*XRAY*, April 1974: 2).

In an effort to break the bottleneck of prosecutions, special courts were set up in 1976 to mete out on-the-spot 'justice' to guerrillas and their peasant helpers. Keeping track was a nightmare for lawyers. The courts were convened at short notice at a time or place of the presiding officer's choosing – he knew that the more remote the venue, the greater the difficulty in finding legal representation. The right of defendants to be represented by their own lawyer could be overruled by the court president if it entailed 'undue delay'.

Some were tried, convicted and sentenced to die within a week of arrest. In the first seven months, the special courts recorded over a hundred convictions, of which 24 were capital cases. Yet if everyone who failed to report the presence of guerrillas had been prosecuted, half the country would have been in prison. The court president, despite his grand title, was an ordinary magistrate, advocate or attorney, sitting with two assessors who did not have to be trained in the law. Much in evidence were hard-line native commissioners, men none too happy at the flouting of their authority. Liberal-minded native commissioners, and they did exist, were not often seated on the assessor's bench.

When IDAF lawyers did appear in a special court or before a magistrate, the impact was startling. Ewen Greenfield, a Bulawayo attorney, recalls cases dismissed because of slipshod presentation of police evidence. It happened more than once that a magistrate acquitted because the accused's confessions were so similar as to be suspect. 'At first, in the early seventies, it was extraordinarily difficult to prove to a magistrate or judge that a confession had been induced,' says Greenfield, whose office was 'engulfed' by Law and Order (Maintenance) Act work. 'The judges were remote, but some of the magistrates, and not just the liberal ones, were realistic, closer to the police and knew how they worked' (Greenfield interview 1992).

The churches identified more uninhibitedly with the struggle than their South African counterparts. Only one in eight Africans was Christian, but three-quarters of these were Roman Catholics. The mission school network ensured that many of the politically-aware rural middle-class were Catholics. The Catholic Commission for Justice and Peace (CCJP) set out to inform the world about life in the war zones. Collective fines imposed on entire villages, the shooting of curfew-breakers, the instant 'justice' imposed by the army, Selous Scouts and other units, all were aired in spite of censorship regulations. Nor were guerrilla atrocities overlooked; they too had a habit of exacting reprisals for non-cooperation. Mission stations offered a bolt hole to freedom fighters – who were often local boys – until the coast was clear. In consequence, a succession of foreign priests and church workers was expelled and their African brothers killed or detained. The Irish Bishop of Umtali, Msgr Donal Lamont, was arrested in 1977 for instructing that the presence of freedom fighters should not be reported. He was gaoled for ten years (the sentence reduced to a year on appeal), stripped of his citizenship and deported. Collins appreciated the desperate straits Smith must have been in to have to take on a Catholic bishop old-fashioned enough to require the faithful to kneel and kiss his ring. Asked to contribute to the defence, he told Joan Darling: 'Certainly, my dear, and immediately please.' IDAF also funded the defence of Fr Dieter Scholz, vice-chairman of CCJP in Salisbury, who, with five other Catholic officials, had publicised government atrocities.[4] They too were expelled (Darling interview 1991).

An interdenominational legal aid office set up by IDAF in 1976 worked through the religious groups. A roster of ten lawyers, black and white, dealt with urgent legal matters, arrests and disappearances. Once the office was informed, the contact lawyer would phone the police station or army camp nearest to the missing person's residence. The voice at the other end was never helpful but a lawyer offered the only chance of making the authorities accountable. The combination of IDAF and the legal profession saved lives and won acquittals against the odds.

Local lawyers, in consultation with IDAF, hoped to stem the tide of official brutality and torture by suing the army, police or minister for damages. In 1975 this became virtually impossible when the Indemnity and Compensation Act gave protection to security force personnel, tribal chiefs and UDI officials against civil claims resulting from acts committed 'in good faith for the purpose of or in connection with the suppression of terrorism or the maintenance of public order'. The protection was made retrospective to 1972. An 'invitation to excess', said the International Commission of Jurists. Chief Jeremy Chirau, president of the council of chiefs, breathed a sigh of relief. Two brothers, members of the ANC, were in the process of suing him for having personally assaulted them, when their lawyer received a certificate signed by Lardner-Burke declaring that the high court action 'shall not be continued'. But IDAF did win R$1,000 damages and costs against Lardner-Burke and a special branch detective.

As in South Africa, the government persisted in the fiction that those in prison were common felons. The 'gung-ho' defence minister, Pieter van der Byl (pronounced 'van der Bile', with a hard 'V', to obscure his Afrikaner origins), declared that there were no political prisoners, 'only people considered a threat to security'. Heavy-handed press censorship and a tight rein on television and radio placed a big responsibility on IDAF and similar organisations. Few Rhodesians were allowed to know who or how many were in prison. Two months after Smith had accepted the principle of majority rule within two years, an IDAF booklet, *Ian Smith's Hostages*, put this pro-mise in perspective by listing 1,839 convicted, detained and restricted political prisoners.

If news of political prisoners was a touchy matter, the fate of executed men and women was a jealously guarded secret. The death penalty was adapted to the changing needs of the time. Petrol bombers had been the first targets. With the invasions, hanging was mandatory for entering the country with weapons of war. In the 1970s, the courts came down heavily on recruitment or failure to report the presence of terrorists. Cooking a pot of *mealie meal* (maize porridge) for a passing guerrilla was a capital offence, though it is not known if anyone was hanged for this – it was simpler to shoot the chef on the spot. In 1975, Smith announced that the names of people sentenced to death or hanged would no longer be released. Van der Byl quipped that it was 'because they are normally dead after it'. One lawyer noted that 'for long stretches guerrillas never seemed to appear in court... they were given the option to co-operate or be shot.' Certainly, there was some leniency in the four years after UDI, with reprieves for 131 of the 173 'politicals' facing execution. But once the war began in earnest, the security forces had to be reassured that ministers were being tough.

In the uncertain period following UDI, Bernard Sheridan applied to the Queen for a reprieve for three men on death row. She obliged through an Order-in-Council, but they were executed nonetheless. Later, Altman attempted to invoke the

Queen as a means of stressing the illegality of the executions. 'Every time we heard that someone had been sentenced to death, I wrote to, and on occasions saw, Foreign Secretary David Owen to ask for the Queen's Pardon. He wouldn't do it. He said we must wait for a political settlement' (Altman interview 1992). When Muzorewa and Sithole joined Smith in government in 1978, they promised to reduce the execution rate. But *Focus*, IDAF's bulletin on political repression in southern Africa, quoting church sources – which might have heard from a black prison chaplain – reported 28 hangings in March 1979 in Salisbury alone (*Focus* No. 23, July–August 1979: 5). Thursday was 'drop day'. IDAF published a list of 109 known death sentences between April 1975 and 1980. Police pressure was such that a father who had heard from his wife of their son's execution was told he should not have been informed.

Not satisfied with the special courts, the military demanded and were given courts martial. The internal settlement, signed in March 1978, had settled nothing, initiating instead a frenzy of killing. Muzorewa and Sithole now had their own private armies, dubbed by Lt-Gen. Peter Walls, commander of combined operations, 'on-side guerrillas', though many had belonged to the security forces and others were turned guerrillas. They were said to be more brutal than the Selous Scouts. The courts martial were unusual in that they tried civilians, which was justified on the grounds that the whole country, except Salisbury and Bulawayo and the corridor between, was under martial law. A ministry of information, immigration and tourism pamphlet explained that 'the State may be compelled by the needs of the moment to disregard to some extent and for a temporary period the ordinary safeguards of liberty in defence of liberty itself and to substitute for the careful and deliberate procedure of the law a machinery more drastic and speedy to cope with a pressing danger.' On the rare occasions that IDAF's lawyers got to hear of courts martial, they had difficulty gaining access. Hearings were in camera, presided over by white farmers. IDAF learnt, in January 1979, of 11 death sentences in the courts martial.

•

The 760 new correspondence courses in 1978 included 57 of the 60 women at Chikurubi prison. Results were mixed, but always morale boosting. 'I managed to squeeze out and passed religious studies with an E,' wrote a grateful student. Told she was free, the future minister Jane Ngwenya asked incredulously, 'You are not releasing me in the middle of my course?' When the gates of Gwelo prison finally opened, everybody, even the elderly, could read and write.

Throughout these years, Collins had to seek permission from the Treasury to transmit money to Christian Care. He was enraged by the annual ritual, the more so as no British Government was ever serious about sanctions. Permission or no, it is a fact that the 'Republic of Rhodesia' received large amounts of money from IDAF, a sworn enemy: the sterling equivalent of R\$500,000 in 1979, and R\$800,000 the next year. It might explain why Christian Care, unlike the South African Defence and Aid committees, was not banned; Smith was desperate for foreign currency.

When Mrs Thatcher moved into Downing Street, she was inclined to recognise Muzorewa's government, but her foreign secretary, Lord Carrington, dissuaded her. Instead, independence was negotiated at a constitutional conference at Lancaster House in London. At its conclusion, Mugabe hosted a thank-you dinner. Phyllis Altman sat on his right. It was the ultimate accolade – though the workers at Amen Court felt a great affinity for Nkomo, founding figure of Zimbabwe nationalism.

Focus published the security forces' final body count: 27,500 killed; 275,000 wounded; 750,000 displaced within Zimbabwe; 225,000 refugees abroad; 225,000 in protected villages; 330,000 lost homes; 500,000 missed years of education.

Mugabe's independence cabinet included 12 graduates of the university behind bars. Eton College never boasted a like domination of British political life. In March 1981 Collins was still actively canvassing funds for the now independent country. The Swedes, Norwegians and Canadians donated additional funds to IDAF, and the £60,000 from the European Community at last featured a British contribution. It went towards the families of 7,000 martial-law detainees, R$300 each to help freed men and women stand on their feet, and a programme to rehabilitate guerrillas. The money was pumped into co-operatives – chicken farms, print shops, the 'All are One' supermarket. Some thrived at first, but by 1985 few were still operating.

In 1982 Mugabe launched an offensive on the ZAPU-dominated Matabeleland region of Zimbabwe, seriously undermining the apparent unity of the new government. He also charged 14 Ndebele, including ZIPRA (Zimbabwe People's Revolutionary Army, the military wing of ZAPU) generals and ZAPU MPs, with treason. When IDAF was asked to fund their defence, it declined, arguing that with white rule overthrown and Mugabe fairly elected to office it would be a gross interference in Zimbabwe's internal affairs. Though the charges were dropped, many in 'Nkomo country' were angered by IDAF's refusal – a sad note on which to end an honourable association with the old Rhodesia and the new Zimbabwe (Altman interview 1992; Judith Todd interview 1992).

Chapter 23

DEATH OF THE CANON

Collins retired as Canon of St Paul's Cathedral on 1 December 1981, in his 77th year. The final months at the Cathedral were as eventful as ever, with the wedding of Oliver Tambo's elder daughter, Tembi, giving him especial pleasure. He officiated at a more historic ceremony, the marriage of Prince Charles, heir to the throne, and Lady Diana Spencer. On the day of the final service, the Queen Mother, her memories stretching back to pre-war days when Collins had been priest-in-ordinary to her father-in-law, George V, drew him aside to offer words of consolation. 'We shall miss you,' she said.

Leaving the Cathedral meant giving up the house in Amen Court. More than just a family home, it was, down the years, the place of incubation for many crusades – CND and Defence and Aid, but others that had achieved a certain notoriety – Radical Alternatives to Prison (RAP), Campaign for the Homeless and Rootless (CHAR) and the Movement for the Ordination of Women (MOW), in which Diana Collins was a prime mover.

The consolation was that the couple would spend more time at Mill House, their hill-top home in Constable country on the Essex–Suffolk border, with its fine views of the Stour valley. The Canon had recuperated there after his coronary. But they also took up residence in a flat in a featureless concrete block on the south side of Blackfriars Bridge, within walking distance of the IDAF office in Newgate Street. Collins had no intention of giving up his extra-curricular activities.

From time to time, over the years, he and Mr X would meet in the Chapter House to drink a glass of sherry in celebration of their survival. Every year, said Frankel, 'we thought the South Africans would tumble to what we were doing and have a blanket restriction on money coming in.' But IDAF seemed to be coping well. According to Altman's summary of activity in South Africa and Namibia during 1980, it had covertly funded 130 trials involving 2,092 people – comparable figures for the previous year were 57 and 295. IDAF-funded lawyers were involved across the spectrum from capital cases to the defence of large groups of school boycotters. The cost of defending was high, but always worthwhile in human terms. Exiled lawyer Albie Sachs said, 'When the attorney appears it is the first time the victim can tell his story – the lawyer will articulate what he is saying, and even if not believed in court, he has said his piece.'

The Terrorism Act was widely deployed against those recruiting and being recruited for guerrilla training. Of 131 on trial for terrorism, only 15 were acquitted, but in less serious cases (strikes, possession of banned literature, boycotts) the acquittal rate was 40 per cent. Convictions and sentences, ranging from 21 lashes to hanging, were invariably taken on appeal. James Mange, alone among 12 in a treason trial in Pietermaritzburg to be sentenced to death, though he had killed no-one, was among the beneficiaries – his sentence was commuted to life.

More trials bred a greater welfare need, with 385 families added to the list in 1980, though some were the parents of sons and daughters who had gone 'under the wire'. The two-monthly allowance was increased by £10 as the price of cooking oil and paraffin climbed and steep rent increases were imposed. There was an extra £10,000 to cover 218 family prison visits. 'Whenever I start panicking and becoming really in need,' a mother wrote, 'then I receive one from you. Then all panics and worries wear off.' It was the sort of letter that made it all worthwhile.

Yet, in a way, IDAF was getting out of its depth, unable to respond adequately to the upsurge in the demand for aid. The gap was partly filled by the South African Council of Churches (SACC) defence fund, *Asingeni*, which had been founded by Steve Biko in King William's Town with Christian Institute backing and World Council of Churches money. At one stage it was bigger than IDAF but then it fizzled out, the target of a security-police inspired judicial commission of inquiry based on spurious allegations of the misuse of funds. The message was clear – without external help, thousands faced destitution.

•

Despite advancing years, Collins had given little consideration to grooming a successor. It is true that he appointed Ioan Evans, a Labour MP unseated in the 1970 general election, to the post of 'Director' of IDAF, at the behest of James Callaghan, when Collins was still hoping to improve matters with the Labour Party. Evans turned out not to be the man for the job, whatever that job was. He signed letters as 'Director' until he was voted back into the Commons in 1974. 'Nice guy,' recalled Hugh Lewin, 'but all he did was serve the sherry. John would say "Poor old Ioan" but he also knew he had been emasculated by Phyllis and Rica (Hodgson).'

After the coronary, Collins continued as if nothing had changed. He was not the first founder of a business to ignore ill health and a creaking memory and believe his shoes were unfillable. But Reddy and the Swedes were worried. Reddy had a chat with Collins at the IDAF conference in Dublin in 1975, and 'persuaded him to set up a small committee of trustees which would reassure the larger donors that their money was properly spent'. Diana, too, sensed he was losing his grip. She tactfully suggested that a serious attempt be made to find a successor. Collins bowed to the inevitable, or so it seemed, and the dance of the heirs apparent was inaugurated.

This was the first time an IDAF post would be advertised and it had to be carefully done. Notices were placed by a member of the Christian Action council, Michael Graham Jones, whose 'Faculties Partnership' provided the cover. Did the Trafalgar Square BOSS-men narrow their eyes at the double column heading: 'International Humanitarian Work – DEPUTY DIRECTOR'? Clues were there in abundance... 'small but well-known international body... administrative headquarters in London... regular contact with the United Nations and with governments... exacting work, essentially charitable but also political.' Applicants were to show 'presence, firmness and diplomacy in discussion, high administrative skills, compassion and political sensitivity'. Starting salary, not less than £6,000.

More revealing was the promise that the appointment could lead 'in due course to the principal executive position'. The advertisement appeared in seven newspapers and magazines, including the *Daily Telegraph* (02.03.76).

The job went to David Mason, a Methodist pastor who seemed to have the required qualifications. He was, like Collins, a man of action, having founded the Notting Hill Gate team ministry after the riots there in 1960. Diana Collins entertained high hopes for Mason, who landed the post in the face of strong contenders – Illtyd Harrington, former deputy leader of the Greater London Council; Tony Smythe of the National Council of Civil Liberties; and Paul Oestreicher, Vicar of Blackheath and Chairman of British Amnesty. Mason was recommended by Abdul Minty, who warned him privately: 'It's OK to work *with* him [Collins], but crazy to work *for* him' (Mason interview 1992).

After a crash course in security procedures, delivered in the penultimate pew at St Paul's by Altman, whispering in his ear from behind, Mason was sent to South Africa on an undercover acclimatisation mission. Collins warned him to take care to disguise his identity but Mason found that the only way contacts would talk to this unknown figure was by mentioning the open sesame word 'IDAF'. So he was able to win the confidence of black consciousness leaders, including Steve Biko. London was horrified. During the visit, he broke another cardinal rule by cabling a request to a friend in England to have IDAF send £6,000 for a black consciousness trial. Altman recalls the Canon asking, 'should I sack him, and I said "Yes" but he gave him another chance.'

Mason had been led to understand that after a year as deputy he would take over as director. An efficient administrator, he improved the staff wage structure, though Altman was upset to discover that his secretary earned more than she did. He survived another 12 months, all the time at odds with Altman, whom he suspected of steaming open his mail. He attributed his eventual departure to his attachment to the Black Consciousness Movement, which was out of kilter with the rest of the office's support for the ANC. But there was more to it than ideology.

Whoever was appointed, Diana recalled, was in an impossible position, 'trapped between John, who was unwilling to delegate, and Phyllis, whose detailed knowledge of South Africa and of all the intricacies of IDAF was unrivalled. We kept having to find something for these unfortunate men to do.' Subconsciously, Collins might have believed he was choosing the candidate he judged least likely to survive the backbiting office tensions.

Of all the would-be supremos, Frank Judd – appointed 'Associate Director' after the 1979 general election – was the weightiest. Foreign Office minister-of-state in the outgoing Labour government, he was blessed with an impressive range of VIP contacts. But as a man who prided himself on being a straightforward administrator, Judd was disturbed by the number of IDAF decisions that went round him rather than through him. He fell into an Altman bear trap by sending copies of her confidential reports to eight London embassies that had not been cleared to have them. She threatened to resign, but Judd beat her to it, announcing that he was off to run Voluntary Service Overseas. His stint at IDAF lasted nine months.

With his departure it became obvious that whoever acquired the title director, associate director or director-designate under Collins was doomed to lightning-quick tenure. Thereafter no serious attempt was made to find a high-profile successor, though Collins enjoyed raising it in certain circumstances, particularly over a decent lunch. Donald Woods was offered the crown over a bowl of sweet and sour pork at the 'Good Friends' in Limehouse. Paul Ostreicher and Ethel de Keyser were also given the come-on. Very probably they were not the last 'candidates' to be button-holed by a now seriously forgetful Canon. He concluded a fulsome introduction to a press conference for the SWAPO president, Sam Nujoma, by looking forward to the day 'when Joshua Nkomo will be prime minister of Namibia'.

Phyllis Altman, for so long the effective chief executive, could not realistically be regarded as a long-term successor. To begin with, she was 63 when Collins stepped down at St Paul's. Her marxist beliefs, her non-Christian background, the lack of a public relations touch, combined with Collins's chauvinistic attitude to women, all seemed to make her unsuitable for what was essentially an English establishment job. Such a person would have to come from further down the IDAF ranks – like Wilfrid Grenville-Grey, an old Etonian who rejoiced in a bizarre Collins job description, 'Chief Executive and Personal Assistant to the President', in the interregnum between Mason and Judd. Grenville-Grey had exemplary South African connections through his marriage to Thabo Mbeki's sister-in-law, but he, as with other outsiders brought in with high-sounding titles, had difficulty ascertaining his place in the pecking-order. Craig Williamson, the South African spy, was sufficiently impressed by Grenville-Grey to air a random story, through his ANC contacts, that his paramount loyalty was to British intelligence.

When Collins tired of him – and hired Judd – Grenville-Grey was shunted sideways across the Atlantic as his 'Chief Representative – United Nations and North America'. It was not as glamorous as it seemed. While the UN and its trust fund were of crucial importance to IDAF, any business that mattered was transacted personally between Enuga Reddy and Collins. So New York was a non-job, though Grenville-Grey did earn merit points by almost making something of it. IDAF at last joined the UN's 600-strong community of non-governmental organisations. Grenville-Grey mounted an exhibition of the work of the exiled sculptor, Dumile Feni, in the UN's main visitors' lobby, which was some relief from the soul-destroying routine that required him to divide up $1,000 a month between half a dozen indigent exiles. As Reddy said: 'John convinced Grenville-Grey that he was coming for something important. But there was nothing here' (Reddy interview 1992).

Forever on the lookout for fresh sources of revenue, and hoping to take the strain off the Swedes, Collins engaged an elegant and well-connected Indian, Mariyam Mahmoud-Harris, to conquer the Middle East, with the non-aligned world thrown in as an added challenge, 'to prevent IDAF being regarded as a western Christian organisation'. The saga of her efforts to open an IDAF office in Delhi or to get the

Saudis to 'disgorge their petro-dollars' was reported back in dispatches to Collins. She met the Saudi foreign minister at a dinner hosted by his Indian opposite number. 'HRH was most affable,' she wrote. 'He claimed me as his sister because of our 'mutual father', the late James Baroody (Saudi representative at the UN), whereupon I claimed a 'sister's privilege' and proceeded to tell him about IDAF.' The minister assured her it was a matter 'close to us', though she did warn Collins of 'many slips twixt cup and lip' (IDAF files). A $75,000 petro-donation arrived in 1977 but over the years the funds she raised barely covered her salary and travel expenses. She was not helped by a hostile climate at IDAF's Newgate Street offices where, with no office of her own, she was forced to work in the waiting room. The final straw was having to report to the rising star, Horst Kleinschmidt. She outlasted Collins by a few weeks.

Collins had taken on Kleinschmidt as a fund-raiser in June 1979 but he quickly made himself useful in other areas. It was Kleinschmidt who reinforced Altman's suspicions of Craig Williamson, effectively denying him access to IDAF. The talent for spy-spotting was hard won, for he had himself once been an object of suspicion. He was a Namibian of German origin. His great-great-grandfather Heinrich arrived in southern Africa as a missionary in 1842, a generation before the formal German colonisation of South West Africa. The old man married a 'half-Griqua', so that, by Pretoria's calculations, Horst was thirty-second part 'coloured'. In the early 1950s Horst's family moved to Johannesburg. In the mid-1960s he attended 'Wits' (University of the Witwatersrand). Despite his conservative upbringing, he was active in student politics, eventually being elected national vice-president of NUSAS.

Whilst at Wits he rejected an attempt at recruitment by the police (by going public to the *Rand Daily Mail* newspaper), though Jewish acquaintances, suspicious of his background, believed there was no smoke without fire. After university, the Progressive Party, looking to expand its youth section, took him on, only to drop him smartly when he was charged with possessing a copy of the banned magazine, *African Communist*. He was then recruited by the Christian Institute, run by the renegade Dutch Reformed Church pastor, Beyers Naudé, which worked closely with the Black Consciousness leadership. Kleinschmidt was put in charge of its white community programme, while Steve Biko ran its black counterpart.

One of Kleinschmidt's tasks was to publicise the names of detainees, something the newspapers were wary of printing. It brought him into the ambit of IDAF. He would ask friends and visiting clergymen and academics to deliver information about detainees to Altman in London. Callers at his home, Kleinschmidt later discovered, had their faces recorded by a camera fitted into the front door of the house of a railway policeman who lived across the road.

Over the years, Kleinschmidt acquired respectable 'struggle honours'. Nelson and Winnie Mandela made him unofficial guardian of their two daughters. He was convicted of possessing 'banned literature'; deprived of his passport; charged but not prosecuted under the Riotous Assemblies Act; detained for 75 days in solitary confinement under the Terrorism Act; and spent three harrowing nights in *Die Gat* ('The Hole'), Pretoria Central's death row, before taking flight (in a friend's Cessna) to Botswana. He ran the Christian Institute's European office in Utrecht, though its influence waned after 1977 when, along with other church and black consciousness groups, it was banned as 'communist' by Pretoria. By the time Kleinschmidt became a staffer at IDAF, the overdue changes were being considered.

The Swedes did not want to be seen to interfere but, in delivering half and more of IDAF's budget, their voice would inevitably be heard. Brought in initially as a trustee, Ernst Michanek, approaching retirement after 14 years in charge of his country's aid agency, identified the need for root and branch reform. He was not impressed with the *laissez faire* way in which Collins, Altman and the treasurer, Reg Gore, ran the office, with 30 employees getting no precise instructions about their day-to-day work. He found Collins 'very authoritarian and the real decisions were never taken at conference'. The topsy-turvy wage structure meant that the longer you stayed, the worse off you were relative to new arrivals. Nothing was worse for security than a rapid staff turnover. The Dutch,

Swiss and American committees were unhappy at the secrecy. Indeed, the Dutch were threatening disaffiliation if IDAF were not reorganised. How, they asked, can we encourage people to contribute to activities that we cannot tell them about? Michanek, a former journalist for whom 'openness has been my gospel', sympathised with this view. It was not just Phyllis Altman. Abdul Minty and Collins 'also supported a high degree of secrecy to protect the recipients' (Michanek interview 1992).

'Memories of Williamson and the IUEF were very painful,' Michanek recalled, 'but the re-organisation of IDAF was necessary anyway.' A new constitution had been adopted at the 1980 Annual General Meeting, but with so many reservations, especially by Swedish Defence and Aid, that it was referred to Sam Silkin, a former Labour attorney-general, who reported that it was 'likely to prove unworkable'. Collins's rearguard action was coming to an end. Tony Gifford, a Labour hereditary peer, joined the group that was searching for a compromise. 'It was an intense transition and I suppose Collins saw in me someone of a like mind, an upper middle class rebel, someone he could talk to.' A committee of Gifford, Minty and Jaap Roosjen, the Dutch chairman, convinced the national committees that IDAF could not function securely under a completely democratic structure. They built in a process of consultation as an alternative to democratic accountability, and the impressive list of independent trustees bedded the process in. On the other side, says Gifford, 'we had to reassure John that what was happening was necessary to put the work he'd pioneered on a basis that could carry the load. It was a very dramatic moment when we passed the resolution to transfer the assets of the old organisation to the new trust, a transition from the old, lovable, but more and more inefficient set-up to something stern, bureaucratic, but capable of winning the confidence of donors and big players' (Gifford interview 1998).

Michanek applied the carving knife to the staff, while salaries were increased and efficiency emphasised. 'There was no longer room for amateurs,' recalled Barry Feinberg. 'IDAF became more and more an adjunct of the struggle in

South Africa rather than a voluntary organisation dishing out charity.' Or, as Reddy put it: 'Ernst did what he thought was right in the Swedish way of dealing with non-governmental organisations, and I do not criticise him, though the concept of voluntary work was lost. Collins was not particularly happy. IDAF had been like a charity operation; now it was being streamlined by bureaucracy.' There was a great showdown at the end between Collins and his successor, whom he referred to dismissively as 'that little man' (Frankel interview 1992).

In the autumn of 1982 Collins went to Vienna, hoping to persuade the Austrian government to contribute directly to IDAF. He returned exhausted. Diana extracted a promise that he would 'really, really' resign as chair of the fund at the end of the year and so make his retirement complete. On New Year's Eve 1982, hours before he was due to deliver on his promise, he died of a heart attack.

'A turbulent priest if ever there was one,' concluded *The Times* (24.02.83), 'whose voice and features were familiar to the whole world.' The *Daily Telegraph* (02.01.83) placed its obituary alongside a report on women peace campaigners arrested at the American Air Force base on Greenham Common. No friend of the Canon in his lifetime, it was nonetheless the *Telegraph* that unwittingly gave him his due. 'Thirty years ago,' it said, 'on racism, nuclear disarmament, social morality, Canon Collins merely stood where the Archbishop of Canterbury and the hierarchy of the Church of England, with a few ifs and buts, stand today.'

For Collins, more than any churchman of his era, had worked against the high grain of public opinion. Rare were the bishops and few the clerical foot soldiers who in the 1950s spoke out on social and political injustice. His fellow priests at St Paul's had signed a round robin to have him ousted. His difficulties were aggravated by the armed struggle. It was no mean feat of funambulism to give it his support while proclaiming pacifist credentials. The British Council of Churches' advisory committee on South Africa long refused to make contact with the ANC, insisting it was controlled by Moscow (Mayson interview 1992). Yet by the time of Collins' death, the politically-influential churches, Anglican, Methodist, and Catholic, were broadly in agreement with him and, incidentally, at odds with Prime Minister Margaret Thatcher's later dismissal of the ANC as 'terrorist'. If any one person was responsible for this sea-change it was Collins. His friend the Scottish theologian George MacLeod of Fuinary spoke of 'the great honour of never having been promoted in the Church.' Collins might not have considered it a sacrifice but given his brains, his wit and his political savvy, he could have gone all the way in the Church of England. No matter. When archbishops are a meaningless roll-call of names in *Crockford's Clerical Directory*, the Canon of St Paul's will be remembered.

He was both admired and criticised. It is not certain whether he had the precious gift of recognising his own failings. John Prevett, a lifelong collaborator, recalls the knowing smiles round the council table when Collins called his old friend Mervyn Stockwood a 'prima donna' for something that had provoked his disapproval. 'There was no bigger prima donna than John,' said Prevett. 'He couldn't see the mote in someone else's eye for the beam in his own' (Prevett interview 1993).

In the last resort, a life is weighed according to how it begins, grows, changes for the better. When he talked of his dry-as-bones Kentish family he was conscious of the distance he had travelled. Conversion to a 1930's socialism coincided with the embrace of High Church Anglicanism, the war experience ushered in Christian Action, the 'Bomb' made of him a pacifist, and apartheid a fellow traveller with the armed struggle. On his visit to South Africa, and thereafter from Amen Court, he listened to the cries of pain and prescribed practical remedies.

A month after his death, all but one of the strands of his life were woven together at a service of thanksgiving in the Cathedral. It was attended by a multi-racial congregation, *The Times* reported, 'many elderly, duffle-coated, the young in anoraks'. The Labour leader, Michael Foot, was there. The Conservative foreign and commonwealth secretary was represented by a former governor of the Falkland Islands. Oliver Tambo read the lesson from Luke: 10, the story of the Good Samaritan – according to Diana, 'more beautiful than I'd ever heard it before'. Anglican prayer and music was interspersed with Africa's tribute – the Lord's Prayer in Xhosa and *Nkosi Sikelel' iAfrika* ('God Bless Africa', now South Africa's national anthem) sung in Zulu by a choir of exiles. CND and Aldermaston were barely mentioned at the service because the Cathedral hierarchy told Diana it would upset Mrs Thatcher. However, once Collins's voice in the nuclear debate had receded, St Paul's was able to tolerate Defence and Aid (*The Times* 24.02.83).

In spite of the publicity attracted by his death, the key secret of IDAF's operation remained intact. Among the regretful non-attenders at the memorial service were the two 'Mr Xs', Martin Bayer and Bill Frankel. It was too risky for them to be publicly associated with Collins, even in death. The obituarists had written of his achievements as being in a distant past. None could have appreciated that until his last months he was actively involved in a covert humanitarian enterprise turning over millions of pounds a year. But if Collins died under-appreciated, Trevor Huddleston's address hinted at the larger role. The Canon's ashes were to be buried in the cathedral, he said, but his monument was not to be found there but 'in the lives of hundreds of thousands, maybe millions, in Africa who never saw him but who because of him and because of his life's work still live in hope and not in despair.' It was the nearest anyone got to the core of his achievement.

The effect of Collins's death on the IDAF power structure was less than dramatic. Bill Frankel remained in place as the pivotal Mr X. Phyllis Altman's name at last appeared as 'Director' on the notepaper, but she too became a victim of the no-frills Scandinavian style that brought much private angst but a whole lot more public alleviation where it really mattered. She was replaced by Horst Kleinschmidt, the leadership candidate reckoned to be most in tune with Michanek's ideas for bureaucratic reform. In July 1983, a 'Dear Wilfrid' letter arrived in New York from IDAF's new chairman, Trevor Huddleston. The cost of maintaining a presence at the United Nations was excessive, he told Grenville-Grey, in spite of his having 'operated it as economically as possible'. The office would close in December, but 'it has not been found possible to offer you a suitable senior position with the new organisation.' There was also rationalisation in London, with the operation integrated into a single headquarters, Canon Collins House, near the Angel, Islington tube station, some way off from the basement in Amen Court where it had all begun, but close enough in spirit.

Chapter 24

PASSIONIST POSTBAG

By the early 1980s, IDAF's letter-writing department, 'Programme Two', had become truly international. By now Rica Hodgson was working at the Solomon Mahlangu Freedom College (SOMAFCO), a school for children of ANC exiles in Tanzania. Under Peggy Stevenson, Hodgson's eventual successor, the task of monitoring the letters was split several ways: Jan Johannes, English wife of an ANC official, liaised with Canada; Carol Trelawny with Denmark, John Hughes with Ireland and Sweden, Margaret Rich with Norway, while Edna Wilcox mopped up the loose ends. The exacting task of filing and microfilming the welfare correspondence was handled by May, wife of the sports boycotter and Chicago-based academic, Dennis Brutus.

Programme staff were social workers in a way, called on, at an ocean's length, to deal with a wide range of problems. They assessed a family's needs almost entirely on the basis of what was in the letters, requiring, Stevenson pointed out, 'a practical and commonsensical approach as well as the ability to empathise with people in a different cultural and political environment many thousands of miles away.' They might be called on to respond to a crisis, as imprisonment or death removed the breadwinner, or parents squabbled over their children. All of this was done through the medium of correspondents, who themselves were being coached at arm's length into building up a trusting relationship with the families they were assisting. With no fieldwork involved, said Stevenson, 'distance itself can bring on stress from a feeling of remoteness and impotence in the face of families' problems.' In a memo, she regretted that 'the social work component of the job has been ignored' (IDAF internal memo).

In June 1983, the British letter writers were given a new 'accommodation address' and a new name to which they were to forward replies from South Africa – Fr JE Sherrington CP. For a change, John Sherrington was a real person, though the initials after his name carried no ideological baggage – they stood for the Congregation of the Passion.

His terraced house in Islington's nondescript New North Road was an easy walk from Canon Collins House. Four times a week, one of Stevenson's team knocked on the front door and came away with a wad of letters. The perceived ordinariness of his life and the fact that Islington council, which employed him as a road sweeper, had no idea he was an ordained priest, made Sherrington an ideal 'dead letter' go-between. But he needed to be careful. When Kleinschmidt told Sherrington and Michael Bold, the other priest living in the house, of his worries about BOSS, they suggested that a brother Passionist should be told of the arrangement. 'If a letter bomb blew up in our face,' said Sherrington, 'the provincial order had the right to know the reason for it.' The two priests ran a project for homeless youths, several of whom lived in the house. The men worried about the letters being opened. By this stage, however, Sherrington's fellow road-sweepers had elected him their National Union of Public Employees (NUPE) shop steward. Sherrington blended another layer of deception into the enterprise, telling curious youngsters that the letters related to union business and the collectors were fellow trade unionists. Some mornings, 40 letters dropped through the letterbox. Those for IDAF were identified through the initial 'E' between the 'J' and the surname. Only when Sherrington opened an incorrectly addressed letter did he understand what he was involved in – families of detainees expressing gratitude for the gifts 'and the considerable amount of aid being given to them.'

'For the situation to change in South Africa,' said Sherrington, 'we had to support the people who were best able to make the change. For me, it was living out the Gospel – it was an honour.' Not that he rated his own contribution highly. 'I felt more like a glorified postman than a secret agent' (Sherrington interview 1992).

Letters might well have been opened in Pretoria, but since they made no mention of IDAF they had scant value as potential evidence. While it was theoretically possible – as critics suggested – that some of the money was diverted to finance terrorist activity, the elaborate method of remitting and acknowledging these small sums made it unlikely in practice. Addressing the UN anti-apartheid committee in 1978, Diana Collins said: 'We never found any evidence to suggest that our humanitarian aid has ever been misused or misdirected. The liberation movements all have huge welfare problems on their hands; no amount of guns is going to help them if they allow all their own people to starve to death' (Diana Collins's address to UN special committee against apartheid, New York 11.10.78).[1]

The basic welfare 'gift' was raised from £50 in 1982 to £60 and then, in March 1984, to £70, with extra available for emergencies. Care was taken to ensure the money's buying power was not diminished. This entailed balancing the improving exchange rate for the pound against the cost-of-living index, which set off at a gallop in the late 1980s. By 1985, IDAF was sending almost £1m a year for family grants and assorted morale-boosters. With apartheid officials eager to cast prisoners' families into the farthest reaches of the bantustans, money was set aside to exploit a change in the law that helped families to buy their rented homes from local councils on a 99-year lease and so retain the right to reside there. Prices ranged from £750 to £1,500. Soon, however, much of this was going on repairing homes wrecked by vigilantes. As township life became ever more fraught, IDAF helped with clothes and bedding for those driven from their homes.

Prisoner education was largely underwritten by IDAF. Mr X sent funds to the Council of Churches, which handled correspondence college payments. The prisons department, unhappy that their wards were accumulating degrees while guests of the government, tried to restrict higher education to first degrees. With IDAF's help, Nambita Stofile obtained a court order to allow her husband, the Rev. Makhenkhesi Stofile (later a provincial premier and cabinet minister), who already had several degrees under his belt, to register for a

University of South Africa LLB. The IDAF budget for the education of the children of prisoners and detainees rose from £28,000 in 1988 to £70,000 a year later.

The Fund was not alone in helping with prison visits, but from 1984 it provided money for more than one a year per family in 'important or desirable' cases. The marked increase in requests for visits was, Stevenson suggested, because families were being more assertive in standing up to the authorities and prison officials.

IDAF was leaving its mark in other areas of the struggle. Many hundreds of children, the youngest seven years old, had been detained, as the police tried desperately to break the school boycotts. Children were of particular concern to Diana Collins, who wrote a report for the UN and the donors based on affidavits provided by the children and smuggled out through IDAF channels. Children were being tortured and, in some cases, sexually abused. Following calls from inside South Africa and more particularly from the ANC, Mrs Collins persuaded Huddleston that IDAF should make an issue of it. The outcome was a conference in the Zimbabwean capital, (now renamed) Harare, in September 1987. Although an IDAF enterprise, it was held under the auspices of the Bishop Ambrose Reeves Trust so that delegates from South Africa could attend without being accused of fraternising with a named enemy. Hundreds crossed the Limpopo and for the first time were able to mingle with foreign anti-apartheid activists from around the world. The conference was well reported in the foreign media, adding to PW Botha's discomfort. Mrs Collins wrote that 'the savagery against the children abated, and by degrees larger numbers of those in prison were released. We felt that this was one of our more worthwhile efforts' (Collins 1992: 376). A year later, the Anti-Apartheid Movement's seventieth birthday concert for Nelson Mandela in London's Wembley Stadium raised £600,000 for children's projects in South Africa.

•

The IDAF of Huddleston and Kleinschmidt came to enjoy a sense of moving forward with a solid body of British public opinion. By the mid-1980s, a new establishment was emerging, encouraged by the first black Dean of St Mary's Cathedral in Johannesburg and General Secretary of the South African Council of Churches, Desmond Tutu, who combined piety and a flinty wit with common sense and uncommon courage. In 1984, Tutu, like Albert Luthuli before him, was awarded the Nobel Peace Prize. (He thereafter became Bishop of Johannesburg, and in 1986 was elected Archbishop of Cape Town.) The following year the British Council of Churches accepted the principle of economic disengagement from South Africa. By now, the Church of England was referred to as 'Her Majesty's real opposition' in the light of its criticism of Thatcherite policies at home and abroad. In 1987 the Trades Union Congress (TUC) awarded its gold badge to Nelson Mandela, an indication that armed struggle had become almost acceptable to the nation's workers, a reflection of the growing solidarity between Britain's trade unions and the mushrooming union movement in South Africa. The TUC had wanted to give the medal to one of Mandela's daughters but settled for Alfred Nzo, the future foreign minister. Even then, the TUC needed to have its arm twisted to allow Nzo on the platform at its annual conference to accept the award on his leader's behalf. And quieter, but scarcely less significant, was the initiative by Collins's long-time Christian Action comrade, John Prevett, a director of Bacon and Woodrow, Britain's largest firm of actuaries, in persuading his professional colleagues to switch the venue of an international conference scheduled for South Africa.

Huddleston, though chairman of the trustees, was at first thought not to have his heart entirely in IDAF. He might have preferred the action-packed world of the Anti-Apartheid Movement – he was, after all, a co-founder and now its president. But IDAF's professionalism won him over and he formed a strong bond with Kleinschmidt. His reputation and that mesmerising oratory meant he was a person world leaders wanted to meet. 'My main job with IDAF in the last years was to fund-raise with governments', he recalled, adding, with a hint of pride, 'I went all over the blimmin' world. I had a meeting with the Canadian cabinet – it took the whole morning' (Huddleston interview 1992).

Big business was suddenly running scared. In 1986, the long campaign against Barclays Bank, which had seen its share of the British student market whittled down from 28 per cent to 18 per cent, ended with withdrawal from South Africa. The British protest groups that had coalesced in the 'End Loans' movement now directed their attention to the merchant banks whose syndicated loans funded South Africa's strategic projects. The pace of events was quickened by PW Botha's failure to deliver on widely heralded political concessions at the Natal congress of the National Party in August 1985. His 'Rubicon speech', as it was ironically termed, plunged the rand into headlong decline. A year later the US Congress's Comprehensive Anti-Apartheid Act – having survived President Reagan's veto – prohibited all loans to South Africa other than for black projects. Without the US banks, there was no rolling-over of the world banking community's loans and, though Pretoria did not default, its credit virtually dried up. When American companies in South Africa were suddenly subjected to double taxation, Kodak, General Motors, Ford, Coca-Cola and other household names held fire sales of their assets and fled. White South Africans were demoralised by this abrupt mood change in their most reliable friend. Even if Pretoria still managed to skirt the UN's oil embargo, it was through go-betweens at extortionate cost. Prospects for the apartheid economy were bleak.

In contrast, the covert economy of IDAF was booming, with the money supply showing a substantial year-on-year increase. In 1983, Johan Coetzee, the scourge of IDAF down the years, became Commissioner of Police, with a seat on the State Security Council, the shadowy group of Afrikaner military and Broederbond leaders who in effect ran the country. But Coetzee's call for drastic action against covert funding of trials and welfare was of no avail. Whenever the proposition was discussed at the highest level, the Treasury demurred. There was an attitude, Coetzee recalls, 'if they want to send money, let them. At least they are not boycotting us in this respect' (Coetzee interview 1992).

Kleinschmidt's sources of income were much the same as Collins's. British Defence and Aid, now managed by Ethel de

Keyser, while still an active fund-raiser, became the conduit for poverty alleviation charities that had quit South Africa or did not want to be seen operating there. Save the Children, War on Want, Christian Aid, even Comic Relief, sent cheques to IDAF via de Keyser. Oxfam, Britain's best-known Third World charity, first contributed direct to IDAF in 1986 with a quiet grant of £50,000 for organisations endangered by the state of emergency. Fearing Mrs Thatcher's wrath, and the displeasure of the middle-class volunteers who ran Oxfam's high street shops, knowledge of this and later grants was restricted to a small circle at headquarters in Oxford. But the bulk of IDAF's money still came from overseas, with the Nordic countries, and Sweden in particular, vouchsafing more than half its budget. The UN Trust Fund supplied the remainder. The British government did not contribute directly but from 1984 the European Community, of which it was part, made regular donations to the UN Fund, and thus to IDAF.

Unlike his predecessor, Kleinschmidt was obliged to respect any condition the donors placed on the use of the money. Ernst Michanek pruned expenditure that did not directly advance the struggle inside South Africa. The stipends Collins had made to exiles were cut at a stroke. But for many, these handouts had become a factor with which to balance a meagre household budget. The ANC exiles, for the most part, chose to suffer in silence, appreciating, perhaps, that the general drift of IDAF beneficence was still very much in their favour. But the PAC hit back venomously.

Collins had always taken care not to state his preference for the ANC too openly. But shortly before joining IDAF, Kleinschmidt had made a speech at the Security Council in New York in which he explicitly sided with the ANC. Later, when he was IDAF's financial director, a roneoed pamphlet entitled 'A Curve in the South African Spy Ring' began doing the rounds in Britain. It was a densely, sometimes stylishly, argued 80-page diatribe against Kleinschmidt, leaning heavily on guilt by association. If Craig Williamson had been dispatched by BOSS to destroy the International University Exchange Fund, it argued, how could one avoid the conclusion that Kleinschmidt was doing the same to

IDAF? They were near contemporaries at university. Both had changed horses 'overnight', from Black Consciousness to the ANC. Michanek's name was brought in to widen the conspiracy. His relationship with Williamson had been 'all but wrapped up in heightened affection'.

The author of the pamphlet was a former PAC representative in London and old friend of Collins, Ngila Michael Muendane. He had attended the national conference and must have had some notion of the secret funds. It seems clear that the drying up of help to individuals in the PAC brought on the gripe. 'Astonishing developments have taken place at IDAF since Horst came in, most particularly since the demise of Canon Collins.' He noted the disappearance of familiar faces: Freda Champion (née Nuell), Collins's secretary; Mariyam Harris; Reg Gore, the bookkeeper; and imminently, Phyllis Altman. He named lawyers in South Africa in dispute with Amen Court over funds. His knowledge of in-house, often confidential, information was impressive. 'It was,' says Al Cook, 'a sinister design to split the resistance.'

Though no one inside IDAF admitted to taking the allegations seriously, the pamphlet caused ripples. Not many copies seem to have been circulated but those that were had a strategic intent. A Danish think-tank requested that any of its correspondence 'with your organisation be removed from your files and returned... as soon as possible.'

Huddleston and Diana Collins called on the PAC's London representative, Hamilton Keke, to disassociate himself from the pamphlet and to 'endeavour to have' it withdrawn. He should also 'consider Mr Muendane's position within the Pan African Congress.' Keke admitted later he was not convinced Kleinschmidt was a spy but the pamphlet, he said, had not been published by the PAC. 'We were only aware of it when it came out. That's why I refused to apologise.'

All external aid to and work with the PAC leadership was frozen, though humanitarian assistance under the two programmes was not affected. The trustees cancelled the monthly payments (and Christmas presents) to Keke and his family. In time the pamphlet was heard of no more, though the curious could obtain a copy from *Editions Azanie* at a private address in Bury, Manchester (Keke interview 1992).

And yet the PAC's sense of being a poor relation of the ANC in the matter of IDAF funding was not wide of the mark. Ernst Michanek tended not to mince words. 'It was the ANC that appeared to be on the move,' he explained later. 'When giving money you must ask yourself the question – who is doing the job? Not the PAC. It was the ANC' (Michanek interview 1992). The truth was that the PAC was considered unreliable and prone to rancorous, sometimes murderous, internal power struggles. It was no accident that not a single PAC adherent was employed in any IDAF department, secret or public.

While IDAF, under both Collins and Kleinschmidt, tried to be scrupulously fair in allocating welfare funds, the ANC benefited from grants that were certainly more political than humanitarian. When Alfred Nzo and Thabo Mbeki asked for £10,000 so that Oliver Tambo, plus two aides and two video cameramen, could travel to America to address newspaper editors and congressmen, Kleinschmidt had no difficulty clearing it with his trustees. Another £5,000 went, with Tambo's blessing, to London-based white draft resisters to set up the Committee of South African War Resisters (COSAWAR). An ANC information conference in Zambia was sponsored by IDAF to the tune of £12,000, though it did say 'no' when the ANC's London man, Reg September, asked for help with the costs of his divorce. On the occasion of the ANC's 75th birthday in 1987, IDAF sent a present of £45,000 (IDAF files).

Pan-Africanist resentment, having boiled over in the spy libel, surfaced again, and in the most sensitive of forums, the United Nations. The PAC still enjoyed influence at the UN where it was accorded equal status with the ANC. In 1988, on the UN Day of Political Prisoners, the PAC used its leverage in a bid to discredit IDAF. It produced Joyce Mokhesi, a sister of one of the 'Sharpeville Six'. She asked the UN Committee on Apartheid to investigate IDAF as its funds were not reaching PAC families (though the 'Six' appear to have been neither ANC nor PAC, simply random people plucked out of a crowd). Another complainant, the wife of PAC leader Zeph Motopheng, maintained that her husband had been in and out of prison since the late 1960s and yet she had never received IDAF's help, directly or indirectly. Kleinschmidt doubled back to London, returning to New York with receipts, signed cheques and other evidence of IDAF's critical role in defending the 'Sharpeville Six' and supporting their families. He also produced proof of money sent to Mrs Motopheng over many years. He showed the evidence to Simon Makana of the PAC, in the presence of UN officials and Anders Ferm, the trust fund chairman. The UN was completely satisfied, though Kleinschmidt received no apology from Makana (Kleinschmidt interview 1992).

The PAC refused to give up. A PAC official brought Julia Ramashamola, mother of Theresa, the one woman among the Sharpeville Six, to Canon Collins House. 'You've let us down,' she told Al Cook, 'we've had to rely on kind friends.' Cook explained that the 'kind friend' was IDAF in disguise, and that the deceit was well meant because her daughter would have faced an additional charge if an IDAF connection had been revealed. By way of proof he showed her a letter that Mrs Ramashamola had written to her Canadian correspondent, Lynda Muir, an IDAF letter-writer. On seeing her own letter, Cook recalls, 'Julia hid her head in her hands. Then she came and put her arms around me and sobbed and sobbed and went back to her seat and said, "I can't look at you." The PAC man kept quiet' (Cook interview 1993; Ramashamola interview 1992).

•

By 1988, the supply of correspondents exceeded demand for the first time. 'People are moved by what is happening in South Africa,' Stevenson wrote, 'and want to do something.' Recruitment was still by word of mouth, from within the magic circle of 'Movement' wives and trusted friends, unions, old school tie and, most of all, the Church, where the Collins tradition lingered on strongly. Theo Kotze, a Methodist pastor who had been Beyers Naudé's deputy at the Christian Institute, held the record. His tally, aided by his wife Helen, was almost 50. Selly Oak Colleges, the inter-denominational complex in Birmingham where he taught, was a recruitment hotbed.

After hearing him lecture on South Africa, students would crowd round asking how they could help. 'A conversation and a cup of tea, and not once did it go wrong. You develop an instinct,' Kotze recalled. No one with theological connections in the West Midlands was safe from this cottage industry. He scored well at the annual Mission Sunday held in many churches. He netted Edward Cadbury, professor of theology at Birmingham University, and an assortment of Christian Aid workers, academics and clerics. Dr Francis Young trusted Theo absolutely: 'There was a certain sense of "do this without asking any questions".' Her father had been a conscientious objector and she had mixed feelings when told of the IDAF links with the ANC and the armed struggle. Louise Asmal's father, Roy Parkinson, ran a small writers' group in central Birmingham based on the St Basil's homeless project, which unusually included West Indians. Kleinschmidt recruited a South African, Jacqueline Theron Malcolm, daughter of General Frank Theron, commander of the South African forces in the Middle East during the Second World War. Gloria Pahad, English wife of the ANC's London security chief, Aziz, used the address of a friend near her flat in Tufnell Park, north London.

For Peggy Preston, the writing slotted into a life-long and worldwide Quaker experience. 'Shattered' by Sharpeville, she had met Huddleston who gave her the money to go to South Africa and work as an occupational therapist at Baragwanath Hospital in Soweto. She repaid the debt by finding bail for political prisoners. There followed five years in a children's hospital in Saigon, remunerated at the local rate and living with a Vietnamese family. Back in England, Preston lived for several years in a caravan outside the Molesworth US missile base, before going to Cape Town to work with the Black Sash women at the Crossroads squatter camp, then under state-orchestrated vigilante assault.[2] 'The blacks called me Mother of Hope, so that when I was expelled and started to write, I used the alias Hope Reston.' It was a mix of the banal and the tragic. Johnson Kola wrote from the Ciskei that the money he received was used to buy a goat and *umqomboti* (home-brewed beer) for his son, Justice, going through the circumcision rite in the bush. A mother with a chest infection brought on by tear gas thrown into her yard, wrote: 'In a way the stressful situation for the family is relieved when the father is in detention because at least now there is a relief because we are not raided at home.'

South Wales was a hive of activity, thanks largely to the exiled Hanif Bhamjee, the local 'Mr Anti-Apartheid'. He recruited Barbara Castle (no relation to the Labour elder) in Cardiff in 1978, hinting at 'a secret fund of money in London to support black prisoners.' Ten years later, living at Gelli-Wrgan Farm, Ynysybwl, in the hills above Pontypridd, the IDAF registered envelope contained almost £1,200 in notes for her eight families. If the parcel arrived on a week day, it was left on the headmistress's desk at Glanffrwd infants' school for Castle to collect. On a Saturday, the postman drove the three miles to her farm. There was a part-time bank in Ynysybwl, 'but half the village would have known by 5 o'clock,' so she bought the money orders at Barclays in Cardiff. At first her letters were thoughtful; about the children, house, weather – once snow held up posting for several days. But over the years the personal touch was lost, reduced to 'we're all really well'. There was the smallholding to look after, the cattle, sheep, ducks. In the lambing season she might pen a letter before dawn while feeding one orphan on her lap as another warmed up beside the Aga. A fresh batch of letters arrived from Dimbaza or Atteridgeville and over tea she would read... 'we don't know how to thank you or we lose our home.'

It was rare for a correspondent to find a well-educated family, fluent in English and at the cutting edge of the drama. Such were the Mashambas who, when not locked up, lived at the University of the North, at Turfloop, near the town of Polokwane (then Pietersburg) towards the Zimbabwe border. For David Armstrong, a lecturer in architecture at Barnet College, north London, Mashamba was just one of 12 indistinguishable names to whom he sent money. Over a series of letters he worked out that the father, George, was in prison for ten years, his wife Joyce for five years, and that the couple had been sentenced in the same (IDAF-funded) trial. When George's mother, who looked after the three sons, wrote to him in prison that friends were helping the family, George supposed it was the ANC or the Council of Churches. In better times, he taught philosophy at Turfloop. A letter from prison mentioning his dissertation for a philosophy MA on 'The Naturalistic Fallacy – a Dialectical Materialist Critique', opened Armstrong's eyes. 'Just too bad Maurice Cornforth at Oxford passed away in 1980,' George wrote, 'otherwise I would have requested you to contact him for me on this matter.' He explained how he 'came from the bush, from a family of heathens who practised polygamy and distrusted Christians, so there was an element of being different.' It was recruiting for MK that landed him in prison. He married Joyce, a Christian, in 1969. He did not see his sons for six years – Robben Island was far away and, besides, children under 16 could not visit.

Joyce was the heart of the family. 'When I left for prison part of them came with me,' she said afterwards. 'I could feel their presence. Imprisonment has such a negative effect... if you cannot handle the stress you might end up going mad, committing suicide, and that was the last thing I wanted to happen because I knew that I had a loving husband, wonderful sons to live for. They said I shouldn't worry, the children will be looked after, we'll explain when you come out.' The old lady signed the letters to Armstrong, but as she could neither read nor write, a neighbour would ask her in Shangaan what she wanted to say, and write it in English. One day an envelope in a different hand arrived for Armstrong. Joyce had been released. She introduced herself, saying what a comfort it was to know that the boys and George's mother were being looked after when she was in prison. She described to Armstrong how, 'coming home from prison she was getting down from the train onto the platform... she saw an old lady and three boys... these were her children and she didn't recognise them.'

The IDAF money kept them under one roof. George had lost his salary, and the Department of Bantu Education were in a hurry to sell his house, but the 'gift' paid off the R27 monthly instalment, and helped the boys' schooling and granny's housekeeping. George needed it when he was released because, as an ex-political prisoner, he could not find a job. In June 1985, Joyce and 14-year-old Nyoka were charged with public violence after being arrested at a civic association committee meeting in a church. They were beaten up, but the charges were withdrawn. The worst times began a year later, with George still in prison and Joyce and Nyoka in detention. Armstrong was beside himself with anxiety for this fractured but closely-knit family. In the year before the thaw, father and sons went into hiding as 'the police kept coming to our home and harassing whoever was there.' Vigilantes ransacked the house. David Armstrong was 'so angry and all I could do was send letters saying it was raining here and how's the weather there' (IDAF files; Armstrong interview 1993).

Then it was over. One day the telephone rang; Joyce was in England on a training course. 'She sat in our dining room telling her story... in and out of prison, harassed, isolated from husband and children. Yet they never broke her. I knew then that my work had been worthwhile, for now I understood the personal dimension of her struggle' (Armstrong interview 1993). Joyce had been expecting 'a minister of religion, one who has gone past being tied by worldly things... I was humbled to see David... when we met he broke down, he cried so bitterly and we ended up sharing the tears. It was such a joyful moment because those tears were not crocodile tears, but tears which cemented the relationship' (Joyce and George Mashamba interview 1993).[3]

Chapter 25

TOTAL ONSLAUGHT

IDAF **outlived its founder** by ten years. It grew to an extent that even its visionary creator could not have imagined. Its annual budget, £3 million at his death, escalated to more than £10 million by the end of the decade. From the mid-1980s, the legal department ('Programme One') in Essex Road channelled an average of 500 new cases to Mr X every quarter. Many were no-hopers but the impact of this courtroom resistance added to the erosion of confidence in the rule of President PW Botha.

With hindsight, it is clear that the moves to improve IDAF's efficiency in the last years of Collins's life had arrived just in time. The temperature of the struggle was rising to boiling point. In the mid-1980s, Botha's 'reform' plan provided a fresh *casus belli* between the races. His solution to the 'black problem', endorsed by a referendum of the white electorate, was the creation of a parliament of separate chambers for whites, coloureds and Asians, leaving Africans to make do with the discredited bantustans, of which four – Transkei, Ciskei, Bophuthatswana and Venda – had a constitutional 'independence' under tribal leaders. To Africans, and indeed to most coloureds and Asians, it was simply a tarted-up version of the old divide-and-rule. Mandela declined an offer of early release in exchange for recognising Transkei's independence.

Opposition to the 'tricameral' parliament coalesced in a broad-based national alliance, the United Democratic Front (UDF). Launched in 1983 at a mass rally at Mitchell's Plain outside Cape Town, it brought together 600 protest organisations – trade unions, student associations, community and church groups, many owing tacit allegiance to the banned ANC. Albertina Sisulu, Walter's wife, was prominent in the UDF leadership. Mandela, recently moved from Robben Island to Pollsmoor maximum security prison on the mainland, was adopted as its patron. From his headquarters-in-exile in the Zambian capital Lusaka, Oliver Tambo exhorted his followers to make South Africa 'ungovernable'.

But western policy was now dominated by a White House–Downing Street axis of Ronald Reagan and Margaret Thatcher, whose sympathies lay unashamedly with white South Africa. Reagan's 'constructive engagement' diplomacy was rationalised on the assumption that, by sweet-talking Pretoria, white 'haves' would be persuaded to make concessions to black 'have-nots'. But when, in June 1984, Mrs Thatcher indulged in a little 'constructive engagement' of her own, the outcome was counter-productive.

She invited Botha, the *'Groot Krokodil'* ('Big Crocodile'), to Britain, the first visit by an apartheid leader in a generation. Sensing that she might have misjudged the national mood, she summoned Huddleston to her presence, hoping the gesture would placate public opinion. They did no more than lecture each other and the meeting ended frostily. Botha was flown from Heathrow Airport to her weekend residence at Chequers, while 100,000 protesters marched through London. Within weeks townships in the Vaal Triangle were in outright rebellion, igniting a forest fire across South Africa that would not be extinguished until after Mandela's release from prison. Mike Terry, secretary of the Anti-Apartheid Movement, organisers of the London demonstration, liked to believe that the uprisings were triggered by reports of faraway Englishmen taking to the streets to protest against the presence of an unwanted guest.

When Collins was first persuaded of the inevitability of the armed struggle, the targets were buildings, not people. Later, *Umkhonto-we-Sizwe* extended its range to township policemen, border guards and defence force personnel. Still Tambo and guerrilla chief-of-staff Joe Slovo ruled out 'soft' targets that risked injury to civilians. But in 1985 the ANC consultative conference in Kabwe, Zambia acknowledged the ferment at home as Tambo warned that distinctions between hard and soft targets could become fudged and 'some innocent people will be killed.' On occasions the hard–soft distinction was difficult to sustain, but even MK's first car bomb attack in May 1983 outside Air Force head-quarters in Pretoria that killed 19 and injured 200, most of them black, was aimed at a strategic installation. After Chris Hani succeeded Joe Slovo as MK chief-of-staff, the policy was rendered yet more flexible. Hani was adamant that the bomb that killed white civilians did not signify a change of policy, but he cautioned that freedom fighters could not be expected to retain the 'coolness of an iceberg'.

Robert McBride, a member of the ANC's special operations unit, appeared to go beyond this remit when he bombed Magoos Bar on the Durban beachfront, killing three people and injuring 80, nearly all of them white. His was a desperate response to Botha's declaration of a countrywide state of emergency in June 1986 that gave the security forces extensive powers of curfew and detention. McBride became – and has remained – the whites' supreme hate-figure. His trial defence was funded by IDAF, though John Collins would probably have had some difficulty selling such a commitment to his original funders. McBride was sentenced to death but escaped execution and was released in 1992 (Rostron 1991; Apelgren interview 1992).

Collins's early followers would have been further dismayed by IDAF's part in defending 'necklacers'. The summary public execution of some suspected police spies, by framing their necks with a burning tyre, was the most gruesome aspect of the uprising. A grim joke translated the acronym for the United Democratic Front as 'Unibond Dunlop Firestone'. Winnie Mandela awarded the practice her seal of approval, but it was disowned by the UDF leadership and condemned unequivocally by Tambo.

Yet even in these trials, judges did listen to imported, IDAF-financed behaviourists explaining the mechanisms of mob psychology. In one case, where a necklacing in an East Rand township had been captured on video, the evidence of an American professor, Edward Diener, mitigated the behaviour of the accused sufficiently to save them from the gallows. An

Eastern Cape judge, hearing an appeal, accepted the evidence of Dr Andrew Coleman, a social anthropologist at Leicester University, on 'de-inviduation', the effects of crowd hysteria on personal behaviour. After taking the concept on board, Judge Jansen explained that 'the person in a group follows the group and becomes anonymous, being inclined to do things which under normal circumstances they would not do.' Five men, having spent two years on death row, were reprieved and their sentences reduced to two years (Coleman 1991).

IDAF now became a branch of the struggle, its funds allowing scores of small 'non-white' law practices to act as creative protectors of resistance. Smith, Tabata & Van Heerden, a firm of two 'coloureds' and an African, worked out of King William's Town, on the border of the Ciskei, the bantustan that had celebrated its 'independence' in 1981 by appointing a state executioner trained by the South African prisons department to preside over its inaugural hangings. This was 'wild east' country (part of the Eastern Cape), where practitioners and campaigners on constitutional and human rights issues found the going especially tough. While still at school, John Smith had been charged with attending an illegal gathering and was defended with funding from the go-between Cambridge solicitor, Rosemary Sands. In 1985, by now a qualified attorney, he made contact with IDAF requesting help in representing 800 blacks who had been expelled to the Ciskei from a 'black spot' (in an area zoned for white occupation) near the city of East London. His counsel argued successfully that though they were 'Ciskeians' they had a right to permanent residence in South Africa. They were given the right to return (Smith and Tabata interview 1992).

Smith was himself detained under the emergency regulations. The town's head of security accused him of interfering in their work. 'Every time we arrest someone in Ginsberg township,' he complained to Smith, 'you phone to make enquiries even before we have time to interrogate him; you and your partners are intimidating my men.' Smith continued the struggle from his prison cell. He had his food analysed by a dietician, who provided the ammunition for another confrontation. 'We made the case that diet was a punitive regime, whereas under the terms of detention you were only allowed to be deprived of your liberty.' A bench of three judges sampled the food in plastic containers and, finding it distasteful, ordered that all detainees should be allowed to eat the same food, from local hotels, as white prison officers did. It boosted detainee morale no end – and some hoteliers might even have had reason to thank IDAF. But Smith's main challenge, the emergency regulations themselves, was rejected.

By law the police were obliged to behave in a civilised manner; in practice they invariably did not. But charges of police brutality, particularly when related to actions inside police stations, were notoriously hard to prove. Ministers backed police methods to the hilt, while the Bench tended to be dismissive. But the climate was changing, and some judges were prepared to see themselves as more than simple guardians of the *status quo*. One day John Smith obtained an affidavit that convincingly described how a detainee had been subjected to protracted torture. In a secret hearing before a judge, Sydney Kentridge argued that defence lawyers should be permitted to arrive unheralded at two East London police stations to search for proof of torture. He cited the Anton Piller order, an English Law Lords' ruling that allowed a company to search a rival's premises for documents in a copyright case before they could be removed. The judge admitted the precedent, but refused an order on the grounds that evidence of torture was so strong that a search was unnecessary.

Some time later, however, Smith was able, again through 'Anton Piller', to search a Ciskei police station for instruments of torture. Smith said 'the beauty of it was that the respondent was not informed, nobody else was allowed in court.' And it worked. 'We arrived with the sheriff and the order of the court and found a blood-stained T-shirt and the plastic hood used to suffocate my client.' Smith won R35,000 from the police for assault.

Although IDAF concentrated its efforts on political trials, it began to intervene in other areas of black and white conflict. In 1986 the South African mining industry's health and safety deficiencies were exposed at Kinross when 177 miners were killed by the ignition of polyurethane foam (a substance banned in UK mines since 1968). It was the country's worst-ever gold-mining accident, and yet the union and representatives of the families of the deceased were not permitted to question witnesses at the official inquiry. The Mines Inspectorate was close to management, so that crucial questions were not canvassed. The hearing was over in three hours. Working through the union, the Johannesburg legal firm Cheadle, Thomson and Haysom, mounted a successful challenge of the procedure and secured greatly improved compensation for the families.

IDAF had a big funding role in the saga of Dr Wendy Orr. Fresh out of medical school and employed by the state health department as a District Surgeon, with responsibility for prisons in Port Elizabeth, she was brought face to face with systematic torture. Orr copied the medical records of 286 detainees, and they became the basis for a successful injunction against the security police and their minister to stop the assaults – though the total compensation paid to the 82 plaintiffs amounted to less than half the fees of the lawyers representing them. Wendy Orr was a rarity. The pattern of abuse she uncovered was certainly not confined to Port Elizabeth but no other medical practitioner working in South African prisons saw fit to speak out against the ill-treatment of the men and women in their charge.[1]

The End Conscription Campaign (ECC) was an area of political activity that had, by its nature, to be exclusively white. In a time of rampant militarism the army required every white male school-leaver to do his patriotic duty of national service in Angola or in the black townships. Some refused at the start of the two-year training period; others refused when ordered to attend the annual camp call-up. The options were to flee the country or go into hiding. But in early 1988, Dr Ivan Toms, a medical doctor working in Crossroads, a riven squatter camp outside Cape Town, came before the court pleading a Christian conscience. Testifying in his defence, John Dugard, Professor of Law at the University of the Witwatersrand, argued that South Africa's military incursions into Angola were illegal, as was the army's occupation of Namibia, following the UN's revocation of Pretoria's mandate in 1966, confirmed in 1972 by the International Court of Justice. Dugard said the military's role in policing the townships inside South Africa could be adjudged contrary to the 1973 Geneva Convention relating to the suppression and punishment of the crime of apartheid. By entering a township as a soldier, Toms rendered himself liable to prosecution in 81 countries. Toms' resistance earned him an 18-month sentence and adoption by Amnesty International as a prisoner of conscience. He was released half way through his sentence, and the minister of justice was obliged to pay him damages for a prison assault. His IDAF-funded defence had provided a damaging show trial for the military state.

In these trials IDAF and the Anti-Apartheid Movement worked together discreetly through the medium of SATIS (South Africa The Imprisoned Society). Tony Trew, IDAF's librarian, was the go-between with Mike Terry, handing over details of current trials and, more urgently, the death row cases. Terry said every death sentence was publicised by the Security Council as a resolution or a statement by the chairman. 'It was the co-operation between us, IDAF and the ANC, that made the difference. It wasn't just the fact of these people being represented in court – if their cases had not been placed under international scrutiny they might have swung. Unlike Rhodesia, where people were executed anonymously for matters like not reporting the presence of a terrorist' (Terry interview 1996).

Although there was no automatic right of appeal against a death sentence, IDAF, as a matter of course, funded reprieve applications in the Appellate Division or, if they failed, to the president himself. Their efforts met with mixed success but they helped keep the administration's paranoia at a high pitch. Botha was forever claiming that South Africa was the object of a 'revolutionary onslaught' aimed at delivering it to the Soviet Union. There was no longer a 'red Canon' to excite his ire but IDAF was still characterised as being an inextricable part of the communist menace. Craig Williamson said few people in the security service actually believed it but it was one of the regime's 'Big Lies – we always did our best to convince anyone we could that IDAF was in fact run by the South African Communist Party and that the South African Communist Party was run by the Communist Party of the Soviet Union, and therefore, if you listened to Defence and Aid or gave them money, you were carrying out the will and aims and objectives, in an international global sense, of the Politburo in Moscow' (Williamson interview 1992).

In reality, IDAF was pretty much the same hotchpotch of ideologies and cultures it had always been, though under more self-effacing management. There were times when Horst Kleinschmidt was perhaps too conscious of the founder looking over his shoulder. 'IDAF under Collins was like a family with a father figure at the top,' he said, 'flamboyant, always bringing colourful people into the office and into the organisation and branching into very interesting things. As director, I certainly didn't match in any way, in any shape or form, the role of John Collins.' In recognition of its growing workload, the trustees created the post of deputy director in 1987. They appointed to the position Al Cook, who had worked for some years in the information department. At its busiest, the staff at Canon Collins House numbered 62, with British recruits outnumbering the exiles (Kleinschmidt interview April 1992).

When Kleinschmidt joined IDAF the staff was largely white. 'John used to say, "The ANC employs blacks, I employ whites"' (Kleinschmidt interview April 1992), though in fact there were several black people, including the Jamaican Maud Henry, bookkeeper to Christian Action, British Defence and Aid and IDAF; Dulcie September[2]; and Wiseman Khuzwayo. Later, at IDAF's Essex Road offices, Afua Boaten, Kleinschmidt's Ghanaian personal assistant, was recruited through the Martin Luther King Employment Agency, which Collins had a hand in setting up in an attempt to improve black job prospects. Another secretary, Zodwa Dabengwa, was the sister of Dumisa Dabengwa, the ZAPU military commander, later Zimbabwean interior minister. Temba Luxoma became treasurer, having previously worked at the ANC headquarters in Lusaka. Shanti Naidoo, an exile whose brothers had been on Robben Island, was in the research library along with Sipho Pityana, a student from an old Eastern Cape ANC family. For security reasons, staff were instructed not to visit South Africa, openly or otherwise, though Ian Robertson, after six years with IDAF, did leave to join a white cell of the ANC. He ended up in Pretoria prison with a 20-year sentence as one of the 'Broederstroom Three', convicted of setting up arms caches for purposes of sabotage.

In man-management terms, Kleinschmidt saw his role as ensuring that 'one flavour didn't win out against another' – the flavours being SACP and non-SACP, or those who were in the ANC and those who were not. But the work was intense enough to allow little time for ideological back-biting – though on Friday nights some of the staff would make it to 'The Half Moon', an Essex Road watering-hole, to imbibe deeply and sing nostalgically with the ANC and assorted exiles. As a work-place, Canon Collins House lacked the style of the Amen Court basement, though the need for security might have been the reason for its austerity. Bombs and arson attacks on the AAM, ANC and SWAPO offices in London heightened IDAF's awareness of itself as a BOSS target. Huddleston's flat in the precincts of St James's Church, Piccadilly, was the scene of a mysterious break-in. Nothing was stolen, but his papers were rifled (and possibly photographed). A feature of these break-ins was that things were rarely stolen. Even if Huddleston was not a hands-on IDAF supremo in the Collins mould, preferring to leave operational matters in the hands of subordinates, the episode brought the BOSS threat closer to home.

The office had a high security rating from Islington borough's fire brigade and police – as did the taxidermist who was a target of animal rights activists. Cook, who was also responsible for in-house security, had the building wired with electronic warning devices and equipped with an array of CCTV cameras in a manner that in those days seemed positively Orwellian. Letter bombs were a real threat. The office believed that a letter it had sent, in July 1979 to a New Zealand priest working in Lesotho, had been tampered with – it arrived loaded with a bomb that blew off his arm, and injured others in the room.[3] Scotland Yard advised Cook to use a mail-scanning machine. When letters and parcels were sorted on the top floor during the mid-morning tea break, workers surplus to requirements made themselves scarce.

Within the building, 'need-to-know' levels of security rose through each floor. The ground floor was the province of the publications department with a shop displaying books, pamphlets and artefacts devoted to the struggle. The first floor housed the library and research department, charged with responsibility for information-gathering and unearthing new cases. Tony Trew, a studious ex-saboteur, ran it. Workers on these lower floors were discouraged from taking too detailed an interest in what was happening on the upper floors, which housed legal defence (now called Programme One), and welfare (Programme Two). Kleinschmidt ordered that the researchers below should not use information collected through these departments, so that secrecy was never compromised. Exchanges between the welfare and legal departments were kept to the bare minimum. Within the legal department, only its head, Hilary Rabkin, knew the identity of Mr X.

As late as 1987, those employed in the lower reaches of the building had only the sketchiest details of the work that was done on the top floor. Then, at the annual conference in London, Kleinschmidt revealed the broad outlines of IDAF's legal and welfare work to the staff, as well as to the donors, national committees and trustees, without mentioning Mr X or the more sensitive links. He was heard in surprised and prideful silence. Huddleston, Michanek and Diana Collins had backed him, Abdul Minty was opposed, Phyllis Altman said he was bonkers. 'At the next break the tea room was buzzing,' recalled Kleinschmidt. It was a calculated risk but it worked. All kept the secret. 'I felt we couldn't say "trust us", when we didn't trust them' (Kleinschmidt interview April 1992).

•

The donors had shown a readiness to sanction year-on-year increases in their funding, but now, as the number of trials proliferated, they questioned whether they were getting value for money. And Enuga Reddy complained that legal aid was starving family welfare by taking the lion's share of the funds. Mr X later acknowledged a loss of quality control. 'The volume of work was so enormous I had no time to think about it much. I would read things and see photographs. There would be the backs of these poor blighters who had been lashed. Electrical torture had been meted out. I would glance at it and then there would be another pile of paper.'

This was in sharp contrast to the days when Frankel and Altman had the leisure to discuss each case in detail, consulting Collins and the liberation movements when necessary, before farming the work out to the small body of lawyers they knew personally or by repute – Jewish, WASP or Asian. Now the uprising brought about an escalation in the number of trials and their geographical extension to places experiencing organised resistance for the first time. The weight of cases created the need to press into action a new army of lawyers who were unknown quantities to their paymasters in London. At the height of the rebellion, 150 firms of attorneys, at least half of them black, were involved in political work. At one stage as many as 80 advocates, nearly all white, were appearing, albeit unwittingly, at IDAF's behest.

There were problems for IDAF in both branches of the two-tier legal profession. The core long-term IDAF advocates such as George Bizos and Sydney Kentridge were satisfied with reasonable fees. But after 1984, as public violence and 'treason' cases soared, a new crop of lawyers who had not previously worked in the field of human rights entered the lists, marking their briefs as if their clients were the Rand mining houses. Attorneys struggled to find counsel willing to work at non-commercial rates, and, said Bizos, 'commercial rates were high'. The attorney Fink Haysom said many 'rising advocates, senior juniors, treated these matters as if they were ordinary commercial cases, so it was a happy confluence of moral and financial reward. With a lot of commercial work around, advocates were reluctant to take on long political cases, especially in country towns, which the state used to inhibit demonstrations and weaken the defendants.' Haysom once phoned 20 advocates before securing the defence of three men facing the death penalty (Haysom interview 1992).

Looking back on this period, Issy Maisels, an original Defence and Aid defender, admitted to being 'ashamed of the Bar... I don't say all of them, but for some of those chaps with no practice this was manna from heaven' (Maisels interview 1992). In all this, IDAF gained an unexpected recruit. Dawid de Villiers, one of Afrikanerdom's favourite sons, represented Tony Yengeni, an MK officer on trial in Cape Town for sabotage. He had led the government's legal team at the Hague International Court of Justice in the dispute over Namibia, and followed with a spell running the white supremacist newspaper group, *Nasionale Pers*. Now he was back at the Bar appearing in what he termed 'under-dog cases'.

The attorneys, or Side Bar, presented a different problem. At Michanek's prompting, IDAF had sought to encourage African attorneys who, as late as 1987, constituted no more than one in 10 of the country's lawyers. They were mostly in small practices, newly qualified and largely dependent on IDAF. In a normal system they would have spent several years learning the trade under the tutelage of experienced senior practitioners. Now they were thrown in at the deep end. Some dog-paddled, some floundered, others showed enormous ability, only to be overwhelmed by events.

The practice with the most substantial slice of IDAF business was known simply as 'P Jana'. Priscilla Jana excited the fury of liberal and reactionary lawyers alike; nor was she loved by the police, having been convicted of *crimen injuria* for calling a security policeman a pig, a conviction overturned on appeal. She worked first for Mandela's attorney, Ismail Ayob, before going it alone in 1979. At the time she was the only woman in human rights work. She numbered many Robben Island prisoners among her clients. 'In the late 80s it became somewhat fashionable to be a human rights lawyer,' recalled Jana, 'but in the 70s it was not very glamorous. You were watched all the time and it wasn't the kind of profession one embarked on if one was ambitious' (Jana interview February 1992).

Caroline Heaton-Nicholls, granddaughter of a Natal senator and former High Commissioner to London, spent five 'exciting' years with Jana at her Johannesburg practice in Commissioner Street, starting as an articled clerk. 'Priscilla was large and flamboyant, and she was courageous, especially before 1981 when she took on cases when not assured of money. She was banned and couldn't leave Johannesburg and rarely appeared in court herself. So suddenly I was involved in an MK treason trial in Pretoria. And then two more. That was a bit chaotic. A clerk should not have been doing one treason trial, let alone three' (Heaton-Nicholls interview 1992).

Jana had an excellent rapport with her clients, never forgetting a birthday cake during a trial and visiting them in prison loaded with presents. Generosity was not limited to her professional life; she raised the daughter of the UDF leader Popo Molefe, naming her 'Tina' after her celebrated client Albertina Sisulu.

> People say that we were more of a welfare than a legal organi-
> sation; that is not quite true. But when you take on a political
> matter one has to put oneself out completely at all hours. I
> bailed out Mrs Sisulu at midnight in Pretoria. During the
> Emergency, the darkest hour in this country, I would put up
> truckloads of youths at my house overnight. There was a stage
> at our office when we could not cope with families virtually
> camping here. They didn't know where their children were.
> We would phone around police stations, government depart-
> ments. The only way we could keep the glimmer of hope and
> the struggle alive was through legal battles, by fighting all the
> harassments imposed on people through the law. Though the
> actual winning of cases was not so important as keeping people
> going. (Jana interview 1993)

Often in MK/ANC membership and recruitment cases, lawyers would plead their client's innocence on the grounds that he or she had been indoctrinated into becoming a member. It was a deeply resented defence; the accused felt they were being treated like children. Jana rejected this line, and would concede that they were members of ANC.

Jana came close to being a defendant herself. On one occasion, an East Rand student, 'young and reckless, considered by the police more dangerous than the ANC', arrived in her office with a grenade in his pocket. It came from a batch that he believed had been booby-trapped by the police, killing one of his gang. Would Priscilla hold it as an exhibit? It went into the office safe. Next day the police arrived on a grenade-retrieval mission, telling the staff they were fortunate not to have blown themselves up.[4]

There was a further close shave when a 'hot', but small student, by the name of Serame, arrived breathless in Jana's office pursued by a posse of policemen. 'They searched every room, under the desks, in the cupboards, but couldn't find him,' Jana recalled. 'They were amazed because they'd seen him coming up the lift and going into our office. They left, and Serame came out from under the typist's very large skirt.'

These events took place while Jana was working on a contract with IDAF. 'I was in a unique situation,' she acknowledged. 'My firm was funded completely and there were no problems whatever we put through to them' (Jana interview 1993). But from 1985 it was getting beyond her ability and resources. She tried farming work out to a string of 20 advocates, claiming they were saving money, though they were doing attorneys' work at steeper Bar rates. She engaged dozens of African, Indian, even Afrikaner, attorneys in the Transvaal, Orange Free State and northern Cape, to handle local trials but there were constant complaints about payment. When IDAF sent in a Johannesburg accountant, Alan Velcich, to restore order, he found, 'not abuse but neglect. Jana herself wasn't ripping off IDAF, but her *modus operandi* was extremely costly. It was too vast and complicated, her records were inadequate, she had an old computer which ran out of capacity, then the bookkeeper left' (Velcich interview 1992). Heaton-Nicholls acknowledged that under pressure of events, the cost appraisal side of things could be slipshod. 'It became very easy to put through fees for work not done. We'd lift up an ample file... hmm, this weighs a lot, how much do we charge IDAF?' (Heaton-Nicholls interview 1992).

With legal costs rising like an untethered balloon, the Delmas Treason Trial was the last straw. As with the Sharpeville Six, it had its origins in the wildfire raging in the Vaal Triangle: six black councillors had been killed in a long-suffering township. But each accused wanted his own attorney and counsel. The trial was expected to be over in a few months, but the methodical Bizos took to contradicting state evidence on virtually every point. It became IDAF's longest and costliest commitment. The ANC were reported to be displeased with the expensive white advocates (Kleinschmidt interview April 1992).

Kleinschmidt was persuaded to act, and at the highest level. In October 1986, an apprehensive Frankel was dispatched to Johannesburg, the first visit by a Mr X to South Africa in 20 years. Times were hazardous, not only for the solicitor but more so for those he met. Victoria Mxenge, an IDAF-listed attorney, had been assassinated a few months earlier, as her husband, Griffiths, also an 'IDAF' attorney, had been in 1981 – a 'Death Squad' policeman later confessed to the murder. Frankel was well aware that if IDAF stepped out of the shadows other lives could be endangered. But he met the key IDAF advocates and attorneys, delivering the message – the donors are fed up and are insisting on economies.

The accountant Alan Velcich, who was given the enforcer's role, recalled Frankel as 'an extremely discreet human being'. His opening words bordered on the pompous: 'I represent several foreign governments who have an interest in human rights matters and fund trials in South Africa'. It may sound improbable, said Velcich, 'but I didn't know it was IDAF until 1990, and I knew of very few attorneys who did know, whatever they say now. Only Priscilla did' (Velcich interview 1992).

When the tariff was published the profiteers were not pleased, though most attorneys recognised the need for it. A senior attorney's monthly retainer was pegged at R9,000, still a considerable figure for the time. As for disbursements (expenses), it was now to be economy air travel only and 3 or 4-star hotels, while 'unreasonably extravagant expenditure on meals and liquor' would not be met. Some felt aggrieved by the demand for a detailed monthly return to Carruthers or Miller & Co. But Rosemary Sands says people had got into bad habits. 'I inherited a system in which IDAF was paying out floats of money without the firm in South Africa having to account for it until the case was finished, and sometimes they went on for years.'

But even with a tariff, how could monitors 6,000 miles away be sure that the hours billed by the attorney had actually been worked? Was the work done by an articled clerk or by the senior partner? How could they verify a two-hour consultation at a prison when there was a strong suspicion it had been conducted on the telephone? Some attorneys covered up their scant accounting with the excuse that it was dangerous to disclose every fact. There were travel claims for Johannesburg to Delmas, a distance of some 50 kilometres, submitted as 250 kilometres. They were not to know their accounts were vetted by South Africans.

If Essex Road had reason to believe someone was not playing the game, Velcich paid a visit. One attorney claimed to have personally worked 45 days in one month. Sometimes it was 18 hours a day, weekends included. 'In our experience South African lawyers don't do more than five hours work a day,' said Velcich, stirring the pot. 'And we would pay them that. We could always say, "Well, Sands insists." It did help that most of the firms were reliant on our funding.' No one was reported to the Law Society but, said Hilary Rabkin at Programme One, a few 'shysters' were dropped. In 1989, she queried 190 bills with 54 firms. Some discounts agreed were staggering, probably saving R1.5 million in all (Rabkin interview 1991).

The Bar was more difficult to tackle. Heaton-Nicholls put her finger on a recurring scam. A political trial is set down for a month and finishes in a week. Some counsel would mark the brief for a month's work, with the justification that it was standard legal procedure. Her firm resisted (she had left Jana by now). 'We would never have the nerve to charge for a full day when the matter was over in half a day, maybe with a postponement. But other firms did not have the resources to check on what happened on a given day. Or counsel might say, "Oh, but other attorneys paid us." Young attorneys found it hard to plead with or, if necessary, harass eminent counsel over fees. But we never assumed that counsel's fees were correct' (Heaton-Nicholls interview 1992).

A senior advocate's monthly retainer, pegged at R16,000, caused yelps of distress at Innes Chambers, home of the Johannesburg Bar. A tariff was an affront to those who cherished the privilege of charging whatever you suspected the client could afford. And now attorneys were actually demanding prior agreement on how a brief was to be marked. 'The advocates were condescending to us,' said Velcich. 'Arthur Chaskalson was great, and Bizos worked in the Delmas trial over several years without any increase. The black advocates were often better, and in Durban they were very much in favour.'

The tariff at first barred the use of senior counsel, the local equivalents of QCs. Despite its manifest social inequalities, South Africa retained the rule inherited from the English that a silk be assisted in court by a junior who by custom marked his brief at two-thirds the amount of his senior's. The pulse of the haemorrhage lay here. White advocates, who dominated the Bar, benefited most as a group from the IDAF millions. But with the death penalty now flourishing in political trials as a leftover of the township turmoil that had been smothered by the Emergency, the IDAF trustees permitted senior counsel to be briefed in capital cases. In 1988, IDAF was running 28 death row appeals involving 55 individuals. Still, some senior counsel complained they could not live on R16,000 a month.

IDAF was not alone in pegging legal charges. In 1988, its tariff was adopted at a meeting in London chaired by Huddleston and attended by Gaye McDougall of the Washington Lawyers' Committee and Beyers Naudé for the SACC's Asingeni Fund and Dependants' Conference. The larger donors, Sweden and the UN Trust Fund, were there, as well as Christian Aid, representing western European Protestant churches. They set up a system aimed at eradicating double, sometimes treble, funding.

Enuga Reddy traced the fees problem to Collins telling the United Nations in 1965 that he was able to finance every trial. 'So advocates marked their briefs high, attorneys were paid more and there was a higher commission for the lawyers in England.' Professor John Dugard thought the defence campaign could have been run at a quarter of the cost by the Legal Resources Centre, which was staffed by lawyers in six main centres. 'The Centre could have expanded, but the Bar would not allow the Centre's lawyers, with advocates of the ability of

Arthur Chaskalson, to take on union work or security trials.' Dugard's own creation, the Centre for Applied Legal Studies (at the University of the Witwatersrand), fought a series of test cases on the Group Areas Act and the pass laws. Shun Chetty, Jules Browde, Dugard himself and others acted free of charge. But when the law was liberalised in 1979 to allow free collective bargaining, the Law Society objected to the Centre's lawyers operating for black trade unions without charge, though their salaries were paid out of Carnegie Corporation and Ford Foundation funding. 'For both branches of the profession,' says Dugard, 'the ultimate crime was to do something without charging' (Dugard interview 1992).

All the while, Michanek was trying to pin down costs at Birkbeck Montagu's in London. Frankel prepared annual statements for fees and disbursements, but they were not itemised. 'It was one of the banes of Michanek, trying to get Bill to provide details of work,' Kleinschmidt recalled. 'He asked Bill direct and there was tension but he did not succeed.' Frankel, responding to a query from the author, said he could not give an accurate estimate of Birkbeck's fees for the IDAF work throughout the 25 years. In the early years, he said 'we charged very little, if anything.' After the Soweto uprising, 'my time involvement in the work became very considerable indeed', but he doubted that his fees would have been more than 50 per cent of the normal commercial rate and probably significantly less. IDAF records show that in 1985, legal fees amounted to £40,000 though this would have included the intermediary solicitors.

•

In early 1988 the security police came close to penetrating the dense world of IDAF funding operations inside South Africa. A police inspector called at the Smith, Tabata & Van Heerden offices in King William's Town to serve a warrant requiring the practice to hand over all correspondence with Miller & Co. The Cambridge firm was by then the principal IDAF go-between. The policeman's authority was the Fund Raising Act, which related to the collection of contributions from the public.

'If the files had been released,' says Dumisani Tabata, 'the whole network of people would have been exposed, from the overseas source of the money to the local activists who referred people to us' – clients were told the money came from 'the church'. The partners bought time by disputing the legality of the warrant. When the policeman returned he was confronted by a local white attorney, Bob Stanford, who assured him that Tabata's firm would not do anything improper. Tabata laughed. 'He was impressed that a white man should say that about us.' But the partners did remove the files to Tabata's house. That afternoon they obtained a temporary stay on the warrant, and a year later won their appeal. It was the last shot in the long-running duel between Pretoria and the Defence and Aid Fund.

On 2 February 1990 the Xhosa chant '*Kaya Hanjwa*' ('We're going home') echoed through the compounds of Robben Island (Walter Sisulu interview 1992). It was true. On that day President FW de Klerk announced that all political exiles would be allowed to return to South Africa and that shortly Nelson Mandela would be released after 10,000 days of imprisonment. He then formally unbanned the ANC, the PAC, the SACP and other 'communist' organisations, including the Defence and Aid Fund.

Chapter 26

CLOSE DOWN

IDAF emerged into the post-apartheid light, blinking, unsure of the next step. It had always been understood that the end of apartheid would mean the demise of John Collins's great undertaking. But now it was all happening so suddenly. Some employees, for whom this was the only working environment they had known, might have believed they would be employed indefinitely, until retirement, like members of the English civil service. But the jolt they were about to receive would be more than offset by the knowledge that they had made a noteworthy contribution to the circumstances that had forced South Africa's President into his historic U-turn.

The trustees initiated a series of soundings. Bill Frankel, liberated from the *nom de guerre* of Mr X, but still overseeing an avalanche of legal work, was dispatched to South Africa to assess what was required by the ANC and others in the internal struggle. He met Mandela at his Soweto home and described to him what IDAF had achieved. 'He was amazed at what he heard and made it very clear he wanted us to continue,' at least through the difficult period of negotiations with De Klerk's government to agree on a democratic constitution. But Frankel detected less enthusiasm for IDAF's continuation at lower levels, where the thinking was that it should be replaced by something more specifically African – or perhaps more amenable to ANC control. Zola Skweyiya, the influential head of the ANC's legal department, was for closing IDAF down, while the treasurer, Tom Nkobi, cautiously favoured its preservation (Kleinschmidt interview February 1992).

This mixed response was mirrored in the board of trustees. Huddleston and Diana Collins were experiencing their first serious policy disagreement. Diana Collins believed strongly that IDAF should continue its work until South Africa could be said to be truly liberated, following free and universal elections. Huddleston blithely suggested that 'it's all solved, Mandela is out of prison, we close down.' With powerful forces ranged on either side – she was supported by Enuga Reddy, while Huddleston counted Ernst Michanek among his adherents – it was by no means clear who would win the argument (Kleinschmidt interviews 1991, 1992).

Kleinschmidt undertook a whirlwind round of consultations with the ANC and friends inside the country. He was of the opinion that IDAF could come into South Africa, but there was resistance from the SA Council of Churches (SACC) as well. 'I was told after the De Klerk speech that it was now the ANC's affair. We were too big and too efficient' (Kleinschmidt interview 1991). At the Namibian independence celebrations in March 1990, Kleinschmidt and three trustees, Michanek, Boudewijn Sjollema of the World Council of Churches, and the Canadian, Renate Pratt, met Frank Chikane of the SACC, Saki Macazoma and others influential in the ANC. The IDAF question, they were told, had still to be 'caucused'. Kleinschmidt complained that 'nobody in the ANC takes a stand until the ANC takes a collective stand.' The visitors were unable to get through to Mandela. When Kleinschmidt asked the ANC for a commendation to help fundraising, Walter Sisulu and Mandela did sign a letter, but on unheaded note-paper, and it made no mention of IDAF, being addressed to 'Frankel, Birkbeck Montagu's, London' and asked to extend 'our heartfelt thanks to your clients for their massive contribution during our many years of struggle' (IDAF files, March 1990).

Seven months later, with the future of IDAF still in the balance, Kleinschmidt received a telephone call at his home in London. He remembers the time – 6:00 in the morning of 18 October 1990. 'Why,' asked a clearly displeased Mandela, 'are you refusing to defend my wife?'

The case of Winnie Mandela had been the cause of one convulsion in IDAF, and was about to generate another. Although Mandela was wholeheartedly supportive of his wife, there had been indications during his final years in prison that she was spiralling out of control. Her endorsement of 'necklacing' had embarrassed the ANC and its supporters abroad. More worrying was her patronage of the '*Mandela United Football Club*', whose mostly teenage members lived in the back of her house in Soweto, charged with her protection. In time, the *Mandela United* boys acquired a fearsome reputation in turf wars with rival gangs. Her house came to be associated with rumours of torture, kidnapping and finally murder. In December 1988, 14-year-old 'Stompie' Seipei was interrogated by Winnie Mandela on suspicion of being a spy. Days later he was found dead in a river bed, with three knife wounds in his body.

IDAF was drawn into the case early in 1990 when Winnie Mandela was formally charged with kidnapping four youths, including Stompie, and with being an accessory after the fact to an assault on the boy days before his murder. Would IDAF fund her defence? Kleinschmidt remembers it as one of the organisation's more fraught decisions. Though keen to help the Mandela family in any way he could, he foresaw difficulties. Frankel recalled that Kleinschmidt had wanted to support her. Frankel argued forcefully against taking on the case. This was a 'criminal crime' and IDAF's trust deed only allowed help in crimes classified as political (Frankel interview with Paul Yule 1993). Kleinschmidt sought the opinion of the trustees, who endorsed Frankel's position. They too felt that this was not a human rights issue.

Kleinschmidt explained this background to Mandela. By the end of the call, however, Kleinschmidt had agreed to try to get the decision reversed by consulting more widely with interested parties in South Africa and with IDAF's principal donors. As part of the consultation process, he and Frankel talked to Ismael Ayob and George Bizos, Winnie Mandela's attorney and advocate, and to anti-apartheid opinion leaders, among them Beyers Naudé, the Afrikaner pastor, and Desmond Tutu, who had become the first black Archbishop of Cape Town. There was a firm consensus that Winnie Mandela should not be judged adversely before she had been tried in court. No one exonerated her behaviour but it was recognised that she had been living under extreme pressure for many years. The donors were less uniform in their response. While the Nordic countries expressed a readiness to sanction the payment for Mrs Mandela's trial costs, the European Community, now a substantial donor with some £800,000 a year, warned Kleinschmidt that if it so much as touched the case IDAF could confidently expect a savage cut in its grant.

Kleinschmidt was able to inform Mandela that IDAF, on reflection, would be prepared to assist with his wife's defence, though there would be damaging funding implications. In quick time Kleinschmidt was surprised by a call from a US multi-national company. Had he heard from Thabo Mbeki? Kleinschmidt was well acquainted with Mbeki, head of the ANC's international affairs department, but there had been no recent communication. Mystified, Kleinschmidt phoned Mbeki. 'You lost money over Winnie,' Mbeki told him, referring to the European Community threat, 'here's another donor for you.' Kleinschmidt understood that the company was keen to get on-side with the ANC as a preliminary to re-establishing its position in South Africa. But under American law the company was not permitted to make a direct contribution to a political movement. It would donate money to IDAF on the understanding that it would benefit the ANC.

The trustees were bemused by the emergence of so unlikely a benefactor. Should they take the money? 'Diana said yes, Huddleston and Michanek were doubtful,' Kleinschmidt recalled. 'But nobody actually said no, largely because the ANC were in favour.' In due course, three men from the company's head office presented themselves at IDAF's Essex Road offices and handed over a cheque for £53,000.

The trial was set for February 1991 but before proceedings were far advanced there was a dispute over the first interim legal bill. The amount requested by Mandela's attorney, Ismail Ayob, was in excess of IDAF's legal tariff. Frankel refused to pay above the limit. However, the message was that as the ANC had raised more than enough money to cover the bill, there was no reason why IDAF should not settle in full. Once again Kleinschmidt went back to his trustees. They were not prepared to break their tariff guidelines. Ayob was instructed to take no more of IDAF's money. IDAF ultimately did not fund Winnie Mandela's trial.

In May 1991 a Johannesburg supreme court judge convicted Mrs Mandela of kidnapping Stompie and of being an accessory to assault and she was sentenced to six years' imprisonment. She was released on bail and on appeal the sentence became a fine of R15,000 (about £3,000). She did not serve any part of the prison sentence.

Though the Winnie Mandela case was not the prime cause of IDAF's shut down, it had the effect of accelerating the centrifugal tendencies in IDAF and hastened its demise. Proponents for its continuation in London and New York lost heart, while in South Africa influential supporters were alienated. Mandela told the author: 'It is unfortunate that some lawyers have gone bankrupt... people who deserve a defence are not getting it. It would have been better if IDAF had kept going but once the organisations were legalised and the prisoners released, IDAF felt it was no longer necessary. There was no pressure within the ANC [to close down]... it was not coming from us at all' (Mandela interview 1992). The one man capable of exerting a calming influence, Oliver Tambo, friend of both Mandela and Defence and Aid, was in a Stockholm hospital recovering from a stroke and would suffer continuing ill-health until his death in April 1993.

The first stage in the official dissolution of IDAF was a special conference in London in December 1990, where donors and other contributing organisations were asked to endorse Huddleston's resolution recommending closure. Ethel de Keyser of British Defence and Aid recalled it as a meeting where 'everyone was unhappy'. The unhappiness became more pronounced when the ANC's treasurer-general, Thomas Nkobi, made a late plea for IDAF to remain in business. This was a surprise, as those present had been under the impression that the ANC was content to go along with a closure plan. The Swedes confirmed their readiness to continue giving money to IDAF, while the Danes, among the early proponents of closure, changed their minds. In the afternoon session, as the mood of the meeting swayed against the resolution, Huddleston warned that he would resign if it was not passed. In the event, there was no call for a dramatic exit.

The specially created South African Legal Defence Fund (SALDEF), based in Cape Town, inherited the work of IDAF's Programme One. The board of trustees, all South Africans, was chaired by Beyers Naudé and included the lawyers Dullah Omar and Arthur Chaskalson, as well as Sheena Duncan of the Black Sash. SALDEF's director, Ntobeko Maqubela, law lecturer and lately of Robben Island, took over the 4,000 live legal files from London.

SALDEF was funded in much the same way as IDAF had been. Its initial annual budget of £5.23 million included contributions from the United Nations, Scandinavia and (a considerably reduced amount) from the European Community. Later, once the ANC and the US government had undemonised each other, it was boosted by funds from USAID.

Even with this impressive send-off, SALDEF struggled to establish an identity. Donors were by now switching from human rights to reconstruction, housing, education and improving the quality of life. But SALDEF saw the funding of the defence in political trials as part of the process of inculcating a civil rights' culture. Louise Asmal, the fund's regional director, spoke of 'a real danger, especially in KwaZulu-Natal, that if people were not defended when they were unjustly accused, more violence could well have happened. We wanted people to feel they could obtain justice through the courts, and not through violent retaliation, which had to stop with the coming demise of apartheid.'

But the optimism was premature. Afrikaner nationalism's hopes of retaining power rested on a strategy of pitting black against black, ANC against the mainly Zulu Inkatha organisation. In the limbo between the dying embers of white rule and the as-yet unachieved electoral democracy, money and arms were pumped into secret police units, whose success as *agents provocateurs* filled the courts to overflowing. With defence money running out, prisoners in rural gaols were mocked with the refrain, *'waar's jou Ee-daf nou?'* ('where's your IDAF now?'). Frankel warned the attorneys that the limited funds should be used to meet current IDAF commitments. As SALDEF moved hesitantly into the driver's seat, he announced tougher qualifications for new cases. One, in particular, appalled the attorneys: bills had to be counter-signed by the client at the bottom of the final page. 'They hated us for it,' said Kleinschmidt.

The belt-tightening was only partially effective. A number of attorneys were heavily committed with on-going cases or appeals. Money management in some firms left much to be desired. Some discovered bills they had previously overlooked. By January 1992, six months after IDAF's closure, John Smith of the National Association of Democratic Lawyers said attorneys were owed R600,000. 'It appears that IDAF's donors, due to certain ideas about South Africa, simply did not pay up at the end. IDAF has offered some lawyers proportional settlements, others, nothing.' Many lawyers faced bankruptcy (Smith interview 1992). A string of advocates were owed R187,000 by Priscilla Jana, herself on the verge of closure. Afrikaner attorneys in the Transvaal and Orange Free State, she said, were 'not interested in this overseas organisation which can't pay and were threatening to sue.' IDAF settled one third of her debt. SALDEF worked out a formula by which it paid more to small firms that were not owed so much but would have had more difficulty surviving than a large firm. Even so, the advocates (predominantly white) took a large proportion of the money (Jana interview 1992).

The larger, sophisticated urban firms were able to re-direct resources. Cheadle, Thompson & Haysom in Johannesburg inherited ANC and trade union work, while in the Cape, Mallinick Ress returned its 'human rights' eighth floor to commercial practice. Essa Moosa in Cape Town and Ismael Ayob, Mandela's attorney, had the cushion of a general practice. But for those who had depended wholly on IDAF defences, indeed, had come into being for that very purpose, the affair of the unsettled bills left a bitter taste. Mandela, who admired Priscilla Jana's spirited defiance, was further distanced from IDAF by these events.

SALDEF covered the diminishing number of trials at a restricted level but never overcame its teething troubles. It was asking too much to step into the shoes of the IDAF legal team, which had worked in the detached serenity of England, for clients whose expectations were pegged at survival level. Some employees were on over-large salaries and maladministration began to rear its head. Announcing SALDEF's closure in mid-1994, Justice Minister Dullah Omar explained that 'democracy has been ushered in to our country and the need for the kind of defence so necessary during the apartheid years no longer exists.'

Programme Two, depending as it did on cash and encouraging words, was more harrowing to terminate. IDAF had offered to carry on the welfare programme from London or South Africa, but was refused. The correspondents were not at first let into the secret of the IDAF connection, though a letter from 'Fr Sherrington' in March 1990 suggested that if 'your families... write about these momentous events... feel free to respond in your own way.' In July, Peggy Stevenson broke cover to address her network directly, revealing that the priests were a front for the International Defence and Aid Fund, 'founded by the late Canon John Collins in response to political trials in South Africa.' They now learnt that hundreds of other volunteers had been writing similar letters every two months, some for 20 years or more. They were asked to tell the families that the grants would end in April 1991, when the last of the political prisoners were due for release. Correspondents were left to devise a form of words apologising for misleading families with whom they may have developed a deep friendship. 'Heartbreaking as it may be,' Stevenson wrote, 'we must remind ourselves that the victims of apartheid repression cannot be assisted indefinitely or until the country provides prosperity for all.' Though many were in desperate straits, they proffered grateful thanks. Some bowed out with dignity. 'Karin, feel at ease,' wrote the Robben Island veteran, Theo Cholo, to Karin Bergengren in Sweden. 'It is not your decision that IDAF should close... it is time for it to wind up its job.'

Kleinschmidt and Stevenson negotiated an agreement with the Dependants' Conference, the only local group capable of taking over the 2,000 families on IDAF's books. Recipients were sent a list of 21 offices to which they might apply for financial help. 'It is up to you to approach them for assistance,' they were advised. 'They will take care of you to the best of their ability; however, there is no guarantee that they will be able to offer assistance at the same rates or on the same long-term basis as IDAFSA has done.' Staff were poorly trained, and local ANC officials were wont to interfere. Kleinschmidt later claimed 'they did not appear to have honoured any commitment.' IDAF received 'sad, often tragic appeals in large numbers of letters from former recipients who could not get help after we ceased functioning.'

So the Essex Road offices were cleared of staff and files. The photo and video libraries, accompanied by Barry Feinberg, were shipped to Cape Town to become the centrepiece of the University of the Western Cape's Mayibuye Centre archive. The mountain of legal files, some in storage in a warehouse in east London, others on Bill Frankel's office floor, were flown to South Africa (at Sweden's expense) to help prepare for the Truth and Reconciliation Commission hearings. And the letter writers? On three consecutive days Peggy Stevenson hosted coming-out afternoons for those who could get to Islington for a glass of wine and a canapé. Sisters Beryl, Dorothea and Caroline Ann of the Anglican order of the Sisters of the Church left their convent on Ham Common, south-west London, to mingle with fellow-conspirators in the silent war. They were given a tour of the top-floor nerve centre. 'We were very conscious of what was going on in the world and wanted to do our bit,' mused Sister Beryl, 'but we are not involved in revolutionary politics. But it was such fun.'

IDAF ran the prison release grant programme to better effect, helped by a UN Trust Fund donation of $200,000 to a charitable trust administered by a Johannesburg legal firm. At the behest of the Association of ex-Political Prisoners, every 'political' in the country, including unbailed awaiting trialists, received £100 for each year inside. The money was placed in the prisoner's hand on the day of release. Kleinschmidt described men stepping onto the quay at Cape Town harbour (off the boat from Robben Island), 'cardboard box under their arm, with whatever rags they'd called clothes when arrested five, ten or twenty years ago.' The money contributed to their self-respect, to the belief that their time in prison was a necessary sacrifice. They came home as heroes, but heroes with money in their pockets. The average payout was £450. In April 1991, the busiest month of the scheme, 238 men and a handful of women returned with £109,000 for their long-suffering families.

And yet, in the uppermost reaches of the ANC, the fund became identified not for what it had done in past years, and more with the dispute over the Winnie Mandela case and the lawyers' payments that characterised its valedictory final months. The degree of upset that these events caused was not at first apparent to IDAF's disbanded army, but after publication in 1994 of Nelson Mandela's autobiography, *Long Walk to Freedom*, it became clear, not from what was said, but from what was omitted. Mandela did not mention Defence and Aid either in relation to himself or the struggle, though the lawyers it had funded, Fischer, Kentridge, Bizos and others, were accorded generous recognition. Neither the name John Collins nor the organisation that raised most of the money for Mandela's two capital trials and helped support his wife and children while he was in prison, appear anywhere in the narrative. Defence and Aid was airbrushed out of the liberation script.

Subsequent histories have hardly remedied this deficiency. Martin Meredith's biography of Mandela, published in 1997, has a one-line reference to Collins in relation to the Treason Trial. Anthony Sampson's authorised biography of Mandela, published in 2000, makes a more generous mention of Collins but gives no idea of the extent of his organisation's achievement (Meredith 1997; Sampson 2000). Neither author provides a hint of the United Nations connection and Defence and Aid's prodigious contribution to the cause after its banning – though a comprehensive account of Collins's secret activities had appeared in the *Observer* newspaper in 1991, followed by a Channel 4 *Secret History* documentary (directed by Paul Yule, researched by the author). However, in 1992 Mandela told the author that IDAF's help was

> absolutely formidable... to be able to get the best lawyers to appear in political trials... for a lawyer to do so is a direct contribution to the struggle... so that those who had perpetrated these acts were encouraged because people know

if things go wrong they will not be abandoned... and they would have a platform to put their views. The fact that funds were available for the success of such lawyers was part and parcel of the struggle.

On the welfare contribution, he said:

> We got news in prison of his [Collins's] help... we knew all that time... People were able to travel from all over the country to see their loved ones. It was absolutely vital that Defence and Aid be there... [it was] a morale booster. (Mandela interview 1992)

The bare statistics of the defending and aiding account for the more visible aspect of IDAF's contribution – tens of thousands of men and women offered the protection of lawyers, an incalculable number of prison family dependants on welfare, adding up to almost £100m orchestrated from London over four decades. A fair proportion of the 3 billion Swedish kroner (£300m) that Sweden spent on the overthrow of apartheid was channelled through IDAF. Indeed, Kleinschmidt told Boris Ersson, the Swedish documentary maker, that over the years IDAF had benefited 45,000 dependants of prisoners and ex-prisoners. In its final six years, from January 1985, the fund helped in 16,551 legal matters – political trials, appeals, detentions without trial, death row stays of execution, inquests, civil claims against the police and the State, group areas appeals, trade union cases, commissions of inquiry, help to communities driven off their land and to people being harassed. In 1990, some 28,000 people were involved; in 1991 they still numbered 20,000 (*Secret Mission*, Swedish television, 1995).

But other factors, less easy to measure, have left their mark on the transformed country. If each defended case dug a small hole in which to sink apartheid, it was at the same time laying down a brick upon which to secure the future of the legal system. This was not a conscious aim on Collins's part, but his relentless support of trial defences helped the courts survive – and adapt – as an inheritable institution. The wonder is that, throughout the period, prisoners were charged and lawyers were able to defend them, even if the judges were openly hostile or incompetent or both, or, being suspected of humanitarian tendencies, were not given political cases to try. The prisoners had their day in court, whereas in East Timor, Argentina or Chile, they would have perished anonymously. This quirky Afrikaner respect for juridical correctness came under strain in the 1980s as the regime lost control. Latin American-style disappearances and the extra-judicial killing of resistance figures became a very real option in the hands of the Civil Co-operation Bureau. But by then enough judges were displaying boldness in protecting individual rights. Judge John Milne, in reactionary Natal, was said to have been elevated to the Appellate Division to prevent him hearing political trials at the first instance.

Though still harbouring exemplars of the *ancien régime*, the courts were on the way to becoming models of non-racial propriety. Modern South Africa has a bill of rights and a constitutional court with powers to test legislation. The first liberation chief justice, Ismael Mohamed, was an Asian, while blacks have moved onto the Bench as magistrates and judges. South Africa might have been a very different place had John Collins not made the solemn undertaking to provide a legal defence wherever possible. At the closing meeting of IDAF, Diana Collins said, in reference to her husband's fund-raising efforts, 'I have always believed, with Shelley, that imagination is the great instrument of moral good; it is imaginative sympathy that enables people to identify with people they don't know, who are suffering in any way, and that prompts them to give generously, which they have always done.'

At the IDAF staff farewell in the Ibis Hotel, Euston in May 1991, Kleinschmidt called for 'a celebration of victory and achievement', not a funeral. They were introduced to the shadowy figure known as 'Mr X'. His self-discipline, said Kleinschmidt, had been crucial to the Fund's success. 'Bill has never featured at an IDAF conference but today I would like you to give him a hand. Bill, would you stand up so people may know who you are.' They saw a mild, bespectacled, by now middle-aged man looking much like the City lawyer that in fact he was. Among the guests was Dullah Omar, who three years later would become South Africa's Minister of Justice.

He said: 'IDAF made it possible for many of our people and organisations to stand on their own feet. Indeed, you have helped to humanise the struggle. Nobody knew where the money came from. Nobody got kudos. This was the key to its success' (Omar speech 25.05.92). The judgement is relevant across the entire anti-apartheid community. The International University Exchange Fund, before its vitiation by Williamson, gave a generation of students the training denied to them at home. The church and union networks, the sporting refuseniks, the campaigns of the Anti-Apartheid Movement with their repercussions in distant townships, the diplomatic leadership of the United Nations and the Nordic states, all aimed at changing South Africa through sanctions and diplomatic pressure. It is the story of an international passive resistance movement in which thousands of people participated, were prepared to go to jail, even sacrifice their careers.

Reddy at the UN believed that the relatively low-key violence of the struggle owed much to the mouthpiece provided by the United Nations and these anti-apartheid campaigners. 'When you have frustration among the people that they cannot do anything, that is the time terrorism develops. But we said at the UN, "your issues will be kept alive by us," and they didn't move into terrorism.' This may equally be a comment on the slowness of the liberation movements to take on Pretoria's military and security machine. But the persistence of small countries and ordinary people finally succeeded in persuading the West that apartheid was not worth the candle. After that, there was no need to go into a pointless final lap of bloodletting.

What a different world from the day in 1952 when John Collins took up the cudgels against an unrecognised tyranny. His spirit was there at the end. As Kader Asmal said: 'The story of the Fund is part of the great South African story of liberation' (Speech at IDAF closing conference, 25.05.91).

Chapter 27

WHERE ARE THEY NOW?

Diana Collins, in her eighties and semi-retired in Suffolk, was made a Dame of the British Empire (DBE) in the 1999 Honours List, for 'services to human rights in southern Africa'. Though dubious about the association with 'Empire', she was pleased that her work and her husband's had been recognised officially at last. 'You need to die or live to a great old age, when you're not a threat to anyone any more,' she observed. When Diana died in 2003, the urn containing her ashes was laid next to her late husband's in the crypt of St Paul's Cathedral. Their eldest son Andrew Collins, now Sir Andrew, the one-time rookie on the Pearce Commission, became a Justice of the High Court (Queen's Bench Division) in 1994. Between 1999 and 2002 he acted as President of the politically-sensitive Immigration Appeal Tribunal and early in 2004 was appointed Judge in Charge of the Administrative Court List.

The most visible reminder of John Collins's work is the office of the Canon Collins Educational Trust for Southern Africa in Islington, run until 2004 by its long-time administrator, the late and lamented Ethel de Keyser OBE. These days, multi-nationals such as Unilever, which once avoided political activists like the plague, are more than willing to sponsor promising black students. The Canon's fan club comes up with occasional legacies; when Nora L'Estrange, widow of a Church of England canon, died in her nineties, she left £40,000 to IDAF, which benefited the Educational Trust.

Of the IDAF inner circle, Bill 'Mr X' Frankel OBE is now a consultant to a large impersonal city law firm, Penningtons, into which the firm Birkbeck Montagu's has been subsumed. Horst Kleinschmidt is Deputy Director-General in the Department of Environmental Affairs and Tourism in South

Africa. On the closure of IDAF, Kleinschmidt's work was recognised by the Swedish government, when he was made the equivalent of a British knight. Abdul Minty is Deputy Director-General in the Department of Foreign Affairs. After a spell in the 1990s as ANC Secretary-General Walter Sisulu's personal assistant, Rica Hodgson lives in retirement in Johannesburg. Barry Feinberg moved back to South Africa in the early 1990s to work at the University of the Western Cape's Mayibuye Centre, location of the former IDAF archives. He is a writer and editor and lives in Cape Town. So too, for at least part of each year (the rest he spends in Lyons), does Neville Rubin, the genius who conceived the clandestine *modus operandi* of IDAF. Since leaving the ILO in 1995 he has written a three-volume *Code of International Labour Law*. Alan Cook now lives in Ottawa, Canada where he is writing a history of IDAF. Tony Trew is employed in the communications section of the Office of the Presidency in Pretoria. Fr John Sherrington has given up sweeping the streets of Islington; these days he is a home help, 'washing, cleaning, ironing and shopping' for AIDS sufferers. Peggy Stevenson stayed on in England, the country that allowed her to become 'a human being'. For many exiles, away so long that their children and grandchildren have grown up British, there was a heartbreaking choice between family and the country for which they had sacrificed so much. For some it was a second, reverse, exile.

Trevor Huddleston, Martin Bayer, the first 'Mr X', and the stalwart Phyllis Altman have since died.

Of the lawyers who worked with IDAF, inside or outside the country, Kader Asmal played a prominent role in the post-1990 political and constitutional negotiations, before becoming Minister of Water Affairs in the first ANC government (1994–1999), then Minister of Education under President Thabo Mbeki (1999–2004). He is no longer a cabinet minister but remains an MP.

Sydney Kentridge practices mainly at the English Bar, perhaps too senior to expect an appointment to the Bench, a position which the profession feels he would grace with authority. He is now Sir Sydney. Arthur Chaskalson is

President of South Africa's Constitutional Court. A colleague on the Bench is the would-be teenage saboteur, Dikgang Moseneke. Another former 'IDAF' attorney, Essop Moosa, was until 2003 a judge of the Free State Supreme Court – a far cry from the days when Asians broke the law if they remained in that province for longer than 24 hours. Priscilla Jana became an ANC MP in the first democratic Parliament and has been Ambassador to the Netherlands since 2000.

If one man exemplified the courtroom struggle against apartheid, it was George Bizos. No lawyer in history can have appeared in more human rights trials. His childhood in Greece, marked by the German occupation and the vicious civil war, helped fashion his patient philosophy. 'When a witness has been in solitary confinement and is then taken to court to give evidence for the prosecution there's no point calling him a traitor. A five-year sentence hangs over him if he doesn't testify and you're not going to turn him round by a frontal attack, because he's gone through far worse interrogation. So we remind him of speeches he once made, of friends, of loved ones, and he begins to leave the personality created in prison and return to his former self. If you succeed, he will give a graphic account of why he is in the witness box.' A case in point was Bizos's defence of a young Briton, Quentin Jacobsen, charged with photographing strategic installations with the intention of committing sabotage. The police had a witness who claimed Jacobsen had tried to persuade him to become a revolutionary. In the witness box, he was asked if he remembered a meeting on the University of the Witwatersrand campus when he shouted, 'Tell it all, tell it all!' Bizos re-enacted the scene, fists clenched, 'and it so transformed him he refused to testify and Jacobsen was acquitted' (Bizos interview April 1992). George Bizos is still in practice and recently appeared for the defence in the trial of the Zimbabwean opposition leader, Morgan Tsvangirai.

One-time IDAF beneficiaries who became MPs in 1994 included Winnie Mandela, Albertina Sisulu, Adelaide Tambo and Joyce Mashamba. The latter left Parliament after the 1999 election to become Minister of Education in the

Limpopo (previously Northern Province) provincial cabinet. Her husband, George Mashamba, is the ANC provincial chairperson in Limpopo.

Of other prominent figures in the story, the gifted doctor and one-time UCT academic, Raymond 'Bill' Hoffenberg, left for Britain on an exit permit in 1968 after being banned, to become, successively, professor of medicine at Birmingham University, president of the Royal College of Physicians, a knight of the realm and president of Wolfson College, Oxford. Hugh Lewin returned home in 1992 and became Director of the Institute for the Advancement of Journalists in Johannesburg. He now works as a freelance media trainer in South Africa and abroad. He was a member of the Human Rights Violations Committee of the Truth and Reconciliation Commission. His book *Bandiet out of Jail* won the Olive Schreiner Prize for the best prose published in South Africa in 2003. Raymond Tucker (who has since died), together with Prof. John Dugard, received an honorary law degree at Witwatersrand University, on 25 March 2004.

Craig Williamson is a businessman with connections in what was once a heartland of resistance to apartheid, Angola. Appearing before the Truth and Reconciliation Commission, he applied for amnesty for his role in the killings by letter-bomb of Ruth First in Maputo in 1982 and Jeanette Curtis Schoon and her eight-year-old daughter Katryn in Angola in 1984. The application was successful, as was that of his former boss, General Johan Coetzee, who died in April 2004 while the principal of a police college in Graaff-Reinet. Michael Ngila Muendane, the former PAC chief representative in London and Horst Kleinschmidt's intemperate accuser, was a PAC MP from 1999 until 2004 and, for some time, was Secretary-General of the PAC.

When Jane Furness, HM Inspector of Probation in Halifax, Yorkshire and clandestine IDAF letter-writer, went to South Africa to advise the new post-apartheid Minister of Correctional Services [Prisons], she called on Martha Mahlangu, mother of Solomon (who was hanged on 6 April 1979, and after whom the 'Freedom College' in Tanzania was named), in Section H, Mamelodi West. 'It was a pretty emotional experience to find myself visiting the family to whom I had written for so many years. It turned into a township party over that weekend and I was made extremely welcome by a whole variety of their relatives and friends.'

Capital punishment was suspended in 1990, sparing the lives of 302 men and women on death row, among them 79 'politicals', 26 of whom had been in two 'common purpose' trials. The foundations of the police state, the Internal Security and Terrorism Acts, have been repealed. Gone are detention without trial, bannings, house arrests, banishments, gaggings and acts 'furthering the aims of communism'. In Britain, Tony Blair's government passed the Criminal Justice (Terrorism and Conspiracy) Act, aimed at exiles operating against nasty regimes in their own countries. If only Mrs Thatcher had thought of it, she could have closed down the ANC and PAC offices and gaoled or expelled their activists. However, when Nelson Mandela came to Britain, the once disdainful Prime Minister queued up to shake the hand of 'the terrorist' and tell him what a fine fellow he was.

The methods pioneered by the 'End Loans' group in exposing collusion with apartheid have helped set higher standards in corporate ethics. EIRIS (the Ethical Investment Research Service) has inspired a trend in which investors ask that their unit trust portfolio exclude companies dealing in arms, tobacco or animal testing, or whose operation pollutes the atmosphere, or any one of 30 'negative criteria'. Conversely, there are 'positive criteria' such as women on the board, environmental initiatives and, coming full circle, investment in South Africa. Much of this campaigning work was led by Christians. Bill Whiffen, once of the Christian Ethical Investment Group, told the Scottish Episcopal Church in 1997, 'Those who live in the free South Africa of today have no doubt that the international pressure on banks and businesses to exercise sanctions on the economy of the white apartheid regime was a very significant factor in bringing about political change.' Peggy Preston, the Quaker activist, joined a group of women peace protestors encamped on the Iraqi–Saudi border before the first Gulf War. She returned to Iraq several times to observe how United Nations sanctions were affecting its people and the dangers they faced from the depleted uranium in unexploded shells. In 2003, at the age of 80, arthritis finally put paid to her front-line activism. Now she speaks out, chirpily and with passion, from her flat in Covent Garden.

The United Nations Trust Fund, once the conduit of tens of millions of pounds through the IDAF bank accounts, is no more, its aims realised. But not before the integrity of its membership had been re-established. After General Augusto Pinochet stepped down in Chile, the successor democratic government appointed a former prisoner of the dictator as a trustee of the fund. That certainly pleased Enuga Reddy. Reddy is now retired but continues to live in New York where he writes books on South Africa's liberation heroes.

The traffic jams around Trafalgar Square are as bad as ever, but no longer are motorists distracted by the 'City of London Anti-Apartheid' 24-hour picket which, to the annoyance of embassy workers and the Anti-Apartheid Movement hierarchy alike, camped for years on the pavement in front of South Africa House. Opening South Africa House in 1933, King George V referred to it as 'the home in London of a united South African nation'. Finally, it is that.

Christian Action, the gadfly that attached itself to many causes, lost and realised, closed down in 1996, its golden jubilee year. It was the creation of one man, and once his compelling genius had gone, the momentum was never regained. Huddleston, though frail, delivered a rousing encomium at the ceremony in the St Paul's crypt. There, the ashes of John Collins are interred, amidst the monuments to Lord Nelson and the Duke of Wellington and the winged and equestrian reminders of battlefield heroism. Collins, for his part, has no need of ostentation. When Diana Collins once reported that members of the congregation at St Paul's had suggested he might harbour saintly qualities, he told her simply, 'I know better.'

Endnotes

Chapter 1

1   On his elevation to the House of Lords, Quintin Hogg assumed the title of Lord Hailsham.

2   Senior appointments to the Church of England, as the established church, are made by the reigning monarch on the advice of the Prime Minister. In effect the ruling government decides who is appointed to posts at the level of Archbishop (of Canterbury and York), Bishop and Dean. In the 1940s when John Collins was appointed, this was the case also for the next level of clergy, that of Canon, but this was later stopped and Canons are now simply appointed by the Church. Like every cathedral, St Paul's has a Dean, and because of its size and importance, it has four Canons.

3   Very Reverend is the title used for a person at the level of Dean (of a Cathedral) in the Church of England hierarchy. Right Reverend is the title used for a Bishop and Most Reverend for an Archbishop.

Chapter 2

1   PRO (Public Record Office) CRO (Commonwealth Relations Office) d: G3210/39, copy 116, 18.11.52

Chapter 3

1   Collins had met Sisulu in London some years earlier and had tried in vain to dissuade him from attending a communist conference in eastern Europe.

Chapter 4

1   In 1936, the few Africans in the Cape Province who qualified for the common voters' roll were disenfranchised. Instead, Africans in the Cape were given the right to elect three white MPs to represent them in the lower house of Parliament, and two in the upper house or Senate. Many of these indirect representatives were either outspoken liberals or communists, such as Ray Alexander, Solly Sachs, Sam Kahn and Brian Bunting.

2   After *Africa South* was banned, Segal switched the operation to

London and, with Collins's support, continued to publish under the name *Africa South in Exile*.
3 In South Africa solicitors are referred to as attorneys, while barristers are advocates.

Chapter 5

1 In 1953, in the face of overwhelming African opposition in the three territories, the British government had merged Nyasaland (Malawi), Northern Rhodesia (Zambia) and Southern Rhodesia (Zimbabwe) into the 'Federation of Rhodesia and Nyasaland' or Central African Federation (CAF), under a constitutional arrangement which located political domination in the hands of Southern Rhodesia's white minority. Unrelenting African opposition to the Federation eventually resulted in the breakup of the CAF at the end of 1963, with Malawi attaining independence in July 1964 and Zambia in October of the same year. The ruling white-dominated Rhodesian Front party unilaterally declared Southern Rhodesia independent (UDI) in November 1965. This action was illegal in international law and recognised only by South Africa.

2 Amongst those abducted by South African agents from neighbouring territories in 1960 were Des Francis from Northern Rhodesia, Rosemary Wentzel from Swaziland, and Anderson and Ignatius Ganyile, and Mohlovoa Matseko from Basutoland (Lesotho). Collins paid for a successful *habeas corpus* application to have the Ganyiles and Matseko returned to Basutoland.

3 At first called the Anti-Apartheid Committee, the AAM programme, issued in April 1960, had as a campaign point to support and raise funds for Defence and Aid.

Chapter 6

1 The fifteenth century Italian religious and political reformer, Girolamo Savonarola, began his religious career with zeal, piety, and self-sacrifice for the regeneration of religious life. He later preached the need for political revolution as the divinely-ordained means for the regeneration of religion and morality, and became known for his fanaticism, obstinacy and disobedience. He was condemned to death, hanged and burned.

Chapter 8

1 16 December was referred to as Dingaan's Day by white, particularly English-speaking, South Africans. The Afrikaans name *Geloftedag* (Day of the Covenant) referred to the vow, or covenant with God, which the Boers allegedly made before

their battle against the Zulu under Dingane kaSenzangakhona ('Dingaan') at Blood River in 1838. They vowed that if they won the battle they would forever keep that day sacred. It is still a public holiday in South Africa, although now known as the Day of Reconciliation.

2   These comments were presaged by Mandela's well-documented statements (quoted in Mary Benson's biography) in Johannesburg in July 1961 – before the sabotage campaign started – when he addressed foreign journalists. 'Soberly, he added: "If the government reaction is to crush by naked force our non-violent struggle, we will have to reconsider our tactics. In my mind we are closing a chapter on this question with our non-violent policy." In the only existing news film of Mandela in an interview given to a London television team later that day, he made the same grave declaration.' (Benson 1986: 104)

Chapter 10

1   Foreign Office records: PRO – FO 371 – 177038
2   The name Defence and Aid Fund (International) was formally changed to Defence and Aid Fund for Southern Africa at the second AGM in London in March 1965, and a year later the name was changed again to the final version: International Defence and Aid Fund (IDAF) for Southern Africa.

Chapter 11

1   Olof Palme was elected to the Riksdag, Sweden's Parliament, in 1958. He became Minister of Communication in 1965 and Minister of Education in 1967, and was always influential with Erlander. Palme was Prime Minister from 1968 until 1976; he was re-elected in 1982, and assassinated in February 1986. Suspicions continue to this day of South African security police involvement in the assassination.

Chapter 12

1   A prominent Liberal Party member and political defence lawyer, Ruth Hayman was banned soon after Defence and Aid was outlawed. She went into exile in England. Helen Joseph, a non-communist member of the Congress of Democrats, became in Oct 1962 the first person placed under house arrest in terms of the General Laws Amendment Act of 1962. She remained banned and under house arrest for the next 20 years. In 1983, she was elected to the leadership of the UDF. She died, aged 87, in 1992.

2 See Minutes, Defence and Aid, Cape Town branch meeting 01.08.64.

3 See *Government Gazette R77*, 18.03.66.

Chapter 13

1 Shortly after the banning of the ANC and PAC in 1960, and the setting up by both organisations of exile structures, a short-lived pact was negotiated by the two parties under the name of the South African United Front. The union was formed largely under pressure from donor governments but never took root.

Chapter 14

1 Following the arrest of John Harris in July 1964, his wife was accommodated by family friends, Walter and Adelaide Hain. Active members of the Liberal Party, both were banned at the time. After the execution of Harris on 1 April 1965, the Hains could not attend the funeral because of their banning orders. An oration on their behalf was given by their 13-year-old son Peter. Three years later the family moved into exile in England where, as a student, Peter became a leading anti-apartheid activist. He later became a member of the British Labour Party and in June 2003 was elected Leader of the House of Commons, while retaining his cabinet post as Secretary of State for Wales.

2 See Collins's letter to Constantine (11.03.58) and Constantine's reply (14.03.58).

Chapter 15

1 See Chapter 8 for a discussion of the ANC and PAC in relation to the armed struggle.

2 '*Spyker*' ('nail' in Afrikaans) van Wyk was a member of the Security Police in the Western Cape for some thirty years beginning in the early 1960s. The Truth and Reconciliation Commission (TRC) conducted an investigation of torture in the Western Cape between 1960 and 1994 and in their *Final Report* (Vol. 3, Ch. 5) wrote the following: 'In the evidence before the Commission, Warrant Officer Hernus JP "Spyker" van Wyk is the individual most associated with torture in the Western Cape over a thirty-year period' (p. 402).

3 The next sentence in the TRC Report on torture refers to Colonel Theunis Swanepoel as 'among those mentioned frequently in submissions to the Commission' (p. 402). An original member of the Security Police's sabotage division formed to investigate

the early-1960s outbreak of sabotage directed at strategic targets, Swanepoel developed a reputation as a brutal torturer. In the mid-1970s he was appointed head of the Riot Unit in Soweto. It was this unit that killed hundreds of schoolchildren in the Soweto uprising of 1976.

4 General Johan Coetzee, later chief of the Security Police and national Commissioner of Police. He was also the handler of the Security Police agent Craig Williamson during the period in the late 1970s when Williamson was based in Geneva working for the International University Exchange Fund (IUEF) (see Chapter 19). Coetzee died in March 2004, aged 75.

Chapter 16

1 Vuyisile Mini, trade-unionist, ANC member, a leader of the Defiance Campaign in Port Elizabeth, and later a Treason Trialist, was hanged in 1964 after conviction, on accomplice evidence, of ordering the shooting of a state witness, and of sabotage. He was executed despite appeals from 2,000 people worldwide, including UN Secretary-General U Thant. His daughter Nonkosi joined the ANC's military wing *Umkhonto-we-Sizwe* and died in a cross-border raid on Lesotho by South African police operatives in December 1986.

Chapter 17

1 Correspondence drawn from Rev. Mpanza's letters to Eileen Wainwright, IDAF files.

2 As one-time commander of the Ermelo security police in the Eastern Transvaal, close to the border with Swaziland; as head of Section C of the security police (the unit responsible for covert operations); and as head of the Port Elizabeth security police in the mid-1980s, General Nicolaas Jacobus Janse van Rensburg participated in or authorised numerous covert operations that resulted in the death of numbers of people in all three areas in which he operated. These included the assassinations of ANC activists based in Swaziland and several important ANC and UDF politicians in the Eastern Cape such as Siphiwe Mtimkhulu, Topsy Madaka and the so-called 'Cradock Four', including Matthew Goniwe. He applied for amnesty for some of these killings. Not all were granted, and he is said to have been on the point of being arrested in April 2004 when he died. He would have stood trial with a fellow member of the Port Elizabeth security police, Gideon Nieuwoudt, who has been arrested and charged.

Chapter 18

1   Eddie Daniels's case is a perfect example of the racist nature of the apartheid era's judicial system. Daniels was one of a handful of coloured members of the largely white African Resistance Movement (ARM). Tried along with a white colleague, Spike de Keller, Daniels received the longest sentence (15 years) of all those meted out to his fellow defendants in this and other ARM trials across the country.
    De Keller was released after serving only two years of his ten-year sentence, while Daniels served out the full sentence. Upon his release he was served with a five-year banning order. Daniels's story is detailed in his autobiography *There and Back; Robben Island 1964–1979* (Cape Town: Mayibuye Books, 1998).

2   For a collection of Eli Weinberg's photos see his *Portrait of a People: A personal photographic record of the South African liberation struggle* (London: IDAF, 1981).

3   According to the *Shorter Oxford Dictionary*, the word 'eleemosynary' means 'charitable' or 'supported by alms'.

4   In the late 1970s, Sibeko was murdered in Tanzania. A member of a leadership triumvirate of the PAC, Sibeko fell victim to the lethal factionalism that plagued the PAC throughout its exile years.

5   In 1960 Sobukwe was sentenced to three years' imprisonment for his role in the anti-pass law demonstrations of March 1960. With his sentence about to expire, Parliament passed legislation to enable the state to continue to detain prisoners beyond the expiration of their sentences. This power was used against Sobukwe who was kept in solitary confinement in a cottage on Robben Island for a further four years.

6   See Joel Carlson: *No Neutral Ground* (New York: Crowell, 1973).

7   See House of Assembly, *Hansard*, 12.05.78, cols. 6847–50.

Chapter 19

1   The 'Muldergate' or Information Scandal took its name from Connie Mulder, the Minister of Information, who used government funds to orchestrate a clandestine pro-apartheid propaganda campaign – and attempted to cover it up.

2   The letter-bomb killings in the same week of 1974 of Tiro in Botswana and John Mvembe in Lusaka were not the work of Williamson. They were killed by the 'Z-squad', a covert hit-unit set up by the head of BOSS, Gen. Hendrik van den Bergh.

Chapter 21

1   In August 1984, nine Sharpeville residents, including a local town councillor, were killed in unrest. In September, six Sharpeville residents were arrested and charged with the councillor's murder in terms of the 'common purpose' legal doctrine. Though the state acknowledged that none of the accused had been directly involved in the actual killing, it alleged that they were responsible in that they had been part of the crowd which besieged the councillor's house at the time he was killed. The six were convicted and sentenced to death. The sentence sparked a local and international protest campaign and in February 1988 – only 18 hours before the six were due to hang – a one-month stay of execution was granted. The sentences were then commuted to life imprisonment and the accused were eventually paroled in 1990.

2   The Delmas treason trial was the second longest of the apartheid era (the longest is dealt with in Chapter 4). It began with the indictment of 22 UDF members in June 1985; the trial itself ran from January 1986 to December 1988, at the end of which 11 of the accused were convicted and given sentences ranging from 5 to 11 years. The judge took four days to read his judgement, but laboured in vain as the appeal court overturned his findings a year later and all those convicted were freed. Amongst them were Mosiuoa 'Terror' Lekota, now Minister of Defence (his nickname earned on the soccer field, not in the arena of 'terrorism'), and Popo Molefe who, in 2004, completed his second and final term as Premier of North West Province.

3   Another 'common purpose' trial, this involved 26 residents of Upington's Pabalello township who were charged with the November 1985 murder of a black policeman. Twenty-five were convicted of murder and one of attempted murder in April 1988. Fourteen were sentenced to death and 11 to jail terms. On appeal in 1991, all but five of the sentences were quashed. By then, the death penalty had been suspended and all the accused were freed soon thereafter.

Chapter 22

1   *In forma pauperis* means that the litigation proceedings are being conducted on the basis that the litigant has no means to pay for the legal services, so that payment is effected by the State, through for example, the Legal Aid Board. It quite literally means *in the form of a pauper.*

2   Daniel Madzimbamuto later became ZAPU's Secretary for Foreign Affairs. He died in the late 1990s and was accorded a 'national hero's' funeral. Other prominent Zimbabweans cited in this chapter are i) Cephas Msipa who became Governor of Zimbabwe's Midland province in 1999; ii) Joseph Msika who in 1999 was appointed Vice-President of Zimbabwe; iii) Maurice Nyagumbo and Josiah Chinamano, both appointed ministers in Zimbabwe's first post-independence Cabinet; iv) George Nyandoro who was General Secretary of ZAPU until 1971 when he joined a breakaway group, the short-lived Front for the Liberation of Zimbabwe (FROLIZI); v) Herbert Chitepo, who became the first National Chairman of ZANU, and led their executive in exile in Lusaka until his assassination in 1975.

3   The ANC guerrillas were members of the Luthuli regiment. The group split into two groups and conducted campaigns in the Wankie (Hwange) and Sepolilo districts. The campaign lasted several months. Most of the guerrillas were either killed or captured. Amongst the few who survived and escaped into Botswana was Chris Hani.

4   The Catholic Commission for Justice and Peace (CCJP), as a church organisation, was one of the few organisations able to continue their opposition to the actions of the Smith regime. It revealed considerable evidence of torture, assault and destruction of property by members of the Rhodesian security forces, and produced numerous booklets, including *Civil War in Rhodesia* (published by the Catholic Institute for International Relations, London in 1976). The CCJP continued to document human rights abuses after independence and produced an authoritative report on the early 1980s ZANU campaign to crush dissent in Matabeleland which resulted in some 20,000 deaths.

Chapter 24

1   The text of this speech is included in the booklet *Freedom and Peace* (London and New York: IDAF and UN Centre Against Apartheid, 1980, p. 66) containing John Collins's addresses to the United Nations. On this occasion he was ailing so Diana spoke on his behalf.

2   The violence in Crossroads and other squatter camps in the Western Cape in 1986 was investigated by the Truth and Reconciliation Commission. It found that though the conflict had its origins in historic rivalries and political differences between groups, these were manipulated and exacerbated by both the security police and the military in terms of an overall

security-force plan, which included 'the covert organising of the *witdoeke* to resist the "comrades"' (See TRC Final Report, Vol. 3, pp. 471–72). The *witdoeke* ('white head-scarves' after their identifying symbol) were a vigilante group armed and organised by the state.

3 George Mashamba is today (2004) a central committee member of the SACP and chairperson of the ANC in the province of Limpopo. His wife Joyce is the Minister of Education in the ANC government in Limpopo.

Chapter 25

1 In South Africa a District Surgeon is a medical doctor employed by the state who is responsible for the care of patients in state facilities, and for medico-legal work, including performing autopsies in cases of unnatural death and providing care for convicted prisoners and those in police custody. Dr Wendy Orr's courage in launching her successful interdict against the state was later recognised by her being appointed one of 17 Commissioners to the Truth and Reconciliation Commission, where she played a substantial part in hearings into the roles of health professionals in human rights abuses under apartheid. She is currently (2004) Director of Transformation and Equity at the University of the Witwatersrand and teaches on issues of medical ethics and human rights.

2 Dulcie September was assassinated in Paris in 1988, by killers hired by South African intelligence.

3 On 6 July 1979 six ANC members in exile in Lesotho were injured in a parcel bomb attack in Maseru. One of the group, Father John Osmers, originally from New Zealand, had his hand and part of his groin blown away by the bomb which was concealed in a parcel containing copies of the ANC journal *Sechaba*. The other victims were a former Durban-based lawyer, Phyllis Naidoo, former South African Students' Organisation (SASO) organiser, Silumko 'Socks' Sokupa and Mbuyisela Madaka, Siphiwe Sithole and Wandile Kallipa.

4 On 26 June 1985, eight members of the Congress of South African Students (COSAS) were killed and seven injured in Tsakane, near Johannesburg, when they threw grenades which the security police had booby-trapped by reducing their timing mechanisms to zero and which had been delivered to them by a police agent who had infiltrated their group. Twelve members of the security police applied to the TRC for amnesty for 'Operation

Zero-Zero' including the then Commissioner of Police, General Johan van der Merwe. In his evidence to the TRC, Gen. van der Merwe claimed that this entrapment killing had been authorised by the then Minister of Law and Order, Louis Le Grange.

References and Other Sources

Books

Alexander, PF (1994) *Alan Paton, a Biography*. Oxford: Oxford University Press.

Altman, P (1952) *The Law of the Vultures*. London: Jonathan Cape; (1987) Johannesburg: Ad Donker.

Benson, M (1963) *African Patriots*. London: Faber.

Benson, M (ed) (1976) *The Sun will Rise: Statements from the Dock by Southern African Political Prisoners*. London: International Defence and Aid Fund.

Benson, M (1985) *South Africa: The Struggle for a Birthright*. London: International Defence and Aid Fund.

Benson, M (1986) *Nelson Mandela*. Harmondsworth: Penguin.

Bernstein, Hilda (1994) *The Rift: The Exile Experience of South Africans*. Jonathan Cape.

Brutus, D (1978) *Stubborn Hope: Selected Poems of South Africa and a WiderWorld*. London: Heinemann.

Carlson, Joel (1973) *No Neutral Ground*. New York: Crowell.

Collins, D (1992) *Partners in Protest: Life with Canon Collins*. London: Gollancz.

Collins, LJ (1966) *Faith under Fire*. London: Leslie Frewin.

Collins, LJ (1980) *South Africa: Freedom and Peace: Addresses to the United Nations 1965–1979*. London and New York: IDAF and UN Centre Against Apartheid.

Desai, B and Marney C (1978) *The Killing of the Imam*. London: Quartet Books.

Dugard, CJR (1978), *Human Rights and the South African Legal Order*. Princeton: Princeton University Press.

ffrench-Beytagh, G A (1973) *Encountering Darkness*. London: Collins.

Henderson, I (ed), (1976) *Man of Christian Action, Canon John Collins: The Man and his Work*. Cambridge: Lutterworth Press.

Herbstein, DM (1979) *White Man, We Want to Talk to You*. London: Andre Deutsch.

Houser, GM (1989) *No One Can Stop the Rain*. New York: The
     Pilgrim Press.

Huddleston, T (1956) *Naught for Your Comfort*. London: Collins.

Joffe, J (1995) *The Rivonia Story*. Cape Town: Mayibuye Books.

Mandela, N (1973) *No Easy Walk to Freedom*. London: Heinemann.

Mandela, N (1994) *Long Walk to Freedom*. London: Little, Brown.

Meredith, M (1997) *A True Gentleman: Nelson Mandela: A Biography*.
     New York: St Martin's Press.

Paton, A (1948) *Cry, the Beloved Country: A Story of Comfort in
     Desolation*. London: Jonathan Cape.

Republic of South Africa (1998) *Report of the Truth and Reconciliation
     Commission (TRC)*. Pretoria: Government Printer.

Rostron, B (1991) *Till Babylon Falls*. London: Coronet.

Sachs, A (1973) *Justice in South Africa*. London: Heinemann.

Sampson, A (2000) *The Long Walk to Freedom of Nelson Mandela*.
     London: Random House.

Scott, Michael (1958) *A Time to Speak*. New York: Doubleday.

Segal, R (ed) (1964) *Sanctions against South Africa*. London:
     Penguin.

Slovo, J (1996) *Slovo: The Unfinished Autobiography*. London: Hodder
     & Stoughton

Troup, Freda (1950) *In Face of Fear: Michael Scott's Challenge to South
     Africa*. London: Faber and Faber.

Winter, G (1981) *Inside BOSS: South Africa's Secret Police*. London:
     Allen Lane.

Journal articles
Coleman, A (1991) Crowd Psychology in South African Murder
     Trials. *American Psychologist 46:10*.

Tham, Carl (1987) Olof Palme and the Struggle against Apartheid,
     Development Dialogue 8:1 (Spring),

Documents
British *Hansard*, House of Commons Second Reading Debate, 16.08.

Christian Action, *The Purge of the Eastern Cape*, ca. 1965
     Focus on Political Repression in Southern Africa, bi-monthly
     News Bulletin of the International Defence and Aid Fund

Focus, IDAF. Copies available at IDAFSA Archives.

International Defence and Aid Fund of Southern Africa (IDAFSA) Archives. Housed at Mayibuye Centre, University of Western Cape, Bellville, Cape Town.

Report of the Commission of Inquiry into the Espionage Activities of the South African Government in the IUEF, (IUEF) Geneva. 1980. 76pp. Mimeo.

South African Directorate of Security, Pretoria. Files relating to the South African Defence and Aid Fund.

South African Prisons and the Red Cross Investigation, IDAF, July 1967.

Survey of Race Relations 1963:51.

Weekly Law Reports, London, 5 Feb 1965 and 6 May 1966.

XRAY: Current Affairs in Southern Africa, monthly fact sheet of the Africa Bureau.

Documentaries

Ersson, Boris (Dir) (1995) *Secret Mission,* for Swedish Television.

Feinberg, Barry (Dir) (1980) *Isitwalandwe: The Story of the Freedom Charter,* IDAF.

Feinberg, Barry (Dir) (1985) *The Anvil and the Hammer,* IDAF

Yule, Paul (Dir) (1993) *White Lies,* a documentary for Channel 4 Television, London.

Interviews and correspondence

The book draws on direct and indirect quotes from interviews conducted by the author; transcripts of filmed interviews for *White Lies,* the Channel 4 documentary, directed by Paul Yule and researched by the author, and personal letters, memos and speech transcripts of the people he interviewed.

Altman, Phyllis: London, 1 March 1991; 24 March 1992; 2 and 9 April 1992; 1 July 1993

Andrews, Raymond: Theydon Bois, Essex, 6 April 2004

Apelgren, Greta: Durban, 28 Jan 1992

Armstrong, David: London, 6 March 1991; 1 July 1993

Asmal, Kader: speech 25 May 1991

Asmal, Louise: Cape Town, 16 Jan 1992; letter 9 Aug 1999

Astor, David: London, 22 Jan 1998

Auret, Mike: Harare, 15 May 1992

Bayer, Martin: London, 8 March 1991

Beer, Chris: London, 27 July 1992

Benjamin, Paul: letter 22 May 92

Benson, Mary: London, 24 Feb 1993

Bizos, George: Johannesburg, 7 Feb 1992; 29 April 1992; 20 June 1993.

Broadbridge, Edward and Hanna: Randers, Denmark, 27 Sept 1993.

Brown, Henry: London, 12 July,1996

Bruce, Gordon: Johannesburg, April 1992; 24 June 1993

Brutus, Dennis: London, 6 Aug 1996

Calder, John: Letter to Collins, 11 April 1962

Calvocoressi, Peter: Bath, 3 March 1997

Campbell, Lord: telephone interview 2 April 1992; Nettlebed, 6 July 1993

Champion, Freda (née Nuell): London, 8 Dec 1992

Cholo, Theo: Soshanguve, 6 Feb 1992

Coetzee, Gen. Johan: Johannesburg, 1 May 1992; Graaff-Reinet, 5 Aug 1993

Cola, Walter: Dimbaza, 23 Jan 1992

Coleman, Max and Audrey: Johannesburg, 30 April 1992

Collins, Diana: London and Suffolk, 28 Feb 1991; 9 March 1992; 22 Oct 1992; 11 June 1993; 9 Feb 1996; 26 Feb 1997

Collins, Canon John: letter to Foot, 16 Oct 1964; letter to Blundell, 11 Nov 1964; letter to Prime Minister Lester Pearson, 26 July 1966; letter to Eriksson, 14 Feb 1976; memo, 30 Nov 1981; in film *Isitwalandwe*, ca. 1979

Cook, Al: London, 3 April 1992; 8 June 1993; 2 July 1993, letter 9 May 2003

Daniels, Eddie: Cape Town, 2 May 1992

Darling, Joan: London, 2 Dec 1991

De Blank, Joost: letter to Collins, 4 Oct 1960

De Keyser, Ethel: London, 25 May 1993; 9 Feb 1997; 14 Aug 1999

De Villiers, Dawid: Cape Town, 23 April 1993

Desai, Barney: Cape Town, 17 July 1997

Dick, Nancy: London, 10 June 1992

Dugard, John: Johannesburg, 1 Feb 1992

Eastwood, Anthony: Harare, 17 May 1992

Elliot, Bryant: Harare, 15 May 1992

Eriksson, Lars-Gunnar: Oslo, 25 March 1992

Evans, Bishop Bruce: Port Elizabeth, 22 Jan 1992

Evans, Mike: Cape Town, 5 May 1992

Feinberg, Barry: Cape Town, 7 May 1992; 24 June 1993

Frankel, William: London, 1 March 1991, 7 April 1992; 1 July 1993; letter 28 March 2002

Futerman, David: London, 25 Feb 1992

Gifford, Lord Tony: London, 27 March 1998

Gilder, Barry: Johannesburg, 4 May 1993

Glasser, Cyril: London, 26 June 1992

Godolozi, Monica: Port Elizabeth, 21 Jan 1992

Goldberg, Dennis: London, 19 Oct 1992

Greenfield, Ewen: London, May 1992

Grenville-Grey, Wilfrid: letter 12 Sept 1992

Gwala, Harry and Lulu: Pietermaritzburg, 28 Jan 1992

Hadden, Eileen and Michael: Harare, 15 May 1992

Hamrell, Sven: Upsalla, 27 March 1992

Hansen, Grethe: Copenhagen, 28 Sept 1993

Harkin, Nora: Ireland, June 1992

Haslam, David: ca. 1996

Haysom, Fink: Johannesburg, 3 Feb 1992

Heaton-Nicholls, Caroline and Malinde, Gcinumuze: Johannesburg, 4 Feb 1992; 23 April 1992

Helander, Gunnar: Vasteras, Sweden, 27 March 1992

Henry, Maud: London, 3 Dec 1991

Hepple, Alex: letter to Collins, 14 Nov 1960

Hjul, Peter: London, 13 Dec 1992

Hodgson, Rica: Johannesburg, 3 Feb 1992; 24 April 1992, 20 June 1993; letter to David Sibeko 10 Aug 1970

Hoffenberg, Dr Bill: letter to David Craighead, 18 Feb 1965

Hogan, Barbara: London 3 March 1992; Johannesburg, 24 April 1992

Houser, George: letter 9 Jan 1996

Huddleston, Trevor: London, 11 Nov 1991; 3 Dec 1992; 28 July 1993

Jana, Priscilla: Johannesburg, 7 Feb 1992; 23 April 1992; 28 July 1993

Johannes, Jan: London, 6 March 1992

Judd, Frank: London, 30 July 1992

Kader, Hassim: Pietermaritzburg, 29 Jan 1992

Katjavivi, Peter: Windhoek, 9 May 1993

Kasrils, Ronnie: Johannesburg, 4 May 1993

Keke, Hamilton: London, 10 Aug 1992

Kentridge, Sydney: Chailey, E Sussex, 24 Aug 1992

Kleinschmidt, Horst: London, Pretoria and Johanesburg, 22 Nov 1991; 6 Feb 1992; 22 April 1992; 9 May 1992; 19 June 1993

Kriel, Ivy: Cape Town, 17 Jan 1992; 31 July 1993

Kumm, Bjorn: Lund, Sweden, letter 14 May 1996

Lane, William: Johannesburg, 5 Feb 1992

Laredo, John: letter to author, 15 Nov 1997

Lazarus, Charles: Bulawayo, 12 May 1992

Legum, Colin: 6 Oct 1995; letters to author, Aug 1996 and 25 Feb 1997

Lewin, Hugh: Harare, 17 May 1992

Lindstrom, Bjarne: Oslo, 25 March 1992

Ling, Margaret: London, 25 Sep 1986

Lister, Richard: Durban, 28 Jan 1992

Lyttelton, Humphrey: letter 24 Sep 1996

Madzimbamuto, Daniel and Stella: Harare, 14 May 1992

Maimane, Jenny: undated letter Aug 1999

Maisels, Issy: Johannesburg, 18 May 1992

Mahlangu, Martha: Mamelodi, 22 April 1992

Malindi, Zollie: Cape Town, 16 Jan 1992

Mallinick, Gerald: Cape Town, 5 May 1992

Mandcla, Nelson: Johannesburg, 23 April 1992; 21 June 1993

Manguni, Rev. Stephen: Bulawayo, 13 May 1992

Maquebela, Ntobeka: Cape Town, 16 Jan 1992

Marsh, Jan: London, 12 Feb 1996

Mashamba, Joyce and George: Turfloop, 26 April 1992; 22 June 1993

Mason, David: 17 July 1992

Mayson, Cedric and Penelope: Johannesburg, 9 May 1992

Mbeki, Govan: Port Elizabeth, 21 Jan 1992

Mcube, Mishek Velaphi: Bulawayo,12 May 1992

Meijer, Berend: letter 5 March 2004

Michanek, Ernst: Stockholm, 6 March 1991; 26 March 1992; 14
    June 1993

Minty, Abdul: Oslo, 25 March 1992

Mitchell, Anne: letter 16 Aug 1992; memo 16 Aug 1992, letters

Molobi, Eric and Martha: Soweto, Feb 1992

Moosa, Essa: Cape Town, 16 Jan 1992

Morgans, Vera: London, 14 Feb 1992

Morrow, Laureen: London, 8 April 1992

Moseneke, Dikgang: Pretoria, 6 Feb 1992

Moshidi, Seun: Johannesburg, 4 May 1993

Moss, Glenn: Johannesburg, 10 May 1992

Mpanza, Rev. Phillipus: Balfour, 2 Feb 1992

Msipa, Cephas: Harare, 16 May 1992

Muir, Lynda: letter 15 July 1992

Musschenga, Bert: letter 13 March 2004

Mutasa, Dydimus: Harare, 17 May 1992

Mxenge, Ngxingweni: Durban, 28 Jan 1992

Mzamo, Elias: interview Khayelitsha, 18 Jan 1992

Nkoane, Matthew: London, 27 July 1992

Nkobi, Thomas: London, 3 May 1993

Nkomo, Joshua: Bulawayo, 13 May 1992

Norman, Alison: 22 Oct 1997

Nuell, Freda (later Champion): 1992; letter to Terence Ranger,
        6 Nov 1962

Ntsele, Henry: Bulawayo, 13 May 1992

Odendaal, Andre: Bellville, 20 Jan 1992

Omar, Dullah: speech, London, 25 May 1991

Parkington, Michael: London, 28 Sep 1992

Paton, Alan: letters, 7 April 1964; 3 Aug 1965

Percival, Lydia: London, 2 June 1993

Pitje, Godfrey: Johannesburg, May 1992

Plouviez, Peter: letter to author, 20 Aug 1996

Preston, Peggy: London, 11 Dec 1991

Prevett, John: London, May 1993

Pulling, Bob: letter to author, 26 Feb 1992

Rabkin, Hilary: London, 28 Feb 1991

Ramashamola, Julia: Sharpeville, 7 Feb 1992; 27 April 1992

Ranger, Terence: Oxford, 16 Feb 1993

Rasool, Aziza: Cape Town, 2 May 1992

Reddy, Enuga: London, 15 March 1992; 5 July 1993; letter 15 March
        2004

Rich, Margaret: London, 10 March 1992

Robb, Noel: Cape Town, 23 April 1993

Rubin, Neville: Windhoek, 6 May 1993; London, June 1993; letter 2
        Sep 2003

Sachs, Dr John: London, 9 Oct 1996

Sakupwanya, Melphy: Harare, 15 May 1992

Sands, Rosemary: Cambridge, 27 Feb 1992

Sanger, Clyde: letter 3 Feb 1996

Schorri, Pierre: Stockholm, 26 March 1992

Senda, Lot: Bulawayo, 13 May 1922

Seglem, Kari: Tromso, Norway, letter 30 March 1992

Shallcross, Jack: letter from Wellington, New Zealand, 18 Feb 1993

Sheppard, Rt Rev. David: Liverpool, 19 Dec 1995

Sheridan, Bernard: London, 8 July 1992

Sherrington, Fr John: London, 31 March 1992

Sibeko, David: letter to Collins, 15 Oct 1978

Sisulu, Walter and Albertina: Orlando, Johannesburg,
    7 Feb 1992; 26 April 1992; London 16 June 1993; Robben
    Island, 1 Aug 1993

Sjollema, Boudewijn: London, 28 July 1998; e-mail 30 April 2004

Smith, John: King William's Town, 27 Jan 1992

Soggot, David: Johannesburg, 9 Feb 1992; 10 May 1992

Spence, Susan: letter 14 Oct 1960

Stephenson, Sir Hugh: letter to Foreign Office, London,
    26 March 1966

Stevenson, Peggy: London, 28 Feb 1991, letters 14 Dec 1964;
    13 March 2004

Storhaug, Kari: 13 Dec 1991; 20 March 1992

Stubbs, Fr Aelred: 31 Oct 1997

Stuyfzand, Do: Zandvoort, Holland, Nov 1991

Tabata, Dumisani: King William's Town, 27 Jan 1992

Tambo, Oliver: Shell House, Johannesburg, 7 Feb 1992;
    23 April 1992

Terry, Mike: London, 29 Aug 1996

Todd, Judith: Bulawayo, 13 May 1992

Van der Post, Laurens: London, 7 Aug 1996

Van Rensburg, Patrick: letter Oct 1993

Velcich, Alan: Johannesburg, 3 Feb 1992

Vigne, Randolph: letter 18 Oct 2002

Wainwright, Eileen: London, 1 March 1991

Wästberg, Anna-Lena: Copenhagen, 23 March 1992

Wästberg, Per: Stockholm, 26 March 1992

Whiffen, Bill: talk to Scottish Episcopal Church, Edinburgh, 11 Jan 1997

Wiberg, Ingrid: letter from Gothenburg to author 22 March 1996

Williamson, Craig: Johannesburg, 8 Feb 1992; 28 April 1992;
    19 June 1993

Woods, Donald: London, 23 July 1992; Feb 1997

Xundu, Rev. Mcebisi: Port Elizabeth, 21 Jan 1992

Zackon, Barney: letter to SERF, Cape Town, 20 July 1960

Ziesler, Anne-Liese and Dr Jan: Oslo, 24 March 1992

Letter Writers

These are some of the people in Europe and Canada who wrote to families in southern Africa. The lists are not complete – the secretive nature of the operation has made it difficult to identify all those involved.

UNITED KINGDOM

Rica Hodgson and
Peggy Stevenson
(*main co-ordinators*)

H Abel
Sue Adler
Kathy Adler
S Aidan
E Alcock
D Archdeacon
David Armstrong
J Armstrong
T Arroyo
Joan Bardsley
Rev. Warren Bardsley
M Barker
J Bays
J Bedford
L Belfast
Barbara Benedikz
Petur Benedikz
P Bentley
Myrtle Berman
Hanif Bhamjee OBE
(*Welsh co-ordinator*)

T Bianchi
I Birney
Prof Dorothy Blair
Claire Blatchford
C Bootland
C Bostock

S Boulds
P Brannigan
S Brearley
Babette Brown
Jenny Brown
Peter Brown
May Brutus
Sonia Bunting
S Burgess
S Burnie
N Burridge
Prof Edward Cadbury
I Campbell
Prof John Campbell
C Carter
Millie Carter
Barbara Castle
R Chalmers
L Chandler
I Clarinbull
B Clarke
I Clason
G Cockle
J Coe
S Colbeck
I Comber
P Conn
C Cowley
Nancy Cowley
M Cropley

H Curtis
M Curwen
E Daffern
Joan Darling
M Davey
A Davie
Eden Davies
O Davies
O Deasy
W de Jong
C Dennis
C Denniston
Nancy Dick
K Dodd
Linda Dolan
Hazel Domb
F Downes
J Drowley
V Drowley
J Drury
B Dutton
A Edwards
E Edwards
Sister Robin Elizabeth
Hazel Elliot
G Ellis
D Emmerson
W Emmett
N Evans
J Eyers
Vanessa Eyre
C Fairmichael
Ann Farr
P Farrell
J and R Fawcett
Rena Feld
Iris Festenstein
Mrs EM Field
L Fifer
P Fitzsimmons
C Ford
D Ford
Sadie Forman
S Fothergill

A Fu
Jane Furness
A Fyall
Brenda Gaine
J G-Hardy
S Garrard
S Garrod
S Gibbons
Vivien Giladi
D Gilbert
M Gordon
Saras Govender
K Gray
M Gray
S Hales
G and C Hall
D Hamilton
Sister Beryl Hammond
H Hampton
Ann Harries
A Harris
J Hasker
C Hawkesworth
H Hawley
Roslyn Hayeem
E Heald
M Heffernan
A Hemingway
N Henry
A Hepburn
S Herbert
Chris Herries
N Hessenberg
T Higgs
E Hill
S Hill
J Hill
D Hillbourne
G Hitchcock
T Holloway
M Holman
M Howells
D Humphrey
J Hunt

Sylvia Hurst
A Hutchinson
M Hutchinson
R Hutchinson
H Hydon
P Jackson
D Jones
Adelaide Joseph
J Joseph
M Kail
P Kattenhorn
S Kearney
A Kelly
T Kendall
Jos King
Rev Theo Kotze
Berry Kreel
Maureen Kreel
E Lambert
E Lawrence
B Lea
J Lee
C Legg
C le Grand-Moir
C Leighton
Freda Levson
P and M Lewis
S Lewis
J Lintell
Mrs Lipschutz
R Littell
June Loewenstein
A Loosemoore
F Love
M Lucas
M Luttrell
I Lyne
Jenny Maimane
Jacqueline Theron Malcolm
V Malcolm
M Maltravers
J Mapp
C Mark-Bell
P A Marshall

S Marshall
H Mason
A Mather
Penelope Mayson
A McCabe
N McCaughen
D McDowell
A McGrath
T McKevitt
H McLeod
J McNaughton
Dr Jenny Meegan
T Merrison
D Metcalf
E Middleton
D Millen
N Miller
Nick Millington
D Moore
Marybel Moore
Vera Morgans
J Moriarty
P Morley
Sister Ruth Morris
C and H Mowbray
L Mqotsi
F Muller
A Mummery
J Murray
S Munn
Hilary Mutch
Prof Kate Myers
C Newman
Len Newman
B Nielson
R O'Brien
C Owen
K Packer
Gloria Pahad
I Palmer
D Parker
Roy Parkinson
L Payan
A Pearce

Elizabeth Pearson
J Pearson
J Perez
G Pettinger
Alan Philips
Margaret Philips
Albert Pierce
E Pierce
K Pindar
Peggy Preston
T Price
M Priestley
Rod Prince
Bob Pulling
Rhoda Pulling
M Quinney
John Raisbeck
S Ramage
Rosemary Ramsay
M Randall
D Rands
D J Reddin
C Rich
P Roberts
M Robinson
Sister Dorothea Roden
D Rogers
E Rogers
Nick Rogers
A Rose
B Rosenberg
Crispin Rose-Innes
Jasmine Rose-Innes
C Rowe
J Rowe
P Rutter
G Sammons
G Scadding
Jean Schurer
B Scott
H Seed
M Senior
Minnie Sepel
D Servini

John Shutt
I Singer
Gilli Slater
L Small
A Smith
J Smith
L S Smith
M N Smith
Hannah Stanton
J Stewart
A Stickings
S Stote
Abby Sullivan
J Sutcliffe
Jean Sutherland
H Sutton
C Swan
D Swift
R Syers
M Taggart
B Taylor
C Tegg
S Tharby
Jacqueline Theron
S Thiele
P Thomas
J Thompson
Violetta Thompson
A Tickell
D Tickell
Ruth Tomalin
Marianne Tomlinson
C Travis
Carole Trelawney
Doreen Tucker
C Tweedy
A Vaugh
I Vickers
Caroline Vogel
E V Vredenburgh
Eileen Wainwright (née Beldon)
D Waldeck
G Wall

D and I Walton
S Ward
C Webb
F Webber
Prof Gabby Weiner
Ian Wellens
J Wellens
Ann Weston
C Whalley
P Whitaker
G White
Clive Wickenden
Mrs Wickenden
B Wigginton
T Wild
P Wilkins
J Williams
J R Williams
E Wilson
R Wilson
Ethel Wix
D Wood
D Woodruff
J Wooliscroft
L Wright
Dr Frances Young
D Zeichner

IRELAND
Louise Asmal
(co-ordinator)

Alicia Carrigy
Mary Clarke
Mary Curtin
Isin Doran
Maire Downey
Ilana Duncan
Bobby Edwards
Berna FitzPatrick
Nora Harkin
Joan Hayes
Garry Kilgallen
Pat MacReamoinn

Sheena McCambley
Marie Meaney
Bill Meek
David Mulhall
Kathleen Murphy
Helen O Murchu
Sean O'Breasail
Bill O'Brien
Louise O'Donovan
Carol Olson
Lily O'Rourke
Susan Redmond
Margo Rice
Orna Shanley
Catherine Smith

CANADA
Barbara Evans
(co-ordinator)

Warren Allmand
Prof Doug Anglin
Mary Anglin
Bruce Archer
Thomas Berger
Chantal Bernier
Andrew Brewin
Catherine Burr
Barbara Evans
Bryan Evans
Ian Fairweather
Joan Fairweather
Gloria Fallick
Karen Flynn
Paula Kingston
Steve Kotze
Larry Kuehn
Sadie Kuehn
Brian Latham
Andrea Levy
Walter MacLean
David Matas
Martha McClure
Howard McCurdy

Mary Ann McGrath
Colin McNairn
Anne Mitchell
Linda Muir
Terry Padgham
Keith Philander
Renate Pratt
Chengiah Ragavan
Don Ray
Keith Rimstad
Brian Rowe
Clyde Sanger
Penny Sanger
Archbishop Edward Scott
Carolyn Thomas
Esmeralda Thornhill
George Tillman
Trish Young

HOLLAND
Berend Meijer
(co-ordinator)

Anneke Andriessen
René Appel
Peter Daniëls
Tjeerd de Boer
Job de Haan
Thom de Ruyter
Hans Geels
Jan Laurens Hazekamp
Henk Kroese
Paul Ligtvoet
Agnes Naber
Pauline Naber
Gerard Ruys
Do Stuyfzand
Eep Talsma
Leen van der Burg
Anton van Harskamp
Christina van Ravenhorst
Pien van Riessen
Hanneke van Vliet
Marie-Helen van Vliet

DENMARK
Randers Group:
Edward Broadbridge
(co-ordinator)

Kirsten Abildgaard
Bente Balle
Lisbeth Breinholt
Edward Broadbridge
Hanna Broadbridge
Lisbeth Bøgh
Bente Nørre Christensen
Malene Dohn
Elsebet Hesselberg
Hanne Hjørlund
Johs Hjørlund
Jane Horning
Henny Foged Hulvej
Lone Jacobsen
Grethe Jensen
Per Knudsen
Mette Kristensen
Henrik Kristensen
Børge Kronborg
Birgit Kruse
Jorgen Kruse
Klaus Langballe
Tove Skærbæk Marcussen
Ole Skærbæk Marcussen
Birgit Mark
Bent Martinsen
Nina Nørgaard
Inger Ørnsvig
Ninna Pedersen
Lene Petersen
Søren Refskou
Henning Simonsen
Ulla Sørensen
Peter Toubol
Jette Trelborg
Kai Vriesema
Copenhagen Group:
Helmer Helmer
(co-ordinator)

Rune Damsager
Grethe Hansen
Birgit Brüel Lorentzen
Helene Fridberg Nielsen
Inger Thorsen

NORWAY

Kari Storhaug
(co-ordinator)

Liv Altman
Ranveig Andersen
Inger Marie Andersen
Turid Eng
Ruth Gurholt
Hermod Haug
Brit Holmberg
Kari Brit Isene
Aase Mette Jamtli
Bjorg Kjus
Marit Kjus
Jan Robert Lund
Eva Naess
Brita Just Nilsen
Torunn Nyrnes
Kari Ormhaug
Wenche Poppe
Mette Sand
Dr Gudrun Sangnes
Kari Seglem
Diana Shutt
Inger Lovise Skaar
Gunnar Skipenes
Beate Sparbo
Kjersti Storhaug
Evy Tonsberg
Anne-Liese Ziesler
Dr Jan Ziesler
Marianne Ziesler

SWEDEN

Anne-Lena Wästberg
(co-ordinator)

Eva Alexandersson
Hans Alfredson
Gunilla Alfredson
Berit Aspegren
Lennart Aspegren
Karin Bergengren
Marta Stina Danielsson
Gosta Ekman
Marie Louise Ekman
Kerstin Fryckstedt
Birgitta Gedin
Ingrid Lilja
Fatima Svendsen
Karin Szamosi

Index